World Economic and Financial Surveys

WORLD ECONOMIC OUTLOOK
May 2001

Fiscal Policy and Macroeconomic Stability

International Monetary Fund

Production: IMF Graphics Section
Cover and Design: Luisa Menjivar-Macdonald
Figures: Theodore F. Peters, Jr.
Typesetting: Choon Lee and Joseph A. Kumar

World economic outlook (International Monetary Fund)
World economic outlook: a survey by the staff of the International
Monetary Fund.—1980– —Washington, D.C.: The Fund, 1980–

v.; 28 cm.—(1981–84: Occasional paper/International Monetary Fund
ISSN 0251-6365)
Annual.
Has occasional updates, 1984–
ISSN 0258-7440 = World economic and financial surveys
ISSN 0256-6877 = World economic outlook (Washington)
1. Economic history—1971–   —Periodicals.   I. International
Monetary Fund.   II. Series: Occasional paper (International Monetary
Fund)

HC10.W7979   84-640155

338.5'443'09048—dc19
AACR 2 MARC-S

Library of Congress   8507

Published biannually.
ISBN 1-58906-032-6

Price: US$42.00
(US$35.00 to full-time faculty members and
students at universities and colleges)

Please send orders to:
International Monetary Fund, Publication Services
700 19th Street, N.W., Washington, D.C. 20431, U.S.A.
Tel.: (202) 623-7430   Telefax: (202) 623-7201
E-mail: publications@imf.org
Internet: http://www.imf.org

recycled paper

CONTENTS

Boxes

Tables

Figures

ASSUMPTIONS AND CONVENTIONS

A number of assumptions have been adopted for the projections presented in the *World Economic Outlook*. It has been assumed that real effective exchange rates will remain constant at their average levels during February 19–March 16, except for the currencies participating in the European exchange rate mechanism II (ERM II), which are assumed to remain constant in nominal terms relative to the euro; that established policies of national authorities will be maintained (for specific assumptions about fiscal and monetary polices in industrial countries, see Box A.1); that the average price of oil will be $25.50 a barrel in 2001 and $22.50 a barrel in 2002, and remain unchanged in real terms over the medium term; and that the six-month London interbank offered rate (LIBOR) on U.S. dollar deposits will average 4.5 percent in 2001 and 4.3 percent in 2002. These are, of course, working hypotheses rather than forecasts, and the uncertainties surrounding them add to the margin of error that would in any event be involved in the projections. The estimates and projections are based on statistical information available through end-March 2001.

The following conventions have been used throughout the *World Economic Outlook*:

. . .   to indicate that data are not available or not applicable;

—   to indicate that the figure is zero or negligible;

–   between years or months (for example, 1997–98 or January–June) to indicate the years or months covered, including the beginning and ending years or months;

/   between years or months (for example, 1997/98) to indicate a fiscal or financial year.

"Billion" means a thousand million; "trillion" means a thousand billion.

"Basis points" refer to hundredths of 1 percentage point (for example, 25 basis points are equivalent to ¼ of 1 percentage point).

In figures and tables, shaded areas indicate IMF staff projections.

Minor discrepancies between sums of constituent figures and totals shown are due to rounding.

As used in this report, the term "country" does not in all cases refer to a territorial entity that is a state as understood by international law and practice. As used here, the term also covers some territorial entities that are not states but for which statistical data are maintained on a separate and independent basis.

FURTHER INFORMATION AND DATA

This report on the *World Economic Outlook* is available in full on the IMF's Internet site, *www.imf.org*. Accompanying it on the website is a larger compilation of data from the WEO database than in the report itself, consisting of files containing the series most frequently requested by readers. These files may be downloaded for use in a variety of software packages.

Inquiries about the content of the *World Economic Outlook* and the WEO database should be sent by mail, electronic mail, or telefax (telephone inquiries cannot be accepted) to:

World Economic Studies Division
Research Department
International Monetary Fund
700 19th Street, N.W.
Washington, D.C. 20431, U.S.A.
E-mail: weo@imf.org   Telefax: (202) 623-6343

PREFACE

The projections and analysis contained in the *World Economic Outlook* are an integral element of the IMF's ongoing surveillance of economic developments and policies in its member countries and of the global economic system. The IMF has published the *World Economic Outlook* annually from 1980 through 1983 and biannually since 1984.

The survey of prospects and policies is the product of a comprehensive interdepartmental review of world economic developments, which draws primarily on information the IMF staff gathers through its consultations with member countries. These consultations are carried out in particular by the IMF's area departments together with various support departments.

The country projections are prepared by the IMF's area departments on the basis of internationally consistent assumptions about world activity, exchange rates, and conditions in international financial and commodity markets. For approximately 50 of the largest economies—accounting for 90 percent of world output—the projections are updated for each *World Economic Outlook* exercise. For smaller countries, the projections are based on those prepared at the time of the IMF's regular Article IV consultations with those countries and updated during the WEO exercise.

The analysis in the *World Economic Outlook* draws extensively on the ongoing work of the IMF's area and specialized departments, and is coordinated in the Research Department under the general direction of Michael Mussa, Economic Counsellor and Director of Research. The *World Economic Outlook* project is directed by David Robinson, Assistant Director of the Research Department, together with Tamim Bayoumi, Chief of the World Economic Studies Division.

Primary contributors to the current issue include Luis Catão, Hali Edison, Maitland MacFarlan, James Morsink, Cathy Wright, Marco Cangiano, Markus Haacker, Michael Kell, Luca Ricci, Torsten Sløk, Arvind Subramanian, and Marco Terrones. Other contributors include Vivek Arora, Tim Callen, Giovanni Dell'Ariccia, Richard Hemming, Sanjay Kalra, Ken Kletzer, Charles Kramer, Prakash Loungani, Paolo Mauro, Blair Rourke, Abebe Selassie, and Mark Zelmer. Mandy Hemmati, Siddique Hossain, Yutong Li, Ning Song, and Bennett Sutton provided research assistance, together with Rikhil Bhavnani and Estella Macke. Gretchen Byrne, Nicholas Dopuch, Staffan Gorne, Toh Kuan, Olga Plagie, Di Rao, and Anthony G. Turner processed the data and managed the computer systems. Celia Burns, Marlene George, Rochelle Gittens, and Lisa Nugent were responsible for word processing. Jeff Hayden of the External Relations Department edited the manuscript and coordinated production of the publication.

The analysis has benefited from comments and suggestions by staff from other IMF departments, as well as by Executive Directors following their discussion of the *World Economic Outlook* on April 5 and 6, 2001. However, both projections and policy considerations are those of the IMF staff and should not be attributed to Executive Directors or to their national authorities.

Since the publication of the October 2000 *World Economic Outlook*, the prospects for global growth have weakened significantly, led by a marked slowdown in the *United States*, a stalling recovery in *Japan*, and moderating growth in Europe and in a number of emerging market countries. Some slowdown from the rapid rates of global growth of late 1999 and early 2000 was both desirable and expected, especially in those countries most advanced in the cycle, but the downturn is proving to be steeper than earlier thought. Given the rapid policy response by the U.S. Federal Reserve and a number of other central banks, and with most advanced countries—with the important exception of Japan—having considerable room for policy maneuver, there is a reasonable prospect that the slowdown will be short-lived. However, the outlook remains subject to considerable uncertainty and a deeper and more prolonged downturn is clearly possible. Against this background, macroeconomic policies—particularly on the monetary side—will need to be proactive to guard against the possibility of a steeper than expected downturn.

Given the strength of activity in early 2000, and with the signs of greater than expected weakening coming late in the year, global output in 2000 grew an estimated 4.8 percent, very close to the projection in the last *World Economic Outlook* (Table 1.1 and Figure 1.1). However, activity in 2001 will slow markedly, with global growth now projected at 3.2 percent, 1 percentage point lower than earlier expected. Within this, GDP growth in the United States has been revised downward by 1.7 percentage points to 1.5 percent, the lowest level for a decade. Growth projections have also been marked down significantly in the other major currency areas. Activity in Europe should nonetheless remain reasonably robust, but in Japan growth is projected to fall to 0.6 percent. In emerging mar-

kets, the revisions to the outlook vary, depending in part on the closeness of linkages with the United States. Growth has been marked down substantially in emerging *Asia* and *Latin America*—although activity in *China* and *India* is expected to remain relatively well sustained, providing an important source of stability. In contrast, most countries in the *Middle East, Central and Eastern Europe, the Commonwealth of Independent States* and *Africa* have been less affected, although growth in *Turkey* is likely to decline sharply as a result of the recent crisis.

Some slowdown in global growth from the very high rates of late 1999 and early 2000 had been long anticipated by most forecasters. By the end of 2000, activity—particularly in the United States—was clearly weakening significantly (Box 1.1). This was in part the result of the appropriate earlier tightening of monetary policy in the United States to address rising demand pressures; and during most of the second half of the year policies appeared broadly on track to achieve this through a moderation in the pace of economic advance. As experience over the past several decades has shown, however, soft landings are not easy to achieve. In the event, a series of shocks—including higher energy prices; a reassessment of corporate earnings prospects, accompanied by a sharp fall in equity markets, particularly of technology stocks, and slowing growth in the technology sector; and a tightening of credit conditions—appear to have combined to generate a marked slowdown in domestic demand growth, and a sharp weakening in consumer and business confidence (Figure 1.2).

The further setback to the already fragile recovery in Japan is an additional source of concern. Following very strong growth in the first quarter of 2000 (partly due to temporary factors), activity appears to have stagnated, weighed down by weak consumer confidence, slowing business investment, and weakening external de-

Table 1.1. Overview of the *World Economic Outlook* Projections
(Annual percent change unless otherwise noted)

	1999	2000	Current Projections		Difference from October 2000 Projections[1]	
			2001	2002	2000	2001
World output	**3.5**	**4.8**	**3.2**	**3.9**	—	**−1.0**
Advanced economies	3.4	4.1	1.9	2.7	−0.1	−1.3
Major advanced economies	3.0	3.8	1.6	2.4	−0.1	−1.3
United States	4.2	5.0	1.5	2.5	−0.2	−1.7
Japan	0.8	1.7	0.6	1.5	0.3	−1.2
Germany	1.6	3.0	1.9	2.6	0.1	−1.4
France	3.2	3.2	2.6	2.6	−0.3	−0.9
Italy	1.6	2.9	2.0	2.5	−0.2	−1.0
United Kingdom	2.3	3.0	2.6	2.8	−0.1	−0.2
Canada	4.5	4.7	2.3	2.4	—	−0.5
Other advanced economies	4.8	5.2	3.0	3.8	0.1	−1.2
Memorandum						
European Union	2.6	3.4	2.4	2.8	—	−0.9
Euro area	2.6	3.4	2.4	2.8	−0.1	−1.0
Newly industrialized Asian economies	7.9	8.2	3.8	5.5	0.3	−2.3
Developing countries	3.8	5.8	5.0	5.6	0.1	−0.7
Africa	2.3	3.0	4.2	4.4	−0.5	−0.2
Developing Asia	6.1	6.9	5.9	6.3	0.2	−0.7
China	7.1	8.0	7.0	7.1	0.5	−0.3
India	6.6	6.4	5.6	6.1	−0.3	−0.9
ASEAN-4[2]	2.8	5.0	3.4	4.7	0.5	−1.6
Middle East, Malta, and Turkey	0.8	5.4	2.9	4.6	0.5	−1.2
Western Hemisphere	0.2	4.1	3.7	4.4	−0.2	−0.8
Brazil	0.8	4.2	4.5	4.5	0.2	—
Countries in transition	2.6	5.8	4.0	4.2	0.6	−0.2
Central and eastern Europe	1.8	3.8	3.9	4.4	—	−0.7
Commonwealth of Independent States and Mongolia	3.1	7.1	4.1	4.1	1.1	0.1
Russia	3.2	7.5	4.0	4.0	0.5	—
Excluding Russia	2.7	6.3	4.2	4.4	2.4	0.3
World trade volume (goods and services)	**5.3**	**12.4**	**6.7**	**6.5**	**2.4**	**−1.1**
Imports						
Advanced economies	7.9	11.4	6.7	6.5	1.1	−1.2
Developing countries	1.6	16.9	8.8	7.9	6.9	−0.3
Countries in transition	−7.3	13.3	8.6	6.9	0.9	0.2
Exports						
Advanced economies	5.0	11.4	6.2	6.2	1.5	−1.4
Developing countries	4.1	15.7	7.1	7.0	6.8	—
Countries in transition	0.6	14.9	4.6	5.1	4.8	−1.4
Commodity prices						
Oil[3]						
In SDRs	36.5	62.6	−7.7	−11.9	10.6	5.3
In U.S. dollars	37.5	56.9	−9.6	−11.8	9.4	3.7
Nonfuel (average based on world commodity export weights)						
In SDRs	−7.8	5.5	2.6	4.4	−0.9	−2.2
In U.S. dollars	−7.1	1.8	0.5	4.5	−1.4	−4.0
Consumer prices						
Advanced economies	1.4	2.3	2.1	1.8	—	—
Developing countries	6.7	6.1	5.7	4.8	—	0.6
Countries in transition	43.9	20.1	15.3	10.0	1.6	2.5
Six-month London interbank offered rate (LIBOR, percent)						
On U.S. dollar deposits	5.5	6.7	4.5	4.3	−0.2	−2.9
On Japanese yen deposits	0.2	0.3	0.3	0.5	0.1	−0.1
On euro deposits	3.0	4.6	4.4	4.1	—	−0.7

Note: Real effective exchange rates are assumed to remain constant at the levels prevailing during February 19–March 16, 2001.
[1]Using updated purchasing-power-parity (PPP) weights, summarized in the Statistical Appendix, Table A.
[2]Indonesia, Malaysia, the Philippines, and Thailand.
[3]Simple average of spot prices of U.K. Brent, Dubai, and West Texas Intermediate crude oil. The average price of oil in U.S. dollars a barrel was $28.21 in 2000; the assumed price is $25.50 in 2001 and $22.50 in 2002.

mand, while deflation has persisted. Activity in 2001 will be helped by policy initiatives, including the November 2000 fiscal stimulus package and the recent shift to a new monetary framework, as well as the depreciation of the yen since late 2000, but business investment and exports appear to be weakening and there is as yet little sign of a pickup in consumer confidence, which is essential to underpin a sustained recovery, or in bank lending. Moreover, with limited room for policy maneuver and continued fragilities in the financial and corporate sectors, the economy remains vulnerable to additional shocks.

In an environment of slowing global growth, commodity prices are expected to weaken (Appendix I). Oil prices have retreated from their late 2000 high, and—while their continued volatility remains a concern and much continues to depend on the production decisions of the Organization of the Petroleum Exporting Countries (OPEC) in coming months—the risks may now be on the downside. Nonfuel prices are expected to remain broadly unchanged, in part reflecting the continued strength of the dollar; however, if global demand slows more than expected, prices would likely weaken, adversely affecting commodity producers, including many poor countries. As oil prices fall back, headline inflation in most industrial countries has begun to stabilize and—with wage increases moderate—underlying inflation remains generally subdued. Inflation remains a concern in some faster growing European countries and in a number of developing and transition countries, but, in general, inflationary risks do not materially circumscribe policymakers' freedom of action at this stage.

In financial markets, after a respite in January 2001 the fall in U.S. equity markets accelerated through early April in the face of continued weak earnings reports, with additional sharp declines in the technology sector and in broader market indices, although sentiment has since stabilized and, as the *World Economic Outlook* went to press, equity prices rebounded in the initial aftermath of the latest cut in U.S. interest rates. Weakness in U.S. equity markets has been mirrored in other mature markets, and broader eq-

Figure 1.1. Global Indicators[1]
(Annual percent change unless otherwise noted)

Global growth is projected to slow markedly in 2001, while inflation remains subdued.

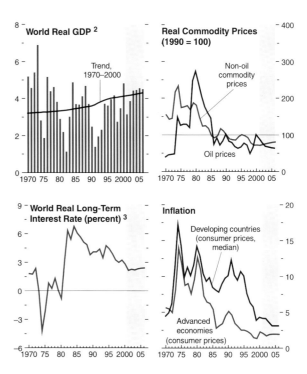

[1]Shaded areas indicate IMF staff projections. Aggregates are computed on the basis of purchasing-power-parity weights unless otherwise indicated.
[2]Average growth rates for individual countries, aggregated using purchasing-power-parity weights; these shift over time in favor of faster growing countries, giving the line an upward trend.
[3]GDP-weighted average of 10-year (or nearest maturity) government bond yields less inflation rates for the United States, Japan, Germany, France, Italy, the United Kingdom, and Canada. Excluding Italy prior to 1972.

Figure 1.2. Selected European Union Countries, Japan, and United States: Indicators of Consumer and Business Confidence[1]

Confidence has fallen back markedly in the United States; in Europe, business confidence has also weakened, although consumer confidence remains reasonably well-sustained.

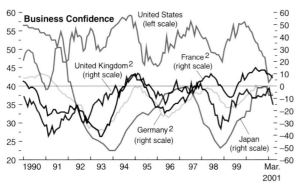

Sources: Consumer confidence for the United States, the Conference Board; for European countries, the European Commission. Business confidence for the United States, the U.S. Department of Commerce, Purchasing Managers Composite Diffusion Index; for European countries, the European Commission; and for Japan, Bank of Japan.
[1] Indicators are not comparable across countries.
[2] Percent of respondents expecting an improvement in their situation minus percent expecting a deterioration.

uity indices have fallen back significantly from earlier peaks (Figure 1.3). Increased expectations of a U.S. slowdown, along with tightening bank lending standards, falling corporate profits, the global downgrading of the technology sector, and a pickup in default rates, have also reduced investors' appetite for risk taking. Although long term government bond yields have fallen—in part also reflecting buybacks and expected Federal Reserve interest rate easing—corporate credit spreads have widened since last summer, and there is much greater differentiation in spreads between risk classes, notably in the high yield market (although high yield rates have fallen back somewhat following the cuts in U.S. interest rates). In currency markets, the euro has strengthened only modestly against the U.S. dollar since its low in October 2000, and still appears undervalued in terms of medium-term economic fundamentals (see Chapter II). As concerns about the sustainability of the Japanese recovery have intensified, the yen has weakened significantly to about its mid-1999 level.

As a result of developments in mature markets, the environment faced by emerging markets has changed for the worse.[1] As technology valuations in mature markets declined, emerging equity markets fell back sharply, in a number of cases also reflecting increased investor concerns about domestic and external risks. In tandem with developments in U.S. high yield paper—widely regarded as a competing asset class—spreads on emerging market bonds widened in the last quarter of 2000, and financing conditions tightened markedly, exacerbated by crises in Argentina and Turkey. Following the cuts in U.S. interest rates in January, emerging equity markets initially strengthened and financing conditions improved, permitting a number of countries to cover a substantial proportion of their annual public sector external financing requirement. However, in parallel with developments in mature markets, equity prices subsequently fell back

[1] See the IMF's February 2001 *Quarterly Emerging Markets Financial Report* (*http://www.imf.org/external/pubs/ft/emf/index.htm*) for a more detailed discussion.

and financing conditions deteriorated (although both have stabilized recently). Spillover effects from the renewed financial crisis in Turkey, culminating in the floating of the Turkish lira in mid-February, have so far been limited, but economic difficulties in Argentina appear to have had more of an impact, particularly on spreads in neighboring countries.

To date, the effects of the global economic slowdown have been seen primarily in those countries with close trade ties to the United States, including Canada and Mexico, and emerging Asia. In Canada and Mexico, the effect will be partly cushioned by solid domestic demand growth; in emerging Asia, where confidence had already been weakened by a variety of domestic and external factors, the impact may be more substantial and would be compounded by a larger-than-expected deterioration in Japan. In other countries, where a key concern is the impact through financial markets and the knock on effects through consumer and business confidence, the effects have as yet been more moderate, although important risks remain. However, looking forward to the remainder of 2001, much will depend on how deep and prolonged the slowdown in the United States proves to be. This remains subject to considerable uncertainty. However, there are a number of reasons to believe that the slowdown may be relatively moderate and short-lived:

- First, long-term interest rates in the United States have fallen during 2000 and, more recently, short-term rates have been cut significantly. This should begin to have a direct effect on U.S. activity in the second half of the year, providing support to the global economy, although the pace of this recovery may be slowed by the recent further decline in equity prices. Lower oil prices will also be helpful.
- Second, with inflationary risks receding, policymakers in most advanced economies have substantial room to maneuver, which some countries, most notably the United States, but also including Australia, Canada, and the United Kingdom, have begun to

Figure 1.3. Financial Market Developments

Notwithstanding lower interest rates, mature and emerging equity markets continued to decline through early April, driven by the fall in the NASDAQ. The euro has modestly appreciated against the U.S. dollar, while the yen has fallen back on rising concerns about the sustainability of the Japan's recovery.

Sources: Bloomberg Financial Markets, LP; European Central Bank; IMF Treasurer's Department, Nikkei Telecom; and WEFA, Inc.

[1] Average of the month.

[2] Three month deposit rate; euro area data prior to January 1999 reflect Germany.

[3] Ten-year government bond rate. To December 1998, euro area yields are calculated on the basis of harmonized national government bond yields weighted by GDP. Therefore, the weights are nominal outstanding amounts of government bonds in each maturity band.

Box 1.1. How Well Do Forecasters Predict Turning Points?

The rapid change in the U.S. economic out-look has taken most people by surprise, with the Consensus forecast for real GDP growth in 2001 falling from 3.7 percent in September 2000 to 1.7 percent in April 2001, the most rapid adjust-ment in expectations since the early 1990s when the United States entered its last recession (see the first figure). As much previous work has in-dicated, the failure to predict major slowdowns or contractions in activity has been a notable feature of forecasts of the U.S. economy for many years.[1] A recent paper reviews the experi-ence with forecasts of a broad sample of ad-vanced and emerging economies during the 1990s, based on the projections published in the private sector Consensus Forecasts.[2] It finds that, in April of the year before a recession year (de-fined as a year of negative real GDP growth), the Consensus mean forecast—averaged across the 60 episodes of recessions—was for 3 percent growth (see the second figure). By October, the mean forecast had been trimmed to about 2 percent, with a further trimming down to zero by April of the year of the recession. These downward revisions suggest that forecasters were clearly aware a slowdown was in progress. By October, the forecasts catch up with the reality of a recession, but still underestimate the actual decline.[3] A similar pattern is observed around business cycle troughs—forecasters are initially slow to adjust their projections, but then steadily

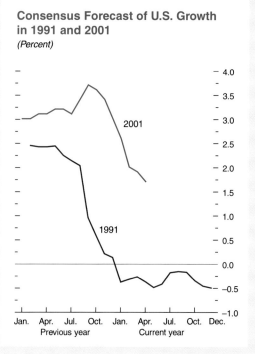

Consensus Forecast of U.S. Growth in 1991 and 2001
(Percent)

[1]See for example, Victor Zarnowitz, "The Record and Improvability of Economic Forecasting," NBER Working Paper No. 2099 (Cambridge, Mass.: National Bureau of Economic Research, July 1987); and David Fintzen and H.O. Stekler, "Why Did Forecasters Fail to Predict the 1990 Recession," *International Journal of Forecasting*, Vol. 15 (July 1999), pp. 309–23.

[2]Prakash Loungani, "How Accurate Are Private Sector Forecasts? Cross Country Evidence from Consensus Forecasts of Output Growth," *International Journal of Forecasting* (forthcoming).

[3]The "actual" values used here are initial estimates, taken wherever possible from the May *World Economic Outlook* of the following year. These initial estimates are used in preference to final GDP data, which often reflect data revisions, re-benchmarking, and other such unforecastable changes.

adjust their forecasts upward to catch up to the reality of an upturn. As the paper also notes, since errors in official and the Consensus fore-casts are highly correlated, such problems are not confined to the private sector.[4]

This evidence on the difficulties forecasters experience in predicting recessions highlights several points. First, identifying recessions is a complex task, even when they are occurring. This is why most recessions are determined to be such after the event, not during it. Even more important, the upward bias in projections is what would be expected if one focuses only on periods of recession. A forecaster needs to assess the probability of an outright recession against

[4]An earlier study of *World Economic Outlook* forecasts also found that they had substantially the same errors as private sector forecasts. See Michael Artis, "How Accurate are the IMF's Short-Term Forecasts? Another Examination of the World Economic Outlook," in *Staff Studies for the World Economic Outlook* (Washington: International Monetary Fund, December 1997).

Consensus Forecast of Growth in Recession Years[1]
(Percent)

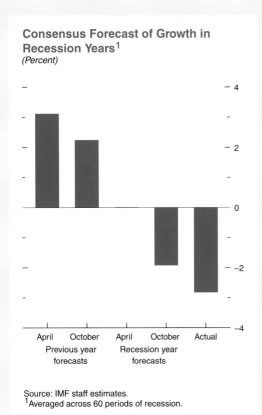

Source: IMF staff estimates.
[1]Averaged across 60 periods of recession.

that of a more mild slowing of activity. Hence, one would expect growth over episodes of recession to be systematically over predicted—essentially, a worse-than-expected outcome does indeed occur when an economy moves into a recession.

However, the fact that forecasters tend to make steady upward or downward revisions to their projections—not just over recessions, but more generally—raises the question of whether forecasts themselves are efficient. As noted cogently by William Nordhaus:

> If I could look at your most recent forecasts and accurately say, "Your next forecast will be 2 percent lower than today's," then you can surely improve your forecast.[5]

[5]William D. Nordhaus, "Forecasting Efficiency: Concepts and Applications," *The Review of Economics and Statistics*, Vol. 69 (November 1987), pp 667–74.

Why might forecasters violate notions of forecast efficiency and prefer to adjust their forecasts in a smooth manner toward the actual? Nordhaus suggests two reasons: fear that "jumpy" or "jagged" forecasts will be treated as signs of inconsistency; and that forecasters tend to stay away from issuing "outlier" forecasts—a strategy that works well in most years since outliers are, by definition, rare events.[6] In addition, reported headline forecasts may not capture shifts in the weights the forecaster attaches to different scenarios, which could change significantly. To the extent that this is the case, such behavior can make the revisions in the Consensus forecast smooth and also guide it away from outlying values and indeed in some instances toward convergence to a forecast value that is far from the actual value.

While this is difficult to test for, in particular because Consensus forecasts by their nature contain a degree of serial correlation, preliminary evidence suggests forecasts may indeed contain a degree of inefficiency.[7] Hence there may be room to improve the Consensus forecasts by adjusting for the degree of serial correlation in forecast revisions in the past (on the other hand, preliminary analysis indicates that the dispersion of forecasts tends to rise only when the level of the forecast has started to fall significantly). For example, a simple correction applied to U.S. growth projections from the Consensus forecasts over the period 1990 to 2000 would reduce the mean absolute error of

[6]Indeed, a recent study finds that individual forecasters tend to conform to the mean (consensus) forecasts; in particular, an individual's forecast is strongly influenced by the consensus forecast of the previous month. See Giampiero Gallo, Clive Granger, and Yongil Jeon, "The Impact of the Use of Forecasts in Information Sets," Working Paper No. 99-18 (San Diego: University of California at San Diego, Department of Economics, August 1999).

[7]Serial correlation is particularly likely in averages of forecasts, because the individual projections may have been made at different times. Even if the individual forecasts do not contain serial correlation, averaging forecasts of different vintages will cause serial correlation.

Box 1.1 *(concluded)*

the forecast by nearly 10 percent, and similar effects appear to be true of other major economies.[8] As forecasters become more aware

---

[8]For this illustration, the corrected forecast is obtained by adding to the recent forecast a multiple of the revision in the forecast made six months ago. The multiple depends on the relationship between past forecast errors and past forecast revisions. For details, see Oliver Kim, Steve C. Lim and Kenneth W. Shaw,

of this bias, it is to be hoped that forecasts themselves will become more efficient and this serial correlation will be eliminated.

"The Use of Forecast Revision in Reducing Built-in Biases in Mean Analyst Forecasts," *Journal of Accounting Research* (forthcoming). The procedure could in principle be generalized to account for more than two forecasts and possible differences in the adjustment factor depending on the stage of the business cycle.

use; Japan, where the scope for adjustment is much less, has also moved to ease monetary policy in the context of its new monetary framework. Moreover, given the substantial strengthening in fiscal positions in recent years (see Chapter III), most countries have room for fiscal easing as a second line of defense, or have already moved to somewhat easier fiscal stances.

- Third, while a number of countries continue to face serious difficulties, external and financial vulnerabilities in emerging markets have been generally reduced since the 1997–98 crises, and the shift away from soft exchange rate pegs has improved their ability to manage external shocks (Figure 1.4). (See Chapter IV.)

Against this background, the *World Economic Outlook's* baseline scenario projects that activity in the United States picks up during the second half of the year, while growth in Europe remains reasonably robust, and the recovery in Japan resumes in 2002. In emerging markets, external financing conditions would gradually improve during the remainder of the year, consistent with a modest pickup in private capital flows. While global growth in 2001 would still slow significantly, it would remain well above earlier troughs and return to close to trend in 2002.

This scenario is certainly plausible, but it is far from assured. On the positive side, if confidence were to rebound quickly, it is possible that the pickup in the United States—and therefore in

the global economy—could be more rapid than presently projected. However, with equity markets weak, the risks of a less favorable outcome are clearly significant. Experience suggests that when turning points are reached, the shift in momentum is often more pronounced than previously expected. As has been highlighted in many previous editions of the *World Economic Outlook*, this may be particularly the case given the substantial imbalances that have developed during the expansion, including the high current account deficit and the apparent overvaluation of the U.S. dollar, the negative personal saving rate, and—despite recent declines—equity markets that are still richly valued by historical standards. These imbalances are closely linked to expectations of continued strong productivity growth in the United States relative to other countries; and the extent, manner, and speed with which they unwind will depend on how those expectations evolve in a climate of slowing growth. In this connection, one risk is that the virtuous "new economy" circle of rising productivity, rising stock prices, increased access to funding, and rising technology investment that contributed to the strong growth in the 1990s (see Chapter II) could go into reverse.

If the slowdown in the United States were to prove deeper and more prolonged, this would pose several interlinked risks for the global outlook that would significantly increase the chance of a more synchronized and self-reinforcing downturn developing:

- First, over the past several years, the strong expansion in the U.S. economy has been instrumental in stabilizing global activity in the face of weak demand elsewhere. Unfortunately, with the recovery in Japan stalling, and potential growth in Europe still modest, the present slowdown in the United States is unlikely to be offset by higher demand growth elsewhere. In these circumstances there would be a greater risk of spillovers to other countries through financial market and confidence effects. The global economy would also become more vulnerable to adverse shocks, such as a sharper-than-expected weakening of activity in Japan.

- Second, as discussed extensively in recent issues of the *World Economic Outlook*, there would be a greater risk that the current account imbalances in the major currency areas, and the apparent misalignments among the major currencies, could unwind in a disorderly fashion. Historical experience suggests that current account deficits of the size that presently exists in the United States have not been sustained for long, and that adjustment is generally accompanied by a significant depreciation. Since the projections in the *World Economic Outlook*, like those of many other forecasters, assume constant real exchange rates, the baseline scenario shows relatively little change in global current account imbalances. As discussed in Appendix II, in a scenario allowing for a gradual adjustment in exchange rates—as has most often been the case in past episodes—these imbalances could adjust in a relatively manageable and nondisruptive fashion, especially if accompanied by stronger growth in Europe and Japan. However, in an environment where U.S. growth slows sharply, the portfolio and direct investment flows that have been financing the U.S. current account deficit could adjust more abruptly. This would heighten the risk of a more rapid and disorderly adjustment, possibly accompanied by financial

Figure 1.4. External Vulnerabilities in Developing Countries

External vulnerabilities have generally declined since the 1997–98 crises, although debt and financing requirements in Latin America remain high, and there has been a general shift toward hard pegs and/or more flexible exchange rate regimes.

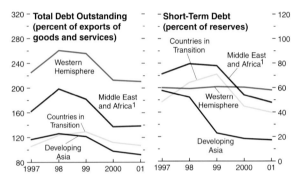

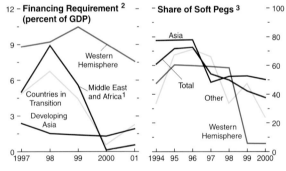

[1] Including Malta and Turkey.
[2] Current account balance plus total amortization due.
[3] Defined as percentage of countries (weighted by purchasing-power-parity GDP) that have a fixed but adjustable exchange rate regime. Covers the major emerging market countries in each region; based on Stanley Fischer, "Exchange Rate Regimes: Is the Bipolar View Correct?" Distinguished Lecture on Economics in Government, AEA Meetings, January 2001 (available at www.imf.org).

market turbulence in both mature and emerging markets. Large swings in exchange rates could also limit the room for policy maneuver.

- Third, given that financial risks often tend to be underestimated in periods of rapid expansion, lower growth could expose fragilities in financial markets. Further downward revisions to expectations of corporate profit growth could intensify pressures on equity markets in the United States and elsewhere, with adverse effects on wealth, investment, confidence, and risk aversion—which would also directly affect demand for emerging market assets. Slower growth would also add to pressures on financial and corporate sectors, particularly in those countries where significant weaknesses remain.

To illustrate these risks, the *World Economic Outlook* also includes a "harder landing" scenario, based on the assumption of a further significant fall in U.S. equity valuations and in consumer and investor confidence in the United States and Japan, associated with a substantial and abrupt depreciation of the U.S. dollar against other currencies. As a result of the abrupt changes in financial market valuations and loss of confidence, the rebalancing of global demand is accompanied by a significant, generalized slowdown in output. Compared to the baseline scenario, global output falls by slightly over 1 percentage point through 2001 and 2002, with the impact varying from 1½ percentage points in the United States to 1 percentage point in other advanced countries. In developing countries, the impact is about one-half of that for the global economy, largely reflecting the fall in demand for net exports, but could be significantly larger if external financing conditions deteriorated sharply. Overall, this would result in a global slowdown broadly comparable to that experienced in 1998. Were the financial weakness to occur but the U.S. dollar depreciation to be delayed, the output loss would be larger in the United States as the increase in net exports would be more limited, and conversely the output losses in other advanced economies would be smaller.

Recent issues of the *World Economic Outlook* have called for policies in the main currency areas to be consistent with a rebalancing of growth and demand among the three main currency areas, supportive of an orderly resolution of global imbalances. This process is now clearly under way; however, it is taking place entirely through lower growth in the United States, with activity elsewhere doing little to offset this decline. With inflationary pressures easing, and downside risks to activity more pronounced, a proactive approach to macroeconomic policies is required, aimed at supporting a reasonably smooth transition to more sustainable growth rates in the United States; strengthening the expansion in Europe; and reenergizing the stalling recovery in Japan:

- In the United States, the aggressive reduction in interest rates that began in January has been appropriate. Monetary policy should remain the first line of defense, and further interest rate cuts may be needed in coming months. Moderate and relatively front loaded tax cuts could also provide useful support to activity, while minimizing the adverse impact on savings and the current account over the medium term.

- In Japan, the new monetary framework introduced in March, including the commitment to maintain it until inflation turns positive, is welcome and should be aggressively implemented. Given the very high level of public debt, the gradual fiscal consolidation under way should be maintained, with fiscal easing a last resort to forestall outright recession. However, the main policy requirement is to vigorously address underlying structural weaknesses, particularly in the financial sector, while seeking, to the extent possible, to minimize the adverse short-term impact on growth. The recently announced package of structural measures is a welcome step forward, but it will need to be implemented forcefully and supplemented with other steps.

- In the *euro area*, with increasing signs that activity is slowing, and underlying inflationary pressures expected to ease looking forward, there is scope for a moderate downward adjustment in interest rates; and the European Central Bank (ECB) will need to move rapidly if signs of weakness become more accentuated or the euro appreciates sharply. Recent tax cuts, fortuitously timed from a cyclical perspective, will also help support activity in some countries and at this point no additional fiscal stimulus appears necessary beyond the automatic stabilizers. A more ambitious approach to structural reform, notably in labor markets, pensions, and health, is needed to raise potential growth and to ensure long-run fiscal sustainability.

- In *emerging markets*, prospects depend critically on maintaining investor confidence. External financing conditions have recently deteriorated and, given the uncertain global outlook and continued economic difficulties in some emerging market countries, are likely to remain volatile in the period ahead. This underscores the need to maintain prudent macroeconomic policies and to press ahead with corporate, financial, and—especially in the transition economies—institutional reforms, particularly in those countries that lag in this process.

The slowdown in global growth will clearly hurt the poor, both directly and through lower commodity prices, although the impact may be mitigated by the fact that two-thirds of the poorest live in south Asia and China, where activity is expected to remain relatively strong. In a number of the poorer countries, debt relief under the Enhanced Heavily Indebted Poor Country (HIPC) Initiative will release substantial resources to finance anti-poverty measures; provided those resources are used efficiently and are supported by comprehensive reform programs, this will help reduce poverty and boost growth over the medium term. To assist these efforts, the advanced economies have a special responsibility to increase aid flows, which are well below the United Nations' target of 0.7 percent of GDP; to promote peace and political stability, particularly in the war-torn regions of Africa; and to provide further assistance to fight the spread of the HIV/AIDS epidemic, which has become the most serious threat to human welfare and economic development on the African continent.

A major barrier to the progress of poorer developing countries remains the trade regimes in the advanced economies, which generally discriminate against the goods that poor countries produce most efficiently, in particular food and textiles and clothing (although quotas under the Multifiber Arrangement are due to be phased out by 2005). With a new round of multilateral trade liberalization on the horizon, it is important to recall that open trade is a major route for providing the benefits of globalization to poor countries. While developing countries also need to improve their trade systems (the case of Africa is discussed in more detail in Chapter II), it is essential for the advanced countries to recognize the substantial benefits that open export markets can provide to developing countries in general and to poor countries in particular. In this regard, the recent decision by the European Union to provide the poorest nations with immediate free access for most products is very welcome, particularly given the importance of the EU market for such countries. In addition, recent measures providing for significant market opening for the poorest nations have also been taken or announced by Canada, Japan, Korea, New Zealand, Norway, and the United States. Still more can and should be done by these and other countries to eliminate remaining barriers to the exports of the poorest countries.

How Hard a Landing in the United States?

After a strong start, economic growth in the *United States* slowed sharply during the course of 2000 (Figure 1.5). Real GDP expanded at a 5¼ percent annual rate in the first half of 2000, outpacing even the most optimistic projections of potential growth, and the Federal Reserve appropriately raised interest rates in response to increasing inflationary risks. Growth slowed to an annual rate of just 1 percent in the fourth quarter, reflecting mainly the surge in energy prices

Figure 1.5. United States: Sharp Slowdown and Persistent Imbalances
(Percent change from four quarters earlier unless otherwise noted)

After a strong start, growth slowed sharply during 2000. Nevertheless, the growth of unit labor costs accelerated, the external current account deficit widened, and the real exchange rate appreciated.

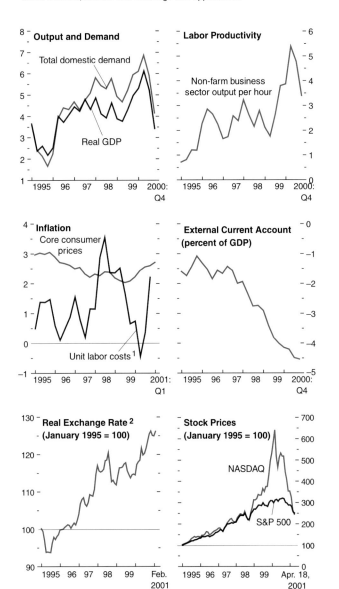

Sources: Bloomberg Financial Markets, LP; Bureau of Labor Statistics; and WEFA, Inc.
[1] Non farm-business sector.
[2] Real effective exchange rate based on consumer prices indices.

and the tightening of financial conditions, including the drop in the NASDAQ and U.S. dollar appreciation. During the course of the year, warnings of slower sales and earnings growth resulted in substantial markdowns in the valuations of many leading high-tech companies, and the U.S. dollar retreated modestly from its peak. At the turn of the year, business and consumer confidence dropped sharply. The downturn in activity has been most severe in manufacturing. While personal spending growth is decelerating, consumer demand and residential construction appear to have provided moderate support to real activity in the first quarter of 2001.

More than the usual amount of uncertainty surrounds the outlook at the current juncture. The *World Economic Outlook's* baseline forecast envisages weak growth in the first half of 2001, reflecting rapid inventory adjustment and a slowdown in investment spending. This is followed by a pickup in activity, supported by lower short- and long-term interest rates, but slowed by the lagged effects of recent declines in equity prices on investment and consumption. This yields growth of 1½ percent for 2001 as a whole and 2½ percent for 2002. An upside risk is the stimulative impact of tax cuts, which have not yet been legislated. However, there is a significant downside risk that the imbalances built up during the long expansion—including equities that have remained richly valued by historical standards, high levels of corporate and household debt, and possible overinvestment in some sectors (notably telecommunications)—could unwind in a less orderly fashion, exacerbated by further declines in confidence and increases in risk aversion in financial markets.

The strength of domestic demand relative to output growth in 2000 led for the third consecutive year to a substantial widening of the external current account deficit. The gap was 4½ percent of GDP in 2000—significantly larger than in other major advanced economies (Table 1.2). With the fiscal surplus increasing, the widening deficit entirely reflected increasing private investment and declining household saving. Substantial capital inflows, partly in response to

Table 1.2. Selected Economies: Current Account Positions
(Percent of GDP)

	1999	2000	2001	2002
Advanced economies	**–0.5**	**–1.0**	**–1.1**	**–1.0**
Major advanced economies	–1.1	–1.6	–1.6	–1.5
United States	–3.6	–4.4	–4.3	–4.1
Japan	2.4	2.5	2.7	2.8
Germany	–0.9	–1.1	–1.2	–1.0
France	2.6	2.1	2.1	2.3
Italy	0.5	–0.6	–0.2	0.1
United Kingdom	–1.1	–1.7	–1.8	–2.2
Canada	–0.4	1.8	1.3	0.8
Other advanced economies	2.0	2.0	1.8	1.6
Spain	–2.1	–3.2	–3.0	–3.0
Netherlands	4.3	3.7	3.7	3.4
Belgium	4.2	4.1	4.3	4.5
Sweden	3.5	2.6	2.4	2.3
Austria	–2.8	–3.0	–2.8	–2.3
Denmark	1.6	2.6	2.5	2.5
Finland	5.9	7.7	7.3	7.6
Greece	–4.1	–6.9	–7.3	–7.1
Portugal	–8.7	–10.4	–9.7	–9.3
Ireland	0.6	–0.5	–2.1	–2.6
Switzerland	11.6	12.8	11.5	11.3
Norway	3.9	13.9	13.4	10.9
Israel	–1.9	–1.7	–2.3	–2.4
Iceland	–7.0	–10.3	–10.6	–8.2
Cyprus	–4.5	–8.0	–5.3	–4.6
Korea	6.0	2.4	2.3	1.2
Australia	–5.8	–4.0	–3.3	–3.2
Taiwan Province of China	2.9	3.0	2.4	2.5
Hong Kong SAR	6.6	5.8	3.0	4.1
Singapore	25.9	23.6	21.0	20.2
New Zealand	–6.6	–5.4	–4.8	–4.2
Memorandum				
European Union	0.3	–0.3	–0.3	–0.2
Euro area[1]	0.4	–0.2	–0.1	—

[1]Calculated as the sum of the balances of individual euro area countries.

the perceived increase in trend productivity growth in the United States, led to further appreciation of the U.S. dollar. Past experience suggests that current account deficits of this magnitude are not usually sustained for very long (see Box 1.2), and that adjustment usually involves slower real income growth and gradual but significant real depreciation over a few years.[2]

Although core CPI inflation has edged up to about 2¾ percent, the slowdown has diminished

[2]Caroline L. Freund, "Current Account Adjustment in Industrialized Countries," International Finance Discussion Paper No. 692 (Washington: Board of Governors of the Federal Reserve System, December 2000).

inflationary risks. If activity continues to grow at below-potential rates, as expected, pressures on resource utilization should ease, albeit with a lag. At the same time, however, labor markets remain tight by historical standards, and the growth rate of unit labor costs is rising. Also, a sharp depreciation of the U.S. dollar could boost import prices. The balance of these factors will depend crucially on the evolution of labor productivity. At the present stage, the risk of an abrupt acceleration in inflation appears modest, allowing policymakers breathing room to reassess the underlying inflation situation as the extent of the slowdown in real activity becomes more clear. With the balance of risks shifting increasingly to slower growth, the timely and significant interest rate cuts in the first four months of 2001 were welcome. Some further easing would be called for if economic and financial conditions remain weak. In the financial system, there has been a slight increase in nonperforming loans and in defaults on corporate paper, partly attributable to the kinds of overreaching typically experienced during strong economic periods. Nevertheless, banks remain quite profitable by historical standards and have an average capital ratio of 12 percent, more than two percentage points above the minimum level required to be considered well capitalized.

At this stage, monetary policy remains the preferred response to cyclical developments. But unlike the situation that prevailed at the time of the October 2000 *World Economic Outlook*, moderate and relatively front-loaded tax cuts guided by structural considerations could now be useful from a cyclical perspective, while minimizing the adverse impact on savings and the external current account balance over the medium term. A multiyear tax plan enacted in phases would be preferable, with each phase put in place only once it is clear that sufficient budgetary resources will be available to finance it. The surpluses of the Social Security and Medicare Health Insurance trust funds should be preserved to help meet future pension and health care costs.

In Canada, the U.S. slowdown is an important factor behind the projected moderation of

Box 1.2. Sustainability of the U.S. External Current Account

The rise in the U.S. external current account deficit to high levels in recent years has raised doubts about its sustainability and concerns regarding the potential impact that a rapid and disorderly correction of this imbalance might have. The deficit rose from 1½ percent of GDP in 1995 to nearly 4½ percent in 2000 (compared with its average during the previous two decades of 1½ percent). The financing of the deficit in 2000 absorbed an estimated 7½ percent of the savings of the rest of the world, in contrast to the 2½ percent absorbed on average during most of the last two decades. Rapid U.S. GDP growth and relatively weaker growth in other parts of the world, notably Europe and Japan, as well as a sharp increase in the real foreign exchange value of the U.S. dollar driven in large part by capital inflows, contributed to the rise in the deficit (see the figure). The domestic counterpart has been a significant rise in investment.

A number of observers have argued that such high levels of the deficit cannot persist.[1] If they were to continue for an extended period, U.S. net external liabilities would rise to an extremely high level and U.S. assets would represent a growing portion of world portfolios that foreign investors might, at some point, become unwilling to hold. This situation would run the risk of large adjustments in the current account and the external value of the dollar, potentially leading to substantial dislocations in the global economy and disruptions in U.S. and world financial markets. Indeed, some observers argue that the risks arise not so much from the size of the U.S. deficit or the outstanding U.S. net liability position as from the suddenness of any adjustment.[2] While the experience of

United States
(Annual percent change unless otherwise noted)

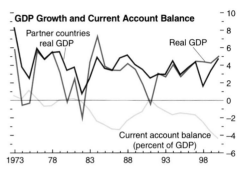

GDP Growth and Current Account Balance

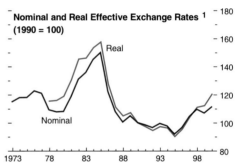

Nominal and Real Effective Exchange Rates [1]
(1990 = 100)

Sources: United States Bureau of Economic Analysis; and IMF staff estimates.
[1] Defined in terms of unit labor cost based on 1989–91 trade weights.

recent decades suggests that external adjustment has typically been gradual, there was a sharp fall in the real value of the dollar associated with the current account adjustment of the late 1980s.

Conventional trade equations imply that trade depends upon economic activity and real exchange rates. Accordingly, mechanisms that might lead to significant external adjustment on the trade side include:

• *Changes in cyclical positions.* After the robust growth in output of the last few years, the U.S. economy in 2000 was probably in a more cyclically advanced state than the euro area and (especially) Japan. While uncertainties about the levels and the underlying growth rates of potential complicate any assessment of the

---

[1]See, for example, Catherine Mann, "Is the U.S. Current Account Deficit Sustainable?" in *Finance and Development* (March 2000), pp. 42–45; and Francis Schott, "Is the U.S. Current Account Deficit Sustainable?" in *Business Economics* (July 2000), pp. 72–73.

[2]Maurice Obstfeld and Kenneth Rogoff, "Perspectives on OECD Economic Integration: Implications for U.S. Current Account Adjustment," paper presented at the Federal Reserve Bank of Kansas City symposium (August 2000).

size of this effect, current staff estimates suggest that "cyclical" factors might currently be adding around ½ percent of GDP to the U.S. current account deficit.

- *Changes in underlying growth performance.* The recent expansion of the U.S. current account deficit has coincided with increases in the estimated potential growth rate of the U.S. economy, and downgrades in the euro area and Japan. Clearly, an increase in potential growth rates in the euro area and Japan could help to reduce the U.S. current account deficit.[3] In addition, even if current potential growth trends continue, the U.S. deficit may not deteriorate as much as implied by conventional trade models, as one of the predictions from these models—that faster growing countries have trend depreciations in their real exchange rates or their external positions—is not consistent with the historical experience.[4]

However, this effect is unlikely to imply a long-term improvement in the U.S. current account deficit.

- *Exchange rate adjustment.* A depreciation of the real value of the U.S. dollar from current levels (which may partly reflect capital inflows associated with robust U.S. growth—see Chapter II) is likely to be the main mechanism by which the U.S. current account deficit is reduced over the medium term. This would presumably be associated with a slowing of U.S. domestic demand, in particular investment. Given the size of the U.S. current account deficit, and the relatively small share of trade in the economy, the implied exchange rate adjustment could be significant.

Appendix II of this Chapter reports a scenario in which the U.S. dollar gradually depreciates against other advanced economies. Over the medium term this generates a significant improvement in the external position of the United States, as domestic demand (in particular, investment) falls and external demand rises. From the historical record, such a gradual adjustment in underlying imbalances remains the most likely outcome.[5] However, a more abrupt adjustment remains a possibility.

[3]See the discussion of alternative scenarios in Appendix II of this Chapter for more on this issue.

[4]Rather, income elasticities for exports appear to vary systematically with long-term growth performance. See Paul Krugman, "Differences in Trade Elasticities and Trends in Real Exchange Rates," *European Economic Review*, Vol. 33 (May 1989), pp. 1031–54. The case of the United States is analyzed in Martin Cerisola, Hamid Faruqee, and Alex Keenan, "Long-Term Sustainability of the U.S. Current Account Balance," in United States: Selected Issues, IMF Staff Country Report No. 99/101 (Washington: International Monetary Fund, September 1999).

[5]See Caroline L. Freund, "Current Account Adjustment in Industrial Countries," International Finance Discussion Paper No. 692 (Washington: Board of Governors of the Federal Reserve System, December 2000).

growth from 4¾ percent in 2000 to 2¼ percent in 2001. The economy is very open to trade, with 86 percent of exports (which amount to 37 percent of GDP) destined for the United States, and it produces non-energy commodities, whose prices are expected to remain weak. While previous interest rate increases will dampen demand for durable goods, housing, and business investment, activity should be supported by the buoyant labor market, income tax reductions, and solid consumer and business confidence. The main downside risk is a deeper and more pro-

longed downturn south of the border. Given the downside risk to growth, and with core inflation remaining around the middle of the 1–3 percent official target range, the interest rate cuts in January, March, and April were welcome. The Bank of Canada will need to remain alert to the possibility that activity slows faster than expected. Recently enacted income tax cuts have been fortunately timed, and the fiscal position remains sound. To further reduce the government debt-to-GDP ratio over time, the government should dedicate the bulk of any projected budget surpluses to debt reduction. To enhance labor market flexibility and lower structural unemployment, new measures are needed to reduce the frequency of employment insurance use and eliminate regional extended benefits.

Will Japan's Fragile Recovery Continue?

In Japan, the recovery is stalling, reflecting in part the global slowdown but also the continuing weakness of consumer confidence and underlying problems with the financial system. The 1¾ percent increase in economic activity in 2000 was driven mainly by a strong first quarter, boosted by one-time factors, including a delay in wage bonuses from December to January and a shift in imports associated with Y2K concerns (Figure 1.6). Thereafter, private consumption was weighed down by uncertainties regarding future economic prospects, and industrial activity was dampened by the slowdown in foreign demand and the downturn in the information technology cycle. Bank lending continued to contract, reflecting weak credit demand and ongoing financial system weaknesses. Public investment and external demand are estimated to have made negative contributions to growth after midyear, reflecting the waning of the November 1999 fiscal stimulus package and the slowdown in partner countries.

The growth forecast for 2001 has been marked down to ½ percent, reflecting the economy's vulnerability to the global electronics cycle as well as the impact of sharp declines in equity prices on confidence. Concerns over unemployment are likely to restrain household spending, and slowing world demand for electronic equipment threatens to dampen business investment. Indeed, the recent *Tankan* survey showed a significant drop in business confidence. Fiscal policy should give a temporary boost to public investment around the second quarter, as the November 2000 stimulus package comes on stream, and the impact of the global slowdown should be cushioned by the depreciation of the yen. An important downside risk is the effect of falling stock prices and deteriorating economic

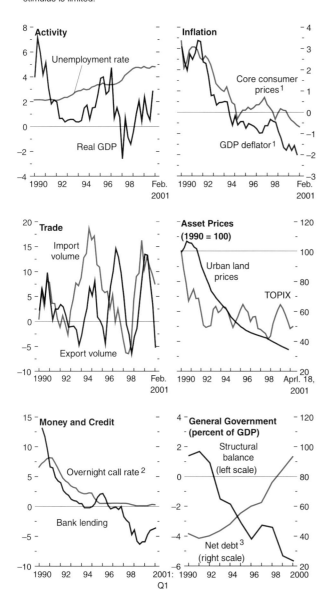

Figure 1.6. Japan: Recovery Faltering
(Percent change from four quarters earlier unless otherwise noted)

Sustained growth will depend on aggressive action to address financial system weakness, especially as the scope for fiscal or monetary stimulus is limited.

Sources: Bloomberg Financial Markets, LP; WEFA; Nomura database; and IMF staff estimates (general government data, 1999-2000).
[1] Adjusted for impact of consumption tax increase in April 1997.
[2] Average of the month.
[3] Excluding social security.

conditions on the financial system. Market analysts are concerned that, at current stock prices, banks and life insurance companies face latent losses on their equity portfolios, which will directly reduce their capital once mark-to-market accounting comes into effect in April 2001, and doubts remain about the extent to which they have recognized and provisioned against problem loans. A sharper-than-expected slowdown in Japan would have a significant adverse impact on the rest of the world, especially Asia.

The faltering recovery is particularly regrettable after a decade of disappointing performance, punctuated by repeated recessions, and characterized by a series of adverse macroeconomic shocks and failures to decisively resolve important structural reform challenges. In particular, current weak growth reflects slow adjustment to the sharp fall in asset prices in the early 1990s, as well as the slow adaptation to globalization and technological change.[3] The prolonged slump in business investment reflects mainly excessive fixed assets and debt in the corporate sector, while lending was undermined by financial system weaknesses, including persistent bad loans and low core profitability, as financial institutions clung to low-margin corporate lending and were slow to expand fee-generating activities. Sluggish performance also reflects the slow shift in the main engines of growth from capital accumulation and exports to innovation and productivity gains.

Weak growth in the 1990s persisted despite expansionary macroeconomic policies. Monetary policy was progressively eased, with the overnight call rate falling from more than 8 percent in 1991 to effectively zero in 1999, but ongoing financial sector problems—which undermined bank lending—largely offset easier monetary policy. Fiscal policy was loosened through a series of stimulus packages, which raised the structural general government deficit by more than 6 percentage points of GDP between 1991–99. However, in practice the impact

was relatively small, reflecting in part the lack of fiscal transparency and increasing concerns about growing fiscal imbalances.

In light of the deteriorating outlook and continued deflation, the introduction of a new monetary policy framework in March was welcome and it should be aggressively implemented (Box 1.3). Given the high level of public debt, the very gradual fiscal consolidation currently under way is appropriate for now, and fiscal easing should only be considered as a last resort in the event that stimulus is needed to forestall an outright recession (Table 1.3). To prepare for the lengthy period of fiscal consolidation that will eventually be needed, the authorities need to take immediate steps to elaborate their medium-term fiscal framework. Key elements of the strategy will need to include the production of consolidated fiscal accounts on a timely basis, the implementation of rigorous cost-benefit vetting of public works, the introduction of taxpayer identification numbers to widen the personal income tax net, and reform of public health care spending.

While macroeconomic policy can play some role, the prospects for a return to sustained growth in the medium term depend most critically on the implementation of fundamental reforms in the banking and corporate sectors. To aid this process, the government recently announced a package of measures—including the accelerated disposal of nonperforming loans by the major banks, measures to reduce banks' equity holdings, and guidelines to aid corporate restructuring and debt forgiveness—which are designed to accelerate the pace of bank and corporate sector restructuring (see Box 1.3). To minimize the adverse short-run impact of these needed structural reforms, the government also announced plans to enhance the social safety net. These new reforms are a welcome step forward, but they will need to be supplemented with other measures. Further, the regulatory and supervisory framework needs to be vigorously applied, particularly in light of the scheduled reimposition of limited deposit insurance in April 2002, including through enforcing more rigorous loan classification standards and more

---

[3]Tamim Bayoumi and Charles Collyns, eds., *Post-Bubble Blues: How Japan Responded to Asset Price Collapse* (Washington: International Monetary Fund, 2000).

Table 1.3. Major Advanced Economies: General Government Fiscal Balances and Debt[1]
(Percent of GDP)

	1984–94	1995	1996	1997	1998	1999	2000	2001	2002	2006
Major advanced economies										
Actual balance	–3.8	–4.1	–3.4	–1.9	–1.3	–1.0	0.1	–0.4	–0.7	0.2
Output gap	–0.7	–2.2	–2.1	–1.5	–1.4	–1.0	0.2	–0.8	–1.1	–0.1
Structural balance	–3.4	–3.2	–2.6	–1.2	–0.7	–0.6	–0.4	–0.2	–0.3	0.2
United States										
Actual balance	–4.9	–3.3	–2.4	–1.3	—	0.7	1.7	1.6	0.8	1.1
Output gap	–1.9	–3.2	–2.9	–1.8	–0.7	0.3	2.0	0.2	–0.5	–0.1
Structural balance	–4.3	–2.2	–1.5	–0.7	0.2	0.6	1.0	1.5	1.0	1.1
Net debt	48.3	59.6	59.2	57.1	53.4	48.8	43.9	40.8	38.1	26.6
Gross debt	62.5	72.9	72.8	70.3	66.6	63.2	57.3	53.8	50.6	36.6
Japan										
Actual balance	0.2	–3.5	–4.2	–3.2	–4.5	–7.0	–8.2	–6.8	–5.9	–2.1
Output gap	0.8	–1.4	0.1	—	–2.9	–3.7	–3.3	–3.8	–3.8	–0.2
Structural balance	0.3	–3.1	–4.2	–3.3	–3.4	–5.7	–7.2	–5.6	–4.8	–2.2
Net debt	16.3	12.7	16.0	17.5	29.5	35.9	43.4	49.7	54.4	58.7
Gross debt	68.9	87.1	92.5	96.8	110.2	120.3	130.4	139.5	145.2	147.6
Memorandum										
Actual balance excluding social security	–2.8	–6.3	–6.7	–5.8	–6.5	–8.8	–9.5	–7.7	–6.6	–3.3
Structural balance excluding social security	–3.3	–6.0	–6.8	–5.8	–5.9	–8.0	–9.0	–7.1	–6.1	–3.4
Germany[2]										
Actual balance[3]	–2.0	–3.3	–3.4	–2.7	–2.1	–1.4	1.5	–2.0	–1.5	–1.3
Output gap	–0.9	0.2	–0.9	–1.4	–1.2	–1.7	–0.9	–1.3	–1.0	—
Structural balance	–1.2	–3.3	–2.7	–1.6	–1.1	–0.4	–0.5	–1.3	–1.0	–1.3
Net debt	22.3	49.4	51.1	52.2	52.0	52.3	51.5	50.3	49.5	46.6
Gross debt	42.6	58.3	59.8	60.9	60.7	61.0	60.2	59.0	58.2	55.3
France										
Actual balance[3]	–3.0	–5.5	–4.1	–3.0	–2.7	–1.6	–1.3	–0.6	–0.8	—
Output gap	–0.1	–2.7	–3.3	–3.1	–2.0	–1.2	–0.5	–0.4	–0.4	—
Structural balance	–2.9	–4.0	–2.3	–1.4	–1.7	–0.8	–0.9	–0.9	–0.6	—
Net debt	24.8	45.8	48.1	49.6	50.0	49.2	48.6	48.6	47.4	37.7
Gross debt	34.4	54.5	57.1	59.3	59.7	58.9	58.3	57.9	55.9	49.0
Italy										
Actual balance[3]	–10.7	–7.6	–7.1	–2.7	–2.8	–1.8	–0.3	–1.3	–1.2	0.8
Output gap	–0.2	–1.1	–2.0	–2.3	–2.4	–2.7	–1.8	–1.8	–1.4	—
Structural balance	–10.7	–7.0	–6.2	–1.7	–1.8	–0.6	–0.7	–0.5	–0.6	0.9
Net debt	85.4	116.6	116.0	113.7	110.1	108.4	104.4	101.8	99.7	87.3
Gross debt	92.5	123.2	122.6	120.1	116.2	114.5	110.2	107.5	105.3	92.2
United Kingdom										
Actual balance[3]	–2.9	–5.4	–4.1	–1.5	0.3	1.5	5.9	1.3	0.3	0.4
Output gap	–0.1	–1.1	–0.9	–0.4	—	–0.1	0.1	–0.2	–0.1	—
Structural balance	–2.0	–4.4	–3.4	–1.0	0.5	1.5	3.4	1.3	0.4	0.4
Net debt	29.5	37.0	46.5	45.0	42.3	39.5	36.5	33.7	31.6	27.4
Gross debt	44.4	52.0	52.2	49.9	47.0	44.4	41.3	38.3	36.0	31.1
Canada										
Actual balance	–7.1	–5.4	–2.8	0.2	0.2	2.2	3.4	2.7	2.5	1.8
Output gap	–2.0	–4.4	–5.3	–3.6	–3.3	–1.6	0.2	–0.3	–0.6	—
Structural balance	–5.7	–2.9	0.1	2.2	1.9	3.0	3.3	2.9	2.9	1.8
Net debt	60.5	88.5	88.2	83.4	81.4	75.3	66.9	61.0	56.0	38.8
Gross debt	92.6	120.6	120.9	117.4	116.2	111.6	101.6	94.3	87.8	65.2

Note: The methodology and specific assumptions for each country are discussed in Box A1.

[1]Debt data refer to end of year; for the United Kingdom they refer to end of March.

[2]Data before 1990 refer to west Germany. For net debt, the first column refers to 1988–94. Beginning in 1995, the debt and debt-service obligations of the Treuhandanstalt (and of various other agencies) were taken over by general government. This debt is equivalent to 8 percent of GDP, and the associated debt service to ½ to 1 percent of GDP.

[3]Includes one-off receipts from the sale of mobile telephone licenses equivalent to 2.5 percent of GDP in 2000 for Germany, 0.6 percent of GDP in 2001 for France, 1.2 percent of GDP in 2000 for Italy, and 2.4 percent of GDP in 2000 for the United Kingdom.

Box 1.3. Japan's Recent Monetary and Structural Policy Initiatives

The Japanese authorities have recently taken a number of welcome steps to enhance the monetary policy framework and to accelerate the pace of bank and corporate sector restructuring. These policy decisions were taken with the aim of ending the current period of deflation and bringing about the fundamental reforms necessary in the banking and corporate sectors to underpin strong, sustained growth over the medium term.

Monetary Policy Framework

On March 19, in response to mounting evidence that the economic recovery had stalled, the Bank of Japan announced that it was adopting a new framework for monetary policy based on:

- A quantitative target for outstanding current account balances at the central bank (mainly consisting of central bank reserves), rather than a target for the overnight interbank call rate. The current target for banks' balances held at the central bank is ¥5 trillion, about ¥1 trillion above the average balance held in the months prior to the policy change.
- Stepped-up outright purchases of long-term government bonds, if needed, to achieve the reserves target. In a significant departure from its earlier policy of purchasing a fixed amount of government bonds in the secondary markets each month, the Bank of Japan signaled its willingness to step up outright purchases of long-term government bonds in the secondary market (*rinban* operations), if necessary, to ensure the smooth provision of liquidity.[1]
- A commitment to maintain this new policy until year-on-year CPI inflation (excluding perishables) has stably reached zero or above.

Following the announcement, the overnight call rate, which is now market-determined, declined to effectively zero. Moreover, the Bank of Japan's increased commitment to combat deflation has underpinned market expectations that

short-term interest rates will stay near zero at least through mid-2002.

The Bank of Japan's willingness to tread new ground and its stated commitment to at least stabilize consumer prices are welcome signs of greater flexibility in dealing with the current deflationary environment. This new approach goes further than merely returning to the zero interest rate policy and provides scope for the Bank of Japan to inject further stimulus to the economy if needed in the future. It also improves policy transparency—the objective of stabilizing consumer prices is more clearly defined than the previous zero-interest rate policy that sought to maintain zero interest rates until "deflationary concerns were dispelled"—and should help to reduce deflationary expectations. However, to be most effective the Bank of Japan will need to follow through in using the scope provided by the framework to clearly demonstrate its determination to combat deflation.

Financial and Corporate Restructuring

On April 6, in response to concerns about the pace of bank and corporate restructuring, the government announced a package of measures designed to accelerate the pace of such restructuring. The main elements of the package were:

- Accelerated disposal of nonperforming loans by the major banks. The plan calls for the major banks to dispose of existing nonperforming loans (NPLs) already classified as "in danger of bankruptcy" and below over a two-year period and new NPLs within three years of their being classified as such. Banks will periodically be required to disclose their progress toward loan disposal, and the situation will be monitored by the Financial Services Agency.
- Measures to reduce banks' equity holdings. To reduce banks' exposure to market risk and curtail cross shareholdings, the plan calls for a yet-to-be-determined limit on banks' equity holdings relative to capital. As a temporary measure, a Bank Shareholdings Acquisition Corporation (BASAC) will be established, with public sector financial support, to buy the banks' excess equity holdings at market prices.

---

[1]However, long-term government bonds effectively held at the central bank cannot rise above the outstanding issue of bank notes.

Box 1.3 *(concluded)*

- The promotion of corporate restructuring. Guidelines are to be established to guide the process of corporate restructuring and debt forgiveness, with the participation of the authorities along the lines of the London Approach.
- Other measures to support restructuring. These include steps to enhance the social safety net and to improve liquidity in the real estate market. Tax reform measures are also under consideration for inclusion in the package at a later date.

While the new emphasis on banking and corporate issues is welcome, the package will need to be implemented vigorously and complemented by additional measures to maximize its impact. One important way to enhance the package would be to broaden coverage to include disposal of NPLs by the regional banks (given that the major banks make up less than half of the assets of deposit taking institutions). In addition, supervision should continue to be strengthened, including to ensure appropriate classification of the large stock of loans to watch

list borrowers a significant part of which—according to market analysts—may in fact be impaired, with appropriate levels of provisioning to reflect a realistic forward looking assessment of prospects of loan recovery. The need to provision against newly downgraded loans may well result in some banks becoming undercapitalized, which could require a further injection of public capital, with appropriately strict conditionality to address moral hazard concerns. The equity purchase scheme in the package needs to be designed to minimize distortions, ensure transparency, and limit the amount of public funds at risk. Finally, it will be essential to ensure that corporate restructuring agreements under the scheme involve sufficiently deep adjustment to restore the long term viability of firms being restructured.

Thus, while the new proposals make a welcome step forward, they will need to be implemented with vigor, and supplemented with other steps to encourage the broad-based bank and corporate restructuring needed to lay the basis for sustained recovery in Japan.

aggressive provisioning against problem loans. To improve the environment for corporate restructuring as banks and firms agree on debt forgiveness in exchange for restructuring plans, a number of complementary reforms are also needed, including to land regulations and to relevant parts of the tax and legal system. Other priority areas for reform include: the deregulation of the telecommunications, power, transportation, and housing sectors; strengthening the role of outside auditors and directors on corporate boards to improve governance; and encouraging private defined-contribution pensions to enhance labor mobility across firms.

Can Domestic Demand Sustain European Growth?

Growth in the euro area is expected to be cushioned by domestic demand, although the

global slowdown and financial market weakness are having an adverse impact on activity (Table 1.4). Real GDP growth eased during the course of 2000, mostly reflecting the negative effect of higher oil prices on purchasing power, particularly in *Germany* (Figure 1.7). In recent months, business confidence has weakened and signs of slowing industrial activity have intensified. Looking ahead, growth in 2001 is expected to remain relatively well sustained at about 2½ percent, exceeding growth in the United States for the first time since 1991. Household spending is expected to be underpinned by expanding disposable income, reflecting both continued employment growth and personal income tax cuts in some countries. While business sentiment has declined markedly in some countries, the vulnerability of business investment is likely to be limited by high levels of capacity utilization and full order books, the fall in long-term interest rates,

Table 1.4. Advanced Economies: Real GDP, Consumer Prices, and Unemployment
(Annual percent change and percent of labor force)

	Real GDP				Consumer Prices				Unemployment			
	1999	2000	2001	2002	1999	2000	2001	2002	1999	2000	2001	2002
Advanced economies	**3.4**	**4.1**	**1.9**	**2.7**	**1.4**	**2.3**	**2.1**	**1.8**	**6.4**	**5.9**	**5.9**	**5.9**
Major advanced economies	3.0	3.8	1.6	2.4	1.4	2.3	1.9	1.7	6.1	5.7	5.9	6.0
United States	4.2	5.0	1.5	2.5	2.2	3.4	2.6	2.2	4.2	4.0	4.4	5.0
Japan	0.8	1.7	0.6	1.5	−0.3	−0.6	−0.7	—	4.7	4.7	5.3	5.2
Germany	1.6	3.0	1.9	2.6	0.7	2.1	2.0	1.3	8.3	7.8	7.6	7.4
France	3.2	3.2	2.6	2.6	0.6	1.8	1.5	1.4	11.3	9.7	8.8	8.2
Italy	1.6	2.9	2.0	2.5	1.7	2.6	2.2	1.6	11.4	10.6	9.9	9.5
United Kingdom[1]	2.3	3.0	2.6	2.8	2.3	2.1	2.2	2.4	6.0	5.6	5.3	5.4
Canada	4.5	4.7	2.3	2.4	1.7	2.7	3.0	2.2	7.6	6.8	7.2	7.1
Other advanced economies	4.8	5.2	3.0	3.8	1.3	2.4	2.8	2.3	7.3	6.3	6.1	5.7
Spain	4.0	4.1	2.9	3.2	2.2	3.4	2.9	2.3	15.9	14.1	12.7	11.7
Netherlands	3.9	3.9	2.9	2.7	2.0	2.3	3.9	2.4	3.2	2.8	3.0	3.0
Belgium	2.7	3.9	2.4	2.4	1.1	2.9	2.2	1.3	8.8	7.0	7.0	7.0
Sweden	4.1	3.6	2.6	2.8	0.5	1.0	1.8	1.9	5.6	4.7	4.1	4.0
Austria	2.8	3.2	2.2	2.6	0.5	2.0	1.7	1.6	3.8	3.3	3.4	3.3
Denmark	2.1	2.9	2.1	2.3	2.6	3.1	2.5	2.1	5.6	5.2	5.3	5.3
Finland	4.2	5.7	4.2	4.0	1.3	3.0	2.6	2.4	10.3	9.8	9.2	8.8
Greece	3.4	4.0	3.8	3.8	2.2	2.9	3.4	3.3	11.7	11.1	10.9	10.7
Portugal	2.8	3.0	2.4	2.8	2.2	2.8	3.8	2.3	4.4	4.1	4.0	4.0
Ireland	9.8	10.7	7.0	6.2	2.5	5.3	4.0	3.3	5.6	4.3	3.7	3.7
Luxembourg	7.3	8.5	4.2	4.3	1.0	3.2	1.5	1.3	2.9	2.6	2.7	2.6
Switzerland	1.5	3.4	2.0	2.0	0.8	1.6	1.4	1.5	2.7	1.9	1.9	1.8
Norway	0.9	2.2	1.9	2.3	2.3	3.0	2.8	2.5	3.2	3.4	3.5	3.5
Israel	2.3	6.0	1.8	4.3	5.2	1.1	0.9	2.5	8.9	8.8	9.4	8.6
Iceland	4.1	3.6	1.9	2.1	3.4	5.0	4.6	3.5	1.9	1.3	1.8	2.1
Cyprus	4.5	5.0	4.5	4.0	1.8	4.1	2.7	2.7	3.6	3.5	3.6	3.8
Korea	10.9	8.8	3.5	5.5	0.8	2.2	4.3	3.0	6.3	4.1	4.2	3.5
Australia[2]	4.7	3.7	1.9	3.5	1.5	4.5	3.7	2.4	7.2	6.6	7.0	6.7
Taiwan Province of China	5.4	6.0	4.1	5.6	0.2	1.3	1.4	1.5	2.7	3.2	3.4	3.2
Hong Kong SAR	3.1	10.5	3.5	4.8	−4.0	−3.7	0.5	2.0	6.3	5.0	4.7	4.1
Singapore	5.9	9.9	5.0	5.8	0.1	1.4	1.9	1.9	3.5	3.1	2.7	2.5
New Zealand[2]	3.9	3.5	2.6	2.7	1.1	2.7	2.8	2.1	6.8	6.0	5.8	5.9
Memorandum												
European Union	2.6	3.4	2.4	2.8	1.4	2.3	2.3	1.8	9.1	8.2	7.8	7.5
Euro area	2.6	3.4	2.4	2.8	1.2	2.4	2.3	1.7	9.9	9.0	8.4	8.1

[1]Consumer prices are based on the retail price index excluding mortgage interest.
[2]Consumer prices excluding interest rate components; for Australia, also excluding other volatile items.

and the relative importance of bank lending (rather than market-based finance). Among the major economies, growth has the greatest momentum in France, driven by relatively strong final domestic demand. In addition, France has more limited vulnerability to external developments, reflecting a lower share of manufacturing in value added, a smaller proportion of capital goods in exports, and weaker trade linkages with the United States and Asia. In Germany and Italy, final domestic demand has been much weaker, although in both countries (particularly in Germany) tax cuts should support private consumption during 2001. Weakening external demand will help reduce overheating pressures in the countries on the periphery, especially *Ireland*, which receives substantial U.S. foreign direct investment and whose economy is relatively technology intensive, but may exacerbate already large current account deficits, including in *Portugal* and—to a lesser extent—*Greece*.

Monetary policy has been on hold since the ¼ percentage point tightening in October 2000. Underlying inflation is expected to remain steady in 2001 at 1½ percent, with little evidence thus far of pass-through effects from last year's

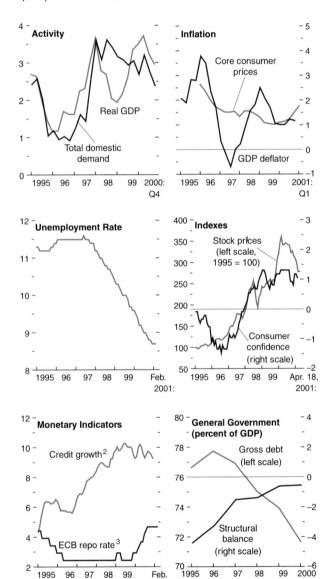

Figure 1.7. Euro Area: Growth Moderating, but Still Reasonably Robust
(Percent change from four quarters earlier unless otherwise noted)

Growth slowed during 2000, with both private consumption and business investment easing. Despite falling unemployment, domestic price pressures remain contained.

Sources: Eurostat; European Central Bank; European Commission; IMF, *International Financial Statistics*; and IMF staff estimates.
1 Dow Jones EURO STOXX index.
2 Three month center moving average.
3 Prior to 1999, Bundesbank repo rate.

higher energy prices or the weaker euro to wages, though inflation is higher in countries on the periphery. The moderation of broad money growth and indicators of underlying inflation—including unit labor costs, profit margins, services price inflation, and core inflation purged of indirect energy effects—point to muted domestic price pressures. At the same time, the fall in external demand has become more pronounced. Given the shift in the balance of inflation risks, a moderate cut in interest rates is now appropriate, with a larger one being in order if the exchange rate were to appreciate sharply or indications of the impact of the global slowdown were to mount.

At this stage fiscal policy is not needed to support activity, given the flexibility to use monetary policy to provide stimulus, though fiscal execution should allow the full play of automatic stabilizers. The structural fiscal balance in the euro area as a whole is expected to remain broadly unchanged in 2001, with a deterioration in Germany (¾ percent of GDP) offset by improvements elsewhere, including in France and *Spain*. Reductions in personal and corporate income taxes in Germany, France, Italy, and *the Netherlands* are expected to improve labor supply incentives, reduce investment distortions, and increase these countries' attractiveness to foreign investors. Tax cuts need to be accompanied by spending restraint in the future to allow medium-term budget targets to be met. In most countries, structural spending cuts should be targeted mainly on subsidies, social transfer programs, and public employment. Countries with overheating pressures should avoid loosening fiscal policies, even if they have a significant fiscal surplus, as in Ireland, and—if monetary policy is eased during the year—may need to consider offsetting fiscal measures.

While the near-term growth outlook in the euro area is still quite favorable relative to North America and Japan, policymakers should not be satisfied with a potential growth rate estimated at 2½ percent. Although important progress has been made in some areas of structural reform, unemployment remains high and a deepening and acceleration of market-oriented reforms are needed, especially of pension systems, labor markets, and product markets. Rising pension and health care costs remain serious medium-term challenges (see Chapter III). In Germany, pension reform that will lay the foundation for a funded "second pillar" to supplement the public pension pillar is moving through the legislative process, albeit with some compromises. In many other euro area countries as well, the establishment of a similar funded "second pillar" will be essential to reduce the burden of aging populations on public pensions and diminish the need for further increases in social contribution rates that could harm labor market performance. Cuts in benefits provided under public pensions—through, among other actions, increases in the retirement age—beyond levels currently envisaged will also be needed in the longer run. Controlling public health care costs will depend on measures to improve cost-sharing and administrative capacity.

Further reductions in unemployment over the medium term will depend largely on additional progress in addressing labor market rigidities. Germany shows signs of greater flexibility in *de facto* working conditions and wages, but legal changes are needed to allow employers and workers to reach wage agreements more in line with firm-level conditions. In France, the 35-hour work week initiative has proceeded relatively smoothly to date, but with the legislation being extended to small firms, flexible implementation—including the relaxation of restrictions on allowable annual overtime hours—will be needed as the labor market tightens. In Italy, the main challenge is to raise employment in the south by linking wages to productivity to achieve greater geographic wage differentiation. In Spain, the priorities are fostering part-time work, reducing dismissal costs to stimulate the growth of employment, and increasing flexibility in wage bargaining.

Additional product market reforms will also be important to increase potential growth rates. Germany has recently implemented impressive reforms in the telecommunications and energy

sectors, but further actions are needed, including the liberalization of shop opening hours, and privatization of financial institutions and of the remaining state holdings in public utility companies. Similarly, in France, the recent progress in privatization is welcome, although there is further scope for liberalization of the financial system, especially with regard to administered interest rates, and of the telecommunications and energy sectors. In Italy, the large privatization program in recent years provides a good basis for additional measures, including further liberalization of the energy sector, reform of the legal framework governing nonlisted companies, and vigorous implementation of the simplifications in public administration and licensing procedures.

With its greater openness to trade and financial flows, the *United Kingdom* is more vulnerable than the euro area to external developments. Growth is showing signs of moderating and the forecast for 2001 is now at 2½ percent, with the balance of risks tilted downward. Domestic demand growth is projected to moderate, despite a strong pickup in public spending, and the external balance is expected to continue to make a negative contribution to growth. Notwithstanding high levels of resource utilization, core inflation has been below target, hovering around 2 percent, reflecting the strength of sterling against the euro, wage moderation, and—more recently—softening economic activity. As inflationary pressures remain subdued, the Bank of England's interest rate cuts in February and April were appropriate, and there remains room for further easing if the growth outlook were to deteriorate further. The March 2001 budget envisages a reduction of the public sector surplus from 1½ percent of GDP in 2000/01 to ½ percent of GDP in 2001/02. While this expansion most likely can be accommodated without overheating, it could contribute to a policy mix that may tend to keep sterling elevated. Over the medium term, the large planned increase in public investment in infrastructure and human capital should help to raise productivity growth. However, it would be better to avoid

Table 1.5. Selected Asian Countries: Real GDP, Consumer Prices, and Current Account Balance
(Annual percent change unless otherwise noted)

	Real GDP				Consumer Prices[1]				Current Account Balances[2]			
	1999	2000	2001	2002	1999	2000	2001	2002	1999	2000	2001	2002
Emerging Asia[3]	**6.3**	**7.1**	**5.6**	**6.2**	**2.1**	**1.8**	**2.8**	**3.2**	**3.7**	**2.7**	**1.9**	**1.5**
Newly industrialized Asian economies	**7.9**	**8.2**	**3.8**	**5.5**	**—**	**1.1**	**2.8**	**2.3**	**7.0**	**5.1**	**4.2**	**3.9**
Hong Kong SAR	3.1	10.5	3.5	4.8	-4.0	-3.7	0.5	2.0	6.6	5.8	3.0	4.1
Korea	10.9	8.8	3.5	5.5	0.8	2.2	4.3	3.0	6.0	2.4	2.3	1.2
Singapore	5.9	9.9	5.0	5.8	0.1	1.4	1.9	1.9	25.9	23.6	21.0	20.2
Taiwan Province of China	5.4	6.0	4.1	5.6	0.2	1.3	1.4	1.5	2.9	3.0	2.4	2.5
ASEAN-4	**2.8**	**5.0**	**3.4**	**4.7**	**10.2**	**3.0**	**5.7**	**4.7**	**9.2**	**7.7**	**6.1**	**4.9**
Indonesia	0.8	4.8	3.5	4.6	20.7	3.8	8.9	5.7	4.1	4.2	3.5	2.0
Malaysia	5.8	8.5	4.5	6.0	2.8	1.5	2.0	2.4	15.9	9.7	6.3	5.6
Philippines	3.3	3.9	3.3	4.5	6.6	4.3	6.1	5.8	10.0	12.4	12.1	11.5
Thailand	4.2	4.3	3.0	4.5	0.3	1.5	2.1	3.6	10.2	7.6	5.9	4.5
South Asia[4]	**6.2**	**6.2**	**5.4**	**5.9**	**4.8**	**4.1**	**4.1**	**5.8**	**-1.0**	**-1.2**	**-1.3**	**-1.5**
Bangladesh	5.2	5.0	4.5	4.5	6.3	4.7	5.8	6.3	-1.7	-1.6	-1.8	-2.1
India	6.6	6.4	5.6	6.1	4.7	4.0	3.8	5.9	-0.6	-1.0	-1.2	-1.3
Pakistan	4.3	5.1	4.4	5.0	4.1	4.4	4.9	4.6	-2.7	-1.6	-1.4	-0.9
Formerly centrally planned economies[5]	**7.1**	**8.0**	**7.0**	**7.1**	**-1.4**	**0.4**	**1.0**	**1.5**	**1.6**	**1.2**	**0.6**	**0.2**
China	7.1	8.0	7.0	7.1	-1.4	0.4	1.0	1.5	1.6	1.2	0.6	0.2
Vietnam	4.2	5.5	5.0	6.0	4.1	-1.7	4.0	4.2	4.5	2.1	-0.3	-4.2

[1]In accordance with standard practice in the *World Economic Outlook*, movements in consumer prices are indicated as annual averages rather than as December/December changes during the year, as is the practice in some countries.
[2]Percent of GDP.
[3]Developing Asia, newly industrialized Asian economies, and Mongolia.
[4]Bangladesh, India, Maldives, Nepal, Pakistan, and Sri Lanka.
[5]Cambodia, China, Lao People's Dem. Rep., Mongolia, and Vietnam.

returning to a budget deficit, so as not to reduce the pool of national savings available for private investment.

Other advanced European economies are even more open than the United Kingdom and thus more vulnerable to external developments. Growth in *Switzerland* is expected to slow sharply from 3½ percent in 2000 to 2 percent in 2001, because of the relatively high importance of the U.S. export market. Growth in Sweden is projected to decline from 3½ percent to 2½ percent, reflecting mainly lower external demand but also the impact of declining stock prices, particularly in the technology sector, on domestic demand. At the same time, low unemployment in both countries, as well as in *Denmark* and *Norway*, is expected to support both consumption and investment in 2001, as firms seek ways around skill shortages. On the whole, monetary policy in these countries is well positioned to react quickly and aggressively to sharper-than-

envisaged weakness in activity. In *Iceland*, where the current account deficit has widened sharply, fiscal policy needs to play a supporting role in addressing domestic and external imbalances, accompanied by early measures to strengthen the financial system; the recent floating of the currency, together with the adoption of inflation targeting, is welcome and will help promote long-term financial stability.

How Will the Global Slowdown Affect Asia?

In emerging Asia, GDP growth rose to 7.1 percent in 2000, buoyed by the continuing recovery from the 1997–98 crisis (Table 1.5). However, following rapid growth in the first half of the year, the pace of activity has since fallen back markedly, and in 2001 regional growth is expected to decline to 5.7 percent. While a slowdown from the high growth rates during the recovery period was expected, this also reflected a series of shocks, including higher oil prices; slowing growth in the United States, the fall in the NASDAQ, and the downturn in the global electronics cycle; political uncertainties; and in a number of countries, concerns over the lagging pace of corporate and financial restructuring. The slowdown was accompanied—and exacerbated—by a sharp decline in regional equity markets, declining portfolio inflows, and in some cases downward pressure on exchange rates.

The impact of these shocks has varied across the region. In *China* and *India*, which account for three-quarters of regional output (excluding Japan), exposure to external developments is moderate and growth in activity is expected to be relatively well maintained. Elsewhere, while activity will in most cases be cushioned by lower U.S. interest rates and to a modest degree by lower oil prices, the effect will be significantly greater. Growth is expected to slow sharply in a number of the newly industrialized and ASEAN countries, with the extent of the slowdown depending on their cyclical positions; vulnerability to external shocks (Figure 1.8); and country-specific factors, such as political uncertainties. Given the improvement in macroeconomic fundamentals over the past three years, combined with more flexible exchange rate management, these countries are in general better placed to manage external shocks than in the past. Nonetheless, the impact of the global slowdown will still be substantial, and would be significantly exacerbated in the event of a harder landing in the United States, a deeper-than-expected slowdown in Japan, or a sharp depreciation of the yen.

In China, the largest economy in the region, activity remained robust during 2000, propelled by rising exports, recovering private consumption, and higher public spending; inflation turned modestly positive as deflationary pressures receded. Given the deterioration in the external environment, GDP growth is expected to moderate to 7 percent in 2001 while inflation remains subdued. The fiscal deficit in the 2001

**Figure 1.8. Selected Asian Countries:
The Impact of Weakening External Demand**

A number of newly industrialized and ASEAN economies are vulnerable to weaker external demand, especially for technology goods.

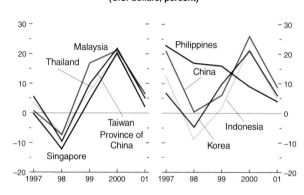

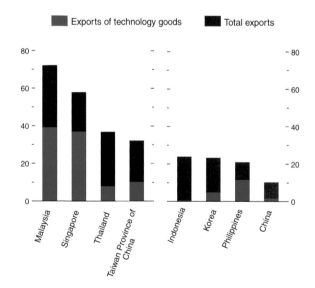

Source: IMF staff estimates.
[1] Goods.
[2] Excluding imported intermediate inputs used in those exports.

budget reflects an appropriately expansionary policy stance, although a modest mid-year spending package may be required if the heightened downside risks to growth materialize. Over the medium term, the scope for further stimulus will be constrained by the need to tackle the substantial off-budget liabilities relating to bank and SOE restructuring, and pension liabilities. As elsewhere, financial and enterprise reforms remain the central priority. Asset Management Companies have now taken over a substantial proportion of nonperforming loans, but need additional powers and political support to move forward with enterprise restructuring. Given the ongoing structural changes in the economy, including those associated with accession to the World Trade Organization (WTO), greater exchange rate flexibility will also be desirable at the appropriate time. In *Hong Kong SAR*, after a strong "V-shaped" recovery, growth is expected to slow markedly to 3.5 percent in 2001, in part reflecting slowing export growth in the Mainland, the weakening regional situation, and falling retail sales. Activity in *Taiwan Province of China* is also expected to weaken, mainly reflecting the downturn in the global electronics cycle, as well as financial sector problems.

Turning to South Asia, GDP growth in India slowed to 6.4 percent in 2000, owing to a second consecutive year of below average monsoons and a weakening of industrial output. Overall activity is expected to slow further to about 5.6 percent in 2001, as a rebound in agricultural production is offset by continued sluggishness in manufacturing and the effect of the devastating earthquake in Gujarat. Inflation increased sharply in 2000 and early 2001, but this appears to have mainly reflected the effects of adjustments in administered fuel prices, and price pressures have recently begun to ease. Despite India's heavy reliance on imported oil, the impact of higher world prices on the current account deficit has been largely offset by buoyant exports and sluggish non-oil imports. The weakness of the rupee and the downward pressure on international reserves that emerged in 2000 have eased, aided by higher remittances from expatriate Indians,

and the Reserve Bank of India was able to lower its Bank rate in February and March 2001. The central challenge for India's policymakers remains to sustain—and indeed improve upon—the economy's strong growth during the 1990s to support meaningful poverty reduction. This will require major structural reforms that improve the environment for private investment and a substantial reduction in the overall public sector deficit, which—at 10–11 percent of GDP—consumed one-half of overall gross domestic saving in 2000/01. The government's 2001/02 budget suggests that the fiscal deficit may remain high, especially once privatization receipts are excluded from the calculation and taking into account the possibility that activity may be slower than expected. Nonetheless, the budget included welcome signs that the commitment to structural reform has been reinvigorated, and proposed fiscal responsibility legislation also signals an encouraging willingness to take the steps necessary to achieve medium-term fiscal consolidation. In *Pakistan*, the depreciation of the rupee and the tightening of monetary policy in the second half of 2000 helped reverse the decline in official reserves, which had reached dangerously low levels. After bumper harvests of major crops last year, manufacturing output has started to pick up, but a severe drought is now casting a shadow over growth prospects for 2001–2002. The recent resolution of tariff disputes with independent power producers will boost investor confidence, but an enduring improvement in consumer and investor sentiment will require accelerated structural reforms to strengthen private sector activity and improve fiscal performance.

Turning to the remaining newly industrialized and ASEAN economies, activity is expected to slow most markedly in those countries where the recovery is furthest advanced; while this is expected, in a number of cases the slowdown has been exacerbated by domestic and external developments. This is particularly the case in *Korea*, where domestic confidence and demand have been weakened by concerns about the pace of corporate restructuring, and exports—

particularly of electronics goods—have slowed sharply. In *Singapore* and *Malaysia*, which are also advanced in the recovery, domestic demand remains relatively strong—notwithstanding some weakening in confidence in Malaysia on account of concerns over corporate restructuring—but slowing external demand is a serious concern. Elsewhere, the recovery has been much slower, and is in danger of weakening further. In the *Philippines*, while recent political uncertainties have now been resolved, they have been accompanied by substantial fiscal slippages. In *Thailand*, the recovery has been held back by weak consumer and investor sentiment, as well as by policy uncertainty and the slow pace of debt restructuring. Despite a pickup in activity in 2000, the economic and political situation in *Indonesia* remains very fragile, with deteriorating market sentiment reflected in continued downward pressure on the rupiah. Debt restructuring and asset recovery remain key to maintaining a sound macroeconomic framework, supported by safeguards to minimize the risks associated with ongoing fiscal decentralization. In a number of these countries, where inflation and fiscal sustainability are not a concern, there has been scope for moderate interest rate reductions, and, in some cases, for easing the pace of fiscal consolidation. However, the central challenge throughout the region remains to accelerate the pace of reform in the financial and corporate sectors. Although further restructuring could hamper activity in the short run, it is critical to boost domestic and external confidence (the gains from which would partly offset the short term negative impact), reduce financial risks, and to provide a basis for a sustained recovery in investment.

In *Australia* and *New Zealand*, strong export growth has continued, underpinned by strong external demand and highly competitive exchange rates, which continued to depreciate during much of 2000.[4] This provided strong support to activity—although in both cases the im-

pact was offset by weakening domestic demand during the year—and also contributed to a significant reduction in current account deficits, which have been quite high by international standards. While activity in New Zealand has remained robust, domestic demand in Australia slowed sharply in the fourth quarter of 2000, although this largely reflected the impact of the mid-2000 changes in the tax regime on housing investment. In both countries, activity in 2001 will be adversely affected by the weakening external environment. With underlying inflationary pressures easing, both countries have reduced interest rates, and there is room for additional cuts if activity were to weaken further. On the structural side, Australia has successfully completed a major tax reform, recently enacted measures aimed at fostering innovation, and is preparing to tackle welfare reform (although less progress is being made on labor market deregulation). In New Zealand, despite some evidence of a pickup in productivity growth in the 1990s, the growth dividend from 15 years of reform appears to have been less than might have been expected. While the new government's focus on human capital development is appropriate, the authorities need to monitor closely the effects of recent measures that could reduce labor and product market flexibility.

How Will the Global Slowdown Affect Latin America?

In Latin America and the Caribbean, GDP growth picked up to 4.1 percent in 2000, aided by buoyant U.S. demand, higher oil prices, and a recovery in domestic demand from the depressed levels of 1999 (Table 1.6). Within this, performance differed markedly across the region, with the strongest growth rates experienced in Mexico, Chile, and Brazil, underpinned by generally sound macroeconomic policy frameworks. Modest expansions are under way in the *Andean region*, with activity hampered in some cases by political uncertainties, while Argentina continues to struggle to escape recession. Notwithstanding the positive impact of

---

[4]See Chapter II, Box 2.1, for a discussion of developments in the Australian and New Zealand dollars.

Table 1.6. Selected Western Hemisphere Countries: Real GDP, Consumer Prices, and Current Account Balance

(Annual percent change unless otherwise noted)

	Real GDP				Consumer Prices[1]				Current Account Balances[2]			
	1999	2000	2001	2002	1999	2000	2001	2002	1999	2000	2001	2002
Western Hemisphere	**0.2**	**4.1**	**3.7**	**4.4**	**8.8**	**8.1**	**6.3**	**4.8**	**–3.2**	**–2.5**	**–3.3**	**–3.2**
South America	**–1.4**	**3.2**	**3.7**	**4.3**	**6.7**	**7.7**	**6.0**	**4.4**	**–3.0**	**–1.9**	**–2.9**	**–2.8**
Argentina	–3.4	–0.5	2.0	3.8	–1.2	–0.7	0.6	0.6	–4.4	–3.4	–3.4	–3.0
Brazil	0.8	4.2	4.5	4.5	4.9	7.0	5.5	3.7	–4.7	–4.2	–4.5	–4.4
Chile	–1.1	5.4	4.8	5.5	3.3	3.8	3.5	3.2	–0.1	–1.4	–1.7	–2.1
Colombia	–4.3	2.8	3.2	3.8	10.9	9.2	8.8	6.9	–0.1	0.2	–1.8	–2.7
Ecuador	–7.3	2.3	3.4	3.0	52.2	96.2	40.6	11.9	6.9	5.3	–1.2	–2.6
Peru	1.4	3.6	2.5	5.0	3.5	3.8	3.3	2.4	–3.5	–3.0	–2.4	–2.4
Uruguay	–3.2	–1.0	2.0	4.0	5.7	4.8	4.9	4.4	–2.5	–2.9	–2.5	–2.1
Venezuela	–6.1	3.2	3.3	2.8	23.6	16.2	12.5	13.6	3.6	10.8	4.3	4.3
Central America and Caribbean	**3.8**	**6.2**	**3.7**	**4.6**	**13.6**	**8.8**	**7.0**	**5.6**	**–3.4**	**–3.4**	**–3.9**	**–3.8**
Dominican Republic	8.0	7.8	6.5	6.4	6.5	7.7	10.9	4.4	–2.5	–6.3	–3.3	–3.1
Guatemala	3.5	3.6	3.0	2.9	5.3	7.0	7.6	10.1	–5.6	–4.7	–4.4	–4.3
Mexico	3.8	6.9	3.5	4.7	16.6	9.5	6.9	5.5	–2.9	–3.1	–3.9	–3.8

[1]In accordance with standard practice in the *World Economic Outlook*, movements in consumer prices are indicated as annual averages rather than as December/December changes during the year, as is the practice in some countries.
[2]Percent of GDP.

higher oil prices for many countries, the regional current account deficit improved only slightly, partly reflecting a strong rebound in domestic demand from the depressed levels of 1999. While vulnerability indicators have generally improved, the regional external financing requirement is the highest among developing country groups (Figure 1.3 and Table 1.7).

Looking to 2001, GDP growth is projected at 3.7 percent, with losses from the slowdown in the United States and somewhat lower oil prices partly offset by the positive impact of lower U.S. interest rates. While the situation differs across countries, the direct impact of the global slowdown on activity will be largest in Mexico (Figure 1.9) and in a number of countries in the Andean region and in Central America, but more moderate in those countries—such as Brazil and Argentina—that are less open and where trade links with the United States are less important. Given the still large external financing requirements across the region, the implications of the U.S. slowdown for financial markets is critical. While external financing conditions improved following the cut in U.S. interest rates in early 2001—allowing a number of countries to cover a substantial proportion of their exter-

nal public sector financing requirements—they have deteriorated following the renewed economic difficulties in Argentina. If a hard landing in the United States were to be accompanied by greater financial market turbulence and a rise in investor risk aversion, or a slowdown in inward foreign direct investment (which finances the bulk of the regional current account deficit), the risks would correspondingly increase. With fiscal sustainability remaining a central concern in many countries, it will be important to maintain prudent fiscal policies, along with structural reforms—particularly in financial and corporate sectors, privatization, and labor markets—to retain the confidence of international investors, increase investment, and reduce the very high unemployment rates across much of the region.

During the latter part of 2000, developments in the hemisphere were overshadowed by the crisis in *Argentina*. Having withstood the Asian crisis relatively well, the economy came under increasing pressure during 1999 and 2000 from the combined impact of large terms of trade losses, the floating of the Brazilian real, the strength of the U.S. dollar (which hurt trade with Europe and Brazil, Argentina's two largest trading partners), and rising international interest rates.

Table 1.7. Emerging Market Economies: Net Capital Flows[1]
(Billions of U.S. dollars)

	1993	1994	1995	1996	1997	1998	1999	2000	2001	2002
Total										
Private capital flows, net[2]	124.5	141.3	189.0	224.2	120.3	53.0	69.8	32.6	56.5	106.2
Private direct investment, net	56.6	80.9	96.8	120.2	144.9	151.0	150.3	143.9	150.5	155.8
Private portfolio investment, net	81.7	110.2	42.8	85.2	42.9	0.7	21.5	25.0	20.2	26.2
Other private capital flows, net	−13.9	−49.8	49.5	18.7	−67.5	−98.7	−101.9	−136.2	−114.2	−75.8
Official flows, net	54.1	8.2	31.3	0.9	56.8	62.1	10.6	4.8	5.9	7.4
Change in reserves[3]	−64.5	−69.0	−118.9	−109.6	−62.4	−34.8	−85.5	−119.9	−85.7	−96.0
Memorandum										
Current account[4]	−116.9	−74.2	−92.2	−96.1	−71.0	−57.3	32.5	112.9	48.9	−3.8
Africa										
Private capital flows, net[2]	3.2	11.4	12.3	12.3	16.8	10.9	12.7	8.6	14.7	14.0
Private direct investment, net	2.2	2.4	2.9	4.7	8.1	7.0	8.9	6.8	10.3	8.4
Private portfolio investment, net	0.9	3.5	3.1	2.8	7.0	3.7	8.7	4.3	3.9	4.4
Other private capital flows, net	0.0	5.5	6.4	4.9	1.6	0.1	−4.9	−2.4	0.5	1.2
Official flows, net	4.5	5.0	3.9	−2.1	−1.8	2.7	1.4	−4.4	−1.5	−2.6
Change in reserves[3]	3.2	−5.4	−2.0	−9.1	−10.6	1.9	−3.5	−14.4	−13.7	−11.0
Memorandum										
Current account[4]	−12.3	−12.3	−16.9	−6.3	−8.0	−20.5	−15.5	1.3	−3.7	−5.5
Developing Asia[5]										
Crisis countries[6]										
Private capital flows, net[2]	20.7	33.4	38.9	64.0	−9.0	−32.7	−9.1	−10.2	−16.8	0.2
Private direct investment, net	6.7	6.5	8.8	9.8	10.5	10.9	7.8	8.6	10.0	11.8
Private portfolio investment, net	17.1	11.3	17.7	23.6	7.2	−9.3	3.6	4.0	−0.6	1.9
Other private capital flows, net	−3.1	15.5	12.4	30.5	−26.7	−34.3	−20.5	−22.7	−26.1	−13.6
Official flows, net	3.3	0.9	14.9	−3.9	14.6	17.8	−5.6	2.5	−0.4	−3.3
Change in reserves[3]	−20.6	−6.1	−19.0	−5.4	39.4	−46.9	−39.3	−22.9	−9.1	−21.2
Memorandum										
Current account[4]	−13.5	−23.2	−39.1	−53.0	−25.5	69.9	62.9	44.8	38.3	30.4
Other Asian emerging markets										
Private capital flows, net[2]	20.9	33.7	35.6	50.0	22.4	−14.3	9.6	8.4	3.4	13.1
Private direct investment, net	26.4	38.2	39.7	45.7	49.7	48.5	42.8	38.5	39.7	43.1
Private portfolio investment, net	0.9	7.6	2.0	3.5	−0.1	−6.3	0.7	8.7	3.1	3.9
Other private capital flows, net	−6.3	−12.1	−6.1	0.8	−27.1	−56.4	−33.9	−38.8	−39.4	−34.0
Official flows, net	8.2	2.3	−3.6	−7.9	−7.3	0.4	3.1	−5.9	0.9	1.4
Change in reserves[3]	−16.7	−51.5	−25.4	−41.7	−46.9	−17.0	−38.7	−25.8	−19.7	−25.2
Memorandum										
Current account[4]	−7.2	18.3	8.1	14.9	51.0	41.5	38.3	33.3	22.3	16.6
Middle East, Malta, and Turkey[7]										
Private capital flows, net[2]	25.1	15.1	11.1	14.6	19.4	8.1	3.7	−16.2	−10.8	0.2
Private direct investment, net	3.3	5.3	7.4	8.3	7.3	7.9	5.0	9.0	8.6	10.5
Private portfolio investment, net	6.9	8.1	3.0	2.7	1.7	−11.4	−4.2	−2.1	−2.5	0.6
Other private capital flows, net	14.9	1.7	0.8	3.5	10.4	11.6	2.9	−23.1	−16.9	−10.9
Official flows, net	5.6	2.3	3.2	4.7	2.0	8.5	5.0	−5.3	−3.3	0.4
Change in reserves[3]	1.2	−4.7	−11.3	−22.0	−20.8	10.3	−6.5	−23.0	−18.7	−12.9
Memorandum										
Current account[4]	−29.9	−7.1	−5.9	4.2	1.9	−29.5	4.2	54.8	45.1	19.8

(continued)

With domestic demand weakening, Argentina became mired in a circle of near stagnation, declining business and consumer confidence, and rising interest rates. As emerging market spreads widened from late September, political uncertainties triggered a sharp deterioration in the country's financing conditions, with investor attention focusing increasingly on the large gross public financing requirement in 2001 and be-

yond. This was accompanied by signs of contagion to other countries in the region.

In response, the authorities moved quickly to strengthen the policy framework. Key elements included a fiscal pact with the provinces, to ensure that budget balance is achieved by 2005; improving product and labor flexibility to facilitate adjustment under the currency board system; reducing fiscal impediments to investment; a re-

Table 1.7 *(concluded)*

	1993	1994	1995	1996	1997	1998	1999	2000	2001	2002
Western Hemisphere										
Private capital flows, net[2]	37.3	42.8	41.6	62.8	68.1	61.8	40.4	39.2	60.6	70.7
Private direct investment, net	12.2	23.1	24.9	39.3	53.8	56.3	64.2	56.9	53.9	53.5
Private portfolio investment, net	47.2	62.4	2.5	38.0	19.0	19.9	10.4	4.7	10.7	11.6
Other private capital flows, net	−22.1	−42.6	14.2	−14.4	−4.7	−14.5	−34.2	−22.3	−4.1	5.6
Official flows, net	30.5	7.8	17.5	6.1	16.2	15.4	7.4	17.1	9.1	8.4
Change in reserves[3]	−20.7	4.0	−23.4	−29.4	−13.8	19.0	9.3	−12.9	−5.0	−11.5
Memorandum										
Current account[4]	−45.9	−52.0	−36.9	−38.9	−66.8	−90.2	−55.7	−47.9	−66.4	−68.7
Countries in transition										
Private capital flows, net[2]	17.4	4.8	49.6	20.5	2.5	19.2	12.5	2.8	5.4	8.2
Private direct investment, net	6.0	5.3	13.1	12.4	15.5	20.5	21.6	24.2	28.1	28.4
Private portfolio investment, net	8.7	17.3	14.6	14.6	8.0	4.0	2.2	5.3	5.5	3.9
Other private capital flows, net	2.7	−17.8	21.9	−6.5	−20.9	−5.2	−11.2	−26.7	−28.3	−24.1
Official flows, net	2.1	−10.1	−4.5	4.0	33.1	17.3	−0.8	0.8	1.0	3.0
Change in reserves[3]	−10.8	−5.3	−37.8	−2.0	−9.8	−2.1	−6.7	−21.0	−19.5	−14.2
Memorandum										
Current account[4]	−8.1	2.2	−1.5	−16.8	−23.7	−28.4	−1.7	26.7	13.5	3.6

[1]Net capital flows comprise net direct investment, net portfolio investment, and other long- and short-term net investment flows, including official and private borrowing. Emerging markets include developing countries, countries in transition, Korea, Singapore, Taiwan Province of China, and Israel. No data for Hong Kong SAR are available.

[2]Because of data limitations, other net investment may include some official flows.

[3]A minus sign indicates an increase.

[4]The sum of the current account balance, net private capital flows, net official flows, and the change in reserves equals, with the opposite sign, the sum of the capital account and errors and omissions.

[5]Includes Korea, Singapore, and Taiwan Province of China. No data for Hong Kong SAR are available.

[6]Indonesia, Korea, Malaysia, the Philippines, and Thailand.

[7]Includes Israel.

form of the health and pension systems; and substantial additional financing from the IMF, other multilateral and bilateral creditors, and the private sector to ease the government's financing needs in 2001 and beyond. The strengthened economic program was well received by financial markets, with an initial sharp decline in spreads. However, spreads have since rebounded as a result of evidence of difficulties in the fiscal area and renewed concerns on external financing issues, and as yet, there is no clear indication of a turning point in economic activity. The authorities' most recent initiatives to strengthen the policy framework are welcome; but with very limited room for policy maneuver it will be critical that fiscal restraint is maintained, and that the authorities at all levels of government adhere to the economic program.

In *Mexico*, activity remained very strong during most of 2000, buoyed by rising exports to the United States and rapid consumption and investment growth. In response to rising demand pressures, monetary policy was tightened steadily dur-

ing the year; inflation was held within the authorities' 10 percent target, but the external current account widened to 3.1 percent of GDP (notwithstanding significantly higher oil revenues). From late 2000, industrial production growth decelerated sharply, particularly in those sectors most closely linked to the United States. With oil prices also declining modestly, GDP growth is expected to fall back to 3.5 percent in 2001, and the current account balance to widen to 4 percent of GDP, increasing vulnerability to external shocks. Against this background, Mexico should maintain—and if possible strengthen—the prudent fiscal stance incorporated in the new administration's 2001 budget. On the structural side, the authorities' plans to reform the budgetary process, simplify the tax system, and move toward international standards for fiscal accounting are welcome. Further measures to strengthen banks' capital base are also a priority, building on the significant progress of recent years.

In Brazil, output growth has remained robust, despite concern about potential for contagion from the Argentine crisis. GDP growth averaged 4.5 percent in 2000, and is projected to reach a similar level in 2001, as slowing export growth is offset by robust domestic demand. With consumer price inflation of 6 percent, inflation was held in line with the target for the second year in a row, which helped the inflation targeting framework to gain substantial credibility. While Brazil remains vulnerable to adverse developments in the external environment, given the sizable current account deficit and external financing requirement, the economy is now in stronger shape to withstand such shocks. The recent tightening of monetary policy underlined the central bank's full commitment to the inflation targeting regime and was appropriate considering, among other factors, the weakening of the real against the U.S. dollar since the beginning of the year. Monetary policy should continue to respond swiftly to developments that could threaten the inflation target. Similarly, the government's proposal to strengthen its fiscal position for 2002–04, and maintain the primary surplus target of the consolidated public sector at 3 percent of GDP, will help to contain the adverse effect of higher interest rates on the budget and put the debt-to-GDP ratio firmly on a downward path. In view of current uncertainties, the authorities should stand ready to take additional action if necessary.

In *Chile*, activity rebounded in 2000 aided by rising exports and investment, although both industrial production and exports have weakened recently and unemployment remains stubbornly high. Given its relatively open economy—and substantial share of exports to the United States and emerging Asia—growth is expected to decline in 2001, although vulnerability to external financial market developments is more modest. Over the medium term, the structural fiscal balance target of 1 percent of GDP may help avoid the procyclical fiscal policy stance that has afflicted many countries in the region.

In the Andean region, GDP growth was generally stronger than expected in 2000, and—notwithstanding lower oil prices—is expected in

Figure 1.9. Western Hemisphere: Exposure to External Shocks
(Percent of GDP)

The extent of trade linkages with the United States varies widely. Most countries have substantial external financing requirements, making them vulnerable to developments in international financial markets.

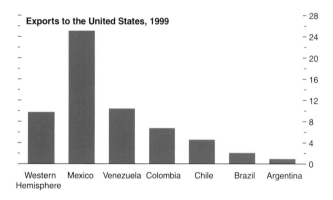

Exports to the United States, 1999

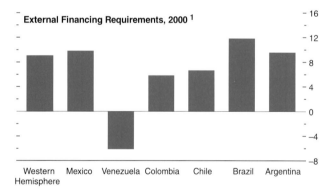

External Financing Requirements, 2000 [1]

Sources: IMF, *Direction of Trade Statistics;* and IMF staff estimates.
[1]External current account deficit plus amortization payments.

Table 1.8. Selected African Countries: Real GDP, Consumer Prices, and Current Account Balance
(Annual percent change unless otherwise noted)

	Real GDP				Consumer Prices[1]				Current Account Balances[2]			
	1999	2000	2001	2002	1999	2000	2001	2002	1999	2000	2001	2002
Africa	2.3	**3.0**	**4.2**	**4.4**	**11.5**	**13.5**	**9.6**	**5.7**	**−3.6**	**0.3**	**−0.8**	**−1.2**
Maghreb	**2.5**	**2.6**	**5.2**	**3.7**	**2.0**	**1.4**	**3.4**	**3.4**	**−0.6**	**7.5**	**5.8**	**3.6**
Algeria	3.2	3.0	3.1	3.1	2.6	0.3	4.0	4.5	0.0	17.3	13.8	9.4
Morocco	−0.7	0.8	7.8	3.3	0.7	2.0	2.8	2.3	−0.5	−1.7	−1.4	−1.0
Tunisia	6.2	5.0	6.2	6.1	2.7	3.0	2.9	2.7	−2.1	−3.7	−3.0	−2.7
Sub-Sahara[3]	**2.4**	**3.0**	**4.0**	**5.0**	**19.1**	**23.3**	**14.5**	**7.3**	**−7.5**	**−3.3**	**−5.3**	**−4.4**
Cameroon	4.4	4.2	5.4	5.7	2.9	0.8	2.0	2.0	−4.1	−1.7	−2.7	−2.4
Côte d'Ivoire	1.6	−2.0	0.3	3.6	0.7	2.5	2.0	2.0	−4.2	−4.6	−4.3	−3.7
Ghana	4.4	3.7	5.0	5.5	12.4	25.0	30.0	17.8	−9.9	−6.6	−3.6	−2.7
Kenya	2.0	−0.4	2.1	2.8	3.5	6.2	5.0	4.5	−2.4	−2.9	−9.3	−5.1
Nigeria	1.1	2.8	1.7	2.5	6.6	6.9	12.5	7.8	−9.5	4.9	−2.1	−0.9
Tanzania	4.8	5.1	5.4	5.7	6.3	6.2	5.0	4.2	−3.9	−2.4	−3.5	−3.3
Uganda	7.6	4.6	5.0	7.2	−0.2	6.3	5.0	5.0	−7.2	−8.1	−8.4	−10.3
South Africa	**1.9**	**3.2**	**3.8**	**3.8**	**5.2**	**5.4**	**5.2**	**4.5**	**−0.4**	**−0.1**	**0.2**	**−0.3**
Memorandum												
Oil importers	2.3	3.0	4.7	4.7	11.0	13.4	8.7	5.1	−3.0	−3.0	−3.0	−2.9
Oil exporters	2.0	3.0	2.8	3.2	13.2	13.7	12.8	7.9	−5.8	9.6	5.6	4.4

[1]In accordance with standard practice in the *World Economic Outlook*, movements in consumer prices are indicated as annual averages rather than as December/December changes during the year, as is the practice in some countries.
[2]Percent of GDP.
[3]Excluding South Africa.

most cases to pick up further in 2001, aided by strengthening domestic demand. In *Venezuela*, activity has been boosted by a sharp increase in government spending. While the authorities have set aside part of the windfall gain in oil prices, with the non-oil balance in large deficit, the fiscal position remains very vulnerable to developments in oil prices. The fiscal position also remains a challenge in *Colombia*, especially given the potential costs of bank restructuring and pension reform. In *Ecuador*, dollarization continues to proceed satisfactorily, and macroeconomic stability has improved. However, further progress is needed to strengthen the banking system, while the recent defeat of the authorities' proposed tax reform in the congress will set back the needed strengthening of the fiscal policy framework unless the partial presidential veto, which seeks to maintain key elements of the tax reform, is sustained.

In Central America, GDP growth slowed in most countries in 2000, as the cost of oil imports rose and world coffee prices remained depressed, although *Honduras* and *Nicaragua* continued to register robust growth as they recov-

ered from the effects of Hurricane Mitch. With the region heavily exposed to developments in the United States, economic growth may be slower than expected, although the impact may be offset by the expansion in access to U.S. markets following the Caribbean Basin Initiative in October 2000 (involving *El Salvador, Guatemala, and Honduras*); and debt relief under the Enhanced HIPC Initiative (Nicaragua and Honduras). The region will need to continue to strengthen fiscal policy, with an emphasis on raising tax revenues, which tend to be low in relation to GDP. On January 1, 2001, El Salvador introduced the U.S. dollar as legal tender, with a view to strengthening the country's integration with the world economy. The other countries in the region, apart from Panama, do not intend to dollarize.

Can Africa Achieve Sustained Higher Growth?

In *Africa*, after two decades of economic stagnation, GDP growth picked up substantially in the second half of the 1990s, underpinned by a

renewed commitment to sound economic policies and more open and better managed
economies. This was accompanied by improved
macroeconomic performance, notably lower inflation and a reduction in fiscal and current account deficits (although, given Africa's still high
debt burden, the latter generally remain substantial—see Table 1.8).[5] However, particularly in
sub-Saharan Africa, the rate of improvement fell
back significantly later in the decade (Figure
1.10). In large part, this deterioration can be
traced to the rising incidence of war and civil
conflict, and to a lesser extent terms of trade
losses from weak commodity prices and latterly
from high oil prices. Countries that maintained
sound economic policies and political stability
(see Figure 1.10) were able to maintain relatively
strong rates of growth—notwithstanding, in
some cases, sizable commodity price shocks.

Growth in Africa is projected to rise to 4.2 percent in 2001 and somewhat further in 2002, with
activity picking up fastest in those countries that
suffered most from domestic or external shocks.
This pickup will, however, depend on the implementation of sound macroeconomic and structural policies, as well as a significant improvement in the security situation in many
countries.[6] Recent improvements remain fragile
(the experience of *Zimbabwe* shows how quickly
macroeconomic gains can be lost); in addition,
Africa would suffer from a steeper than expected global slowdown, particularly as a result
of falling commodity prices. Nonetheless, the recent strengthening of economic policies—supported by debt relief through the enhanced
HIPC initiative and the IMF's Poverty Reduction
and Growth Facility (Box 1.4)—has helped to
improve the environment to achieve sustained
growth. This is an important beginning, but

[5]See Chapter IV for a detailed discussion of the factors
underlying the improvement in inflation in developing
countries.

[6]Over the past decade, partly because these conditions
have not been satisfied, the IMF's forecasts for growth in
Africa have been consistently over optimistic; growth projections made at the beginning of the forecast year have
averaged about 1 percentage point higher than the actual
outcome.

**Figure 1.10. Sub-Saharan Africa: Why Has the
Recent Expansion Slowed?[1]**
(Per capita real GDP growth, percent)

After a strong pickup in 1995–96, per capita GDP growth has slowed
markedly, mainly due to war and civil disturbances and commodity
shocks. However, growth in countries with strong policies has been
better-sustained.

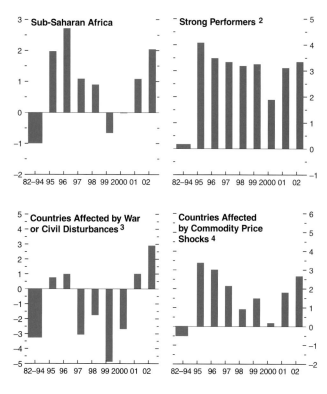

[1]Excluding South Africa.
[2]Countries with generally strong macroeconomics and structural policies;
comprises Benin, Botswana, Burkina Faso, Cameroon, Mali, Mauritius,
Mozambique, Rwanda, Tanzania, Senegal, Seychelles, and Uganda (24 percent of
sub-Saharan African GDP).
[3]Countries experiencing war or significant civil disturbances during 1998–2000;
comprises Angola, Burundi, Comoros, Congo, Dem Rep. of, Congo, Rep. of,
Côte d'Ivoire, Ethiopia, Guinea-Bissau, Lesotho, and Sierra Leone (20 percent of
sub-Saharan African GDP).
[4]Countries experiencing adverse commodity price shocks exceeding 10 percent
in 2000 compared with the 1995–97 average; comprises Benin, Burundi, Burkina
Faso, Central African Rep. , Chad, Côte d'Ivoire, Ethiopia, Ghana, Madagascar,
Mali, Mauritius, Rwanda, São Tomé and Príncipe, Tanzania, Togo, Zambia, and
Uganda (33 percent of sub-Saharan African GDP).

African countries continue to face enormous development challenges. Strong domestic policies, undertaken in an environment of peace and reasonable political stability, additional international assistance, and more open markets in industrial countries, will all be needed in order to raise growth to the levels necessary to support a meaningful reduction in poverty.

In *South Africa,* activity is recovering well from a series of adverse shocks, including higher oil prices, unfavorable weather conditions, and contagion from the crisis in Zimbabwe. GDP growth is estimated at 3.2 percent in 2000, and should rise to 3.8 percent in 2001. However, with global demand slowing, and consumer and business confidence still quite weak, there are downside risks to the outlook. Moreover, while the current account deficit is modest, persistent capital outflows—linked in part to the Zimbabwe crisis—have contributed to a steady weakening in the rand. With inflation having peaked at about 8 percent, the Reserve Bank appears on track to meet its target of 3 to 6 percent in 2002; with direct inflationary pressures easing, there may be scope to ease interest rates later in the year, once it is clear that second round effects from rand weakness and oil price hikes are dissipating. Over the medium term, to address high unemployment, poverty, and extreme income inequality, the challenge is to increase growth to above 6 percent through accelerated structural reforms, particularly in the labor market and privatization.

Elsewhere in Africa, developments continue to depend importantly on commodity prices. The oil exporting countries of north and west Africa have experienced a large improvement in their terms of trade, resulting in much stronger fiscal and external balances. However, GDP growth has generally increased only modestly, constrained by structural weaknesses in non-oil sectors and in some cases war and political uncertainty. In *Nigeria,* the democratically elected government that took office in May 1999 initially took important measures to address macroeconomic imbalances and began to tackle corruption. However, signs of sustained economic recovery remain elusive; federal government

spending has risen sharply, primarily due to higher wages; reserve money growth has accelerated, leading to rising inflation and pressures on the naira; and structural reforms have fallen behind schedule. Higher oil prices temporarily boosted the current account, but the medium term external situation remains difficult. To restore macroeconomic stability, strict financial discipline—through limiting expenditure by federal government—remains critical, supported by market-based reforms—especially in the conduct of monetary and exchange rate policies, privatization, trade policy, and governance—and additional debt relief. In *Algeria,* where unemployment is estimated at 30 percent, the main challenge is to achieve a sustained increase in growth, without jeopardizing the hard won progress toward macroeconomic stability in recent years. While the fiscal position remains in strong surplus, recent substantial increases in the minimum wage and civil service salaries may increase vulnerability to developments in oil prices (as well as exacerbate labor market imbalances). It will also be important to accelerate the pace of structural reform, particularly in the areas of banking and privatization.

In much of the rest of Africa, the terms of trade have deteriorated substantially in recent years. While this has been partly offset by rising export volumes—particularly in the Horn of Africa and eastern and southern Africa—much of the impact has been absorbed through lower domestic demand and growth. In 2001–02, non-fuel commodity prices are projected to remain weak, albeit offset to some extent by lower oil prices. Macroeconomic stability has in general improved, but remains a concern in some countries, particularly in southern and eastern Africa. In a number of these—notably *Angola,* the *Democratic Republic of the Congo,* and Zimbabwe—conflicts or domestic political turmoil have contributed to a substantial weakening in macroeconomic policies, and in some cases—especially Zimbabwe—have had adverse effects on neighboring countries.

For the region as a whole, the central policy challenge remains to improve the environment

Box 1.4. The Enhanced HIPC Initiative in Africa

To address the problem of unsustainable debt burdens in poor countries, mainly in Africa, the IMF and the World Bank launched the Initiative for the Heavily Indebted Poor Countries (HIPC Initiative) in 1996. This was enhanced in the fall of 1999 in the context of strengthening the links between debt relief and poverty reduction by providing faster, deeper, and broader debt relief, supported by country-owned and participatory strategies designed to help these countries reach the International Development Goals for poverty reduction and other key social indicators.[1] The main goals are reducing the proportion of people living in extreme poverty by at least one half by 2015 (from the 1990 level); achieving universal primary education in all countries by 2015; eliminating gender disparity in primary and secondary education by 2005; and reducing child mortality by two-thirds and maternal mortality by three-fourths by 2015 (from the 1990 level).

For Africa, the enhancements to the HIPC Initiative resulted in a broadening of the number of countries that could qualify for debt relief to 33.[2] So far, 18 African countries reached the point where they qualify for and can start to receive HIPC debt relief—their so-called decision points—and will receive total debt service relief amounting to $25 billion in nominal terms ($15 billion in net present value terms). On average,

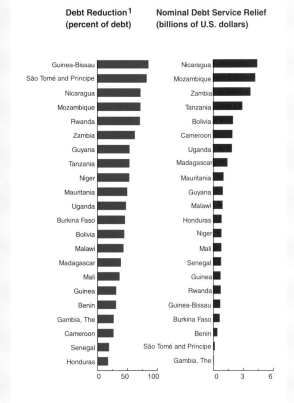

Enhanced HIPC Initiative: Comparative Debt Reduction and Debt Relief for 22 Decision Point Countries, December 2000

Debt Reduction[1]
(percent of debt)

Nominal Debt Service Relief
(billions of U.S. dollars)

[1] In terms of net present value.

[1]See "The New Approach to Poverty Reduction", Chapter IV in the May 2000 *World Economic Outlook* for a detailed description of the Enhanced HIPC Initiative. See also http://www.imf.org/external/np/HIPC.

[2]Of these, 18 have reached the point at which they qualify for debt relief (Benin, Burkina Faso, Cameroon, The Gambia, Guinea, Guinea-Bissau, Madagascar, Malawi, Mali, Mauritania, Mozambique, Niger, Rwanda, São Tomé and Príncipe, Senegal, Tanzania, Uganda, and Zambia), 12 have still to qualify (Burundi, Central African Republic, Chad, Republic of Congo, Democratic Republic of Congo, Côte d'Ivoire, Ethiopia, Liberia, Sierra Leone, Somalia, Sudan, and Togo), and two are expected not to require assistance (Angola and Kenya). Ghana decided in 1999 not to seek debt relief under the Initiative.

HIPC relief combined with existing debt relief mechanisms will reduce countries' debt service by two-thirds (see the figure), equivalent to between 1 and 2½ percent of GDP per year. The debt relief allows significant increases in pro-poor expenditure, in particular, in education and health, for which today's public spending levels in sub-Saharan Africa average about 6 percent of GDP (compared with 6.5 percent for the average of all IMF-supported program countries).

All African countries that have reached their decision points are significantly increasing the budget allocations for social and other program spending, in several countries by more than the

Box 1.4 *(concluded)*

HIPC debt relief through a reallocation of resources from lower-priority uses. But it is equally, if not more, important to ensure that such spending is efficient and reaches the poor. This involves major efforts to strengthen the budget process, including through the introduction or strengthening of medium-term expenditure frameworks (such as in Uganda, Malawi, and Zambia). It also involves the systematic tracking of government expenditure to the intended programs and their beneficiaries (for example, special surveys are being undertaken with donor support in Cameroon, The Gambia, and Madagascar). And more generally, it involves steps to enhance accountability in the use of public resources (including HIPC relief) through the establishment or strengthening of the general accountant's office (like in The Gambia, Niger, Rwanda, and São Tomé and Príncipe) or the introduction or strengthening of financial management systems (like in Zambia and Malawi).

A critical element in the HIPC Initiative is that every country prepares an *Interim Poverty Reduction Strategy Paper* (IPRSP) and then a *Poverty Reduction Strategy Paper* (PRSP) through a consultative process. These papers focus on:

- Maintenance of macroeconomic stability and achievement of equitable growth, both essential for sustainable poverty reduction.
- Greater specification of measurable targets for poverty reduction and social indicators and incorporation of the costs of reaching these targets in the budget.
- Increases in the level and efficiency of pro-poor spending. HIPC relief permits countries to continue the upward trend in such spending shown in recent years, while maintaining overall fiscal balances consistent with debt sustainability.
- Clearer identification of pro-poor spending in the budget and improvements in monitoring. This typically involves adopting new budget classifications, introducing medium-term expenditure frameworks, undertaking regular public expenditure reviews, decentralizing social services provision to local governments,

and holding regular beneficiary "tracking" surveys.

The focus on poverty reduction and safeguarding the efficient use of debt relief are also reflected in triggers for reaching the point at which HIPC debt relief becomes fully and irrevocably available to the country—the so-called completion point. The triggers for African HIPCs have typically covered:[3]

- *Governance.* Measurable progress in public expenditure management, accountability, anticorruption safeguards, and tracking of expenditures to beneficiaries.
- *Education.* Measurable progress in public spending levels/efficiency; number of teachers and classrooms; improved incentives for rural teachers; and enrollment rates.
- *Health.* Measurable progress in public spending levels/efficiency; number of health workers and equipped health centers; provision of drugs; immunization rates, mortality, and morbidity rates.
- *Other reforms* essential for poverty reduction, such as the implementation of AIDS action plans; rural road maintenance: improvements in micro finance institutions; and privatization of essential public enterprises.

In the period ahead, the critical issue for countries that have reached the decision point is to ensure that poverty reduction strategies are fully implemented. They need also to improve their expenditure systems to ensure that available resources (including HIPC relief) are used efficiently and reach the poor. Assistance from countries' external partners for the PRSP process and expenditure management is essential. For the 12 HIPC-eligible African countries that still have to qualify for HIPC relief, however, there are many obstacles to overcome. Nine of these countries are affected by ongoing or past armed conflicts, many have poor eco-

---

[3]For reaching their completion points, it is necessary that countries have maintained macroeconomic stability, as evidenced by satisfactory implementation of the PRGF-program, and have prepared, and implemented satisfactorily for one year, a full PRSP.

nomic performance linked to weak governance, and several have large and protracted arrears, including to the World Bank, IMF, and African Development Bank. Through technical assistance and policy advice, often under staff-monitored programs, the IMF is helping these countries, where possible, to establish a minimum track record of good economic policies and to regain access to financing from multilateral institutions and bilateral donors. In all of the HIPC countries, however, debt relief by itself is not enough. As stressed in Chapter I of this *World Economic Outlook*, additional foreign aid is needed, and, even more important, advanced economies must provide these countries greater access to their markets to ensure that the poorest countries can begin to share more fully in global prosperity.

for private investment, which remains very low compared with other developing country regions. The priorities are to strengthen public service delivery, including education and poverty relief, financed by debt relief and improved tax administration; to improve infrastructure (including through privatization); and to continue to open up to the outside world. There is also a pressing need to improve governance, which remains a pervasive problem, including through greater transparency in public sector resource management (under way in *Kenya* and *Mozambique*); developing sound and efficient civil services and legal frameworks (in progress in *Cameroon* and *Zambia*); and attacking corruption (where *Senegal*, *Tanzania*, and *Uganda* have taken important steps).

For many countries, AIDS has become a major threat to sustainable development, with between 20 and 36 percent of the adult population of countries in southern Africa now infected with the virus. Since combination therapies to prolong life are generally not available, due to the high cost of anti-retroviral drugs and weak medical infrastructure (particularly in rural areas), deaths in the adult population will rise sharply over the next 10 years, with severe social and economic consequences.[7] Prevention efforts—which are relatively inexpensive and have proved quite effective in some countries, including

Uganda and Senegal—have been stepped up in many countries, but only a few countries—including South Africa recently—provide drug treatments to pregnant women to reduce transmission to unborn children. While budgetary resources are generally very limited, every effort will need to be made to reduce nonproductive outlays to finance additional health-related expenditures. Given the scale of the problem, substantial external support will also be essential.

The Middle East: Managing Terms of Trade Volatility

In the Middle East, oil price fluctuations continue to dominate economic developments, resulting in sharp terms of trade volatility. After falling by 20 percent in 1998, the terms of trade for the region soared by some 50 percent in 1999–2000, as oil prices rebounded. Higher oil revenues have largely been saved, leading to a substantial improvement in fiscal and external imbalances in many countries (Figure 1.11 and Table 1.9). The strengthening terms of trade, and several increases in OPEC oil production quotas during 2000, also boosted activity, with GDP growth rising by 2.1 percentage points to 4.8 percent in 2000, the highest since the early 1990s.

While oil prices have fallen back somewhat from their peaks in late 2000, they are expected to remain relatively high in historical terms in 2001. Since the windfall gains from higher oil prices have in general been prudently used, the

---

[7]See Box 1.4 of the October 2000 *World Economic Outlook* for a discussion of the macroeconomic consequences of AIDS in Africa.

Figure 1.11. Middle East: Responding to Oil Price Volatility[1]
(Percent of GDP)

In most countries, the recent windfall increases in oil prices have been prudently used, and the projected decline in 2001–02 will be manageable.

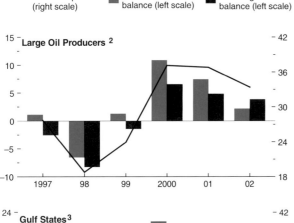

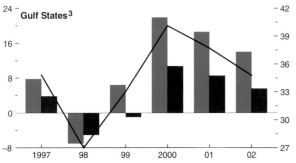

[1] Data for 2001 and 2002 are IMF staff projections.
[2] Iran, Islamic Rep. of, Libya, and Saudi Arabia.
[3] Bahrain, Kuwait, Oman, Qatar, and United Arab Emirates.

impact of somewhat lower prices in most countries is expected to remain manageable. Thus, growth is projected to remain reasonably robust in 2001 and 2002, and in most cases fiscal and external positions would be able to absorb the bulk of the oil price fall. However, given the continued volatility in oil prices and recent production cuts, there may be downside risks to the outlook. Hence, a prudent approach to fiscal policy remains desirable, especially in those countries—such as *Saudi Arabia*—that need to reduce government debt.

More generally, recent oil price volatility continues to underscore the need for reforms to promote economic diversification and growth. In the *Gulf Cooperation Council* countries (*Bahrain, Kuwait, Oman, Qatar, Saudi Arabia,* and *United Arab Emirates*), efforts should continue to focus on encouraging the expansion of the non-oil private sector, including through removing impediments to foreign direct investment; strengthening labor markets; and accelerating privatization. In other countries, where growth and employment are constrained by dominant state sectors and widespread controls, the challenge is more wide ranging. *Iran,* in a clear break with the past, is enacting a welcome program of reforms, although in some areas—notably price and trade liberalization, privatization, and the development of a social safety net—a bolder approach could pay dividends.

Turning to other countries in the region, GDP growth in the *Mashreq* (comprising Egypt, Jordan, Lebanon, Syria, and the West Bank and Gaza Strip) increased to 4.2 percent, while inflation remained well under control. Growth in the region has been the strongest in *Egypt,* spurred by broad-based economic reform in the mid-1990s. However, from late 1997, external shocks, including the appreciation of the U.S. dollar, combined with relatively expansionary fiscal and monetary policies and a slowdown in structural reforms, resulted in a deterioration in the external position, and a decline in international reserves. After allowing the currency to depreciate by about 12 percent in 2000, the authorities adopted an adjustable band (of +/−1 percent)

Table 1.9. Selected Middle Eastern Countries: Real GDP, Consumer Prices, and Current Account Balance
(Annual percent change unless otherwise noted)

	Real GDP				Consumer Prices[1]				Current Account Balances[2]			
	1999	2000	2001	2002	1999	2000	2001	2002	1999	2000	2001	2002
Middle East[3]	2.7	4.8	4.8	4.5	12.0	11.2	9.8	8.9	1.4	11.0	7.8	3.8
Oil exporters[4]	2.1	5.0	5.0	4.4	15.7	14.6	12.4	11.0	3.0	15.2	11.5	6.5
Saudi Arabia	−1.0	4.1	4.8	3.0	−1.2	−0.6	—	0.8	−1.2	8.6	7.3	1.3
Iran, Islamic Rep. of	2.5	3.6	4.0	4.5	20.4	18.5	15.5	13.0	4.7	14.8	7.2	3.0
Kuwait	−2.4	3.6	1.9	2.0	1.8	1.5	2.5	2.5	16.7	29.7	25.9	22.0
Mashreq[5]	4.1	4.2	4.1	4.9	2.0	2.2	2.6	3.1	−3.6	−3.0	−4.3	−4.9
Egypt	6.0	5.1	4.5	5.3	3.8	2.8	2.8	3.0	−2.0	−1.2	−1.8	−2.2
Jordan	3.1	4.0	3.0	4.5	0.6	0.7	1.8	2.3	5.0	1.6	−2.2	−1.7

[1]In accordance with standard practice in the *World Economic Outlook*, movements in consumer prices are indicated as annual averages rather than as December/December changes during the year, as is the pratice in some countries.
[2]Percent of GDP.
[3]Middle East, Malta and Turkey *World Economic Outlook* grouping excluding Malta and Turkey.
[4]Bahrain, Iran, Islamic Rep. of, Iraq, Kuwait, Libya, Oman, Qatar, Saudi Arabia, and United Arab Emirates.
[5]Egypt, Jordan, Lebanon, and Syrian Arab Republic.

against the U.S. dollar from February 2001; this new regime should be operated in an appropriately flexible manner. Credit to the private sector has slowed substantially, which, along with the depreciation of the Egyptian pound, is helping to strengthen the balance of payments position. In addition, somewhat tighter fiscal policies would be desirable. After what appears to have been a temporary slowdown in growth in early 2000, some modest signs of recovery have emerged, although much will depend on the speed with which investor confidence strengthens and on developments in the region. In both Egypt and other countries in the Mashreq, which have yet to share fully in the benefits of globalization, further reform of trade and investment regimes remains a priority. Recent regional trade initiatives—including the negotiation of Association Agreements with the European Union, so far completed with *Jordan* and Egypt—are encouraging, and, along with entry into the WTO, could provide external anchors to underpin reform efforts more generally. In Lebanon, the very high fiscal deficit and public debt ratios remain a serious concern.

In *Israel*, activity rebounded strongly in 2000, led by buoyant technology sector exports. However, the economic impact of the deterioration in the security situation, as well as the political uncertainties in the run up to the recent elections, contributed to a sharp decline in GDP growth in the fourth quarter of 2000, and activity is expected to slow sharply in 2001. Domestic demand is weakening, and tourism bookings have dropped; in addition, export growth is slowing due to weakening external demand and the turndown in the global electronics cycle. With inflation running below the 3–4 percent target band, the Bank of Israel has room to continue with cautious interest rates cuts, while monitoring the possible repercussions in currency markets. Continued budgetary consolidation remains important given Israel's very high public debt.

Rebalancing the Policy Mix in Europe's Emerging Markets

Growth surged in Europe's emerging markets in 2000, but in many countries high inflation persisted and external current account deficits remained wide, reflecting strong domestic demand and higher world oil prices (Table 1.10). Current account deficits were largely financed by foreign direct investment, which in turn was supported by the prospect in many countries of eventual accession to the European Union (see Box 1.5 and Chapter III in the October 2000 *World Economic Outlook*). In late 2000, the European Commission presented a detailed

Table 1.10. European Union Accession Candidates: Real GDP, Consumer Prices, and Current Account Balance
(Annual percent change unless otherwise noted)

	Real GDP				Consumer Prices[1]				Current Account Balances[2]			
	1999	2000	2001	2002	1999	2000	2001	2002	1999	2000	2001	2002
European Union accession candidates	**−0.1**	**4.8**	**1.9**	**4.5**	**25.3**	**24.4**	**20.5**	**12.7**	**−4.1**	**−5.1**	**−2.9**	**−2.7**
Turkey	−4.7	7.2	−2.6	4.9	64.9	54.9	48.4	28.4	−0.7	−4.8	0.4	0.1
Excluding Turkey	1.9	3.8	3.9	4.3	11.2	13.1	9.9	6.4	−5.8	−5.2	−5.0	−4.8
Bulgaria	2.4	5.0	5.0	5.0	2.6	10.4	8.5	3.2	−5.5	−5.5	−4.4	−3.9
Cyprus	4.5	5.0	4.5	4.0	1.8	4.1	2.7	2.7	−4.5	−8.0	−5.3	−4.6
Czech Republic	-0.8	3.1	3.0	3.5	2.1	3.9	4.2	4.4	−3.0	−4.8	−4.7	−4.3
Estonia	−1.1	6.4	5.5	5.5	3.3	4.0	5.0	2.8	−5.8	−6.7	−7.2	−6.7
Hungary	4.5	5.3	4.9	4.7	10.0	9.8	8.5	6.4	−4.3	−3.5	−5.1	−5.1
Latvia	1.1	5.5	6.0	6.0	2.4	2.7	2.1	3.0	−9.7	−7.2	−6.6	−5.5
Lithuania	−4.2	2.7	3.2	3.8	0.8	1.0	1.3	2.6	−11.2	−6.9	−6.7	−6.3
Malta	3.5	3.2	4.3	3.3	2.5	2.5	2.5	2.5	−3.7	−3.9	−3.7	−3.1
Poland	4.1	4.1	4.0	4.5	7.3	10.1	7.0	5.0	−7.5	−6.1	−5.4	−5.0
Romania	−3.2	2.0	3.0	4.0	45.8	45.7	34.2	16.4	−3.8	−3.7	−4.4	−4.8
Slovak Republic	1.9	2.2	3.1	4.4	10.7	12.0	6.9	6.0	−5.7	−3.6	−4.8	−4.9
Slovenia	5.2	4.9	4.5	4.0	6.2	8.9	7.0	5.0	−3.9	−3.2	−2.7	−2.4

[1]In accordance with standard practice in the *World Economic Outlook,* movements in consumer prices are indicated as annual averages rather than as December/December changes during the year as is the practice in some countries.
[2]Percent of GDP.

timetable for accession, which aims at concluding the negotiations on all chapters of the *acquis communautaire*[8] by mid-2002, and EU heads of state agreed to internal reforms that set the stage for admitting new members in the coming years. Turkey experienced two financial and currency crises in late 2000 and early 2001, but the spillovers to other countries appear to have been relatively limited thus far.

In most countries, growth is expected to remain relatively well sustained in 2001, although activity is vulnerable to a faster-than-projected slowdown in western Europe and external current account deficits are forecast to remain large. A rebalancing of the policy mix toward a relatively tighter fiscal policy would help restrain domestic demand while limiting upward pressures on interest rates and exchange rates, which would adversely affect net exports and private investment. To promote sustainable growth in the medium term and ensure continued progress toward EU accession, further structural and insti-

tutional reforms are needed, notably in privatization, enterprise restructuring, financial regulation and supervision, labor market reform, and pension and health care systems.[9]

In Turkey, growing problems in the banking system and the widening external current account deficit led to a financial and currency crisis in late 2000. Under the economic program adopted in 1999, good progress was made in strengthening public finances, lowering inflation, and reviving growth. However, the current account deficit grew from ¾ percent of GDP in 1999 to an estimated 4¾ percent of GDP in 2000, reflecting a combination of policy, domestic, and external factors. The introduction of a preannounced exchange rate path helped reduce nominal interest rates, but the effect on inflation expectations was not as strong, and the resulting sharp decline in real interest rates spurred domestic demand, which—combined with the rise in world energy prices and the global slowdown—contributed to the drop in

[8]The detailed body of laws and regulations that underpins the European Union.

[9]These issues were discussed in Chapter IV of the October 2000 *World Economic Outlook.*

Box 1.5. Large Current Account Deficits in Transition Countries Seeking Membership in the European Union

Most Central and Eastern European (CEE) transition countries have in recent years registered current account deficits of magnitudes that have often been associated with balance of payments crises both within the region and elsewhere (see the figure).[1] While in most countries these current account deficits have more recently narrowed, owing to a mixture of policy adjustment, slower domestic activity, and strong export performance, with few exceptions they remain at relatively high levels—with a median deficit of just under 5 percent in 2000. This box examines the factors behind the current account deficits, their financing, and policies to mitigate vulnerability.

In general, the composition of financing (predominantly inward foreign direct investment or FDI) and exchange rate regimes (primarily hard pegs or relatively free floats) suggest that the vulnerability of the CEE countries to a full-fledged balance of payments crisis may be limited. Indeed, the resilience of these countries to the fallout from the Russia crisis is testament to this. However, as inward foreign direct investment is partly linked to prospects of early EU accession, changes to those expectations could affect the financing of current account deficits. Continued strengthening of both financial systems and, in most cases, fiscal positions will be necessary in the coming years. Policymakers will also need to be alert to a possible shift in the composition of financing toward more liquid and thus readily reversible flows.

Some Facts

With the exception of Slovenia and Bulgaria, current account deficits as a ratio to GDP in the other eight countries seeking EU membership peaked at more than 7 percent in the mid- to

[1]For example, the Czech Republic experienced a balance of payments crisis in 1997, Hungary in 1993–94, and the Slovak Republic in 1998. The European Union has accepted 10 CEE countries as candidates for accession: Bulgaria, Czech Republic, Estonia, Hungary, Latvia, Lithuania, Poland, Romania, Slovak Republic, and Slovenia.

Selected Countries in Transition[1]
(Percent of GDP)

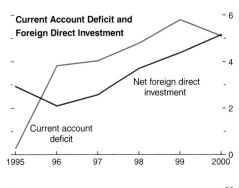

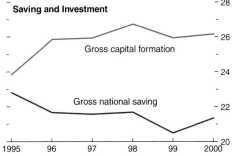

[1]GDP-weighted average of Bulgaria, Czech Republic, Estonia, Hungary, Latvia, Lithuania, Poland, Romania, Slovak Republic, and Slovenia.

late 1990s. By and large, this reflected rising investment to GDP ratios and to a lesser extent greater consumption (see the figure). Large general government deficits, especially in Lithuania, Romania, and Slovakia, also contributed to wide current account deficits.

The current account deficits of the CEE countries have generally been financed without much difficulty, and largely through private resources. In the 1995–99 period, the median net private capital flow to the 10 countries in the process of accession (6½ percent of GDP) was considerably higher than to other emerging and transition countries (some 3 percent of GDP). In addition, FDI—a large part of which was related to privatization—has been a major component (about

Box 1.5 *(concluded)*

half) of the inflows to the CEE countries, again more than recorded to other transition and emerging market countries.

Factors Behind the Large Capital Flows

The role of policy. The CEE countries have with few exceptions coped well with the massive upheaval entailed by the transition process, securing in less than a decade macroeconomic stability while transforming themselves into investor friendly locations. And indeed the rewards to resolute policy implementation have been evident among the CEE countries, with the strong reformers (among them Estonia, Hungary, and Poland) receiving significantly more capital inflows than weak reformers (Romania).

Proximity to the European Union and capital accumulation. The proximity of the CEE countries to the European Union and their eligibility for membership have made these countries an attractive location for investment.[2] The large and persistent differences in output per worker between the European Union and the CEE countries are partly due to differences in capital stocks. Thus, the potential magnitude of flows necessary to equalize the rate of return on capital can be estimated using a Cobb-Douglas production function framework. On this basis, cumulative capital flows in the range of 147 percent of GDP (Slovenia) to 825 percent of GDP (Latvia) would have been required to equalize output per worker between Germany (representing the European Union) and the CEE countries at the start of the transition period.[3] The actual level of capital flows has, of course, been considerably less. Nevertheless, the fact that most of the inflows appear to have financed rising investment is consistent with this story.

Country size. Another distinguishing feature of the CEE countries is the fact that half are particularly small, with populations of less than or close to five million. Small countries tend to show greater volatility in their external balances, reflecting their higher degree of openness. Even modest capital flows from the perspective of creditors can generate large capital flows from the perspective of small countries, inducing large changes in their current account balances. Recently, current account deficits in the smaller CEE countries have been markedly high.

Mitigating Vulnerability

With a median current account deficit of 5 percent of GDP and the possibility that consumption and investment ratios may rise in the coming years, the CEE countries should attempt to mitigate their vulnerability by adopting appropriate policies. In terms of exchange rate policy, the picture is broadly appropriate.[4] The CEE countries have over time moved toward either strong fixes (Bulgaria, Estonia, and Lithuania have currency boards) or relatively free floating regimes (Czech Republic, Poland, Romania, Slovakia, and Slovenia). Latvia has a conventional peg but for all intents and purposes follows quasi-currency board rules, while Hungary has a crawling peg. The countries with pegged exchange rates have relatively flexible product and labor markets.

A stronger fiscal position will be necessary to avoid rising imbalances and to cope with the demands of accession. Most CEE countries will need considerable investment to bring their infrastructure to EU standards. To the extent that private saving will be broadly stable, public savings will need to rise to facilitate the potentially higher public and private investment needs. At the same time, fiscal policy has to be ready to re-

---

[2]See Stanley Fischer, Ratna Sahay and Carlos Végh, "How Far is Eastern Europe from Brussels?" IMF Working Paper 98/53, (Washington: International Monetary Fund, April 1998).

[3]See Leslie Lipschitz, Timothy Lane, and Alex Mourmouras, "Capital Flows to Transition Economies: Servant or Master?" IMF Working Paper (Washington: International Monetary Fund, forthcoming).

[4]See Robert Corker, Craig Beaumont, Rachel van Elkan, and Dora Iakova, "Exchange Rate Regimes in Selected Advanced Transition Economies—Coping with Transition, Capital Inflows, and EU Accession," IMF Policy Discussion Paper 00/3 (Washington: International Monetary Fund, April 2000).

spond to and manage shocks that the CEE countries will inevitably encounter.

Finally, the composition of financing may shift away from FDI (in part as privatization is completed) to more liquid flows intermediated by local financial institutions in the coming years. Vulnerability to speculative attacks and conta-

gion can be mitigated by strengthening financial systems in the CEE countries. While the financial sectors in many CEE countries have improved considerably over the years, strengthening their health and the manner in which they are supervised remains a challenge.

net exports. In November 2000, the worsening external position and weakening confidence led to growing liquidity problems in the banking system, which were exacerbated by asset/liability maturity mismatches. The central bank's provision of liquidity supported increased purchases of foreign currency, which—given the preannounced exchange rate—led to declining official foreign reserves.

In response, the Turkish government announced in December 2000 a revised economic program, supported by additional financing from the IMF. The revised program included tighter macroeconomic policy settings and accelerated structural reform. While the program elicited a positive initial response from financial markets, a combination of events in late January and early February 2001, including delays in privatizing key telecommunications and energy companies, the implications of these delays for the government budget, increased political uncertainty, and a worsening of external financing conditions, undermined investor confidence. In response to rapidly declining official foreign reserves, the authorities allowed the currency to float. The situation remains difficult, with a contraction in activity likely in the aftermath of the crisis.

Contagion from the crises in Turkey to other emerging markets through trade and financial links has so far been modest. Turkey's imports from trading partners are expected to fall and the real depreciation of Turkish lira will make Turkey's exports more competitive, possibly reducing other countries' exports to third markets. However, both of these trade effects are

likely to be small, as Turkey is not a major export market for any other country, and Turkey's second largest export is tourism (after textiles). The crises in Turkey hurt investors' perceptions of emerging market borrowers in general, put upward pressure on the spreads of large borrowers, and reinforced concerns about the vulnerability of pegged exchange rate regimes. However, international investors and leveraged players are believed to be less involved in Turkey than in the Asian or Russian crises, partly because some investors have been unwinding positions since last fall, and investors are seen as discriminating more between different fundamentals among emerging market borrowers. Finally, Turkish-owned banks' lending in other markets, particularly in the Commonwealth of Independent States (CIS), could be reduced, but such banks do not account for large shares of those banking systems.

In *Romania* and *Bulgaria* sovereign bond spreads rose moderately and temporarily in response to the crises in Turkey. Romania has close business and financial ties with Turkey, and some investors may have perceived a parallel between the currency board arrangements in Bulgaria and Argentina. Other external developments strongly influenced both countries in 2000: expanding exports to the European Union and the improved security situation in Kosovo boosted growth, while the oil shock fueled inflation and put pressure on the external current account deficit. In Bulgaria, important progress in stabilization and structural reform since 1997—including the currency board arrangement, wage restraint in state enterprises, enter-

Figure 1.12. Selected European Countries: Domestic Demand Growth and General Government Balances[1]

With accelerating domestic demand expected to support growth in 2001, a rebalancing of the policy mix toward tighter fiscal policy would help reduce upward pressures on interest rates and exchange rates.

■ 1999   ■ 2000   ☐ 2001

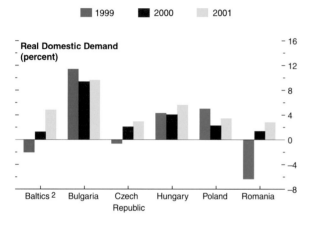

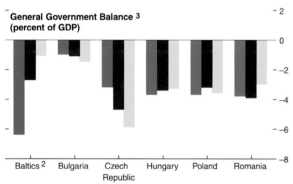

[1] Data for 2001 are IMF staff projections.
[2] Weighted average of Estonia, Latvia, and Lithuania.
[3] The data should be treated with caution, as some quasi-fiscal activities are not reflected in the general government balance and countries have not yet adopted ESA-95.

prise restructuring, and privatization—provide the basis for solid growth, declining inflation, and a narrowing current account deficit over the next few years. By contrast, in Romania, the momentum of economic reform was interrupted in 2000; durable growth, disinflation, and an improved external position require fiscal consolidation, prudent monetary policy, wage and financial discipline in state-owned enterprises, and accelerated restructuring of the enterprise and banking sectors.

In Central Europe, current account deficits are expected to remain substantial in 2001, ranging from 4¾ percent of GDP in the *Czech Republic* to 5½ percent of GDP in *Poland*. To support growth in the near term, restrain inflation, and help narrow the current account deficit, the macroeconomic policy mix in most countries needs to be rebalanced toward relatively tighter fiscal policy (Figure 1.12). In the Czech Republic, which has an inflation targeting framework, additional fiscal consolidation would allow interest rates to decline, helping to alleviate upward pressures on exchange rates. In *Hungary*, which has a crawling exchange rate, tighter fiscal policy would help reduce inflationary pressures and contain the current account deficit. In Poland, given falling inflation and inflationary expectations, the recent interest rate cut was welcome, though real interest rates remain at regional and historical highs.

In the Baltic countries, growth accelerated sharply and inflation remained moderate in 2000, with cross-country variation determined in part by different hard currency pegs. The depreciation of the euro against other major currencies boosted inflation in *Estonia*, which pegs to the euro, but had little effect on inflation in *Latvia*, which pegs to the IMF's special drawing right or SDR, or *Lithuania*, which pegs to the U.S. dollar. While current account deficits remained large in all three countries, they were mostly financed by non-debt creating capital flows. Fiscal positions improved substantially and important progress on structural reform continued to support a conducive environment for foreign direct investment. Prospects for 2001 are favorable, in part because oil prices have declined from last year's highs, though a sharper slowdown in the advanced economies of Europe could curb net exports and harm confidence. An appreciation of the euro against other major currencies would improve competitiveness in Latvia and Lithuania and have only a limited adverse effect on Estonia, as the euro area is the main export market. Notwithstanding recent progress, further fiscal consolidation is under way in all three countries to allow for the government spending needed in connection with EU accession, and in light of looming pension liabilities.

In the *Federal Republic of Yugoslavia*, the economy is devastated after years of regional conflicts, international isolation, and economic mismanagement. In 2000, economic activity stood at less than half of its 1989 level, end-year inflation exceeded 100 percent, and the ratio of external debt to GDP was about 140 percent. The key source of inflationary pressures was the monetary financing of quasi-fiscal deficits of state-owned enterprises. The immediate macroeconomic strategy aims to bring inflation under control by limiting the growth of credit, strengthening the underlying fiscal position, and preventing a further accumulation of expenditure arrears. Achieving a viable balance of payments position will require, in addition to prudent macroeconomic policies and bold structural reforms, a restructuring of external debt. Peace and economic stability will provide the foundation for economic growth in Yugoslavia, which will have important spillover effects on other countries in the region, including *Albania, Bosnia and Herzegovina,* and *FYR Macedonia.*

Commonwealth of Independent States: Oil Prices Are Key

Strong economic performance in Russia in 2000, reflecting a combination of higher world energy prices and the real exchange rate depreciation following the 1998 crisis, helped to boost growth and external positions in most CIS coun-

tries (Table 1.11). In addition, robust foreign demand contributed to these favorable outcomes, while spillovers from the crises in Turkey were limited. However, some oil-importing countries were adversely affected by the rise in oil prices.[10] Also, the record on inflation was mixed: there was a sharp decline in Russia, but it rose in Ukraine. In line with the decline in oil prices from their recent highs and slowing growth in partner countries (mainly Europe), growth and external positions in many CIS countries are projected to be lower in 2001. In most countries, a substantial structural reform agenda remains, and many countries appear to be stuck in a reform trap, with further progress blocked by vested interests that benefit from a situation of partial reform (see Chapter III of the October 2000 *World Economic Outlook*). In *Russia*, the rise in world energy prices and the depreciated currency spurred growth and generated exceptionally large current account and fiscal surpluses in 2000 (Figure 1.13). Prudently, most of the oil windfall appears to have been saved, with the rise in the current account surplus being almost as large as the increase in energy exports. About two-thirds of these savings were captured in official foreign reserves—gross reserves more than doubled during the year—though private capital outflows remained high. Foreign exchange purchases were partly sterilized through a combination of the central bank deposit facility and a buildup of government deposits at the central bank. Notwithstanding these efforts, the strong balance of payments position led to rapid monetary expansion, which added to inflationary pressures.

Lower oil prices, the global slowdown, and the real appreciation of the ruble during the course of last year are expected to reduce growth in Russia to 4 percent in 2001. The general government surplus is expected to decline sharply though remain in overall surplus, reflecting lower oil tax receipts, the revenue loss

[10]See the IMF Research Department's "The Impact of Higher Oil Prices on the Global Economy," available at *http://www.imf.org/external/pubs/ft/oil/2000/index.htm.*

Table 1.11. Commonwealth of Independent States: Real GDP, Consumer Prices, and Current Account Balance
(Annual percent change unless otherwise noted)

	Real GDP				Consumer Prices[1]				Current Account Balances[2]			
	1999	2000	2001	2002	1999	2000	2001	2002	1999	2000	2001	2002
Commonwealth of Independent States	**3.1**	**7.1**	**4.1**	**4.1**	**70.6**	**25.0**	**19.1**	**12.5**	**7.8**	**14.0**	**9.0**	**6.2**
Russia	3.2	7.5	4.0	4.0	85.7	20.8	17.6	12.3	12.4	18.4	12.0	8.2
Excluding Russia	2.7	6.3	4.2	4.4	41.8	34.6	22.2	12.8	−1.5	1.9	−0.3	−0.3
Armenia	3.3	6.0	6.5	6.0	0.7	−0.8	4.5	3.0	−16.6	−14.5	−14.1	−12.1
Azerbaijan	7.4	10.3	8.5	8.0	−8.5	1.8	2.5	2.5	−13.0	−0.3	−14.7	−19.6
Belarus	3.4	6.0	2.5	3.1	293.7	169.0	75.0	23.7	−2.2	−2.6	−2.9	−4.0
Georgia	2.9	1.5	3.8	5.0	19.1	4.0	7.6	4.0	−8.0	−8.1	−7.1	−6.2
Kazakhstan	2.8	9.4	5.0	5.0	8.4	13.4	9.2	5.8	1.0	7.4	3.3	4.9
Kyrgyz Republic	3.7	5.0	5.0	5.2	36.8	18.7	9.1	7.2	−16.3	−12.2	−9.3	−4.5
Moldova	−3.4	1.9	5.0	6.0	39.3	31.3	12.7	10.0	−2.6	−5.6	−7.0	−4.9
Tajikistan	3.7	8.3	5.0	5.0	27.6	34.0	39.6	8.8	−3.4	−6.4	−6.0	−6.2
Turkmenistan	16.0	17.6	10.0	6.0	23.5	8.0	15.0	15.0	−16.0	2.7	2.0	2.0
Ukraine	−0.4	4.2	4.0	4.5	22.7	28.2	15.1	12.1	2.7	4.8	2.3	2.1
Uzbekistan	4.3	4.0	1.0	1.0	29.1	25.4	35.5	24.7	−1.0	0.6	2.4	3.5

[1]In accordance with standard practice in the *World Economic Outlook,* movements in consumer prices are indicated as annual averages rather than as December/December changes during the year as is the practice in some countries.
[2]Percent of GDP.

associated with the implementation of desirable tax reform, and additional expenditures that are appropriate in light of the strong expenditure compression in recent years. The external position is expected to remain strong, so the central bank will have to actively sterilize its foreign exchange interventions to help contain inflationary risks.

The present favorable macroeconomic environment offers the opportunity to move ahead with structural and institutional reform, where progress has been modest. In July 2000, the government adopted a long-term reform program covering the period through 2010, but the program remains to be fully developed in a number of key areas, including the banking sector and measures to reduce arrears. Major tax code revisions included in the government's program were approved by the Duma in August 2000, while the remainder—including revisions to the profit tax and amendments to strengthen tax administration—are still under preparation. There is a need to ensure that the cost of tax reforms does not become too high. There has been backtracking in the energy sector, with export restrictions reintroduced in August.

In *Ukraine,* the economy grew in 2000 for the first time since independence, as net exports were boosted by rapid growth in Russia—the main export market—and the substantial real depreciation of the hryvnia in 1998–99. The fiscal position improved markedly, as strong economic growth boosted tax revenue, and government expenditure was kept in check. Extensive unsterilized foreign exchange intervention stemmed the appreciation of the currency and contributed to the acceleration of inflation. Growth is expected to remain strong in 2001, with domestic demand boosted by improved consumer and business confidence, and the current account surplus should narrow, as slower growth in Russia and elsewhere dampen exports. The targeted reduction in inflation will depend on prudent fiscal policy, including the use of privatization proceeds primarily for debt reduction, and greater exchange rate flexibility. Further progress on structural reform, especially in the banking system, privatization, and payment arrears, is needed to bolster private investment.

In other CIS countries, exports to Russia also grew rapidly in 2000, though economic performance differed depending largely on the role of oil. In energy-exporting countries, including *Kazakhstan*, *Azerbaijan*, and *Turkmenistan*, growth was supported by the increase in oil and natural gas prices, with the exceptional growth in Turkmenistan reflecting primarily greater success in securing payment for its energy exports. Conversely, the direct effect of the oil shock on energy-importing countries, including *Armenia*, *Georgia*, *the Kyrgyz Republic*, *Moldova*, and *Tajikistan*, was negative. Growth in 2001 will be influenced mainly by the moderation of energy prices since 2000 and the prospect of somewhat weaker but still robust growth of exports to Russia.

Sustainable growth in the medium term depends on structural and institutional reform, especially deregulating small and medium-sized enterprises, hardening budget constraints, improving corporate governance, introducing greater competition, developing financial systems, and transforming the role of the state. Inflation has moderated somewhat, but it remains high in many countries, reflecting mainly fiscal problems. Although government expenditures have generally been trimmed, quite extensively in some countries, revenue collection remains weak. Directed credit continues to undermine monetary policy in *Belarus*, Turkmenistan, and *Uzbekistan*. External debt burdens are especially high in Armenia, Georgia, the Kyrgyz Republic, Moldova, and Tajikistan.

Appendix I: The Global Slowdown and Commodity Prices

The volatility in the spot price of oil and the associated uncertainty about its future price path continue to constitute a major issue for the global forecast. This volatility has shown no sign of abating and prices remain high despite slowing global growth. Developments in other commodity markets generally receive less attention, although a prolonged period of comparatively weak prices for most nonfuel prices has hurt many developing countries (as discussed in Chapter II of the October 2000 *World Economic Outlook*). The projected slowing of global

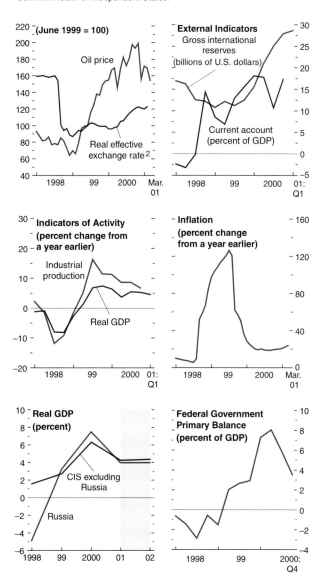

Figure 1.13. Russia: Recovery Driven by Exchange Rate Depreciation and Oil Prices [1]

Higher oil prices and a depreciated exchange rate boosted economic activity in Russia in 2000, which supported growth elsewhere in the Commonwealth of Independent States.

Sources: National authorities; and IMF staff calculations.
[1] Shaded area indicates IMF staff projections.
[2] Real effective exchange rate based on consumer prices indices.

Figure 1.14. Primary Commodity Prices and Selected Economic Indicators[1]

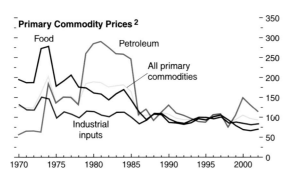

Primary Commodity Prices [2]

Food

Petroleum

All primary commodities

Industrial inputs

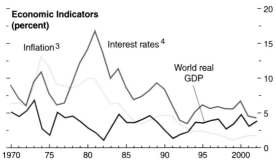

Economic Indicators (percent)

Inflation [3]

Interest rates [4]

World real GDP

[1]Data for 2001 and 2002 are IMF staff projections.
[2]Indices measured in real U.S. dollars.
[3]Advanced economies GDP deflator.
[4]London interbank offered rate (LIBOR) on six-month U.S. dollar deposits in percent.

growth, and hence demand for commodities, could further harm economic prospects of many poorer nations, as well as producers of computer chips, which have many of the attributes of "traditional" commodities.

Prices of both oil and other commodities were strong in the mid 1990s, in part because of the strength of world growth (Figure 1.14). For metals (which are the most cyclically sensitive commodities) the stock overhang was all but eliminated. In addition, rapidly increasing incomes in Asia led to higher demand for meat, contributing to a buoyant market for livestock and associated feed stuffs. Subsequently, the economic problems associated with the 1997–98 financial and economic crises led to a fall in demand growth for most commodities and a slump in commodity prices. By the end of 1998 oil prices had fallen by nearly one-half to around $11 per barrel—their lowest nominal levels since the early 1970s, and in real terms even lower—while prices of nonfuel commodities were about 25 percent below their peaks only two years earlier, and stocks accumulated.

Since 1998, however, the price of oil and natural gas has soared while prices for most other commodities have remained in a slump. The turn around in energy prices has been led by oil, with natural gas prices following with a brief lag (gas prices are often linked to past oil prices).[11] Rapid oil price increases were largely the result of supply constraints, although demand growth and low levels of oil stocks were also contributing factors. After some false starts in 1998, in early 1999 members of Organization of the Petroleum Exporting Countries (OPEC) and a few non-OPEC cooperating countries reached an effective agreement to restrain production. During 2000, however, against a background of growing energy demand associated with accelerating global economic growth, oil producing countries increased production targets on four occasions. Despite these actions, in September 2000 oil prices moved well above the $22 to $28 reference price range that OPEC views as consis-

[11]Coal has recently also risen in price.

tent with long-term market stability, in part because stocks of crude oil and petroleum products remained low.

In December 2000, the upward movement in petroleum prices was reversed. Increases in production appeared to offer consumers some relief and there were worries about a slowdown in the rate of growth of the world economy, in particular in the United States. OPEC countries responded by announcing plans to lower production targets early in 2001. Despite weakening demand, these announcements, a marked slowing in Iraqi exports, and political uncertainties in the Middle East pushed oil prices up in late January and early February, although not back to levels seen between September and November 2000 (Figure 1.15). Given the large moves in spot oil prices over the last few months, the likely path for oil prices over the future remains highly uncertain. The futures market indicates a gradual reduction in prices, but further significant movements in spot prices (particularly downward as the world economy slows) cannot be ruled out.

Unlike energy, prices of other commodities have regained little of their mid-1990s luster since the Asian crisis. By the beginning of 1999, the IMF's price index of industrial inputs—mainly metals, timber, and fibers—had fallen 25 percent below its 1995–97 average. A 10 percent increase during 1999 was mostly erased during 2000 and early 2001 in U.S. dollar terms. The largest price changes have been in the prices of metals and timber. Prices of metals have weakened despite lower levels of stocks, apparently reflecting pessimistic expectations of demand. Food prices, comprising cereals, edible oils, meat, sugar, coffee, cocoa, and tea, saw a small upturn at the end of 1999, which was more than offset in U.S. dollar terms by a decrease in 2000, mostly attributable to declines in coffee prices.[12] Stocks of coffee have accumulated and prices have fallen as a result of a series of good har-

[12]See Chapter II of the October 2000 *World Economic Outlook* for a discussion of the impact of these price changes on poorer countries.

Figure 1.15. West Texas Oil: Spot Price and Futures Contacts
(U.S. dollars per barrel)

Source: Bloomberg Financial Markets, LP.

vests. Consumption of beef has also been adversely affected by health concerns, particularly in Europe, and stocks of cereals (while generally declining) remain high relative to consumption. At the same time, some of this weakness in commodity prices reflects the strength of the U.S. dollar. Prices of many commodities have remained relatively buoyant in terms of euros. This has cushioned the impact of recent U.S. dollar price declines, particularly in countries whose main trading ties are with Europe (which is often true of African nations).

Toward the end of 2000 and increasingly in the first months of 2001, concerns about the slowing of global economic growth have become more central to assessments of prospects for non-energy commodity prices, particularly metals. Estimates of U.S. demand for a number of metals—steel, aluminum, copper, nickel, and zinc—in the first quarter of 2001 are about 5 percent lower than the first quarter of 2000, and slowing growth elsewhere will exacerbate this situation. For other commodities, which are typically less cyclically sensitive than metals, the signals are less clear, as commodity-specific factors tend to dominate the near term prospects (the most visible example of this being the oil markets, discussed earlier).[13] Nevertheless, weakening global demand can be expected to put generalized downward pressure on prices, exacerbating the problems of many poor nations.

Finally, the slowdown in activity also negatively affects another market with many features in common with "traditional" commodities, namely computer chips. In mid-2000 the market for chips for use in personal computers, cell phones, and digital cameras appeared very strong. Prices for the dynamic random access memory chips (DRAMs), often described as

---

[13]Unexpected and often large movements in prices generally based on supply factors remain an important feature of world commodity markets. Over the past 30 years, the average annual change has varied between 9 percent (for bananas) to 37 percent (for sugar in the "free market"), and this variability has not decreased in recent years.

"workhorse" memory chips, and the modules made from these chips had increased by about 50 percent from March to July 2000 on rising demand (Figure 1.16). The five leading Japanese chip producers were in the process of increasing investment by more than two-thirds over the previous year.

By October, however, slowing growth in the U.S. information technology market was becoming evident. Production targets for personal computers were reduced and there was a buildup of DRAM inventories. The leading Japanese microchip companies were cutting by half their forecasts of operating profits on semiconductor sales. By January 2001 DRAM prices were one-third the level six months earlier. In response, chip manufacturers have been cutting back on investment in new capacity and are reportedly trying to shift their production away from chips for personal computers to chips for cell phones and digital cameras, markets where rapid rates of growth are expected to continue. However, the fall in both price and slowing in demand for chips is significantly affecting economic prospects in several countries, most notably in Asia.

Appendix II: Reducing External Imbalances

The baseline forecast in this *World Economic Outlook* contains a scenario in which, after a significant slowdown in global activity in 2001, growth rebounds back to close to its underlying potential in 2002 and is broadly stable subsequently (Figure 1.1). However, the accompanying path for domestic demand implies that existing trade and exchange rate imbalances across the major currency regions continue to remain large over the future (see Statistical Appendix Table 44). An important reason for the limited progress in addressing existing trade imbalances is that the *World Economic Outlook* forecasts are predicated on the assumption that real exchange rate is fixed over the future. This convention, which is also used by other forecasting publications, such as the OECD's *Economic Outlook*, follows existing evidence on short-term exchange rate dynamics.[14] However, when exchange rates across the world's currency areas—particularly the United States and the euro area—appear significantly different from the values implied by medium-term fundamentals, it is useful to explore the consequences of a gradual movement in exchange rates that leads to a reduction in international trade imbalances.[15]

This appendix describes two simulations using MULTIMOD, the IMF's international macroeconomic model, to examine alternative paths by which these imbalances are reduced at a faster rate. The first is a "soft landing with imbalance adjustment" scenario, illustrating the consequences of a resolution of these imbalances through a gradual change in the values of major currencies and equity markets over the next three years. Next comes a "harder landing" scenario, in which existing tensions associated with imbalances in currency and stock markets lead to these changes in exchange rates occurring abruptly, with associated reductions in confidence and equity market valuations.[16]

These simulations should be taken as only illustrative for a number of reasons. In addition to the obvious fact that the future is inherently uncertain, it should also be recognized that the changes in external balances contained in these scenarios, while significant, are in all probability not large enough to fully address the trade imbalances that are currently present in the world

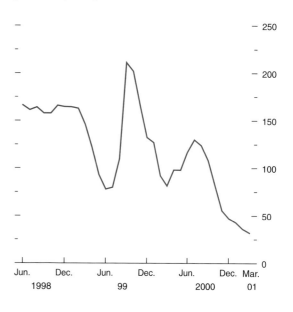

Figure 1.16. Computer Chip Prices[1]
(U.S. dollars per unit)

Source: Primark Datastream.
[1]Dynamic random access memory (DRAM) modules, 128 MB, 100 MGHZ bus, 16 by 64, U.S. spot price.

[14]The difficulties of forecasting short-run exchange rate dynamics was highlighted in a seminal paper by Richard Meese and Kenneth Rogoff, "Empirical Exchange Rate Models of the Seventies: Do They Fit Out of Sample," *Journal of International Economics*, Vol. 14 (1983), pp. 3–24. More recent work has found evidence for some reversion to underlying values over time, but at a relatively slow rate (see Ronald MacDonald, "Long Run Exchange Rate Modeling: A Survey of the Evidence," *IMF Staff Papers*, International Monetary Fund, Vol. 42 (1995), pp. 437–89).

[15]The IMF's approach to calculating exchange rate misalignments is discussed in Peter Isard and Hamid Faruqee, eds., *Exchange Rate Assessment: Extensions of the Macroeconomic Balance Approach*, IMF Occasional Paper No. 167 (Washington: International Monetary Fund, 1998).

[16]This has been a recurring theme in previous editions of the *World Economic Outlook*. See, for example, "Alternative Scenarios," Appendix I, Chapter I of the October 2000 edition.

Figure 1.17. Global Imbalances Adjustment Scenarios
(Deviation in percent from baseline real GDP)

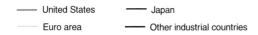

United States
Euro area
Japan
Other industrial countries

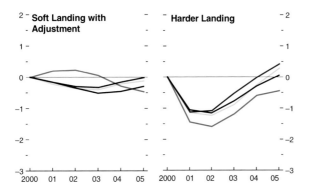

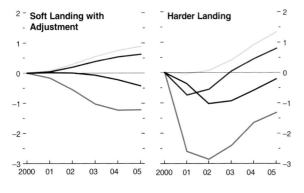

Source: IMF MULTIMOD simulations.

economy. Other factors, in addition to exchange rate movements, could also contribute to resolving these imbalances. In particular, faster growth in potential output in the euro area and Japan brought about by more rigorous structural reforms can help. A MULTIMOD simulation in which potential growth rate in these regions was raised by ½ percent a year indicates that this could have a significant impact on trade imbalances, reducing the deficit in the United States by some $50 billion after five years (see Appendix I of Chapter I of the October 2000 *World Economic Outlook*). Finally, the increase in potential growth in the United States may also imply some change in underlying trade elasticities (see Box 1.2, which discusses the sustainability of the U.S. current account deficit).

The results of the "imbalance adjustment" scenario are reported in Table 1.12 and Figure 1.17. The real value of the U.S. dollar is assumed to steadily depreciate over the next three years by a cumulative total of 20 percent against the euro and the yen, and 15 percent against the other industrial countries (reflecting the fact that exchange rates of these countries tend to be linked more directly with the U.S. dollar).[17] This leads to a gradual adjustment in international imbalances, and in 2005 (by which time this adjustment is relatively complete) the U.S. trade balance has improved by over $85 billion, the main counterpart being a reduction in the trade balances of the euro area (slightly over $45 billion) and Japan (about $30 billion). By contrast, there is relatively little impact on the trade balance of the other industrial countries group, as the real effective exchange rate remains relatively unchanged, with the depreciation against the U.S. dollar being counterbalanced by appreciations against the euro and yen.

The adjustment in trade balances occurs primarily through a gradual rebalancing of world demand. Focusing initially on the United States, real exports rise and real imports fall compared

---

[17]The largest four members of the other industrial country group are Australia, Canada, Sweden, and the United Kingdom.

Table 1.12. Alternative Scenario: Soft Landing with Imbalance Adjustment
(Percent deviation from baseline unless otherwise specified)

	2001	2002	2003	2004	2005
World Real GDP	−0.1	−0.2	−0.3	−0.3	−0.3
United States					
Real GDP	0.2	0.2	0.1	−0.3	−0.5
Real Domestic Demand	−0.2	−0.5	−1.0	−1.2	−1.2
Real Investment	−0.5	−2.0	−3.5	−4.1	−4.3
Real Effective Exchange Rate	−6.1	−11.4	−15.1	−14.5	−14.4
Trade Balance ($billion)	3.1	16.4	42.9	67.0	85.2
CPI Inflation (percentage points)	0.5	0.7	0.7	0.3	0.3
Short-term interest rate (percentage points)	0.3	0.8	1.2	1.2	1.2
Equity Prices	−3.4	−7.4	−9.5	−9.6	−9.8
Euro Area					
Real GDP	−0.2	−0.4	−0.4	−0.2	−0.1
Real Domestic Demand	0.1	0.3	0.5	0.8	0.9
Real Investment	0.3	1.0	1.8	2.3	2.3
Real Effective Exchange Rate	3.2	6.0	8.3	8.5	9.4
Real U.S. Dollar Exchange Rate	7.5	14.9	20.5	20.4	21.0
Trade Balance ($billion)	−3.7	−12.1	−25.5	−37.2	−47.9
CPI Inflation (percentage points)	−0.3	−0.5	−0.6	−0.5	−0.5
Short-term interest rate (percentage points)	−0.6	−1.3	−1.9	−2.1	−2.2
Equity Prices	1.8	4.1	5.7	6.2	6.0
Japan					
Real GDP	−0.2	−0.3	−0.3	−0.2	—
Real Domestic Demand	—	0.2	0.4	0.6	0.6
Real Investment	0.2	0.7	1.2	1.4	1.5
Real Effective Exchange Rate	4.5	8.9	11.4	10.1	9.8
Real U.S. Dollar Exchange Rate	7.7	15.4	20.5	19.0	18.8
Trade Balance ($billion)	1.4	−1.0	−10.2	−21.6	−27.9
CPI inflation (percentage points)	−0.2	−0.2	−0.2	−0.1	−0.2
Short-term Interest Rates (percentage points)	−0.2	−0.6	−0.9	−1.1	−1.2
Equity Prices	1.3	2.4	3.4	3.5	3.6
Other Industrial Economies					
Real GDP	−0.2	−0.3	−0.5	−0.5	−0.3
Real Domestic Demand	—	—	−0.1	−0.2	−0.4
Trade Balance ($billion)	−3.7	−8.3	−14.0	−15.0	−13.9
Industrial Countries					
Real GDP	−0.1	−0.1	−0.2	−0.3	−0.3
Real Domestic Demand	—	−0.1	−0.1	−0.2	−0.1
Trade Balance ($billion)	−2.8	−5.0	−6.8	−6.8	−4.5
Developing Countries					
Real GDP	−0.1	−0.2	−0.3	−0.4	−0.4
Real Domestic Demand	−0.2	−0.4	−0.6	−0.7	−0.8
Trade Balance ($billion)	3.4	6.0	8.0	11.4	7.8

to baseline through 2005, as trade responds to current and lagged exchange rate movements. The impact on real GDP is relatively small. It initially rises slightly above baseline values and subsequently falls below them. This is because the main counterpart to the change in real net exports is a reduction in real domestic demand compared to baseline. This comprises a fall in both real investment and, to a rather lesser extent, real consumption, resulting from a monetary policy tightening (to counteract imported inflationary pressures) and an erosion in equity prices (as lower investment reduces potential output and hence future expected profits). The opposite adjustment mechanism can be seen in the euro area and Japan. Real exports fall, real imports rise, and real domestic demand is boosted by a loosening of monetary policy and a rise in equity prices, while real GDP falls slightly below baseline.

Elsewhere, the other industrial country group experiences fewer benefits than the euro area and Japan, reflecting its closer trade and financial links with the United States. Both real GDP and real domestic demand fall compared to baseline. Developing countries see a medium-term reduction in real GDP and domestic demand compared to baseline, both because higher U.S. dollar interest rates reduce access to borrowing (and lead to a small improvement in the current account) and because the demand for exports falls as demand is switched from the United States, which trades relatively heavily with developing Asia and Latin America, to other countries that are mainly in Europe, whose trade is more directed to other advanced economies, the countries in transition, and Africa. For the world as a whole, the overall impact is to marginally reduce global growth, as reductions in U.S. investment are not fully offset by higher capital spending elsewhere.

The "harder landing" scenario assumes that these exchange rate adjustments (a fall in the real value of the dollar of 20 percent against the euro and yen, and 15 percent against currencies of other industrial countries) occur precipitately some time in early to mid-2001,[18] and are accompanied by:

- A fall in *global equity values* as investor confidence declines, with the United States being hit the hardest (a 20 percent fall in values), and the euro area and Japan the least.
- An accompanying erosion of *consumer and investor confidence* in the United States (due to the fall in equity prices) and in Japan (as weakness in global demand does further damage to an already weak economic situation).

- A gradual appreciation in equity values over the next three years as investor confidence is gradually restored, with this effect being again most pronounced in the United States.

The results from this scenario, reported in Table 1.13 and Figure 1.17, indicate that the adjustment of international imbalances and global demand is achieved more rapidly than in the "soft landing," but at the cost of significant short-term reductions in global growth.[19] World output falls by slightly over 1 percentage point compared to baseline in 2001 and stays at this level in 2002, after which it slowly recovers to baseline values by 2005. Although the larger falls in equity market values and confidence lead to a somewhat larger short-term reduction in real GDP compared to baseline in the United States than elsewhere in the advanced countries, the short-term losses in output are relatively similar across the advanced country regions, as the rapid depreciation of the U.S. dollar leads to largely offsetting movements in real net exports. Weaker output leads to a generalized fall in core inflation, and monetary policy is loosened throughout the advanced world. It is also possible that the decline in the U.S. dollar will be delayed, however, as capital continues to flow into the United States based on future growth prospects. In this case, the reduction in output and real demand in the United States would be larger in the short term as the benefits to real activity from a depreciation in the currency are delayed. Correspondingly, the real effects on other advanced country regions would be smaller.

Returning to the main "harder landing" scenario, the loss of confidence in the United States translates into more rapid divergence in relative levels of real domestic demand than in the "soft

---

[18]No particular event is postulated as starting this adjustment, as significant asset price movements can, and often do, occur without such a trigger once underlying imbalances have built up. For example, the recent global correction in equity valuations in the technology sector (discussed further in Chapter II) does not appear to have been driven by a significant specific macroeconomic event—nor were the 1929 and 1987 U.S. stock market crashes.

[19]The impact on global growth is somewhat smaller than in the harder landing reported in the last *World Economic Outlook*, particularly in the United States, reflecting the significant slowing of global growth and reduction in equity values already seen. Adjusted for the lower underlying forecast, the current simulation implies significantly weaker growth in 2001 than was implied by the earlier scenario.

Table 1.13. Alternative Scenario: Harder Landing
(Percent deviation from baseline unless otherwise specified)

	2001	2002	2003	2004	2005
World Real Growth	−1.1	−1.1	−0.8	−0.3	—
United States					
Real GDP	−1.4	−1.6	−1.2	−0.6	−0.4
Real Domestic Demand	−2.5	−2.7	−2.3	−1.6	−1.3
Real Investment	−9.8	−9.9	−7.7	−6.0	−4.7
Real Effective Exchange Rate	−14.0	−15.2	−15.6	−15.4	−15.4
Trade Balance ($billion)	6.6	33.9	54.0	70.1	85.4
CPI Inflation (percentage points)	0.9	−0.5	−1.0	−1.2	−1.1
Short-term interest rate (percentage points)	−2.8	−3.0	−3.0	−2.3	−1.5
Equity Prices	−19.1	−14.9	−12.1	−10.5	−10.0
Euro Area					
Real GDP	−1.1	−1.2	−0.9	−0.3	0.3
Real Domestic Demand	—	0.1	0.4	0.9	1.4
Real Investment	−0.1	—	0.5	1.3	2.3
Real Effective Exchange Rate	8.5	9.7	10.1	9.7	9.2
Real U.S. Dollar Exchange Rate	20.0	22.0	22.3	21.6	21.3
Trade Balance ($billion)	−18.4	−30.3	−38.0	−46.6	−58.6
CPI Inflation (percentage points)	−1.1	−0.8	−0.5	−0.2	−0.1
Short-term interest rate (percentage points)	−2.9	−3.0	−3.0	−2.8	−2.7
Equity Prices	−0.4	0.3	2.6	5.0	7.4
Japan					
Real GDP	−1.1	−1.1	−0.5	—	0.4
Real Domestic Demand	−0.7	−0.6	0.1	0.5	0.8
Real Investment	−4.0	−2.6	0.2	1.0	1.7
Real Effective Exchange Rate	6.3	9.1	9.9	9.2	9.0
Real U.S. Dollar Exchange Rate	14.9	18.5	19.4	18.5	18.2
Trade Balance ($billion)	0.8	−1.0	−7.4	−13.3	−18.8
CPI inflation (percentage points)	−0.3	−0.4	−0.4	−0.4	−0.4
Short-term Interest Rates (percentage points)	−0.5	−0.7	−0.9	−1.4	−1.6
Equity Prices	−0.1	2.8	3.2	4.0	3.9
Other Industrial Economies					
Real GDP	−1.1	−1.2	−0.8	−0.3	0.1
Real Domestic Demand	−0.4	−1.0	−0.9	−0.6	−0.2
Trade Balance ($billion)	−6.0	6.4	11.5	13.3	8.1
Industrial Countries					
Real GDP	−1.2	−1.3	−0.9	−0.3	—
Real Domestic Demand	−1.1	−1.3	−0.9	−0.3	—
Trade Balance ($billion)	−16.9	9.0	20.1	23.5	16.1
Developing Countries					
Real GDP	−0.5	−0.5	−0.4	−0.3	−0.2
Real Domestic Demand	−0.8	−0.8	−0.6	−0.4	−0.3
Trade Balance ($billion)	18.5	−5.4	−14.1	−14.7	−5.2

landing" scenario, and by 2002 the adjustment in trade balances is twice as large. However by 2005, when the process of trade balance adjustment is essentially complete, the differences between the two scenarios have been largely erased. The U.S. trade balance improves by $85 billion compared to baseline (almost identical to the other scenario), with the main counterparts again being the euro area (almost $60 billion) and Japan (almost $20 billion). By this time, sig-

nificant differences are also apparent in the path of real activity. Compared to baseline, real output recovers much more slowly in the United States than elsewhere, particularly in the euro area and Japan, as differential movements in real investment translate into changes in the level of potential output.

There is also a significant fall in real GDP and real domestic demand in developing countries, although it is only about half of that in the advanced world. Compared to the results in the "soft landing" scenario, the fall in real GDP and (in particular) real domestic demand is larger initially but smaller over the medium term. This reflects two competing forces. The larger initial fall in output in the advanced countries reduces demand for exports from developing countries, lowers commodity prices, and reduces capital flows. Over several years, however, the loosening of global monetary conditions coming from weakness in activity provides a boost to the developing world, particularly to regions that are heavily dependent on foreign borrowing, such as Latin America. The decline in output, however, could be significantly greater if the hard landing in the United States was accompanied by a substantial deterioration in financing conditions for emerging markets.

CHAPTER II

THREE CURRENT POLICY ISSUES

This chapter contains three essays on current policy issues. Each essay addresses different aspects of the impact of globalization on economies and each provides some new empirical evidence. Globalization is one of the major forces affecting economic behavior, and its effects can be seen across a wide range of topics. In many cases, however, there has been relatively little empirical work done to measure its impact on underlying economies. The empirical results reported here are by necessity preliminary, since the phenomena being examined are so recent, but may still provide useful insights to policymakers.

The first essay examines how the correction in technology stocks affects real activity. A major development in the world economy over the last year has been the global correction in technology stocks in both advanced and emerging markets, which has been the main force in reducing equity values. The essay explores whether technology stocks have a different impact compared to nontechnology stocks on real consumption, real investment, and as a leading indicator of industrial production.

The second essay examines exchange rate movements across the three major currencies—the U.S. dollar, the euro, and the yen. The recent weakness of the euro against the dollar appears to defy conventional exchange rate analysis—for example, increases in euro area interest rates have been associated with weakness in the currency. This has led many commentators to suggest that the bilateral rate is being driven by portfolio equity flows reflecting expectations of higher profits and output growth in the United States. This explanation, while plausible, seems difficult to reconcile with the fact that the yen has remained relatively stable against the dollar at a time when expected growth rates have been marked down. The essay examines how the diverging trends between the euro-dollar and the yen-dollar exchange rate can be reconciled.

The final essay looks at open trading regimes, focusing on sub-Saharan Africa. Sub-Saharan Africa's growth rate per capita has been negative over the past 25 years, and one of the leading explanations for this disappointing result is that the region did not embrace openness to international trade. Over the last decade, however, there have been substantial moves toward such opening, including a host of regional trade initiatives. The essay evaluates the success of these initiatives, suggests how policymakers could build on the existing momentum to open African trade, and examines the role of advanced economies in lowering their barriers to Africa's exports.

Impact of the Global Technology Correction on the Real Economy

Stock market valuations have risen significantly in the 1990s, and advanced economies, in particular, have experienced dramatic increases in their main stock price indices (Figure 2.1). A striking feature of developments in the late 1990s has been the global rise and fall in valuations of technology stocks, which raises the question of what these swings—especially the latest corrections in technology valuations—imply for global activity. This section describes recent trends in global equity markets and presents some preliminary results as to whether changes in technology stock valuations have a different impact on consumption, investment, or future output trends compared with the effect from the rest of the stock market.

Recent Developments

Impressive world growth at the turn of the millennium and, in particular, the strong economic performance of the U.S. economy in the late 1990s, generated a rally in stock valuations from 1998 that came to a peak in early 2000. Subsequently, stock prices began falling in most countries and continued sliding into the current year. Technology stock valuations have fallen most; for example, the technology intensive NASDAQ index fell by about 70 percent between early March 2000 and early April 2001.

The run-up and subsequent fall in technology stocks (called Telecommunication, Media, and Information Technology and Software equities in this essay and referred to as TMT hereafter) occurred in a wide range of markets, not just the United States (Figure 2.2).[1] Furthermore, TMT returns have become increasingly linked over the last decade (Figure 2.3).[2] For the non-TMT segment as a whole, correlation also rose from the mid-1990s to early 1999, although it has fallen somewhat subsequently. However, correlations across individual non-TMT segments remain relatively low.[3] In addition, domestic correlations between weekly returns in the TMT segment and the rest of the stock market have gone down, especially for the United States and Europe.

The fall in TMT stock valuations throughout 2000 was a worldwide phenomenon, but this masks important regional differences (Figure 2.4). First, stock markets are different in size relative to GDP. The United States has throughout the period had a relatively large stock market

Figure 2.1. Equity Price Indices
(1995=100)

Stock prices rallied between late 1999 and early 2000, but have come down since in most countries.

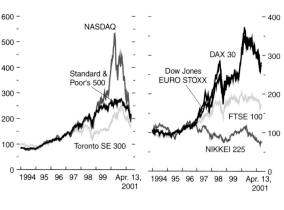

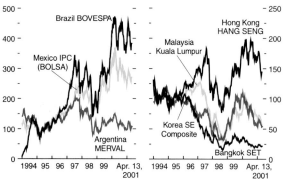

Source: Primark Datastream.

---

[1]The data on these sectors used in this essay come from Datastream, which provides consistent data across a wide range of countries. For more on the strengths and weaknesses of the data see Chapter II of the October 2000 *World Economic Outlook.*

[2]Calculated as a rolling 100-day correlation window. A closer look at the return correlation of components of TMT reveals that correlations have been generally rising most in the telecommunication and the information technology and software sectors, but less so in the rather more diverse media segment.

[3]See Robin Brooks and Luis Catão, "The New Economy and Global Stock Returns," IMF Working Paper 00/216 (Washington: International Monetary Fund, 2000), who find evidence of a much larger global common factor driving returns in TMT segments of stock markets than in other sectors.

valuation, and at the end of 2000 capitalization stood at around 130 percent of GDP, with about one-third in TMT shares, while Canada has a lower capitalization ratio but a similar composition. In the major European economies stock market capitalization varies widely as a ratio to GDP, with the United Kingdom well above the United States ratio, and the three large continental economies well below. For Europe and Japan, TMT stock valuations make up 20 to 25 percent of overall valuations. In the emerging market economies of Asia, markets are on average about the same size as in continental Europe, whereas in Latin America they are, with a few exceptions, significantly smaller. For emerging markets in both Asia and Latin America, the size of the TMT stock market capitalization as a share of GDP remains in single digits for most countries.

A second regional difference between stock markets is the composition of the TMT sector. In Europe, telecommunication companies constitute the largest share of the TMT sector, although the share of information technology (i.e., hardware manufacturing) and software has increased since mid-1999.[4] In contrast, in the United States the valuation of the TMT sector throughout the 1990s has been more broad-based in the information technology and software sectors. In the Asian countries, the technology sector has been broadly equally divided between telecommunication and information technology and software stocks, reflecting the significant production of semiconductors and other computer components. Finally, in Latin America, the TMT sector is dominated by telecommunication companies.

These differences in size and composition of the TMT sector are important, not only because

---

[4]Relative market valuation is not the same as relative production, but it reflects financial markets' valuation of the relative potential of the components of the TMT sector. These data only measure companies that are listed on stock exchanges, not privately held firms. This may bias the data in particular for emerging markets in Asia, where a substantial number of firms are not listed on the stock exchange.

Figure 2.2. Stock Price Indices for Technology, Media, and Telecommunications (TMT) vs. Non-TMT Sector[1]
(1995=100)

A global phenomenon is the rise and fall in technology stock valuation.

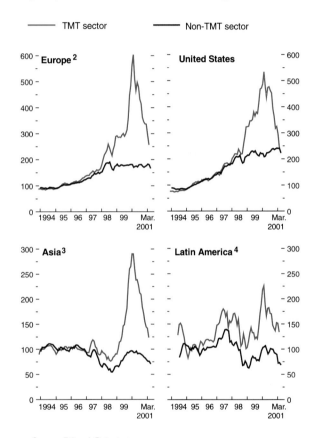

Source: Primark Datastream.
[1] Weighted by market value.
[2] Includes Austria, Belgium, Denmark, Finland, France, Germany, Greece, Ireland, Italy, Luxembourg, Netherlands, Norway, Portugal, Spain, Sweden, Switzerland, and the United Kingdom.
[3] Includes China, Hong Kong SAR, India, Indonesia, Japan, Korea, Malaysia, Philippines, Singapore, Taiwan Province of China, and Thailand.
[4] Includes Argentina, Brazil, Chile, Colombia, Mexico, Peru, and Venezuela.

Figure 2.3. Correlation Between Technology, Media, and Telecommunications (TMT) and non-TMT Returns Across Regions[1]

Correlations between technology stock returns have increased globally, but domestic correlations between technology returns and nontechnology returns have fallen.

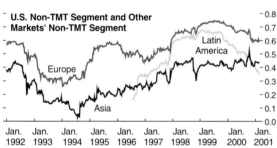

Sources: Primark Datastream; and IMF staff estimates.
[1]Calculated as a rolling 100-day correlation window.

they influence the long-run growth rate of the regions but also because they may have a different impact on the real economy. For example, the relatively higher concentration of telecommunications in Asia, Latin America, and Europe makes these regions less vulnerable to changes in views on the "new" economy, but more vulnerable to sentiment surrounding the telecom sector. In addition, given the relatively small size of TMT sectors in Asia and Latin America, the impact on aggregate consumption and investment will probably be smaller than in continental Europe and the United States, Canada, and the United Kingdom.

Stock Market Valuations and Economic Activity

As can be seen in Table 2.1, the magnitude of the recent fall in stock market values (measured relative to GDP) has been severe, especially in the United States, Canada, and Japan, and has been focused in the TMT sector. Indeed, in many countries non-TMT values rose over this period. Given the very different behavior of these two sectors, a natural question is whether changes in TMT valuations have a different impact on consumption, investment, and future trends in output than the rest of the stock market.

Changes in stock market valuations affect consumption through wealth effects and investment through the cost of capital.[5] Identifying the exact channels of transmission from TMT and non-TMT valuations to the real economy is difficult, and there is not yet an established literature analyzing these phenomena. The following constitutes a preliminary attempt to assess how the two stock market segments affect consumption and investment, and whether they have different properties as leading indicators of the business cycle.

[5]See Chapter III of the May 2000 *World Economic Outlook*. An overview of the channels of transmission between the real economy and stock prices is also provided in Peter Christoffersen and Torsten Sløk, "Do Asset Prices in Transition Countries Contain Information About Future Economic Activity?" IMF Working Paper 00/103 (Washington: International Monetary Fund, 2000).

Table 2.1. Change in Market Capitalization from March 2000 to March 2001

(In percent of GDP)

	Total Market	TMT	Non-TMT
United States	−19	−28	9
Canada	−20	−28	8
Japan	−32	−19	−15
Germany	−15	−11	−4
France	−12	−9	−3
Netherlands	−28	−28	−2
United Kingdom	−27	−32	5
Argentina	−2	−3	1
Brazil	−7	−5	−1
Mexico	−5	−1	−4
Indonesia	−9	−2	−7
Thailand	−8	−1	−6

Note: The numbers may not add up due to rounding.

Effect on Consumption

A change in stock prices affects private consumption through changes in households' income and wealth. The magnitude of the impact generally will be larger the greater the share of households owning stocks and the larger the stock market relative to GDP. In the United States and several other English speaking countries, these factors are quite pronounced, whereas this is less the case in continental Europe. In Latin America and Asia there are only a limited number of households owning stocks and markets are on average smaller and less liquid, which suggests that the impact from stock price changes to consumption is smaller than in the advanced economies.

It is at least plausible to suppose that the impact of changes in the value of TMT and non-TMT equities could be different given that there is considerable evidence that households have different propensities to consume out of stocks and other types of wealth.[6] However, the sign of

[6]For example, Flint Brayton and Eileen Mauskopf, "Structure and Uses of the MPS Quarterly Econometric Model of the United States," *Federal Reserve Bulletin*, Vol. 73 (February 1987), pp. 93–109, find that the propensity to consume out of changes in stock valuations is about half that of other types of wealth. For a more recent documentation of the FRB/US model see David Reifschneider, Robert Tetlov, and John Williams, "Aggregate Disturbances, Monetary Policy, and the Macroeconomy: The FRB/US Perspective," *Federal Reserve Bulletin*, January 1999, p. 1–19.

Figure 2.4. Technology, Media, and Telecommunications (TMT) as a Share of GDP
(Percent)

Stock markets are bigger in Anglo-Saxon countries than elsewhere.

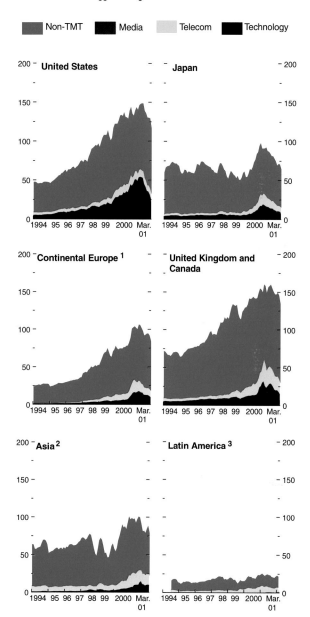

Sources: Primark Datastream; and IMF staff estimates.
[1] Includes Austria, Belgium, Denmark, Finland, France, Germany, Greece, Ireland, Italy, Luxembourg, Netherlands, Norway, Portugal, Spain, Sweden, and Switzerland.
[2] Includes Hong Kong SAR, Indonesia, Korea, Malaysia, Philippines, Singapore, Taiwan Province of China, and Thailand.
[3] Includes Argentina, Brazil, Chile, Colombia, Mexico, Peru, and Venezuela.

Table 2.2. Impact of a Rise in Equity Valuations on Consumption
(Increase in real U.S. dollar spending from a one U.S. dollar increase in equity values)

	TMT Capitalization	Non-TMT Capitalization	Total Market[1]
Average North America and United Kingdom	**0.04**	**0.05**	**0.05**
Average continental Europe	**0.04**	**0.01**	**0.01**
Japan	0.06	**0.13**	**0.12**

Note: Bolded estimates are statistically significant. North America and United Kingdom covers the United States, Canada, and the United Kingdom and "continental Europe" covers Germany, France, and the Netherlands. Effect after 2 years. A reduced-form vector autoregression was estimated for each country over the period 1990: 1 to 2000:10 with monthly retail sales, real TMT stock market capitalization, real non-TMT stock market capitalization, and industrial production. Three lags were used and all variables are in logs. The two year effect was calculated for each country as the level of the impulse-response function after 24 months. The effect of the experiment was calculated using private consumption for 2000 and market capitalization in December 2000. For the details of the statistical analysis see Hali Edison and Torsten Sløk: "Wealth Effects and the New Economy" IMF Working Paper (Washington: International Monetary Fund, forthcoming).

[1]Total Market is the effect of a one U.S. dollar increase, where the one dollar increase is split between TMT and non-TMT using their share of total stock market capitalization in December 2000.

this effect is unclear. On the one hand, TMT equities are more volatile, and households may view them as risky investments, implying a smaller propensity to consume. On the other hand, the increasing use of stock options and bonuses based on performance as a means of paying employees in the technology sector could imply a higher propensity to consume from changes in TMT share values.

There has been a large amount of casual evidence linking changes in TMT equity prices to consumption, but much less formal work on this issue.[7] Accordingly, the IMF analyzed the impact of stock market valuation on consumption, focusing on differentiating between the effect from TMT and non-TMT stock market valuations. The analysis examined the interaction between monthly retail sales, real TMT stock capitalization, real non-TMT stock capitalization, and industrial production (as a proxy for income) over the period January 1990 to October 2000.[8] The short sample period reflects the recent emer-

gence of the TMT sector as an important factor in stock markets. The analysis was limited to seven advanced economies; United States, Canada, and the United Kingdom, three continental European countries (Germany, France, and the Netherlands), and Japan, because in emerging markets the quality and coverage of retail sales data is limited and, as discussed above, stock market valuations are smaller.

Table 2.2 reports the results of an increase in TMT and non-TMT valuations on consumption after two years (a typical time period for households to react to increases in wealth). Given the uncertainty in estimates for individual economies that are seldom individually significant, it is most useful to report estimates for broad groups of countries, namely North America and United Kingdom and the three continental European countries, as well as for Japan. For North America and United Kingdom, the results indicate that an increase of one U.S. dollar in TMT stock market valuation raises consumption by 4 cents. The opposite also holds, with a $1 decline resulting in a 4-cent fall in consumption. A similar change in non-TMT values changes consumption by 5 cents (both are statistically significant). Studies for the United States

[7]See, for example, HSBC, *World Economic Watch* (February 2, 2001), p. 5; Morgan Stanley Dean Witter, *Global Equity Research*, (February 1, 2001), p. 4; and Bridgewater *Daily Observations* (January 4, 2001), p. 1.

[8]A reduced-form vector autoregression (VAR) was estimated with the logarithms of retail sales, real TMT stock market capitalization, real non-TMT stock market capitalization, and industrial production. Using stock price indices instead of market capitalization did not change the results significantly. A VAR was chosen as it presents a flexible and simple way of analyzing the underlying characteristics of data. Based on evidence from U.S. data, it is assumed that half of the estimated elasticities for retail

sales can be applied to aggregate consumption in order to find the aggregate cents-per-dollar impact. For the details and robustness checks of the statistical analysis, see Hali Edison and Torsten Sløk, "Wealth Effects and the New Economy," IMF Working Paper (Washington: International Monetary Fund, forthcoming).

have found a total stock market wealth effect between 3 to 7 cents, and the estimates found here suggest that the propensity to consume out of total stock market wealth has been in this range in the 1990s, so, despite their relative imprecision, the results appear broadly plausible.[9] In the continental European countries an increase (decrease) in non-TMT equity values of one U.S. dollar is estimated, on average, to lead to an increase (decrease) in consumption of 1 cent, consistent with the view that wealth effects are generally less important in these countries. For TMT the effect is higher, statistically significant, and similar to the impact estimates for North America and United Kingdom. As TMT stock market valuations in continental Europe are significantly smaller as a ratio to GDP, however, the implied impact on activity is generally smaller (Table 2.1).

A possible interpretation from these admittedly preliminary results is that the fall in TMT stock valuations could have a larger impact on consumption in continental Europe than has been generally expected. They suggest that, even though the underlying impact on activity is generally larger in North America and United Kingdom, changes in TMT valuations have played a role in both groupings whereas changes in non-TMT valuations have had a significantly higher impact on consumption in North America and United Kingdom. The result for the continental European countries could reflect the widespread ownership of TMT shares (including the telecommunications sector) and rising share ownership over time, which may come through more in the TMT results, as the main changes in TMT valuation are focused in the post–1995 period.

For Japan, the estimated impact on consumption of both TMT and non-TMT stock values are large, too large to be plausible as a direct wealth effect given that households are not significant owners of equities and most equities are held by financial institutions. Part of this may reflect the imprecision of the underlying coefficient estimates. However, the coefficient on non-TMT stocks is significantly different from zero, suggesting that some connection does exist between stock values and consumption. This may well reflect the significant impact of stock market valuations on banks' balance sheets. Given the fragility in Japan's banking sector since the asset price bubble burst in the early 1990s, and the importance of bank lending in financial intermediation, the impact on bank lending could affect overall activity and hence consumption.[10]

Effect on Investment

Stock markets affect investment through the cost of capital. If the ratio of market valuation of capital to the cost of acquiring new capital (also referred to as Tobin's q) rises, so will investment. The increase in TMT stock valuation has been a key source of funding for information technology companies in the late 1990s through IPOs, as their access to other capital markets (bonds and bank loans) has been limited. The dramatic increases in valuations of TMT firms led to easier access to resources and consequently also to higher investment.[11] In addition, at least for the United States, changes in TMT valuations have been correlated with changes in investment in information technology products, presumably because TMT valuations reflect beliefs about the value of this "new" technology (Figure 2.5).

[9]James Poterba, "Stock Market Wealth and Consumption," *Journal of Economic Perspectives*, Vol. 14, No. 2, (Spring 2000), pp 99–119, and Martha Starr-McCluer, "Stock Market Wealth and Consumer Spending," Finance and Economics Discussion Series Working Paper No. 1998–20, (Washington: Federal Reserve Board of Governors, April 1998), provide an overview of this literature. It has also been argued that most estimates of the wealth effect for the United States are upward biased because they omit a variable to proxy consumer access to credit; See Martin Cerisola and Paula De Masi, "Determinants of the U.S. Personal Savings Rate," Section V in *"United States—Selected Issues,"* IMF Staff Country Report No. 99/101 (Washington: IMF, 1999), available at http://www.imf.org/external/pubind.htm.

[10]See Tamim Bayoumi, "The Morning After: Explaining the Slowdown in Japanese Growth in the 1990s," *Journal of International Economics*, Vol. 53 (April 2000), pp. 241–259.

[11]Also, venture capitalists generally take an equity stake in a company, again implying a link with TMT equity valuations.

Figure 2.5. NASDAQ Stock Price and Private Fixed Investment in Computers and Peripheral Equipment
(Quarterly percent change from a year earlier)

NASDAQ has been highly correlated with information technology investment in the late 1990s.

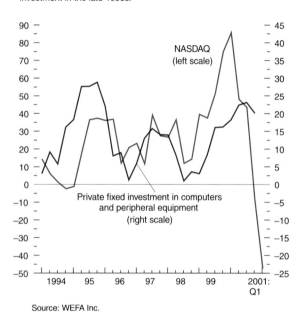

Source: WEFA Inc.

Figure 2.6. The "New Economy" Cycle of the Late 1990s

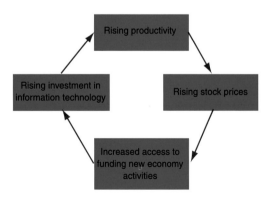

Higher investment in information technology in turn affected productivity, again affecting stock market valuations, giving rise to a virtuous cycle of an expanding economy, rising investment, rising productivity, and a rising equity market (Figure 2.6). This cycle, which has been more pronounced for the information technology sector than the telecom and media sectors, has been documented best in the United States, where many TMT companies with limited access to bond markets or bank finance used stock markets as a source of funding. The rapid rise in investment in TMT goods has been directly correlated with changes in the technology-intensive NASDAQ index, suggesting that TMT valuations may affect investment more than non-TMT valuations.[12] Such a cycle may well also operate as TMT equity values fall.

The link between TMT and non-TMT equity values and investment was tested using a model similar to that discussed earlier, except with quarterly investment substituting for monthly retail sales and adding short-term interest rates to reflect the cost of capital. The initial results reported in Table 2.3 again suggest that in North America and United Kingdom changes in TMT valuations have had a statistically significant impact on investment similar in size to their non-TMT counterparts. For the continental European countries, the results suggest that changes in non-TMT equity values have little or no impact on investment, but that for TMT equities the effects are statistically significant and similar to North America and United Kingdom in cents per dollar (although smaller absolute value for the reasons discussed earlier). The results for Japan are not statistically significant. The results for TMT values, however, are incorrectly signed for Japan, emphasizing the lack of precision of estimates for individual countries. That said, the large estimated impact from non-

[12]Evidence for such a relationship is also provided by several market commentators such as Deutsche Bank, *World Outlook* (December 1, 2000), pp. 12–18; HSBC, *World Economic Watch* (February 2, 2001), p. 5; and JP Morgan, *Global Data Watch;* (January 5, 2001), pp. 11–12.

Table 2.3. Impact of a Rise in Equity Valuations on Investment
(Increase in real U.S. dollar investment from a one U.S. dollar increase in equity values)

	TMT Capitalization	Non-TMT Capitalization	Total Market[1]
Average North America and United Kingdom	**0.04**	**0.05**	**0.05**
Average continental Europe	**0.05**	0.00	0.01
Japan	−0.06	0.08	0.04

Note: Bolded estimates are statistically significant. North America and United Kingdom covers the United States, Canada, and the United Kingdom and "continental Europe" covers Germany, France, and the Netherlands. Effect after 2 years. A reduced-form vector autoregression was estimated over the period 1990:1 to 2000:3 with quarterly real investment (private gross fixed capital formation), real TMT stock market capitalization, real non-TMT stock market capitalization, industrial production, and short interest rate. Three lags were used and all variables are in logs, except the interest rate. The two year effect was calculated as the level of the impulse-response function after eight quarters. The effect of the experiment was calculated using investment (private gross fixed capital formation) for 2000 and market capitalization in December 2000. For the details of the statistical analysis see Hali Edison and Torsten Sløk "New Economy Stock Valuations and Investment in the 1990s," IMF Working Paper (Washington: International Monetary Fund, forthcoming).

[1]Total Market is the effect of a one U.S. dollar increase, where the one dollar increase is split between TMT and non-TMT using their share of total stock market capitalization in December 2000.

TMT equity values to investment is consistent with views about the impact of bank lending on activity discussed above.

One possible explanation for the relatively smaller impact of non-TMT share prices on investment in continental Europe compared to North America and United Kingdom is the difference in corporate laws and traditions, as witnessed by less frequent takeovers, the greater importance accorded to employees in decision making, and the higher gearing ratios. These features could suggest that managers tend to be less responsive to the stock market relative to their counterparts in North America and United Kingdom. What these results suggest, however, is that these differences apply less to the TMT market, possibly because the structure of these sectors is much more similar across countries. This may reflect a more general shift as pressures build for firms to restructure and raise productivity, so as to take full benefit of the single-currency European capital market.

Stock Prices as a Leading Indicator of Activity

In addition to affecting consumption and investment directly, changes in stock valuations can also serve as a leading indicator of the business cycle. To the extent that stock valuations reflect the value of anticipated future profits of listed companies, expectations about the business cycle will affect the current value of firms. Again, it is of interest to examine if there is a difference in

the predictive power of TMT and non-TMT stocks in explaining the business cycle in the 1990s. To test this, a statistical model was formulated using monthly data since 1990 in which industrial production was explained by historical values of real TMT stock capitalization, real non-TMT stock capitalization, the short interest rate, and lagged values of industrial production. Given the wider access to reliable data on industrial production, the analysis encompassed a broader range of countries, with the limited time frame being generally compensated for by using panel estimation across a number of countries.

The preliminary analysis suggests that TMT stock valuations, together with short-term interest rates, have generally been the more robust leading indicators of the business cycle in most regions of the world, while non-TMT stocks have been less successful at predicting cyclical performance (Table 2.4).[13] Indeed, both short-term interest rates and TMT stocks appear to be a statistically significant indicator of changes in the cycle in all countries or regions examined. By contrast, non-TMT stock valuations appear as a leading indicator only in the United States, Asia, and Latin America. Given the correlation in

[13]Splitting up the TMT sector into Telecommunications, Media, and Information Technology stocks does not provide more useful results. In other words, the TMT sector is a leading indicator of the business cycle, but there does not seem to be general evidence that any one component of the TMT sector predicts industrial production better than others.

Table 2.4. Are Stock Valuations a Leading Indicator of the Business Cycle?

	TMT Stocks Significant at Any Lag Length	Non-TMT Stocks Significant at Any Lag Length	Short Term Interest Rate Significant at Any Lag Length
United States	X	X	X
Continental Europe	X		X
United Kingdom	X		X
Latin America	X	X	X
Asia	X	X	X
Japan	X		X

Note: At a 15 percent significance level. In the panel regression "Continental Europe" covers Germany, France, and the Netherlands, "Latin America" covers Argentina, Brazil, and Mexico, and "Asia" covers Indonesia, Korea, Malaysia, and Thailand. All variables are in dlogs (except the interest rate which is in simple differences) and four lags were included of variables on the right hand side (except the lagged dependent variable which only has one lag). Coefficients for groups of countries are estimated in fixed-effects panel regressions with country-specific variances. The p-values are calculated using White's heteroscedasticity and autocorrelation consistent estimator and this estimator was applied both in panel regressions and for individual countries.

movements in TMT stocks across countries, it remains unclear whether the apparently superior performance of TMT stocks reflect local considerations or the global technology cycle. In any case, the implication that the worldwide fall in TMT stocks in 2000 is a precursor of a slowdown in activity indeed appears to be coming true.

Some Policy Considerations

The empirical analysis reported in this essay suggests the following:
- Stock market developments may have a significant impact on consumption and investment in North America and United Kingdom with little differences between the TMT and non-TMT sectors.
- Non-TMT valuations do not appear to have a large impact on activity in continental Europe. Measured in cents-to-the-dollar, TMT valuations may have a similar impact to North America and United Kingdom, but the overall effect is smaller as valuations are a lesser share of GDP.
- The results for Japan are relatively imprecise, but are consistent with a view that

changes in equity valuations are translated to activity through their impact on bank capital and lending.
- TMT stocks in the last decade may have been a leading indicator of economic activity.

The links from stock markets to the real economy found in this essay raise a number of issues for policymakers.[14] In particular, the analysis suggests a strong link from equity markets to consumption and investment in countries with widespread stock ownership, large stock markets, and where stock options are used as payment to employees. A similar relationship appears to hold in the TMT sector for continental Europe. Together with the close correlation of TMT valuations across the world, this could imply that the TMT sector is capable of providing significant generalized disturbances to global activity.

What Is Driving the Weakness of the Euro and Strength of the Dollar?

A concern of policymakers over the past year has been the pronounced weakness of the euro against the U.S. dollar and the potential implication a hard landing of the U.S. economy might have on the value of the euro (Figure 2.7). From a value of $1.04 per euro in early 2000 (already well below the $1.17 at its inception on January 1, 1999), the euro fell to a low of $0.83 in October 2000. Even after a subsequent rebound, its trading range remains $0.88–$0.95, well below estimates of the value consistent with medium-term economic fundamentals (some consequences of this situation are explored in the alternative scenarios reported in Appendix II of Chapter I). More broadly, this reflects generalized euro weakness (including against the yen

[14]The challenges are even greater if the effect on the real economy is larger for falls in equity values than for increases, because the sales of stocks triggers a taxable event or consumers/firms face liquidity constraints. Hassan Shirvani and Barry Wilbratte, "Does Consumption Respond More Strongly to Stock Market Declines Than to Increases?" *International Economic Journal,* Vol. 14, No. 3 (Autumn 2000), pp. 41–49, present these arguments and find that the hypothesis of asymmetric effects is confirmed by data for Germany, Japan, and the United States.

and the pound sterling) and equally generalized strength of the U.S. dollar (including against currencies of other major trading partners, such as Canada, Australia, and New Zealand—Box 2.1 discusses the latter two currencies).

What makes the weakness of the euro against the dollar of particular interest is that it seems to defy explanations from conventional exchange rate models.[15] These models link exchange rate movements to changes in the market for current transactions (usually proxied by the current account)[16] and interest rate differentials (which drive portfolio flows in fixed income assets such as bonds).[17] Over the period of euro weakness, however, the U.S. current account balance has deteriorated to record lows, and fallen significantly relative to that of the euro area. Even more striking, interest rate hikes by the European Central Bank in the second half of 2000 were generally associated with a weakening of the euro. Finally, the argument that the depreciation of the euro reflected disorderly market conditions and associated bandwagon effects has been dented by the failure of intervention to lead to a rapid appreciation of the currency and by the persistence of euro weakness.[18]

[15]See Peter Isard, *Exchange Rate Economics* (Cambridge: Cambridge University Press, 1995).

[16]Other "autonomous" capital flows can be included. Indeed, this was the foundation of a literature on the "basic balance" active during the 1950s and 1960s, but the "basic balance" rarely included portfolio equity flows, as they are potentially highly volatile.

[17]These models are relatively unsuccessful empirically. Indeed, the dominant view is that short-term exchange rate movements are largely unforecastable, implying that only contemporaneous events have systematic influence. The seminal paper is by Richard Meese and Kenneth Rogoff, "Empirical Exchange Rate Models of the Seventies: Do They Fit Out of Sample?" *Journal of International Economics*, Vol. 14 (February 1983), pp. 3–24.

[18]Initially, intervention was coordinated with other central banks, including the U.S. Federal Reserve. Even coordinated intervention, which is more effective than its unilateral counterpart, is generally found to have a short-lived impact on the exchange rate unless markets are disorderly or it is accompanied by policy changes. See Hali Edison, "The Effectiveness of Central-Bank Intervention: A Survey of the Literature After 1982," *Special Papers in International Economics* (Princeton: International Finance Section, Department of Economics, Princeton University, 1993).

Figure 2.7. Movements of the Euro and Yen

A key feature in major currency markets has been the pronounced weakness in the euro.

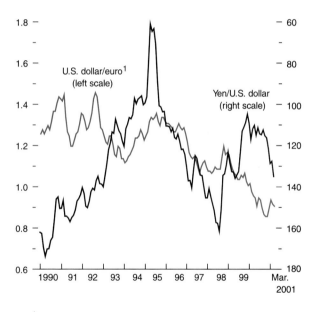

[1]A synthetic euro is used through the end of 1998.

Box 2.1. The Weakness of the Australian and New Zealand Currencies

In 2000, the Australian dollar and the New Zealand dollar have weakened sharply, especially against the U.S. dollar. The Australian dollar dropped from around US$0.65 at the end of 1999 to around US$0.50 by mid-November; over the same period, the New Zealand dollar dropped from around US$0.51 to around US$0.39 (See the Figure). In 2001 after a short-lived rebound, both currencies have remained around their end-2000 levels, below their end-1996 peak levels by 30–40 percent.[1]

Against a background of generally sound fundamentals and relatively favorable economic prospects (and for Australia strong economic growth) the recent fall in these currencies has confounded policymakers and market analysts alike. In particular, the variables believed to be the main driving forces of both the Australian and the New Zealand dollar in the past—commodity prices, the current account deficit and associated external imbalances, and interest rate differentials—do not appear to explain the recent movement of the currencies. In 2000, prices of Australia's and New Zealand's commodities strengthened, the countries' terms of trade have improved, the (admittedly large) current account deficits look set to narrow, and interest rate differentials versus the United States have not moved significantly since 1997. In that respect, the weakness of the two currencies has not been unlike that of the euro, which has also defied traditional explanations based on interest rate differentials and current account imbalances.

The weakness of the Australian dollar and New Zealand dollar has been seen in part as the reflection of the unilateral strength of the U.S. dollar (between the beginning of 1999 and the end of 2000, all the major currencies with the exception of the yen depreciated against the U.S. dollar).[2] In that context, the correlation between the

Recent Movements in the Australian Dollar and New Zealand Dollar
(U.S. dollar per local currency)

Source: IMF, *International Financial Statistics.*

Australian dollar–U.S. dollar exchange rate and the euro–U.S. dollar exchange rate rose in 2000 from about 0.25 to about 0.75. Consequently, analysts examining the Australian dollar and the New Zealand dollar have looked to similar explanations to those used for the euro, such as relative expected growth rates. In addition, local factors have been cited to help explain the particularly sharp and prolonged depreciation of the two currencies. In particular, the medium-term weakness of these currencies has been attributed to the following three factors:[3]

---

[1]Although it is not discussed in this box, the Canadian dollar also weakened against the U.S. dollar in 2000.

[2]Donald Brash, "The Fall of the New Zealand Dollar: Why Has It Happened, And What Does It Mean?" *Reserve Bank of New Zealand Bulletin,* Vol. 63, (December 2000).

[3]In that respect, the IMF's preliminary results from medium-term analysis find that the fiscal consolidation of the 1990s played a significant role in the determination of the real exchange rate for Australia (see "Sources of Fluctuations in Australia's Real Effective Exchange Rate" in *Australia: Selected Issues and Statistical Appendix,* IMF Staff Country Report, No. 01/55). Similarly, a switch in the composition of growth from domestic demand to net export can partly account for the weakness of the Australian dollar in 2000.

- *The gap in relative medium-term growth prospects* between the United States on the one hand and Australia and New Zealand on the other has been considered the chief driving force behind recent exchange rate movements, although Australia has matched the U.S. economic performance over the last few years. In particular, downward revisions of expectations of Australia's output growth relative to the United States have been thought to be at the root of the sharp exchange rate depreciation at the beginning of the year. Equity flows offer weak support for this view: in 2000, net foreign equity outflows increased for Australia, but not for New Zealand.

- *Technology divide.* In Australia, and more so in New Zealand, a smaller share of the economy is involved in the development and production of information technology products and services relative to the United States, although spending on such products has been high in both cases.[4] Australia and New Zealand may have suffered from a weakening of investor sentiment reflecting the perception that they are relatively less well positioned to benefit from the productivity gains associated with the development of the "New Economy," although the depreciation of the Australian dollar and the New Zealand dollar in the second half of 2000 coincided with a sharp correction in the price of U.S. technology stocks.[5] In addition, the small number of "New-Economy" companies traded on Australia's and New Zealand's stock markets may have reduced portfolio equity inflows.

- *The net foreign asset positions* of Australia and New Zealand may help explain the medium-run behavior of the countries' respective currencies. It may be that larger net foreign liabilities require a relatively more depreciated real exchange rate to generate a larger surplus on goods and services to meet net factor payments. However, this view has not found much support in the data. In Australia, the long-run worsening of the net foreign asset position has been accompanied by a weaker exchange rate. However, the factor income deficit increased only moderately in the 1970s and has remained roughly constant in more recent years. Regression analysis suggests that net foreign liabilities do not significantly affect the real exchange rate after interest rate differentials and the terms of trade are taken into account.[6] For New Zealand, the real exchange rate was at the beginning of 2000 roughly the same as at the beginning of 1980, while the net foreign asset position followed a trend similar to Australia's. Moreover, as in Australia, in New Zealand the various components of the current account did not exhibit any particular trend in recent years.

In conclusion, as it is the case for the euro, it is difficult to relate the recent weakness in the Australian dollar and the New Zealand dollar to the factors that explained the behavior of these currencies in the past. While there is too little evidence to say whether there has been a structural break in the exchange rate determination process, partly because of the recent nature of the hypothesized change there are indications that, especially for Australia, the terms of trade, although still predominant, are becoming relatively less important and that factors characteristic of more mature economies, possibly including equity portfolio flows, are increasing their weight in the determination of the exchange rate.

---

[4]See Chapter II "Current Issues in the World Economy" of the October 2000 *World Economic Outlook* for information on Australia.

[5]Ian Macfarlane, "Recent Influences on the Exchange Rate," Reserve Bank of Australia *Bulletin* (December 2000).

[6]The fact that in recent years interest rate spreads on Australia's bonds narrowed may be part of the explanation.

An alternative explanation for the weakness of the euro against the dollar suggested by many commentators is that it reflects bilateral portfolio equity flows (including mergers and acquisitions) out of the euro area.[19] It has been suggested that these equity flows are driven by the perception of greater prospects for growth and profits in the United States. Certainly, the sheer size of the global currency market, where *daily* flows involving all currencies are $1½ trillion, one and a half times *annual* exports of goods and services from the United States, imply that changes in investor sentiment could have an impact on exchange rates. However, although this explanation has gained considerable attention and is rapidly becoming the received wisdom, most of the evidence supporting it is anecdotal, and subject to little rigorous analysis.

In addition, if the euro is being driven down by expectations of higher U.S. growth, what explains the path of the yen against the U.S. dollar and euro? The weakness of the Japanese economy over the last two years has not led to a corresponding depreciation of the yen, which until quite recently had remained relatively firm against the U.S. dollar and had appreciated significantly against the euro. This divergence between the euro-dollar exchange rate and its yen counterpart is unusual, although not unprecedented.

Recent Trends in International Capital Flows and Current Accounts

Globalization during the 1990s has led to a generalized increase in cross-border capital flows. In particular, over the past few years the United States has been the recipient of increasing net capital inflows. The dominant factor behind these net portfolio flows has been moves in or out of U.S. assets.[20] Net portfolio flows—U.S. government bonds and notes, U.S. government agency bonds, U.S. corporate bonds, and U.S. equities—increased from less than $25 billion in the early 1990s to almost $500 billion in 2000. The composition of these flows has changed over time, shifting toward agency bonds, corporate bonds, and (in particular) equities, at the expense of government bonds and notes. Indeed, while net flows into U.S. government bonds have gradually contracted over the 1990s, turning negative since 1999 as the market for such government bonds shrank due to buy-backs, the corresponding net flows into U.S. stocks have risen by a factor of 12 since 1995 (Figure 2.8). The rapid expansion in international equity flows has also coincided with a boom in cross-border mergers and acquisitions, which rose from around $300 billion in 1997 to announced deals worth $1,200 billion in 2000.

There are also important differences when comparing bilateral net portfolio flows into assets in the United States by country.[21] Bilateral

---

[19]For example, Lehman Brothers, *Global Foreign Exchange Strategies* (May 18, 2000), pp. 2–4; Lehman Brothers, *Global Foreign Exchange Strategies* (July 27, 2000), pp. 2–4, Lehman Brothers, *Global Foreign Exchange Strategies* (October 5, 2000), pp. 9–11; Lehman Brothers, *Global Foreign Exchange Strategies* (March 1, 2001), Morgan Stanley Dean Witter, *Currency Strategy and Economics* (November 22, 2000), pp. 7–8; Goldman Sachs, *European Weekly Analyst* (November 17, 2000), pp. 1–8; Deutsche Bank, *Global FX Outlook and Strategy—Special Edition* (November 10, 2000), pp. 21–23; and Deutsche Bank, *Global FX Outlook and Strategy* (December 1, 2000), pp. 16–18.

[20]While generally true, there are some instances where capital flows into foreign assets have been important—such as the move by U.S. investors into Japanese equities in 1999.

[21]Bilateral data on flows, which come from the U.S. Treasury International Capital (TIC) reporting system, have a number of shortcomings. In particular, they reflect only the location of the transactor, so it is necessary to assume that the recorded transactions for a country are conducted for a domestic resident. While this assumption seems reasonable for flows from countries lacking large financial centers, it is more problematic for countries with such centers, such as the United Kingdom, Hong Kong, or Singapore. In addition, any transactions carried out through such a center—for example, a German purchase of U.S. assets that is organized through London will be recorded as a flow from the United Kingdom, not Germany. Finally, the data for U.S. assets are differentiated between government bonds, government agency bonds, and corporate bonds, while foreign assets are only divided between bonds and equities.

net flows into U.S. equities from the euro area increased dramatically, while there is little evidence of a similar shift for Japan. A similar pattern holds for mergers and acquisitions. About 40 percent of the companies originating mergers and acquisitions are from the euro area and the implied capital flows are significant; Japan has not been a significant player in this area. Mergers and acquisitions announced in 2000 imply an aggregate net flow into the United States estimated at about $200 billion (on the same basis, the net outflow from the euro area is roughly $300 billion).

There have also been different current account developments across the three regions. The United States has experienced a large and growing overall current account deficit, as well as rising bilateral current account deficits against both the euro area and Japan. Japan has had a large and relatively stable overall current account surplus in recent years (on the order of $100 billion a year), while the current account of the euro area has deteriorated from a surplus of $100 billion in 1997 to around balance in 2000. Given the need to finance these transactions through the capital account, the deterioration in the external balance of the United States might be expected to have created pressure for U.S. dollar depreciation.

Empirical Results

This section reports some preliminary analysis of the importance of the current accounts and various capital account flows in tracking the behavior of the exchange rates of the euro and the yen against the dollar. The motivation for this work is the paucity of empirical evidence on the relative importance of these different net flows, in particular equity flows, in determining exchange rates.[22] Given data limitations and the short period over which higher capital flows have occurred, scope for econometric analysis is

[22] The only other empirical estimates that could be located were reported in Lehman Brothers, *Global Foreign Exchange Strategies* (May 2000).

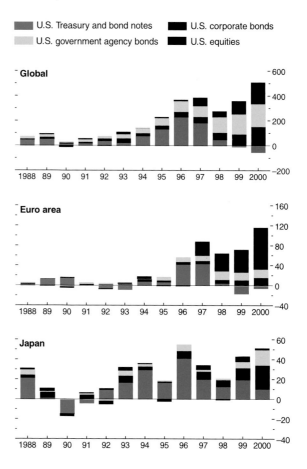

Figure 2.8. Global Net Portfolio Flows to the United States by Asset Class
(Billions of U.S. dollars)

Net portfolio flows into the United States have grown dramatically during the 1990s and the change in the composition of those flows has been even more pronounced.

Source: U.S. Treasury Department.

limited.[23] Nonetheless, simple bivariate regression analysis on data since 1988 (to provide some perspective from before the late 1990s surge in capital flows) can still shed some light on the extent to which movements in exchange rates are associated with particular current account and capital flows, as well as variables that might be expected to explain these movements.

The explanatory variables were the U.S. bilateral current account balance and bilateral net bond flows (covering traditional explanations of exchange rate movements), bilateral net equity flows, and net foreign investment (for equity flow explanations of exchange rate movements). In addition, similar regressions were estimated for variables that might explain these flows. Current cyclical conditions, short-term interest rate differentials, and long-term interest rate differentials were used to investigate the validity of traditional explanations of exchange rate dynamics. Relative equity returns and expected real growth differentials were included to investigate the newer view that portfolio equity flows are important for exchange rates.[24]

This exercise (reported in Table 2.5) yields the following results:[25]

- *There is evidence that equity flows matter for the euro-dollar rate, but not for the yen-dollar rate.* Movements of the euro-U.S. dollar exchange rate are significantly correlated with net portfolio flows and some associated underlying variables, but the same is not true for

Table 2.5. Explaining Bilateral Exchange Rate Movements

	Euro Area Coefficient	Japan Coefficient
Current account and capital flows		
Current account[1]	—	+
Capital account		
Net bond flows[2]	+	—
Net equities flows[3]	++	+
Foreign direct investment[4]	+	+
Traditional underlying factors		
Long-term interest differential	++	++
Short-term interest differential	+	+
Relative current growth	+	—
Alternative underlying factors		
Relative stock returns	—	+
Relative expected growth[5]	++	—

Note: The symbols ++, +, and — indicate the coefficient is correctly signed and significant, correctly signed and insignificant, and incorrectly signed, respectively. The equations regress the change in the logaritm of the bilateral exchange rate on a constant and the contemporaneous value of the explanatory variable using quarterly data since 1988.
[1]Bilateral current account vis-a-via the United States.
[2]Net bond flows are defined as U.S. bond flows less foreign bond flows.
[3]Net equity flows are defined as U.S. equity flows less foreign equity flows.
[4]The sample period starts in 1994: Q1.
[5]Expected growth rates were calculated by taking a weighted average of the expected current and future year growth rate of the Consensus Forecast since 1990. The weights being 11/12 on the current year forecast in January and 1/12 on the next year's forecast, in February 10/12 and 2/12 respectively, and so on until in December the full weights on the next year's forecast. Regressions were run since 1990.

the yen-dollar rate. Specifically, for the euro, the coefficients on net equity flows and expected growth are correctly signed and significant, although relative equity returns are not significant (Figure 2.9).[26] For the yen, none of these variables is significant.

---

[23] This task was made even more complicated because of the short sample period since the inception of the euro. In this work, data for the euro area on the bilateral current account and various capital account flows were extended back to the start of 1988 by aggregating data over the 11 initial members of Economic and Monetary Union (EMU), and calculating a corresponding synthetic version of the euro. An equivalent data set was then constructed for Japan.

[24]Given the data problems associated with identifying bilateral capital flows that go through major financial centers, multilateral versions of the regressions (where flows to and from financial centers get netted out) were also estimated, with broadly similar results.

[25]See Robin Brooks, Hali Edison, Mohan Kumar, and Torsten Sløk, "Exchange Rates and Capital Flows," IMF Working Paper (Washington: International Monetary Fund, forthcoming).

[26]There are potential problems interpreting the empirical results based on aggregating data for individual euro area countries. As a check on euro area results, versions of the regressions were also estimated for all 11 members of the euro area separately, yielding similar results. For the period since 1995, when capital flows expanded rapidly, the results suggest that a $10 billion increase in net equity inflows into the United States has been associated with a 2 percent depreciation of the euro vis-à-vis the dollar. For the first three quarters of 2000, this implies that equity flows could have reduced the value of the euro against the dollar 15 percent, more than half of the actual depreciation. This result is somewhat stronger than those reported in Lehman Brothers (May 2000).

• *There is little evidence that merger and acquisition flows are important for exchange rate determination.* The coefficients on net foreign direct investment (FDI) flows are correctly signed, but statistically insignificant for both the euro and yen. The lack of explanatory power of FDI flows suggests that mergers and acquisitions flows (which are a major component of the FDI data) may have not played an important role in euro weakness. Initially, several private sector analysts pointed to the size of mergers and acquisitions flows as an important element in explaining the path of the euro against the dollar. The empirical results, however, are more consistent with the more skeptical view taken by other private analysts, who note that the majority of cross-border mergers and acquisitions flows are financed through share-swaps that have no immediate impact on the demand for currencies.

• *Net bond flows appear to have no significant effect on the euro- or yen-dollar rate.* Similarly, bilateral current account positions are not statistically significant for either exchange rate. However, when multilateral current account positions were used, there was some evidence of an effect, suggesting that currency demand associated with current transactions may matter.

• *The movements of euro- and yen-U.S. dollar exchange rates are significantly correlated with the long-term interest rate differential, but not their short-term equivalent* (Figure 2.10). The results are supportive of the traditional approach to exchange rate determination. In the case of the euro, however, the explanatory power of this interlaying variable is "weaker" than for equity portfolio flows.

The analysis is admittedly preliminary but is relatively supportive of the new conventional wisdom that net equity flows are important for the euro-dollar exchange rate, although long-term interest rate differentials also appear to matter. For the yen, however, there is little evidence that net equity flows have been an important deter-

Figure 2.9. Net Portfolio Flows into U.S. Stocks from Euro Area and the Exchange Rate
(Billions of U.S. dollars)

Increases in European purchases of U.S. equities have been associated with euro weakness.

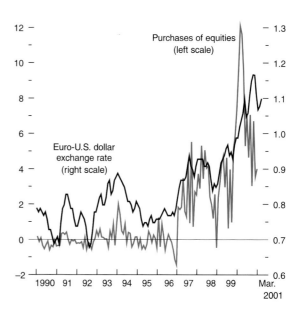

Sources: IMF Treasurer's Department; and U.S. Treasury Department.

minant of the bilateral exchange rate with the U.S. dollar.

Policy Considerations

Are exchange rate movements getting more sensitive to capital flows? It is difficult to answer this question, partly because exchange rates are notoriously hard to analyze. In addition, given the recent nature of the hypothesized changes in behavior, any empirical results are inevitably highly preliminary. That said, it does appear that there is some evidence that an important factor driving exchange rates between the euro area and the United States over the past few years may have been net equity flows, apparently based on perceptions of future growth. Between the yen and the dollar, however, these factors appear to play little or no role. Rather, relative interest rates and current demand for currency appear to matter. At first blush, this seeming inconsistency appears to add a further level of uncertainty to the already difficult world of exchange rate analysis.

On further reflection, however, there are at least two ways of reconciling these results. The first is the desire to hold a diversified international portfolio to minimize the risk for a given level of expected returns. With the advent of the euro and hence a common monetary policy across the euro area, returns across euro area stock markets have become more correlated. As a result, investors (particularly those in the euro area) who wish to diversify their portfolios will tend to move some of their original intra-euro area investments outside of the region, consistent with the recent increase in net equity investment from the euro area to the rest of the world. As there has been no shift in underlying conditions in Japan, no similar impact would be seen on the yen, explaining the differential behavior of the euro and the yen currencies—although the explanation does not help explain the strength of the U.S. dollar. It also implies that the weakness of the euro may continue for some time, as the stock adjustment driven by the

Figure 2.10. The Euro and Long-Term Interest Rate Differential

The euro has defied traditional explanations of exchange rate determination.

Sources: European Central Bank; IMF Treasurer's Department, Nikkei Telecom; and WEFA Inc.
[1] German long-term interest rate as a proxy for the euro long-term interest rate prior to 1994.

desire for portfolio diversification is gradually achieved.

An alternative explanation is that investors in the euro area are seeking to increase their returns and have been investing in United States equities because of perceived higher returns. There is also anecdotal evidence that this may be important for explaining the weakness of the Australian and New Zealand dollars (Box 2.1). In Japan, however, particular conditions may have made equity holders (which are mainly financial institutions) considerably more risk averse. Because of the fragility of the Japanese financial system, banks or insurance companies may have been more focused on their capital base than on maximizing high rates of return. This explanation implies that euro weakness and dollar strength reflect perceptions of growth differentials between the euro area and the United States, perceptions that could potentially change quite rapidly—as was graphically illustrated during the Asian crisis.

These views are not incompatible. Maximizing expected returns and minimizing risk are the two basic objectives of investing, and hence can occur concurrently. Even if much of the outflow of equity investment from the euro area reflects a desire to rebalance portfolios, the allocation of these investments abroad will be affected by perceptions of relative rates of return. As this outflow occurred at a time of perceived higher expected returns in the United States, a relatively large part has been invested in that direction. There must also be a proportion of the euro area outflows that would be repatriated if returns abroad turn out to be disappointing, while financial sector fragility may also help explain the continued appetite from Japan for U.S. government bonds and paper. What remains uncertain, however, is the relative weight of these factors in the overall patterns that has been seen over the past few years.

Trade Integration and Sub-Saharan Africa

In a period of global integration, sub-Saharan Africa (hereafter, Africa) has continued to lag behind the rest of the world in the level and rate of growth of per capita income (indeed, real GDP per capita in Africa has fallen by over 1 percent a year in the last 25 years). While this performance reflects a variety of factors, such as unfavorable geography, poor quality of institutions and governance, political turmoil and civil conflict, extensive government controls, falling real commodity prices, and bad management of commodity price cycles, one of the leading explanations of this disappointing outcome has been the failure of the region to embrace open international markets.[27]

Given the continent's lack of access to international capital markets, openness to trade is one obvious mechanism through which the benefits of international integration could be felt. There is strong evidence that greater openness to trade can boost long-term growth, largely through the impact on domestic competition and investment.[28] This suggests that increasing Africa's openness to trade is an important part of the overall strategy to boost growth and reduce poverty. Advanced economies need to open their trade regimes to products where poor nations have an advantage, such as agricultural goods, and recent moves by the European Union have been helpful (see

[27]There is, however, some evidence of sustained improvements in macroeconomic performance and a turn-around in growth performance in the mid-1990s. See Ernesto Hernández-Catá, "Raising Growth and Investment in Sub-Saharan Africa: What Can Be Done," IMF Policy Discussion Paper 00/4 (Washington: International Monetary Fund, 2000).

[28]For empirical support for the benefits of openness based on individual country experiences, see Jagdish Bhagwati, *Foreign Trade Regimes and Economic Development,* (Cambridge, Mass: Ballinger, 1978); on cross-country growth analysis, see Jeffrey Sachs and Andrew Warner, "Economic Reform and the Process of Global Integration," *Brookings Papers on Economic Activity: 1,* Brookings Institution (1995), pp. 1–118; and Sebastian Edwards, "Openness, Productivity and Growth: What Do We Really Know?" *Economic Journal,* Vol. 108 (March 1998), pp. 383–98. The cross-country evidence is disputed by Francisco Rodriguez and Dani Rodrik, "Trade Policy and Economic Growth: A Skeptic's Guide to the Cross-national Evidence," in *NBER Macroeconomics Annual 2000,* ed. by Ben Bernanke and Kenneth Rogoff (Cambridge: MIT Press, 2000).

Chapter I). The focus of this essay, however, is on what African nations can do to open their own trading systems. During the 1990s, Africa has developed a number of regional initiatives aimed at expanding trade, but the impact to date has been limited, prompting further consideration of the way in which trade liberalization has been approached.

Is Africa Undertrading?

Several indicators point to a deterioration in Africa's trade performance over time. In particular, Africa's share of world trade has declined steadily from more than 2 percent in the early 1970s to less than 1 percent in the late 1990s (Figure 2.11). A recent study by the World Bank estimates that the loss of world market share since 1950 represents forgone income opportunities to Africa of $68 billion, or about 21 percent of its GDP.[29] Another estimate, based on cross-country growth regressions, suggests that increasing openness to trade could have increased long-run growth by 1.4 percentage points.[30]

Other researchers, however, question the view that Africa is being marginalized from global trade, pointing out that openness (measured as the ratio of trade to GDP) has been rising broadly in line with that of the world, and that Africa may have simply taken advantage of trading opportunities consistent with evolution in its income and development.[31]

Figure 2.11. Africa: Trade Indicators
(Percent)

Africa's share of world trade has declined, although its openness ratio has evolved in line with that of the world.

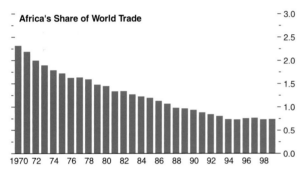

Africa's Share of World Trade

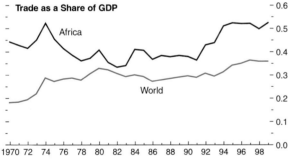

Trade as a Share of GDP

[29]World Bank, *Can Africa Claim the 21st Century?* (Washington: World Bank, 2000).

[30]Jeffrey Sachs and Andrew Warner, "Sources of Slow Growth in African Economies," *Journal of African Economies*, Vol. 6, No. 3 (October 1997), pp. 335–76. See also Paul Collier and Jan Gunning, "Explaining African Economic Performance," *Journal of Economic Literature*, Vol 37 (March 1999), pp. 64–111. For South Africa, there is evidence that a 1 percent cut in prices due to trade liberalization increases annual total factor productivity growth by about 0.2 percentage points (see Gunnar Jonsson and Arvind Subramanian, "Dynamic Gains from Trade: Evidence from South Africa," *IMF Staff Papers*, International Monetary Fund, Vol. 48 (2001).

[31]Dani Rodrik, *The New Global Economy and Developing Countries: Making Openness Work* (Baltimore: Johns Hopkins University Press for the Overseas Development Council, 1999).

Table 2.6. Measures of Trade Policy Regimes in Africa and Other Regions: Sachs-Warner Openness Index[1]

	1980s	Late 1990s	Number of Countries
Number of open countries:			
Sub-Saharan Africa	7	18	25
Asia	7	11	15
Middle East and North Africa	2	1	9
Western Hemisphere	3	22	22
Advanced economies	22	24	24

Sources: Arvind Subramanian, *Trade and Trade Policy in Eastern and Southern Africa*, IMF Occasional Paper No. 196 (Washington: International Monetary Fund, 2000); and IMF staff calculations.

[1]IMF staff's calculations applying the Sachs-Warner criteria of openness for tariffs and nontariff barriers (Jeffrey Sachs and Andrew Warner, "Economic Reform and The Process of Global Integration," *Brookings Papers on Economic Activity: 1*, 1995, pp. 1–118). That is, a country is classified as closed if its nontariff barriers covered 40 percent or more of the value of trade or if its average tariff exceeded 40 percent.

These contrasting views on Africa's marginalization from trade have distinct policy implications. The former sees Africa's declining trade share as an independent source of concern—distinct from other factors that have caused low growth—and accordingly places considerable emphasis on policy measures to expand trade opportunities. The latter view sees causality running from growth, and other determinants, to trade, and hence places emphasis on promoting economic growth rather than trade, per se.

There are two main approaches to evaluating trade openness. The first investigates the trade *regimes* in place, by examining a combination of tariffs and quantitative restrictions. Despite the well-known difficulties of aggregating different trade restrictions into a single measure, such a combination of tariff and qualitative restrictions provides a broad indicator of the stance of trade policy. Two such measures, reported in Tables 2.6 and 2.7 highlight a number of points:

- Africa has recently made significant strides in increasing its openness to international trade. For example, on the basis of one classification of trade policy regimes, the number of African countries with open regimes has risen from seven out of 25 in the 1980s to 18 currently.
- Notwithstanding this progress, Africa is currently among the most protected regions in the world. On the IMF's assessment of trade regimes, Africa has the most restrictive tariff regime, with the highest average level of tariffs and tariff revenue as a ratio to GDP. On the aggregate index, which takes account of nontariff barriers, Africa ranks third to last, just above the Middle East and North Africa

Table 2.7. Measures of Trade Policy Regimes in Africa and Other Regions: IMF's Trade Restrictiveness Index, 2000

	Overall Rating	Nontariff Barriers Rating	Tariff Rating	Average Tariff (percent)
Sub-Saharan Africa	4.7	1.6	3.0	19.2
Eastern and Southern Africa	5.6	1.8	3.5	20.3
Central and Western Africa	4.3	1.4	3.0	18.9
Fast growing countries of Asia[1]	3.4	1.7	1.3	7.2
Asia, excluding fast-growing countries	5.0	1.9	2.4	13.8
Eastern Europe (early transition) and Baltic countries[2]	1.9	1.1	1.4	8.0
Eastern Europe (late transition)	2.9	1.4	1.8	11.5
Former Soviet Union	4.2	1.8	1.8	10.2
Middle East and North Africa	5.6	2.0	3.0	18.1
Western Hemisphere	4.1	1.8	1.8	11.7
Industrial countries	3.9	2.0	1.0	5.4

Sources: Arvind Subramanian, *Trade and Trade Policy in Eastern and Southern Africa*, IMF Occasional Paper No. 196 (Washington: International Monetary Fund, 2000); and IMF staff calculations. For details on the methodology used in constructing this index, see Appendix I in Robert Sharer, *Trade Liberalization in IMF-Supported Programs*, World Economic and Financial Surveys (Washington: International Monetary Fund, 1998).

[1]Comprises Hong Kong, Indonesia, Korea, Malaysia, Philippines, Singapore, and Thailand.

[2]Comprises Czech Republic, Hungary, Poland, Slovak Republic, Estonia, Latvia, and Lithuania.

Box 2.2. Africa's Trade and the Gravity Model

A variety of trade issues have been analyzed using the gravity model, which has become one of the workhorses of empirical trade analysis. Applications include assessing whether countries "undertrade," examining the effects of preferential trade agreements on creating and diverting trade, weighing the desirability of preferential trade agreements, and uncovering the effects of currency unions on trade and growth.[1] In its basic form, the model relates trade between two countries to the product of their incomes, size (typically proxied by population), and to the costs of trade (proxied by the distance between them).[2] These terms are analogous to Newton's equation for the force between two objects—hence the term gravity model. Dummy variables are included to control for geographical contiguity, cultural affinities, common language, and free trade agreements.

The model was used to examine three aspects of African trade:

- *Does Africa undertrade and has this changed over time?* This can be tested by running a gravity model over a wide range of countries and then introducing dummy variables identifying trade between all African countries and other groups of countries and separately for the two subgroups of Africa: eastern and southern Africa, and central and western Africa. The sign on these variables indicate whether African countries over- or undertrade compared to other similar countries, while the evolution of these dummy variables over time can shed light on how this is trending over time. In the results reported in the text, the dummies for Africa's trade as well as those for eastern and southern Africa and central and

western Africa were negative and significant, and fell over time, indicating that African trade was below that of the average trader and that this problem had been getting worse over time. These level results were particularly pronounced for African countries' trade with the advanced economies.

- *The effect of active regional free trade agreements.* This was examined by introducing a dummy variable for trade between members of the regional agreement and another dummy for trade between members of the agreement and the rest of the world for each of three active regional agreements in the 1990s. The impact of the trade agreement was then examined by observing the coefficients before and after implementation. Results indicate that members of the Regional Integration Facilitation Forum (RIFF, formerly the Cross-Border Initiative) have not significantly expanded their intraregional trade during the 1990s, but have reduced their trade with outsiders by about 15 percent—consistent with trade diversion. In the case of Western African Economic and Monetary Union (WAEMU) and the Central African Monetary and Economic Community (CAMEC), the performance of intratrade could not be tested because of the poor quality of trade data. However, the coefficient of the dummy for their trade with the advanced economies did not decline over time, suggesting an absence of diversion, but also no trade creation.

- *Evaluation of prospective African regional groupings.* The original model is augmented by including dummy variables for intragroup trade to examine if these countries are "natural trading partners," which would reduce the likelihood that preferential integration will lead to trade diversion.[3] The dummies for the

---

[1]A short history of the gravity model is given in Jeffrey Frankel, and Andrew Rose, "Estimating the Effect of Currency Unions on Trade and Output," CEPR Discussion Paper No. 2631 (London: Centre for Economic Policy Research, December 2000).

[2]Trade between two countries is expected to be an increasing function of their incomes and a decreasing function of trade costs. The sign of the population coefficient is ambiguous, although it is observed in general that small countries trade more than large ones.

[3]The natural trading partner hypothesis was advanced by Paul Krugman, "The Move Towards Free Trade Zones," in *Policy Implications of Trade and Currency Zones*, Federal Reserve Bank of Kansas City (1991); and by Lawrence Summers "Regionalism and the World Trading System," in *Policy Implications of Trade and Currency Zones*, Federal Reserve Bank of

Kansas City, 1991. It has been applied to gravity models by, among others, J. Frankel, *Regional Trading Blocs in the World Economic System*, (Washington: Institute for International Economics, 1991). The validity of the hypothesis is, however, contested (see J. Bhagwati, and A. Panagariya, "Preferential Trading Areas and Multilateralism—Strangers, Friends or Foes?" in J. Bhagwati and A. Panagariya, eds., *"The Economics of Preferential Trade Agreements"* (Washington: American Enterprise Institute Press, 1996).

SADC group and all eastern and southern African countries were positive and significant, indicating that member countries already trade substantially more with each other than the average set of countries. This is not true, however, for COMESA, which includes countries that do not appear to be natural trading partners with other each other.

group and the slower growing countries in Asia group.[32]

- Countries in (largely English-speaking) eastern and southern Africa are more highly protected than those in (largely French-speaking) central and western Africa, where liberalization has proceeded rapidly recently in the context of regional integration arrangements.[33]

A second approach to measuring openness to trade and changes over time is to use a statistical model of trade. One such approach is to use a gravity model (one of the standard empirical models of trade, see Box 2.2), that explains bilateral trade in terms of the economic mass of the two countries and their distance apart (hence the name "gravity" model), as well as other fixed characteristics such as language. Using this benchmark estimate of what trade might be expected to be, one can then evaluate the degree to which actual trade patterns deviate from this norm.

Recent work by the IMF using a wide set of countries to analyze African trade, (paying particular attention to the low quality of African trade data)[34] yields the following conclusions:[35]

- Africa does indeed undertrade when compared with the average set of countries. For example, in the period 1997–98, sub-Saharan Africa's trade is about 65 percent less than what would be expected given Africa's income and geography.
- The degree to which Africa undertrades has steadily increased since the 1980s. By contrast, other developing countries have generally outperformed the model benchmark.
- Undertrading is more pronounced for countries in central and western Africa than in eastern and southern Africa, even though the former appear (on average) to have

[34]For example, smuggling and bad record keeping lead to a substantial under-recording of intraregional trade, particularly in central and western Africa. Indeed, many intraregional observations are zero, which creates statistical complications. As data on trade with advanced economies is less prone to these problems, especially if trade of African countries is measured on the basis of that reported by partner countries, results relating to trade with advanced economies may be more reliable.

[35]Arvind Subramanian and Natalia Tamirisa, "Africa's Trade Revisited," IMF Working Paper 01/33 (Washington: International Monetary Fund, 2001). Previous gravity model research, which is limited by only focusing on particular aspects of African trade, yielded the result that Africa's trade was not unusual. See Faezeh Foroutan and Lant Pritchett, "Intra-Sub-Saharan African Trade: Is it Too Little?" *Journal of African Economies*, Vol. 2 (May 1993), pp. 74–105, which focuses on intra-African trade; and David Coe and Alexander Hoffmaister, "North-South Trade: Is Africa Unusual?" *Journal of African Economies*, Vol. 8 (July 1999), pp. 228–56, which focuses on extra-African trade.

[32]See Robert Sharer, *Trade Liberalization in IMF-Supported Programs*, World Economic and Financial Surveys (Washington: International Monetary Fund, 1998), for a description of how this index is constructed.

[33]Notably, the West African Economic and Monetary Union (WAEMU) and Central African Economic and Monetary Community (CAEMC). Insofar as some of the nontariff barriers in central and western Africa are not adequately captured in the trade restrictiveness index, this assessment of the two sub-regions may need to be qualified.

more open trade regimes (this issue is discussed further below).

- Undertrading is marked in Africa's trade with the advanced countries. This is particularly significant because trade with, or more specifically imports of capital goods from, advanced economies represents an important channel for transmitting the benefits of globalization.[36]

Why Does Africa Undertrade?

A number of factors can account for the low level of African integration with global markets. First, as noted above, Africa's trade policies are more restrictive than those of other developing countries, which itself contributes to lower levels of trade.[37] A second factor could be the high level of transactions costs, particularly those related to trade. Key infrastructure sectors—telecommunications and transport—are less well developed, owing in part to domestic policies that have been detrimental to efficiency, and access to finance and trade credits is difficult.[38] The model finds evidence for this effect: African countries appear to face a trade-related cost disadvantage relative to Asia of about 20 percent. Surprisingly, Africa's heavy reliance on commodity exports does not seem to contribute to undertrading, although the income elasticity on commodity exports is often thought to be smaller than for manufacturing. A dummy for

primary commodity exporters is insignificant and does not affect the results relating to Africa's undertrading.[39]

It is striking that Africa's undertrading seems to have risen during the 1990s, at a time when African governments intensified their policy and institutional reforms with a view to enabling Africa to benefit from globalization. This could reflect in part the persistence of nontariff barriers, which are not adequately captured in the measures of trade restrictiveness. For example, marketing boards or monopoly purchasing agencies in key sectors (such as cotton in several countries in central and western Africa) continue to impede trade. In addition, other developing countries also liberalized their trade regimes, so Africa's relative level of openness may not have increased significantly. This may also help explain the greater undertrading in central and western Africa compared to eastern and southern Africa.

The contrasting evolution in trade between central and western Africa and eastern and southern Africa raises the possibility that other factors may also have played a role in trade marginalization in central and western Africa. For example, exchange rate misalignments, caused by large aid inflows, and particularly evident in the overvaluation of the CFA franc prior to 1994, may have had a debilitating effect on trade performance. It is also possible that trade restrictiveness in central and western Africa is understated because of nontariff barriers cited above are not fully captured.

Another reason for Africa's undertrading may be that Africa's regional agreements—which have proliferated in the 1990s—increased intra-African trade at the cost of reducing trade with the rest of the world, helping to explain the continued underperformance of African trade

---

[36]The technology embodied in capital goods increases productivity growth in the importing country (see David Coe, Elhanan Helpman, and Alexander Hoffmaister, "North-South R&D Spillovers," *Economic Journal*, Vol. 107 (January 1997), pp. 134–39).

[37]See Rodrik, *The New Global Economy and Developing Countries*.

[38]Sub-Saharan African policy regimes in two key infrastructure sectors—financial and telecommunications services—are highly restrictive both in absolute terms and relative to other developing countries. See Aaditya Mattoo, Randeep Rathindran, and Arvind Subramanian, "Measuring the Impact of Services Sector Liberalization on Growth: An Illustration," (unpublished; Washington: World Bank, 2001).

[39]Africa has witnessed more conflict and civil unrest than other countries, which could contribute to its undertrading; however, the gravity model captures the impact of these forces on trade to the extent that it is a consequence of reduced income.

with the advanced economies.[40] Regional trade agreements that lower tariffs within a group of countries but not with the rest of the world give rise to two opposing effects. When partner country production displaces production from more efficient non-members, there is trade diversion, which reduces welfare; however, when partner country production displaces higher cost domestic production, there is trade creation, which enhances welfare. While the relative magnitudes of these two effects are uncertain, trade diversion may be more likely in Africa than elsewhere because of higher trade barriers and relatively lower levels of efficiency. Figure 2.12 indicates that intra regional trade shares are low across most of the regional agreements, but gravity models allow for a better evaluation of the trade diversion and trade creation effects.

For three blocs that have made progress on integration—the RIFF (formerly, the CBI) in eastern and southern Africa and CAEMC and the WAEMU in western and central Africa—a preliminary gravity model exercise indicates that the RIFF may have reduced trade with the rest of the world while creating a relatively small expansion of intra-bloc trade. For CAEMC and WAEMU, by contrast there appears to have been no contraction in extra-regional trade. The results for RIFF are particularly striking because intra regional trade liberalization was accompanied by reductions in external barriers. While it is too early to tell, the overall implication is that regional trade integration has not as yet been a vehicle for substantial extra-African trade creation, particularly in enhancing links with the advanced economies.

[40]Agreements that have been active in the 1990s have been WAEMU, CAEMC, and the Regional Integration facilitation Forum (RIFF), formerly the Cross-Border Initiative (CBI). Regional integration is also envisaged under the auspices of the Economic Community of West African States (ECOWAS), the Southern African Development Community (SADC), the East African Community (EAC), and the Indian Ocean Commission (IOC). The Southern African Customs Union (SACU) is a long-standing regional agreement.

Figure 2.12. African Trade Arrangements: Intra and Extraregional Trade, 1980–98
(Percent of GDP)

Intraregional trade in African trade arrangements is probably quite low, even allowing for likely underrecording.

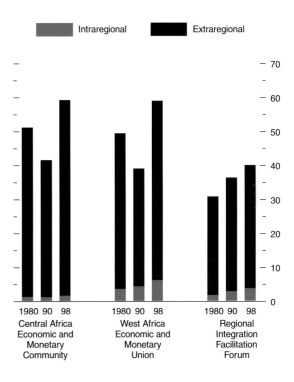

Source: IMF, *Direction of Trade Statistics*.

The Road Ahead

Africa stands to gain if its marginalization from trade can be reversed. How can trade and other policies, including regional integration, help secure this objective?

First and foremost, a large unfinished agenda of trade liberalization lies ahead. Pervasive quantitative restrictions, high tariffs, and widespread exemptions continue to characterize trade regimes in a number of countries (in particular, Ethiopia, Kenya, and Zimbabwe), reducing tariff collection efficiency and leading to wasteful rent seeking.[41] And trade restrictions in the form of marketing boards, particularly in the cotton sector in western Africa (Mali, Burkina Faso, Benin, and Chad) and Kenya, and export taxes (in Mozambique) impede the development of key export sectors.

Second, a key to improving trade prospects lies in reducing transaction costs, particularly those related to trade. This can be achieved by enhancing the efficiency of important infrastructure sectors through a combination of privatization and effective, pro-competitive regulation. The latter is especially important in Africa because its small markets, combined with the natural economies of scale in infrastructure sectors, may not be able to sustain effective competition.

Third, the extra-national institutional anchors created by a trade agreement can help gain credibility for an open trade policy, thereby promoting and maintaining sound trade policies.[42] Given the history of trade policy reversals in Africa, establishing credibility is essential to foster a stable climate for private enterprise.[43] For

Africa, in addition to the use of multilateral commitments under the WTO, locking-in mechanisms could include regional agreements (with peer pressure serving as an agency of restraint as being developed in WAEMU and CAEMC) and free trade agreements with industrial country trading partners.

The Role of Regional Integration

Given the renewed political impetus for regional integration, how can it be channeled in a way that maximizes the benefits and minimizes risks? First and foremost, countries should steadfastly implement their regional liberalization commitments. The track record of compliance, while improving, could be better. At the same time, progress on external liberalization will lessen the risks of inefficient trade diversion. In eastern and southern Africa, the overlapping set of trade arrangements (known as the "spaghetti bowl") creates a number of problems (Figure 2.13). First, some countries face conflicting obligations: as members of a future customs union (COMESA) they will not be able to offer preferences to non-members with whom they are partners in another free trade arrangement (SADC). Second, implementation can be difficult when countries are simultaneously members of several arrangements. Customs officials face the difficult task of establishing the origin of goods coming from different groups of countries, while rules of origin will also complicate marketing and production decisions, creating an uncertain climate for investors. Third, the sheer administrative and political costs and distraction stemming from multiple initiatives create difficulties.

Given that the countries in eastern and southern Africa may be a natural trading bloc, rationalization of the current situation, possibly in the form of a single arrangement, may be worth considering. At the least, there needs to be harmonization of the measures adopted by the different arrangements, including common rules of origin, external tariffs that are similar in structure and rates, and compatible standards. As the largest economy in the region, the country with the strongest links with neighbors, and

---

[41]In a number of countries in eastern and southern Africa, less than half of tariff revenues are collected, owing to exemptions (see Arvind Subramanian, *Trade and Trade Policies in Eastern and Southern Africa*, IMF Occasional Paper No. 196 (Washington: International Monetary Fund, 2000).

[42]See Paul Collier and Jan Gunning, "Trade Policy and Integration: Implications for the Relations between Europe and Africa," *The World Economy*, Vol. 18 (May 1995), pp. 387–410.

[43]For example, eight out of 21 countries in Eastern and Southern Africa reversed, albeit not permanently, some of the trade liberalization during the 1990s (see Subramanian, *Trade and Trade Policies in Eastern and Southern Africa*).

Figure 2.13. Africa: The Regional Trade Integration Quilt

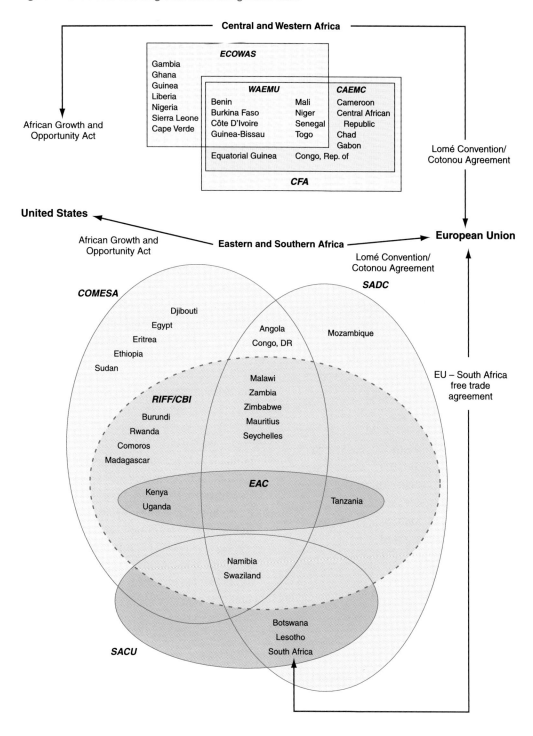

Note: *ECOWAS* is the Economic Community of West African States; *WAEMU,* the West African Economic and Monetary Union; *CAEMC,* the Central African Economic and Monetary Community; *CFA,* Communauté Financière d'Afrique, or African Financial Community; *COMESA,* the Common Market for Eastern and Southern Africa; *SADC,* the Southern African Development Community; *RIFF,* the Regional Integration Facilitation Forum, formerly the Cross-Border Initiative in Eastern and Southern Africa (CBI); *SACU,* the Southern African Customs Union; *IOC,* the Indian Ocean Commission; and *EAC,* the East African Community.

one that has signed a free trade agreement with the European Union, South Africa would be the most likely anchor for such an initiative, although it is not a member of the largest regional initiative, COMESA.[44]

African countries could also seek reciprocal free trade agreements with advanced industrial country partners.[45] The agreement between South Africa and the European Union presages wider reciprocal agreements between countries in Africa on the one hand, and advanced economies on the other. The advantages of such an approach over regional integration confined to Africa are threefold. First, the locking-in benefits will be stronger because of the presence of strong anchors with the ability and willingness to ensure compliance with policy commitments.[46] Second, a reciprocal agreement would provide more secure market access for African exports, access which under current arrangements is conditional, partial, and unilaterally granted rather than contractually committed to by advanced economies. Third, as discussed previously, integration with advanced economies is more likely to elicit growth-enhancing foreign direct investment and technology flows.[47] The more outward oriented the

African trade regime, the more comprehensive the product coverage under regional agreements, and the greater number of advanced economies involved in the agreements, the greater the benefits of such an approach.

Africa's trading partners can also play an important role in facilitating Africa's integration with the world economy. It is estimated that if the European Union, Japan, Canada, and the United States eliminated their trade barriers (tariff and nontariff) on African trade, exports would rise by about $2.5 billion or (14 percent), raising African income levels.[48] The recent move by the European Union to lower tariffs for African countries on a wide range of products is very welcome, following significant market opening measures by Canada, Japan, Korea, New Zealand, Norway, and the United States. Still more can and should be done by these and other countries to eliminate remaining barriers to exports of the poorest countries.

Finally, trade policy does not occur in a vacuum. In particular, increasing global trade integration will present Africa with some domestic economic challenges. Given the high level of tariff barriers, trade liberalization will create fiscal pressures. In addition, the gains from integration will inevitably be accompanied by the short-term costs of adjustment, as resources are relocated within the economy, with accompanying economic uncertainties. Strengthening the tax base and instituting effective social safety nets are thus necessary complements to promoting trade integration and to the substantial benefits that more open trade policies will provide.

---

[44]On integration going beyond trade, governments in Africa will need to identify areas where the regional approach will have the maximum benefits, such as reducing wasteful tax competition between countries, cooperating on infrastructure projects (especially transportation and electrical grids), and promoting competition in services by creating an integrated market so that suppliers—be they domestic or foreign—can exploit economies of scale.

[45]This point is forcefully made by Collier and Gunning, "Trade Policy and Integration." Reciprocal trade integration is envisaged as part of the Cotonou Agreement and also under the U.S. Africa Growth and Opportunity Act.

[46]The locking-in of reforms has been argued to be the most important benefit for Mexico under the North American Free Trade Agreement (NAFTA).

[47]Of course, even this approach would be inferior to the first-best approach of liberalization on a most-favored-nation (or nondiscriminatory basis) by African countries

and the elimination of all market access barriers by the advanced economies.

[48]See Elena Ianchovicina, Aaditya Mattoo, and Marcelo Olarreaga "Unrestricted Market Access for Sub-Saharan Africa: How Much Is It Worth and Who Pays," World Bank Policy Research Working Paper (Washington: World Bank, forthcoming).

CHAPTER III

FISCAL IMPROVEMENT IN ADVANCED ECONOMIES: HOW LONG WILL IT LAST?

Countries around the world have significantly improved their fiscal positions since the early 1990s. This development has been particularly striking in the advanced economies, where several countries have attained sizable surpluses for the first time in nearly half a century (Figure 3.1).[1] This chapter describes the forces behind these gains and the challenges that lie ahead.

A defining characteristic of the recent fiscal adjustment is that it has been based primarily on expenditure restraint. Revenue rose as a share of GDP in the 1990s, but, compared with the role of spending, its contribution to fiscal adjustment was much less than during similar efforts of the 1980s. Instead, the emphasis in many countries, particularly in Europe, has been on changing the tax structure, shifting from direct taxes on labor and capital income toward indirect taxes. Furthermore, recent fiscal developments have been accompanied by widespread reforms directed at strengthening fiscal frameworks. These include measures focused on debt ceilings and deficit targets, on expenditure rules, and on the transparency of fiscal management.

Several factors may have underpinned this general strengthening of fiscal positions and fiscal institutions. The government's role in the economy expanded during much of the twentieth century, both in producing goods and services and, especially, in providing transfer payments.[2] In the 1980s and particularly the 1990s, however, many countries appeared to change their view, preferring a more limited role of government. In part, this change may reflect concerns about the extent to which government could ameliorate the effects of market failure and improve the distribution of

[1]See Chapter IV of this *World Economic Outlook* for some discussion of fiscal developments in emerging markets.

[2]The evolution of the role of government in the twentieth century was reviewed in Chapter V of the May 2000 *World Economic Outlook*.

Figure 3.1. Fiscal Trends in OECD Countries
(Percent of GDP)

Fiscal balance in advanced economies has been restored for the first time in a generation.

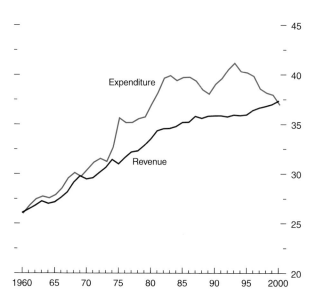

Sources: OECD Analytical and Economic Outlook Databases; and OECD Historical Statistics.

income. In addition, there may have been increased recognition of potential distortions arising from high rates of taxation and from public sector competition for economic resources, including the financing needed to support ongoing deficits. Competitive pressures from the growing international integration of goods and capital markets, together with generally lower rates of inflation, may have further constrained government's ability to raise taxes, monetize deficits, and build up public debt.

A key issue looking ahead is whether this recent fiscal adjustment will endure or whether—as in the 1980s—it will be reversed during a future economic slowdown. There is some reason for optimism in this regard, but also a need for caution. On the positive side, empirical assessments of earlier fiscal consolidations have identified a number of factors that tend to be associated with durable adjustment. These include a focus on expenditure reductions rather than tax increases; cuts in transfer spending and in the public sector wage bill; and an urgent need to address high levels of public debt. To varying degrees, these are characteristics of the recent period of fiscal improvement. Furthermore, such forces have been associated with better overall macroeconomic performance, including stronger investment and employment growth. The decline in private saving associated with an increase in public saving was apparently stronger during the 1990s than in earlier periods. This response may also point to the latest fiscal adjustment being more credible, although other factors (such as rising stock market wealth) may also have lowered private saving. It is likely that the strengthening of fiscal frameworks, combined with public sector management reforms that have improved the prioritization and control of public spending, has also contributed to greater fiscal discipline, and should help sustain these improvements.

Nevertheless, these fiscal and institutional measures have yet to face the test of a cyclical downturn. The recent buoyancy of revenue in some countries, notably the United States, is due in part to an exceptionally well-sustained period of economic growth and to the contribution of "new economy" factors whose durability has yet to be fully demonstrated. As a further note of caution, lower interest payments and capital outlays have made an important contribution to the recent decline in expenditure, most significantly in Europe where, for example, a number of countries have seen sizable reductions in interest rate risk premiums associated with the introduction of the euro. Substantial additional fiscal improvements from lower interest rates cannot be expected, and further reductions in capital outlays are not necessarily desirable. Recent experience with the new fiscal frameworks is too limited to identify which approach, if any, might best help to withstand prospective pressures for an expansion of spending over the short to medium term. Some further refinement of rules may also be needed—for example, to ensure ongoing emphasis on restraining discretionary expenditures.

Looking to the longer term, the pressures of aging populations on pension, health, and other areas of public spending will impose a challenge to fiscal positions and underlying fiscal frameworks in almost all advanced economies. While some countries, such as the United Kingdom, Canada, and Sweden, have reformed their public pension systems to improve significantly their financial viability, others, such as Germany and France, still have a long way to go to ensure the future of these schemes. The challenge of aging populations need not be insurmountable, however, if timely and wide-ranging policy measures are taken. Part of this response, already taken in a number of countries, is to limit prospective retiree claims on future output by scaling back pensions or increasing contributions. A more far-reaching approach, though, would be to boost output growth so that future retirees and workers will have a larger pie to share. Measures directed at this goal would include comprehensive labor market reforms, particularly in the euro area, to reduce unemployment and to increase participation both of older workers and—in some countries—of females. Increased prefunding of pension liabilities could help if this led to higher overall saving and investment; this approach would also improve the intergenerational equity in pension provision and allow a smoother profile of contribution rates.

Increasing globalization can also provide opportunities for countries to tackle the challenge of aging. Trends in projected dependency ratios and national saving-investment balances in the advanced economies are the opposite of those in many developing countries, which, in aggregate, are projected to provide nearly half of global output by 2050. By building up national saving and foreign assets in advance of age-related economic pressures, advanced economies would both support incomes and consumption in their own countries as dependency ratios reach their peak and would also contribute to investment and growth in developing economies. The pressures of aging populations on employment and output could also be reduced through increased migration from countries with younger population structures.

The capital and labor flows implied by this global approach would be largely unprecedented, at least in modern times. But making full use of these prospective benefits of globalization, as well as pursuing pension system reforms and other structural adjustments, would go a long way toward enabling countries to cope with the aging challenge.

Fiscal Improvement in OECD Countries: A Retrospective

The fiscal positions of almost all industrial countries have improved markedly since the early 1990s.[3] Only Japan has not contributed to this area-wide adjustment, reflecting the use of expansionary fiscal policy during much of the 1990s to promote and sustain economic recovery (see Box 3.1). Taken together, other industrial countries have seen an improvement in the overall structural balance of the general government of about 4½ percent of GDP (Figure 3.2).[4]

---

[3]This section focuses on OECD data sources because they provide details on the composition of general government revenue and expenditure, particularly on a cyclically adjusted basis.

[4]The figures cover the original OECD member countries plus those that joined in the 1960s (Finland) and in

Figure 3.2. Fiscal Developments in the OECD Area
(Percent of GDP unless otherwise noted)

Industrial countries have experienced a marked improvement in fiscal positions since the early 1990s, mostly due to expenditure reduction.

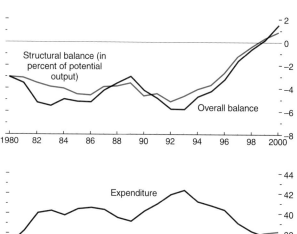

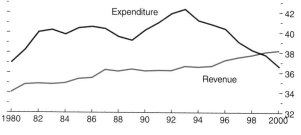

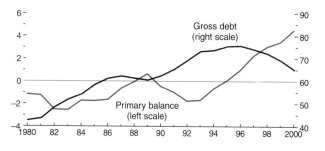

Sources: OECD Analytical and Economic Outlook Databases.

Figure 3.3. Fiscal Developments in Groups of OECD Countries

(Percent of GDP unless otherwise noted)

Recent fiscal improvements have been similar among industrial countries, although surpluses have been smaller in the euro area.

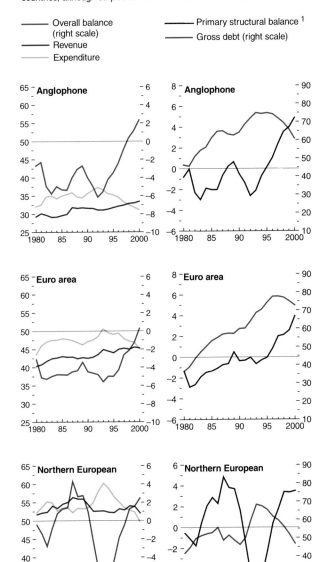

Sources: OECD Analytical and Economic Outlook Databases.
[1]Percent of potential GDP.

As primary surpluses began emerging toward the end of the 1990s, the overall government debt ratio has declined from its peak of about 75 percent of GDP. However, fiscal adjustment has not been as large in the euro area, where the overall surpluses that are now commonplace among other OECD countries have yet to be seen in the three largest member countries: France, Germany, and Italy (Figure 3.3).[5]

Since 1980, there have been two periods of fiscal adjustment (1983–89 and 1993–2000), separated by a period of fiscal expansion triggered by the economic slowdown of the early 1990s (Figure 3.4). Precise comparisons between the two periods of adjustment are complicated by the decline in inflation over this period and its differential impact on the various fiscal indicators.[6] Nonetheless, the two episodes differ in key respects:

- The more recent fiscal adjustment has been the result of a sharp reduction in primary expenditure, especially wages and transfers, and a marked reduction in interest payments, especially in the euro area countries with relatively high levels of government debt;[7] in contrast, the fiscal adjustment in the 1980s was driven mainly by revenue increases.

the early 1970s (Australia and New Zealand). In addition to Japan and the new non-industrial country members of the OECD, Luxembourg, Switzerland, and Turkey have been excluded because comparable data are not available. All aggregate measures are weighted averages based on 1995 GDP and purchasing power parities as reported in OECD *Economic Outlook 68* (Paris: Organization for Economic Cooperation and Development, 2000).

[5]The groups are as follows: mainly Anglophone countries (Australia, Canada, New Zealand, the United Kingdom, and the United States); euro area countries; and northern European countries that do not participate in the euro area (Denmark, Iceland, Norway, and Sweden).

[6]A decline in inflation can affect the fiscal position through various channels, most notably through lower nominal interest rates. The primary fiscal deficit is less subject to such an effect and is therefore a more useful indicator for fiscal comparisons across periods with different inflation levels.

[7]In the euro area, the move toward European Economic and Monetary Union contributed to reducing the real interest rate by enhancing the credibility of the exchange rate peg.

- Debt dynamics in the 1990s have been favorably influenced by the emergence of primary surpluses, lower interest rates, and buoyant growth. In the earlier fiscal adjustment, government debt ratios generally increased, as primary deficits more than offset the effect of negative real interest rates. Recent trends have raised questions in the United States and elsewhere about the implications of a diminishing supply of government securities (Box 3.2).

- Discretionary fiscal policies have played more of a role during the recent fiscal adjustment (Figure 3.4).[8] This may reflect the smaller size of automatic fiscal stabilizers in the 1990s, partly due to reforms that have reduced the overall progressivity of the tax system, lowered social benefits, and improved the targeting of benefits.[9]

- Changes in estimates of potential output growth in the second half of the 1990s should also be noted. In the United States, a portion of the improvement in the structural balance can be attributed to upward revisions to estimated potential output growth, as part of the increase in revenues and of the fall in spending resulted from underlying improvements in the economy. Hence, the increase in the structural fiscal balance may overstate the extent of discre-

[8]According to the OECD methodology, the difference between the actual and cyclically adjusted (structural) balances, corrected for net interest payments, provides a measure of automatic stabilizers. The change in the structural primary balance measures the change in the stance of fiscal policy; see *OECD Economic Outlook* Sources and Methods at http://www.oecd.org/eco/sources-and-methods/index.htm. A discussion of the differences between the OECD, the European Union, and the IMF methodologies used in assessing the fiscal stance can be found in Bank of Italy, *Indicators of Structural Budget Balances* (Rome: Bank of Italy, 1999).

[9]This point is discussed in Paul van den Noord, "The Size and Role of Automatic Fiscal Stabilizers in the 1990s and Beyond," OECD Economics Department Working Paper No. 3 (Paris: Organization for Economic Cooperation and Development, January 2000). The cyclical adjustment may not take full account of other factors, such as the stock market boom in the United States and related revenues from realized capital gains, together with the increase in effective tax rates as incomes increase.

Figure 3.4. Actual and Structural Balances in Groups of OECD Countries

(Changes within each period)

Compared with the fiscal adjustment in the 1980s, the recent improvement has resulted from discretionary policies, particularly reductions in primary expenditures.

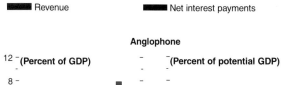

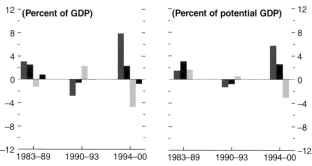

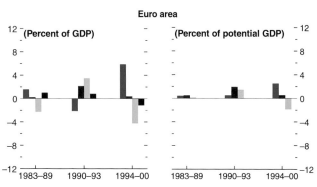

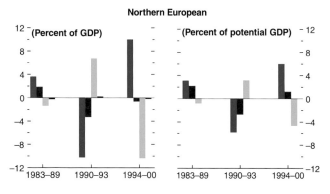

Sources: OECD Analytical and Economic Outlook Databases.
[1]Primary structural balance when evaluated as percent of potential GDP (right column).

Box 3.1. Japan: A Fiscal Outlier?

Japan adopted a conservative fiscal policy for most of the postwar period. A golden rule budget policy, in which borrowing through "construction bonds" was used only to finance investment, was in place until the mid-1960s, when the first "deficit-financing" government bonds were issued to make up for a revenue shortfall. The first oil shock and the revenue weakness in the wake of the subsequent recession prompted a buildup in the deficit (see the first Figure).

By FY1979, the general government deficit (excluding social security) had risen to 7 percent of GDP.[1] With the rapid expansion of the economy during the 1980s, however, significant fiscal consolidation was achieved, eliminating the need for deficit-financing bonds in the FY1990 budget. This strengthening was reflected in an approximately balanced fiscal position (excluding social security) in FY1990.

Japan has experienced a substantial deterioration in its fiscal position over the 1990s, however, in contrast to other major industrial countries. The main proximate causes were a decline in tax collections following the bursting of the "bubble" economy at the beginning of the decade and the countercyclical policy measures undertaken to help resuscitate the economy:[2]

- Revenues were affected by the decade-long stagnation of economic activity and by tax cuts. General government tax revenue fell from a peak of 22½ percent of GDP in FY1990 to 18¼ percent in FY1994, and has yet to recover. The bulk of the fall in tax revenue was due to a fall in tax elasticities, particularly the impact of declining profitability on corporate tax receipts. The revenue losses also reflected, in part, policy decisions. These include temporary income tax cuts in FY1994–96 and FY1998; an upward shift in income tax brackets in FY1995; a reduction in the top marginal income tax rate from 65 percent to 50 per-

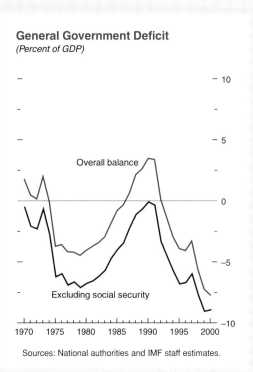

General Government Deficit
(Percent of GDP)

Sources: National authorities and IMF staff estimates.

cent with proportional reduction in other income tax brackets; and a progressive reduction in the corporate income tax rate to 40 percent from 50 percent in 1990.[3]

- Countercyclical increases in expenditure also boosted the deficit. Stimulus packages, including significant amounts of public works spending, were used as an instrument to quickly boost aggregate demand in view of the relatively weak automatic stabilizers in the Japanese economy. The packages involved significant "headline" spending figures—reaching ¥18 trillion (3½ percent of GDP) in November 1998—although the "real water" content (i.e., new measures that directly stimulate activity) was often significantly lower. Besides greater public investment spending at

---

[1]The Fiscal Year (FY) runs from April to March.
[2]See Martin Mühleisen, "Too Much of a Good Thing? The Effectiveness of Fiscal Stimulus," in *Post-Bubble Blues*, ed. by Tamim Bayoumi and Charles Collyns (Washington: International Monetary Fund, 2000).

[3]An effort to shore up the fiscal position—when in FY97, the consumption tax rate was hiked from 3 percent to 5 percent and the tax rebates were revoked—was given up as the economy sank back into a recession after a short-lived revival in growth.

both central and local government levels, these packages contained financial measures, such as loans provided through the Fiscal Investment and Loan Program (FILP).

Reflecting these economic developments, the budget deficit increased sharply. The general government balance (excluding social security) rose from near balance in FY1990 to a deficit of over 7 percent of GDP in FY1998. The structural balance (excluding social security) is estimated to have deteriorated by about 6 percent of GDP over the same period.

Japan's public debt has risen sharply as the deficit deteriorated, and on some measures now surpasses that of other major industrial countries. By the end of 1999, *gross debt* had reached 120 percent of GDP (see the second Figure). However, the sizable assets of the general government have kept *net debt* (around 35 percent of GDP at the end of 1999) at a relatively low level by international standards. The difference between gross and net debt is accounted for by the assets of the pension system (valued at 50 percent of GDP) and financial assets held by the central and local governments (35 percent of GDP). An alternative definition of net debt would treat the social security system as independent and exclude its assets—which for Japan are more than offset by the projected net future liabilities of the pension system (estimated at 60 percent of GDP through 2050)—from public debt calculations.[4] On this definition, net debt would be around 85 percent of GDP at the end of 1999. However, the general government's net obligations may be considerably higher than suggested by the net debt figures, as liabilities arising from loan guarantees and bank support may have to be met and assets may be overvalued.

Uncertainties about the extent of public indebtedness highlight the need for improving fiscal transparency. The problems include a significant time lag in the presentation of fiscal

[4]See Martin Mühleisen "Sustainable Fiscal Policies for an Aging Population," in *Japan: Selected Issues,* IMF Staff Country Report No. 00/144 (Washington: International Monetary Fund, November 2000).

Public Debt
(Percent of GDP)

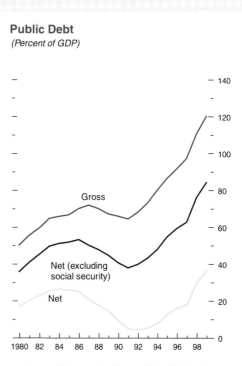

Sources: National authorities and IMF staff estimates.

information, a confusing distinction between initial and supplementary budgets, and concerns over the quality of general government financial assets. The authorities have taken some steps to improve transparency, including the publication of a consolidated central government balance sheet, initial steps toward the application of cost-benefit analysis for project selection, and Fiscal Investment and Loan Program reform legislation that provides for greater reliance on market financing of public works projects. However, these measures need to be supplemented with further steps to increase the coverage of the government's balance sheet, through, among other actions, consolidating central government data with those of local governments, placing budget planning in a medium-term policy framework to reduce uncertainty about future plans for deficits and debt levels, overhauling the system of central and local government accounts, and ensuring timely compilation of consolidated general government accounts.

Box 3.1 *(concluded)*

Japan's unfavorable demographic trends are also adding to fiscal pressures. As discussed in the main text, under current projections Japan is likely to experience the most rapid increase among the Group of Seven countries in the share of the elderly in its total population, implying increasing pressure on health care as well as pension costs.[5] Moreover, slower growth of the labor force will lower potential output growth, which will complicate the task of bringing government debt down to a more manageable share of GDP.

The rise in public debt and pressures from unfavorable demographic trends have put the spotlight on the need for fiscal consolidation. Given the trade-offs between the very high level

of public debt and the still fragile recovery, the very gradual withdrawal of fiscal stimulus currently under way is appropriate for now. However, it is important that the authorities map out a strategy for consolidation to improve confidence in Japan's medium-term growth prospects and to reduce the risks of volatile financial market conditions. An appropriate strategy is likely to involve a substantial scaling back of spending on public works, combined with revenue increases secured through a broadening of the personal income tax base and some increase in the consumption tax rate. Some progress was made toward improving the solvency of the public pension system in 2000 through reform legislation that, among other measures, provided for an increase in contribution rates. However, additional social security reforms are likely to be needed, not only on the pension side, but also in the area of public health care expenditures.

[5]See Hamid Faruqee, "Population Aging and its Macroeconomic Implications" in *Japan: Selected Issues,* IMF Staff Country Report No. 00/144 (Washington: International Monetary Fund, November 2000).

tionary policy actions. Conversely, in the euro area, a decline in estimated potential output growth implies that the fiscal effort has been larger than shown by the change in structural balances.[10]

Expenditure Contribution to Adjustment

The most striking feature of the recent fiscal consolidation has been the downtrend in gov-

[10]See "Growth Divergences in the United States, Europe, and Japan: Trend or Cyclical?" Chapter III of the October 1999 *World Economic Outlook.* Between 1994 and 2000, estimates of potential output in 1999 have increased by 1.7 percent in the United States and decreased between 1½ and 2 percent in the euro area. Assuming a revenue elasticity slightly higher than one and an elasticity of current spending in the range of 0 and ¼, and bearing in mind all the uncertainty surrounding potential output and elasticity measures, about ½ of a percent of GDP of the fiscal adjustment in the United States would be accounted for by higher potential output, whereas euro area countries would have adjusted their structural balances by about of a percent of GDP more than would have been justified by changes in estimated potential output.

ernment expenditure. On average, general government expenditure in the advanced economies (excluding Japan) declined by close to 6 percent of GDP during 1993–2000, with the sharpest reduction in the northern European countries (10½ percent of GDP). The bulk of adjustment has fallen on expenditure categories that contributed to the earlier long upward trend in the expenditure ratio: wages and salaries, current transfers, and interest payments (Figure 3.5).

- Expenditure on *wages and salaries* contributed substantially to the latest fiscal adjustments, largely due to a slowdown in government employment growth; these expenditures were almost constant as a share of GDP throughout the 1980s.
- In the Anglophone and northern European countries, the increase in the share of GDP absorbed by *current transfers* in the 1980s and early 1990s was largely reversed during 1993–2000. This change reflects privatization, increased targeting of social spending,

and, in some cases, major pension reforms (for example, Sweden).

- The decline in the share of *interest payments* as a percent of GDP coincided with the reduction of primary deficits and the subsequent emergence of primary surpluses. This reduction was more accentuated among euro area and northern European countries, due to their higher level of public indebtedness and, for some euro area economies, to sharp declines in interest rates in the run-up to monetary union.

- *Public investment* declined in the euro area and, to a lesser extent, in northern European countries, both in percent of GDP and as a ratio to primary outlays.[11]

- There was also a reduction in *defense spending*, largely driven by the United States and the United Kingdom, where the peace dividend amounted to some 2 percent of GDP.[12]

Reforms in public expenditure management, including mechanisms to strengthen budgetary procedures and to enhance budget flexibility while strengthening expenditure control, have contributed significantly to expenditure restraint.[13] Furthermore, reconsideration of the role of government has led to an expanded role

[11]On the other hand, in some countries of the euro area, the reduction in public investment may have reflected the privatization process or changes in the classification of public utilities and other units from the general government to the private sector, as pointed out in Daniele Franco and Fabrizio Balassone, "Public Investment, the Stability Pact, and the 'Golden Rule'," *Fiscal Studies*, Vol. 21 (June 2000), pp. 207–29. The same authors also point to the increasing use of project financing, which, in the case of the United Kingdom, appears to explain about a third of the decline in public investment. That being said, the United Kingdom has recently adopted a golden rule (government should borrow only to finance investment) as part of its fiscal framework to facilitate public investment, which had fallen to historically low levels.

[12]For most countries, data on the functional breakdown of expenditure are available only through 1995, largely reflecting problems associated with shifting national accounting standards from SNA93 to ESA95.

[13]Measures have included *ex ante* and *ex post* program evaluation (Australia), creating responsibility centers (France), and performance agreements (New Zealand and the United Kingdom). For a discussion of these measures, see Jim Brumby, "Budgetary Devices That Deliver,"

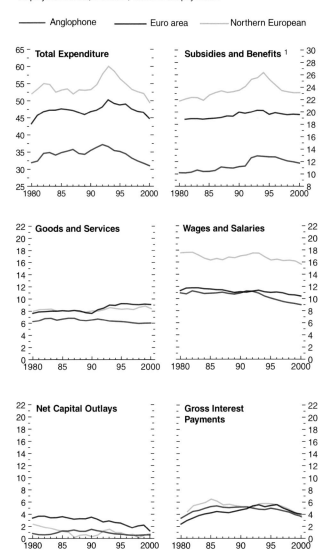

Figure 3.5. Expenditure Developments in Groups of OECD Countries
(Percent of GDP unless otherwise noted)

The recent reduction in expenditure has been driven by lower public employment costs, transfers, and interest payments.

Sources: OECD Analytical and Economic Outllook Databases.
[1]Cyclically adjusted, in percent of potential output.

Figure 3.6. Revenue Developments in Groups of OECD Countries
(Percent of GDP)

The modest rise in fiscal revenues in the 1990s has comprised increasing indirect taxes in Europe, and rising direct taxes on households in the Anglophone countries.

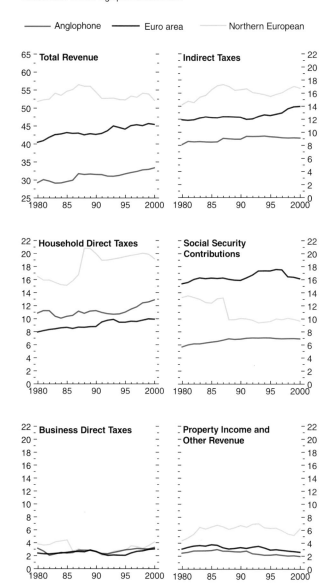

Sources: OECD Analytical and Economic Outlook Databases.

for markets in the provision of public goods and services, including contracting out of government services, liberalizing public procurement, introducing user charges, and using vouchers in the distribution of merit goods and services.

Revenue Contribution to Fiscal Adjustment

Unlike in the 1980s, revenue growth has made a relatively small contribution to the fiscal adjustment that has taken place since 1993. Revenue to GDP ratios rose only modestly in the 1990s in the euro area and mainly Anglophone countries, and generally stabilized in northern Europe (Figure 3.6). While revenue ratios from the business sector increased slightly across all countries, European countries have shifted toward taxing consumption, whereas in Anglophone countries direct taxation of households has risen.

The limited recent contribution of revenue increases reflected a wave of tax reforms that started in the United States, Canada, and the United Kingdom in the first half of the 1980s and then moved to other industrial countries. These reforms were directed at strengthening tax administration and improving the overall tax structure.[14] Marginal tax rates on personal and corporate income were reduced, but tax exemptions, reliefs, and credits were drastically curtailed to offset revenue losses. Many countries lowered taxes on capital income, both to contain capital flight and to achieve greater neutrality in the taxation of income accruing from different financial assets. The value added tax, or VAT, has become

Oxford Policy Institute Policy Brief No. 3 (June 2000); and OECD, "Modern Financial Management Practices," PUMA/SBO (98)8 (Paris: Organization for Economic Cooperation and Development, 1998), available at http://www.oecd.org/puma.

[14]A more detailed account of tax and tax administration reforms over the last two decades can be found in Ken Messere, "Half a Century of Changes in Taxation," *Bulletin for International Fiscal Documentation*, Vol. 53 (August/September 1999); Jeffrey Owens, "Emerging Issues in Tax Reform: the Perspective of an International Bureaucrat," *Tax Notes International*, Vol. 15 (December 1997); and Vito Tanzi, "Globalization, Tax Competition, and the Future of Tax Systems," IMF Working Paper 96/141 (Washington: International Monetary Fund, December 1998).

Box 3.2. Financial Implications of the Shrinking Supply of U.S. Treasury Securities

The recent and prospective reduction in the supply of U.S. treasury securities has attracted considerable attention, in part because of the international role of the U.S. dollar, and in part because the U.S. treasury market is the largest, deepest, and most liquid government securities market in the world.[1] Reflecting these features, U.S. treasury securities currently play several important roles in U.S. and global financial markets, including as a benchmark for the prices of private securities, an asset for holdings of official foreign exchange reserves, a major instrument of U.S. monetary policy implementation, and a safe haven for domestic and international investors during times of financial stress.

The shrinking supply of U.S. treasury securities and the associated decline in liquidity in the secondary market have made these securities less useful in the above roles.[2] In particular, their prices increasingly reflect the scarcity of treasury securities and technical factors. As a result, treasury securities are becoming poorer market benchmarks, increasingly expensive to use as collateral (because their yields have declined relative to the cost of funds to finance their purchase), and less attractive to portfolio managers.

In this environment, while questions have arisen about what instruments could substitute for U.S. treasury securities if the supply continues to shrink, markets are already successfully shifting away from treasuries:

- In the U.S. dollar markets, a variety of non-treasury benchmarks, including swaps, securities issued by large U.S. "agencies" (such as Fannie Mae, Freddie Mac, and the Federal Home Loan Bank), and some large corporate issues, can be and are being used as reference points both for *quoting* yields on new and existing fixed-income instruments and for the *pricing* of new issues.
- Market participants have significantly shifted short-term liquidity and funding activities toward high-quality, liquid alternatives to the treasury bill and treasury repo markets—mainly agency securities (as noted above) and some corporate bonds. As a result, cash and repo markets in agency securities have become more liquid and active.
- Portfolio managers that have long-maturity liabilities face a dearth of high-quality, long-maturity assets. These managers—including those at pension funds and insurance companies—may need to shift to shorter-maturity assets, and would need to manage the resulting maturity mismatch between assets and liabilities.
- Central banks in the United States and elsewhere have expanded the menu of securities that they use for liquidity and foreign exchange reserve management to include U.S. agency securities and asset-backed securities.

In summary, it is clear that private securities can readily serve as the benchmark and in most other roles in U.S. dollar markets, as they did before the treasury market existed. It is less clear what instruments might serve as the U.S. dollar safe haven. Market participants might use bank deposits or high-grade corporate bonds, although neither has the minimal credit risk and strong market liquidity of U.S. treasuries. Alternatively, they might use whatever the Federal Reserve decides to use in place of treasuries in its operations. In addition, the financial implications of shrinking government securities markets may be different outside the U.S. dollar markets. Government securities markets may play more important benchmark roles in countries that lack well-developed markets for private instruments than the treasury market does in the United States. These questions will be more fully explored in the 2001 issue of the IMF's *International Capital Markets* report.

[1]The U.S. treasury market has daily turnover of about $200 billion, five times greater than daily turnover on the New York Stock Exchange.

[2]The gross federal debt held by the public declined from about 50 percent of GDP in 1995 to about 36 percent in 2000, and is projected to decline further during the current decade.

an increasingly important source of indirect tax revenues in almost all advanced economies.[15] Particularly in the euro area, standard VAT rates have gradually been increased to partially offset the downward trend in marginal income tax rates.

The Role of One-Off Factors

Several forces, such as privatization and tax amnesties, that may not be repeated in the future have helped to drive the recent fiscal adjustment. While such moves may have been significant in particular countries, the overall influence of these one-off sources of revenue has been limited. Privatization proceeds during the 1990s were modest for the countries covered in this chapter (0.3 percent of aggregate GDP a year on average), with about two-thirds generated within the European Union.[16] Although the scope for further revenue from privatization is limited, new income sources such as spectrum license fees have recently emerged, particularly in the European Union.[17] A number of countries have also used tax amnesties to raise revenue and remove backlogged tax appeals, but the payoff was generally small (often less than ½ percent of total revenue) and voluntary tax compliance rarely increased, probably because of the expectation of future amnesties.[18] Various "creative accounting" measures—such as moving

spending off budget, making payments to the government for assuming pension liabilities, and shifting taxes forward—helped some EU countries meet the Maastricht deficit and debt targets, but the fiscal impact in countries pursuing such measures averaged a modest ½ percent of GDP in 1997.[19] Such measures have not contributed significantly to fiscal outcomes in subsequent years.

The Success of Fiscal Consolidations

Reductions in fiscal deficits do not always guarantee a significant and enduring strengthening of public finances. While some attempts at fiscal consolidation result in a persistent improvement in the fiscal balance and a sizable reduction of the public debt, others are soon reversed. Recent economic analysis suggests that, in advanced economies, a fiscal improvement is more likely to be successful when based on cuts in expenditure, especially reductions in the wage bill (via lower public employment) and in transfers (such as pensions), and when undertaken by countries with high levels of debt.[20] The same factors appear to be important in determining the impact of fiscal consolidation on macroeconomic performance more generally (Box 3.3). This analysis has identified successful fiscal consolidations mostly in the 1980s and 1990s, possibly reflecting growing opposition to the progressive enlargement of public sector participation in the economy and, for some countries, grow-

---

[15]The United States central government is now the only one in the OECD without a VAT or equivalent tax.

[16]In EU countries, privatization receipts do not count toward reducing the general government deficit in the Maastricht definition. Furthermore, these are gross proceeds that do not necessarily correspond to net proceeds to government. For further detail, see Ladan Mahboobi, "Recent Privatization Trends," OECD *Financial Market Trends*, No. 76, (Paris: Organization for Economic Cooperation and Development, June 2000).

[17]IMF staff estimates indicate that revenue in 2000 from the allocation of third-generation licenses amounted to 1½ percent of GDP in the euro area.

[18]Countries offering amnesties include France, Ireland, Italy, Australia, and New Zealand, as well as most states in the United States. See John Hasseldine, "Tax Amnesties: An International Review," *Bulletin for International Fiscal Documentation*, Vol. 52, No. 7 (July 1998) and the references therein. The 1988 general amnesty carried out in Ireland stands out because it raised about $700 million or 4½ percent of total revenue.

[19]Eurostat, "Statistics on Convergence Criteria-Assessment by Eurostat," (Luxembourg: Eurostat, March 1998).

[20]See Alberto Alesina and Roberto Perotti, "Fiscal Adjustments in OECD Countries: Composition and Macroeconomic Effects," *IMF Staff Papers*, International Monetary Fund, Vol. 44 (June 1997), pp. 210–248; IMF, *World Economic Outlook* (May 1996), Ch. III "Fiscal Challenges in Industrial Countries," pp. 44–62; Alberto Alesina and Silvia Ardagna, "Tales of Fiscal Adjustment," *Economic Policy* (1998) pp. 488–545; Roberto Perotti, Rolf Strauch, and Juergen Von Hagen, *Sustainability of Public Finances* (London: Centre for Economic Policy Research, 1998); and Juergen Von Hagen, Andrew Hughes Hallett, and Rolf Strauch, "Budgetary Consolidations in EMU," Economic Papers No. 148 (Brussels: European Commission, March 2001).

Box 3.3. Impact of Fiscal Consolidation on Macroeconomic Performance

This box reviews the broader aspects of economic performance—notably, trends in output, saving, and external balances—that have been associated with the recent fiscal improvements. The focus is on the euro area and the Anglophone countries.

While there is widespread agreement that a sound fiscal position is conducive to improved economic performance over the medium to long term, the impact of fiscal consolidation on output in the short term is an area of some dispute.[1] The standard Keynesian analysis suggests that fiscal contraction will result in lower employment and output over the short term, as it reduces aggregate demand (partly offset by the decline in real interest rates and by the anticipation of a reduction in the future tax burden). A more recent economic literature (often labeled "non-Keynesian") has emphasized the distortions arising from government intervention. In this view, the short-term macroeconomic impact of fiscal consolidation can be positive under the same circumstances that help make such adjustments successful—when they occur with high initial levels of public debt or are expenditure-based. As high public debt raises interest rates and enhances expectations of future increases in taxation or possible default (especially if certain thresholds of public debt are perceived as unsustainable), a reduction in public debt can increase aggregate demand of the private sector via wealth effects.[2] Reductions in public expenditure and the associated public wage compression (which can impact private sector wages) can reduce production costs, which raises profitability and competitiveness, thus stimulating investment and

exports.[3] Reducing public spending can also raise the confidence of the business sector, to the extent such consolidations are perceived as more successful.

Considering the experience of the past 20 years, there is some evidence for the United States suggesting that in the short term the standard Keynesian effect may dominate, with fiscal contractions (achieved through either a reduction in expenditure or an increase in taxes) estimated to have had a negative effect on output, although the multipliers are generally small.[4] This result plausibly reflects the relative stability of fiscal policy and government debt in the United States and the limited role of government in the economy, characteristics that are shared by other Anglophone countries—at least over recent years. Even in these countries, however, one part of the non-Keynesian story does appear to hold, namely reductions in government spending have a strong positive effect on investment spending.[5]

The evidence for other countries is more mixed, with several authors finding evidence that some fiscal contractions can be associated with somewhat higher growth even in the short term, particularly if the contraction is associated with falls in government spending.[6] Most of these cases occur in euro area countries characterized by high levels of government debt and large governments, where non-Keynesian effects

[1]See Richard Hemming, Michael Kell, and Selma Mahfouz, "The Effectiveness of Fiscal Policy in Stimulating Economic Activity—A Review of the Literature," (unpublished; Washington: International Monetary Fund, March 2000); and Chapter III in the May 1996 *World Economic Outlook.*

[2]See, among others, Roberto Perotti, "Fiscal Policy in Good Times and Bad," *Quarterly Journal of Economics,* Vol. 114 (November 1999), pp. 1399–1436.

[3]See, for example, Alberto Alesina, Silvia Ardanga, Roberto Perotti, and Fabio Schiantarelli, "Fiscal Policy, Profits, and Investment," NBER Working Paper No. 7207 (Cambridge, Mass.: National Bureau of Economic Research, July 1999).

[4]See Olivier Blanchard and Roberto Perotti, "An Empirical Characterization of the Dynamic Effects of Changes in Government Spending and Taxes on Output," NBER Working Paper No. 7269 (Cambridge, Mass.: National Bureau of Economic Research, July 1999). Small multipliers are also a property of the IMF's large econometric model (MULTIMOD) when monetary policy is assumed to primarily stabilize inflation.

[5]This result has also been found for other countries. See Alesina and others, "Fiscal Policy, Profits, and Investment."

[6]For a survey, see Alberto Alesina, Roberto Perotti, and Jose Tavares, "The Political Economy of Fiscal Adjustments," *Brookings Papers on Economic Activity,* No. 1, Brookings Institution, pp. 197–266 (1998).

Box 3.3 *(concluded)*

are likely to be particularly important. Although governments remain large in many euro area countries, recent reductions in government debt ratios and fiscal deficits, and the associated improvements in the long-term fiscal outlook, may have reduced the effectiveness of non-Keynesian channels. In addition, other factors that have supported output during times of fiscal consolidation—such as exchange rate depreciations in the 1980s and reductions in real interest rates in the run-up to the European Economic and Monetary Union in the 1990s—are less likely to play a significant role in the future. These arguments suggest that broad-based fiscal contractions are now less likely to be associated with short-term output expansions, even in the euro area. Indeed, the improvement in fiscal balances in most euro area countries over the late 1990s to achieve the Maastricht treaty criteria was associated with a period where output remained below potential. As for Japan, it is notable that the attempted fiscal consolidation in 1997 was followed by a sharp contraction in output.

Turning to saving and the current account, improvements in the fiscal balance are generally not fully reflected in higher aggregate saving, as part is offset by the decline in private saving, presumably induced by the anticipation of future tax reduction. This offset is likely to be bigger when the fiscal consolidation is expected to be larger and more successful.[7] Numerous empirical analyses have attempted to estimate the average extent of the impact: most contributions have concluded that in industrial countries about half of a reduction in fiscal deficits is offset by a decrease in private saving.[8]

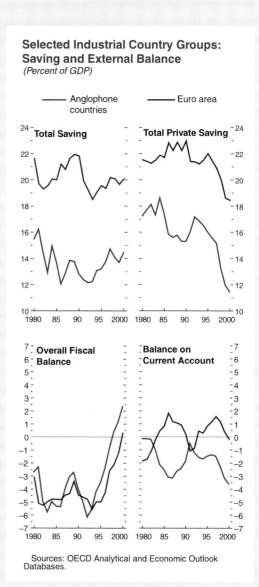

Selected Industrial Country Groups: Saving and External Balance
(Percent of GDP)

—— Anglophone countries   —— Euro area

Sources: OECD Analytical and Economic Outlook Databases.

[7]For a formal analysis of Ricardo's suggestion that the private sector tends to neutralize the impact of fiscal adjustments on total saving, see Robert J. Barro, "Are Government Bonds Net Wealth?," *The Journal of Political Economy*, Vol. 82 (November–December 1974), pp. 1,095–1,117. Subsequent literature has identified several reasons suggesting a limited extent of the offset—see, for example, Olivier Blanchard and Stanley Fischer, *Lectures on Macroeconomics* (Cambridge: MIT Press, 1985).

[8]See Douglas Bernheim, "Ricardian Equivalence: An Evaluation of Theory and Evidence," in *NBER Macroeconomic Annual 1987*, ed. by Stanley Fischer

The substantial improvement of fiscal balances in industrial countries (excluding Japan) since 1993 has been associated with an offsetting

(Cambridge: MIT Press, 1987) pp. 263–303. For a survey of the literature and more recent empirical results, see Paul R. Masson, Tamim Bayoumi, and Hossein Samiei, "International Evidence on the Determinants of Private Saving," *The World Bank Economic Review*, Vol. 2, No. 3, pp. 483–501 (The World Bank: Washington, 1998).

fall in private saving that appears somewhat larger than the average estimates reported above (see the Figure). This sizable offset may partly stem from the wealth effects associated with booming stock markets but it may also reflect the perceived success of recent fiscal consolidations—partly associated with their size, their composition, and the institutional support provided by fiscal rules and improved transparency.

Fiscal developments do not appear to have been the driving force behind current account trends across advanced economies, despite the past popularity of the "twin deficits hypothesis" to explain the U.S. current account deficit in the 1980s and early 1990s (see the Figure). Estimates of the impact of changes in relative fiscal positions on the current account in industrial countries show a small effect (not always significant) of between 10 and 40 percent.[9] In

any case, fiscal positions for the Anglophone and the euro area countries have been highly correlated over time, so that relative fiscal positions have varied much less than their external counterparts. Hence, whatever the fiscal offset might be, factors other than fiscal policy—such as relative business cycles and asset market developments—appear to be the primary drivers of external positions.

---

[9]For recent empirical analysis of the impact of fiscal balance on external balance over the past decades, see, for example, Menzie D. Chinn and Eswar S.

Prasad, "Medium-Term Determinants of Current Accounts in Industrial and Developing Countries: An Empirical Exploration," IMF Working Paper No. 00/46 (Washington: International Monetary Fund, March 2000); Hamid Faruqee and Guy Debelle, "Saving-Investment Balances in Industrial Countries: An Empirical Investigation," in IMF Occasional Paper No. 167, *Exchange Rate Assessment: Extensions of the Macroeconomic Balance Approach,* ed. by Peter Isard and Hamid Faruqee (Washington: International Monetary Fund, 1998); Philip Lane and Roberto Perotti, "The Trade Balance and Fiscal Policy in the OECD," *European Economic Review,* Vol. 42 (1998) pp. 887–895; and Michel Normandin, "Budget Deficit Persistence and the Twin Deficit Hypothesis," *Journal of International Economics,* Vol. 49 (1999) pp. 171–193.

ing concerns about the sustainability of public debt.[21]

These considerations suggest that the fiscal consolidations of the 1990s are more likely to be successful than those of the 1980s. However, caution is needed. Successful consolidations are defined over a relatively short period and can be reversed over time. Many of the consolidations of the 1980s unraveled during the early 1990s— for example, in the United Kingdom. This highlights the importance of factors other than just the composition of fiscal adjustment. In particular, sound fiscal frameworks—considered in the following section—may help reinforce political

commitment to fiscal restraint in the face of pressures for expansion.

The Role of Institutional Reform[22]

The reductions in fiscal deficits since 1993, and associated macroeconomic benefits, have occurred in the context of widespread reforms to fiscal frameworks.[23] These institutional reforms have been aimed primarily at achieving and maintaining fiscal consolidation, while continuing to leave room for fiscal policy to dampen the business cycle through automatic

---

[21]Examples of successful fiscal consolidations include the fiscal adjustments experienced by the United Kingdom in 1979–90, Ireland in 1987–89, and Denmark in 1983–86. For examples of unsuccessful fiscal consolidations, the literature points to Ireland in 1982–84 and Sweden in 1983–90.

[22]This section draws on Richard Hemming and Michael Kell, "Promoting Fiscal Responsibility: Transparency, Rules, and Independent Fiscal Authorities," paper prepared for a Bank of Italy workshop on fiscal rules held in Perugia, Italy (February 1–3, 2001).

[23]The major exception, in terms of both consolidation and institutional reform, is Japan.

stabilizers and (if necessary) policy actions. This section discusses the nature of these reforms and the role they have played in the recent fiscal consolidations.

Recent institutional reforms can be classified into three broad, but not mutually exclusive, groups (details of these reforms in some advanced and developing economies are set out in Box 3.4).

- *Formal deficit and debt rules.* The main examples of this approach are the countries of the euro area, which are bound by the Maastricht Treaty and subsequent Stability and Growth Pact limit of 3 percent of GDP on the deficit; and the United Kingdom, which since 1997 has operated a golden rule (borrowing only to finance capital spending) and a sustainable investment rule, which limits net debt to 40 percent of GDP over the cycle. Several countries have deficit and debt rules at the subnational level.[24]

- *Expenditure limits.* Other countries, such as Sweden and the United States, as well as Finland and the Netherlands in the euro area, have put more emphasis on expenditure limits, supported by procedural requirements, whereby proposals resulting in overruns in certain expenditure areas must be accompanied by offsetting expenditure cuts elsewhere or by revenue increases. Canada has also focused on instituting a rigorous expenditure review process.

- *Transparency.* New Zealand pioneered an approach to fiscal management that places primary and explicit emphasis on transparency (generally defined as being open to the public about the structure and functions of government, public sector accounts, and fiscal policy intentions and projections), with the Fiscal Responsibility Act of 1994.[25] Australia and the United Kingdom have since adopted similar approaches. The key elements that these frameworks share are an explicit legal basis, an elaboration of guiding principles for fiscal policy, a requirement that objectives are clearly stated, an emphasis on the need for a longer-term focus to fiscal policy, and demanding requirements for fiscal reporting to the public.

These approaches have often been combined and have, in some instances, evolved over time in the light of experience. For example, the United Kingdom, Australia, and New Zealand combine legally mandated transparency with rules or objectives for deficits and debt, and the Netherlands uses expenditure and revenue rules to meet its requirements under the Stability and Growth Pact. The United States now places relatively more emphasis on expenditure rather than deficit rules, while the deficit and debt criteria of the Maastricht Treaty have been complemented by the provisions of the Stability and Growth Pact. The evolution of fiscal frameworks has been driven in some cases by a change in focus from improving an initially weak fiscal position toward maintaining a sound position over the medium term. In the former case, fairly inflexible ceilings on deficits or expenditure have typically been applied; in the latter, more sophisticated considerations generally come into play, including imposing debt ceilings, specifying rules in cyclically adjusted terms, and emphasizing fiscal transparency.

There are two main justifications for these institutional reforms. First, fiscal rules and transparency strengthen fiscal discipline, thus helping governments maintain commitments to improve public finances: while rules limit the influence of contingent events on fiscal outcomes, transparency increases accountability for the design

---

[24]All but two U.S. states have laws requiring the submission, passing, or signing of balanced budgets and limiting the ability of states to issue debt. Nine provinces and territories in Canada have fiscal rules, with balanced budgets being required in all but one case. Italian local governments are allowed to take on debt only for the purpose of financing investment projects. In the euro area, Austria, Belgium, Italy, and Spain have internal stability pacts to ensure that the finances of subnational governments are consistent with commitments under the Stability and Growth Pact.

[25]George Kopits and Jon Craig, *Transparency in Government Operations*, IMF Occasional Paper No. 158 (Washington: International Monetary Fund, 1998).

Box 3.4. Fiscal Frameworks in Advanced and Emerging Market Economies

Following the classification set out in the main text, countries and regions can to some extent be grouped according to whether their respective fiscal frameworks emphasize deficit and debt rules, expenditure rules, or transparency. This categorization is somewhat arbitrary, however: some countries could be assigned to more than one group, and the categories are not mutually exclusive.

Frameworks Emphasizing Deficit and Debt Rules

Euro area. Under the 1992 Maastricht Treaty, countries seeking to participate in the Economic and Monetary Union (EMU) had to aim to achieve general government deficits not in excess of 3 percent of GDP and gross government debt not in excess of 60 percent of GDP. These reference levels could be exceeded, if the excess deficit was small and either temporary or had declined significantly, and if debt was on a clear downward path. Building on these gains in fiscal discipline, the 1997 Stability and Growth Pact requires euro area countries (and other countries in the European Union) to achieve fiscal positions that are close to balance or in surplus, so that they can respect the 3 percent deficit ceiling during normal cyclical downturns. There is a commitment to achieve this target by 2002 at the latest. In addition, some euro area countries have their own fiscal rules. For example, in Germany, the Basic Law requires a balanced current budget (i.e., a golden rule) which limits borrowing to investment expenditure under normal economic circumstances.

Canada. Since 1993, the federal budget has been based on three key elements: a two-year planning horizon based on systematically prudent macroeconomic assumptions and an ex ante balanced budget target; the inclusion of an annual contingency reserve; and a commitment to use the latter, when it is not needed, to pay down public debt. The government's *Budget Plan 2000* included commitments to maintaining balanced budgets in 2000/01 and 2001/02 and to keeping the debt-to-GDP ratio on a permanent downward path.

Switzerland. A constitutional amendment in 1998 required the federal government to attain budget balance by 2001. Once this has been achieved, a new constitutional amendment will require that a year-by-year ceiling be set on the level of central government expenditure, with the aim of ensuring budget balance over the cycle.

Frameworks Emphasizing Expenditure Rules

United States. The 1990 Budget Enforcement Act (BEA) replaced the relatively unsuccessful deficit targets of the 1985 Gramm-Rudman-Hollings Act with more complex limits on spending (excluding social security and Medicare). Discretionary spending categories are defined and capped in nominal terms for five years ahead; if these caps are exceeded, a uniform percentage reduction in spending in that category is required. For revenues and mandatory spending (spending controlled by permanent laws such as Medicare), the BEA requires that changes be financed on a pay-as-you-go basis, implying that any law that reduces revenue or increases spending must be offset by other measures to avoid triggering uniform cuts in certain mandatory spending programs. Discretionary spending caps and pay-as-you-go legislation are set to expire in 2002.

The Netherlands. The 1998 Coalition Agreement, supported by subsequent budget memoranda, sets ceilings for real central government expenditure over the period 1999–2002. There is also a rule that mandates how deviations in projected revenue from its baseline path will be allocated (in the case of "upturns") and offset (in the case of "downturns").

Sweden. The 1996 State Budget Act sets a ceiling for total central government expenditure (consistent with a surplus of 2 percent of GDP on average over the cycle) for the coming budget year and the following two years. Indicative nominal funding levels are set for each of 27 expenditure areas, together with a "budget margin" to provide a buffer against forecasting errors. Cost overruns in one program have to be financed by reductions in other expenditure areas or by increases in revenue.

Box 3.4 *(concluded)*

Frameworks Emphasizing Transparency[1]

United Kingdom. The current fiscal strategy embeds deficit and debt rules within a framework that places particular emphasis on transparency. In 1997, the government introduced two fiscal rules that apply over the cycle: a golden rule, which requires that the government should borrow only to finance investment, and a sustainable investment rule, which requires that net public sector debt as a proportion of GDP should be held at a stable and prudent level, currently set at 40 percent of GDP. A complementary Code for Fiscal Stability, emphasizing transparency, was added in 1998. The Code commits the government to specify its fiscal objectives and operating rules, and justify any changes to them; disclose any decisions and circumstances that might have a material impact on the economic and fiscal outlook; ensure best practice accounting methods are used; and publish a range of fiscal documents.

Australia. The Charter for Budget Honesty enacted in 1998 requires the government to publish an annual fiscal strategy statement that indicates long-term fiscal policy objectives and sets fiscal targets for the following three years. The Charter does not specify any particular fiscal rule or numerical targets. However, under the current fiscal strategy, the primary objective is to achieve fiscal balance on average over the economic cycle. Supplementary objectives are to maintain fiscal surpluses over the forward estimates period while economic growth prospects remain sound; to avoid an increase in the overall tax burden from its 1996–97 level; and to improve the general government net asset position over the medium to longer term.

[1]The frameworks of the United Kingdom, Australia, and New Zealand, which are described in this section, have motivated a more general effort to improve fiscal transparency. In particular, these frameworks provided the starting point for work at the IMF that resulted in the *Code of Good Practices on Fiscal Transparency—Declaration of Principles,* which was published in 1998. The Code provides a benchmark for assessing fiscal transparency and as such represents a standard of fiscal transparency to which all countries should aspire.

New Zealand. The Fiscal Responsibility Act of 1994 mandates that the government should be clear about the objectives and consequences of its policies, through, among other actions, strengthened reporting requirements. The Act also stipulates that the government should be judged against its ability to reduce debt to prudent levels by achieving operating surpluses each year; ensure that over a reasonable period of time total operating expenses do not exceed total operating revenues; achieve appropriate levels of government net worth; manage risks prudently; and maintain predictable and stable tax rates. While the Act does not contain numerical targets, the government must set out each year its "broad strategic priorities" for the budget and for the next two years and its long-term fiscal policy objectives.

Recent Improvements in Fiscal Frameworks in Emerging Market Economies

Argentina. The 1999 Fiscal Responsibility Law, as modified in December 2000, sets a ceiling for the deficit and requires that it should decline so that balance is achieved in 2005. Provincial governments undertook to enact similar laws. The 1999 legislation also established a Fiscal Stabilization Fund, financed through tax revenues, to dampen the impact of cyclical fluctuations and external shocks on government revenues. In addition, the law prohibits the creation of off-budget items, sets out new reporting requirements, and provides for penalties for civil servants who do not implement the budget.

Brazil. The 2000 Fiscal Responsibility Law prohibits financial support operations among different levels of government, sets limits on personnel expenditure, and requires that limits on the indebtedness of each level of government be set by the senate. It also includes measures to improve transparency and accountability.

Peru. The 1999 Fiscal Transparency Law sets limits on the deficit and the growth of government expenditure. It also established a fiscal stabilization fund to ensure that fiscal savings in good years can be used during recessions and contains measures to encourage transparency.

Similar fiscal responsibility legislation is being drafted in *Colombia* and is before parliament in *India.*

and implementation of fiscal policy. The United Kingdom, for example, introduced deficit and debt rules after having experienced in the early 1990s the unwinding of a sizable fiscal adjustment achieved during the 1980s. Second, problems caused by lax fiscal policy can spill from one jurisdiction to the next within a currency area or a federation. This would provide justification for the deficit and debt limits in a European framework under the Maastricht Treaty.

Assessing Institutional Reforms

The advantage of deficit rules is that, compared with other approaches, they are clear and focus on a generally well-understood macroeconomic aggregate. The main criticism of deficit rules in general, and balanced budget rules in particular, is that they are inflexible and therefore tend to be procyclical.[26] This is an important issue for national governments, although less so for subnational governments owing to the openness of regions within a country.[27] Deficit rules for national governments have increasingly been refined to address this problem and now generally apply either to a cyclically adjusted deficit measure or an average over the economic cycle. Thus, these rules allow the operation of automatic stabilizers and possibly provide some room for discretionary policy within the cycle.[28] This increased flexibility comes at a cost, how-

ever, since the benchmark against which fiscal performance is to be judged is made more complicated (especially if estimates of potential output are revised, as discussed earlier). This increases the scope to bypass the rules, making them potentially harder to enforce, which in turn undermines credibility.

Debt ceilings can be a useful adjunct to deficit rules, although the definition of an appropriate ceiling is difficult.[29] In practice, debt ceilings have been driven not by calculations based on theory but rather by concerns about reducing high debt levels, and have thus generally been chosen on the basis of circumstances of individual countries.[30] However, if debt is well below the ceiling, there may be significant room for maneuver in the short term and little restraint on policy.[31]

Expenditure rules typically impose ceilings on specific areas of expenditure—for example, discretionary as opposed to nondiscretionary and, in some cases, for particular programs.[32] The principal advantages of capping expenditure are that this process is well understood by players in

[26]Alberto Alesina and Roberto Perotti, "Budget Deficits and Budget Institutions," in *Fiscal Institutions and Fiscal Performance*, ed. by James Poterba and Jurgen Von Hagen (Chicago: University of Chicago Press, 1999).

[27]Tamim Bayoumi and Barry Eichengreen, "Restraining Yourself: The Implications of Fiscal Rules for Economic Stabilization," *IMF Staff Papers*, International Monetary Fund, Vol. 42 (March 1995).

[28]According to the 1997 Resolution of the European Council on the Stability and Growth Pact (European Council Resolution 97/C), the "close to balance requirement" under the Pact also leaves room for automatic stabilizers to operate (and in some cases for discretionary measures) without breaking the 3 percent of GDP deficit limit under the Maastricht Treaty. See Michael Artis and Marco Buti, " 'Close to Balance or in Surplus': A Policy-Maker's Guide to the Implementation of the Stability and Growth Pact," *Journal of Common Market Studies,* Vol 38, No. 4 (November 2000).

[29]Theory provides little guidance. Three distinct approaches are contained in Robert J. Barro, "On the Determination of Public Debt," *Journal of Political Economy*, Vol. 87 (October 1979) pp. 940–71; Gian Maria Milesi-Ferretti and Nouriel Roubini, "On the Taxation of Human and Physical Capital in Models of Endogenous Growth," *Journal of Public Economics*, Vol. 70 (November 1998); and S. Rao Aiyagari and Ellen R. McGrattan, "The Optimum Quantity of Debt," *Journal of Monetary Economics,* Vol. 42 (October 1998) pp. 447–69.

[30]See, in this regard, the debate on eliminating the U.S. federal government debt summarized in recent papers prepared for the September 2000 Brookings Panel on Economic Activity: for example, Vincent Reinhart and Brian Sack, "The Economic Consequences of Disappearing Government Debt," *Brookings Papers on Economic Activity*: 2, Brookings Institution (2000) and, in the same issue, Michael J. Fleming, "Financial Market Implications of the Federal Debt Paydown."

[31]The choice of debt measure is also an issue: gross debt can be easily measured and compared across countries, but net debt is the best indicator to assess fiscal sustainability, although it presents substantial measurement difficulties (in terms of which assets to consider and how to value them).

[32]This interpretation excludes the medium-term expenditure frameworks that some countries (e.g., the United Kingdom) have put in place.

budget negotiations and the wider public, and it tackles deficit bias by addressing the principal source of rising deficits, namely political and institutional pressures to increase expenditure. Governments are also made accountable for what they can control most directly, which is not the case with deficits, given that they are highly dependent on economic developments. Ceilings on specific expenditure items can impose fiscal discipline while allowing the operation of automatic stabilizers on both the revenue and on the expenditure side, and can therefore operate in effect like a cyclically adjusted deficit rule. In contrast, caps on overall spending could force unwarranted cuts in discretionary spending items during a cyclical downturn in order to support higher transfer spending.

Fiscal transparency helps to relax the trade-off between the need for flexibility and discipline in fiscal policy. A commitment to transparency should improve credibility generally and increase the chances that a government can retain credibility in the event that it needs to temporarily deviate from, or substantively change, its fiscal rules or targets. In this context, it is noteworthy that Japan introduced a rules-based approach in 1997 without a commitment to transparency, but was forced to abandon this approach in the wake of the Asian crisis. As noted above, New Zealand, Australia, and the United Kingdom have recently introduced legislation specifically directed at enhancing transparency. Among other things, these frameworks address the standard criticism of rules—namely, that rules encourage creative accounting—by adopting uniform accounting and classification standards and setting demanding reporting requirements as a means of encouraging independent scrutiny.[33] Hence, transparency legislation can complement other elements of a fiscal framework, such as deficit

rules. Legislation, however, is not the only means to achieve fiscal transparency; in other advanced economies, such as Canada, Sweden, and the United States, transparency is associated with a long tradition of open government.

The Impact of Institutional Reform

As fiscal developments in OECD countries in the 1990s have shared a common pattern, it is difficult to see substantial differences in behavior between countries such as Australia, New Zealand, and the United Kingdom, which have most emphasized fiscal frameworks based on transparency; the overall group of EU countries, with the strongest rules-based approach to fiscal policy; and North America, where the United States in particular places more emphasis on procedural rules. Against this background, the specific role of fiscal rules and transparency in contributing to fiscal adjustment is not immediately obvious. However, some other evidence points in this direction, especially for the euro area and North America.

For the euro area, one recent study notes that fiscal rules have been associated with stronger fiscal performance and have been less reactive to cyclical fluctuations and monetary policy changes in the 1990s than in earlier periods.[34] This difference has been ascribed to a "Maastricht effect." The effect appears to have been more pronounced in high-debt countries— Greece, Italy, and Belgium—as well as in countries that experienced large increases in debt ratios in the period preceding Maastricht, such as Finland, the Netherlands, and Portugal. This may be viewed as evidence of the effectiveness of strict quantitative targets, but one could also argue that the underlying political commitment to qualify for EMU and concerns about high debt levels were the real forces behind the large fiscal

---

[33]See Gian Maria Milesi-Ferretti, "Good, Bad, or Ugly? On the Effects of Fiscal Rules with Creative Accounting," IMF Working Paper 00/172 (Washington: International Monetary Fund, October 2000). The elaborate peer review process in the European Union, combined with common principles of fiscal accounting, is intended in part to limit the scope for creative accounting.

[34]Von Hagen, Hallett, and Strauch, "Budgetary Consolidation in EMU." The empirical evidence presented in this and in similar studies should be regarded cautiously because the effectiveness of both transparency and fiscal rules, and especially rules supposed to apply over the cycle, can only be assessed over an extended period.

adjustment during the 1990s. [35] Evidence from U.S. state governments also indicates that balanced budget rules have lowered fiscal deficits and public debt, but at the cost of more limited automatic stabilizers.[36]

For the U.S. federal government, several studies have concluded that the specific expenditure ceilings embodied in the Budget Enforcement Act have played a significant role in reducing expenditure. This approach was better suited to the U.S. budget process than the earlier deficit reduction targets contained in the Gramm-Rudman-Hollings Act, which were so sensitive to economic and technical factors that they threatened large sequestrations that could not be implemented, thereby undermining credibility.[37] In Canada, expenditure reviews across government to identify specific areas where permanent cuts would be feasible and reforms to the expenditure management system were deemed largely successful in contributing to fiscal improvements.[38]

Transparency also seems to have played a central role in locking in fiscal adjustment and pre-

venting the unwinding of previous reforms, as in New Zealand, for example. However, the New Zealand legislation did not prevent recent slippage relative to long-term fiscal goals, and this has cast some doubt on whether transparency by itself is sufficient to promote fiscal responsibility.[39] In the United Kingdom, the combination of transparency and fiscal rules has supported the adjustment process. The use of deliberately prudent forecasting assumptions, together with unexpected structural improvements to the level of receipts, has now created substantial room for maneuver within current fiscal rules; hence, the role of transparency in sustaining fiscal policy credibility will continue to be very important.[40]

Fiscal rules and frameworks are a recent innovation, so definitive statements are difficult to make. Nevertheless, the real test appears likely to come during an economic slowdown when pressures emerge to unwind recent fiscal adjustment by more than can be justified under the established rules. In particular, the expenditure reductions that have spearheaded recent adjustment may be significantly reversed. Such a circumstance is tailor made for fiscal rules, and especially expenditure ceilings, which can help to directly contain reversals on the spending side while providing scope for countercyclical fiscal policy, and a debt ceiling, which addresses longer-term sustainability. One conclusion is clear. The credibility of fiscal rules and objectives is strengthened if such measures are accompanied by enhanced fiscal transparency, as this openness complements a rules-based approach in three ways: by removing any tendency to be nontransparent to meet rules; by facilitating judgments of actual fiscal performance against

[35]However, note that while adjustment in the Netherlands may have been primarily driven by EMU considerations, the switch to a fiscal framework emphasizing expenditure ceilings in 1994 has been judged to have resulted in a smoother and more predictable budget process, as discussed in *OECD Economic Surveys: The Netherlands* (Paris: Organization for Economic Cooperation and Development, 1998).

[36]See James M. Poterba, "State Responses to Fiscal Crises: The Effects of Budgetary Institutions and Politics," *Journal of Political Economy*, Vol. 102 (1994); James E. Alt, "Credibility, Transparency, Accountability, Institutions," paper prepared for the Annual Meeting of the American Political Science Association, Washington, DC (September 2000); and Bayoumi and Eichengreen "Restraining Yourself."

[37]James M. Poterba, "Do Budget Rules Work?" in *Fiscal Policy: Lessons from Empirical Research*, ed. by Alan Auerbach (Cambridge, Mass.: MIT Press, 1997), pp. 53–86; *OECD Economic Surveys: The United States 1999* (Paris: Organization for Economic Cooperation and Development, 1999); and Allan Schick, "A Surplus, If We Can Keep It," *The Brookings Review*, Brookings Institution, Vol. 18, No. 1 (2000).

[38]See *OECD Economic Surveys: Canada 1998–1999* (Paris: Organization for Economic Cooperation and Development, 1999); and OECD, "Managing Structural Deficit Reduction," Public Management Occasional Paper No. 11 (Paris: Organization for Economic Cooperation and Development, 1996).

[39]*OECD Economic Surveys: New Zealand 1999* (Paris: Organization for Economic Cooperation and Development, 1999.)

[40]IMF, "United Kingdom: Staff Report for the 1999 Article IV Consultation" (Washington: International Monetary Fund, 2000), available at http://www.imf.org/external/pubind.htm. Finland and the Netherlands also incorporate cautious growth assumptions in their fiscal projections.

rules, which makes transparency an essential requirement for rules to be effective; and by allowing justifiable flexibility in the application of rules.

Future Fiscal Performance

A much more significant test to fiscal positions and frameworks will come from the economic pressures arising from the substantially older demographic structure that the advanced economies will face in the first half of the twenty-first century. The economic challenges associated with aging populations are unique—not simply because of the unprecedented nature of these developments, but also because the pressures are fairly predictable. Of even greater significance is that a number of reasonably well-recognized policy measures could, if implemented in a timely manner, largely offset the adverse consequences of aging on output growth and fiscal balances. Unfortunately, though, while some countries (e.g., the United Kingdom and Sweden) have taken substantial steps in recent years to put their public pension systems on a sounder financial footing, reforms efforts elsewhere (e.g., Germany and France) have been of only limited scope and marked by controversy and delay. Such delays will only increase the cost of the adjustments that will eventually be required.

Demographic and Fiscal Outlook

Because of the dramatic rise in births immediately following World War II and the subsequent fall in fertility, the advanced economies face a significant aging of their population structure over the next several decades. The coming retirement of the baby boom generation will lead to a steady rise in elderly dependency ratios, initially in Japan and then in the European Union and the United States (Figure 3.7).

Though interrelated in practice, it is useful to distinguish between the consequences of aging for fiscal balances (considered in this section) and for the real economy (considered below).

Figure 3.7. Elderly Dependency Ratios[1]
(Percent)

Elderly dependency ratios will rise significantly over the next few decades as the baby boom generation retires.

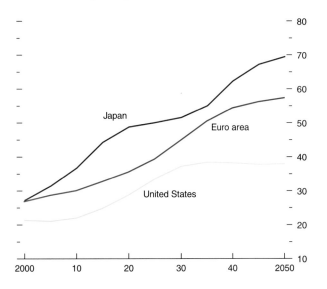

Source: United States Census Bureau.
[1]Ratio of population aged 65 and older to population aged 20–64.

In terms of fiscal balances, public pension systems in the advanced countries have been established either with partial pre-funding (as in the United States, Japan, and Canada) or on a largely unfunded "pay-as-you-go" basis (as in many EU countries).[41] In general, however, virtually all pension systems face substantial net liabilities in the decade ahead, even after taking into account asset positions and projected contributions from current and future workers. Fiscal projections produced by the OECD and European Union, each using global macroeconomic models, suggest generally similar patterns.[42] As a direct result of meeting liabilities generated by current pension schemes, fiscal positions over the next 50 years would reach a peak deterioration of around 2 to 3 percent of GDP in the United States, 4 to 5 percent in the European Union (although very little change in the United Kingdom), and 10 percent in Japan (OECD projections are shown in Figure 3.8).[43] Recent reforms to pension systems—notably in Japan—have helped to reduce these projected

[41]With pre-funding, contributions to the pension scheme exceed payouts while dependency ratios are still relatively low, leading to asset accumulation by the pension fund. These assets, possibly combined with contributions from concurrent workers, can then be drawn on to provide pensions to individuals retiring when dependency ratios are high. With a purely unfunded system, contributions from concurrent workers are the sole source of finance for public pensions of concurrent retirees.

[42]See Dave Turner, Claude Giorno, Alain De Serres, Ann Vourc'h, and Pete Richardson, "The Macroeconomic Implications of Ageing in a Global Context," OECD Economics Department Working Paper No. 193 (Paris: Organization for Economic Cooperation and Development, 1998); and Kieran McMorrow and Werner Roeger, "The Economic Consequences of Ageing Populations," Economic Papers No. 138 (Brussels: European Commission, November 1999). National-level pension simulations for EU countries, using a generally similar set of underlying economic assumptions, are reported in Economic Policy Committee, "Progress Report to the Ecofin Council on the Impact of Ageing Populations on Public Pension Systems," EPC/ECFIN/581/00 (Brussels: European Commission, November 2000).

[43]The OECD's reference scenario draws on United Nations' population projections to 2050. These show population growth turning negative in Japan and the European Union after 2010, declining to around zero in the United States and other "fast-aging" regions by 2050, while

Figure 3.8. Direct Effects of Aging on Government Finances
(Percent of GDP)

Population aging is likely to impose a significant fiscal burden, especially through increases in pension and health expenditures.

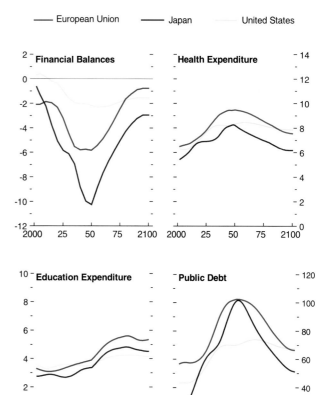

Source: Dave Turner, Claude Giorno, Alain de Serres, Ann Vourc'h and Pete Richardson, "The Macroeconomic Implications of Aging in a Global Context," OECD Economics Department Working Paper No. 193 (Paris: OECD, 1998).

imbalances, but substantial pressures remain (see Box 3.1).

In addition to pension benefits, rising health care costs as the population ages will impose a further burden on public finances. Health care costs per capita for the elderly are several times those for the non-elderly; furthermore, overall health expenditures have been rising as a share of GDP over recent decades, despite much more favorable demographic trends.[44] In the relatively optimistic scenario (compared with recent trends) where per capita treatment costs rise at the same rate as real GDP, public health spending in most advanced economies could increase by around 2 to 3 percent of GDP over the next 50 years as a direct result of aging (Figure 3.8). Little if any offset can be expected from reduced public education expenditures: these are projected to remain roughly constant as a share of GDP (Figure 3.8).

Without reforms to boost revenue or contain spending, the age-related expenditure pressures would lead to a rapid and significant buildup of public debt. Net debt as a share of GDP could in-crease by around 80 percent in Japan by 2050, by 45 percent in the European Union, and 30 percent in the United States (Figure 3.8). These projections assume, however, that the debt buildup is limited through tax increases.[45] EU estimates, prepared without such a constraint, indicate that debt in the European Union could increase by around 150 percent of GDP by 2050.[46]

Generational accounting provides further insights into the fiscal pressures arising from aging populations. By explicitly taking into account the government's intertemporal budget constraint, this methodology assesses the present value of taxes (net of transfer payments received) that individuals of different age cohorts need to pay over their remaining lifetimes to finance the future stream of public expenditures. Recent studies have drawn attention to the very high remaining net taxes facing young and middle-aged members of many advanced economies under current tax and transfer policies, partly because current transfers to the elderly are often generous compared to earlier payments into the system.[47] Moreover, on the basis that net government liabilities not met by current generations will have to be paid by future generations, current policies imply that generations yet to be born could face much higher lifetime net taxes than those arising at present. Restoring generational balance would require either substantial reductions in government spending on current generations, increases in taxes, or some combi-

---

staying above 1 percent per year in the remaining "slow-aging" parts of the world until the 2040s. By around 2080, population growth is assumed to converge at around ½ percent per year. Age-specific participation rates are assumed to be constant, as are unemployment rates. Growth in labor-augmenting technical progress converges to about 1½ percent per year. On this basis, annual GDP growth in Japan and the European Union falls to under ½ percent in the 2030s, and to around 1.5 to 1.7 percent in the United States and other fast-aging regions, while growth in slow-aging regions remains above 2 percent until the mid-2050s. Growth in each region converges to just below 2 percent in the final quarter of the century.

[44]The OECD estimates that the ratio of health costs for the elderly compared with the non-elderly is 4¾ in Japan, 4¼ in the United States, and 3 in the European Union. If per capita treatment costs were to rise at a one percent faster rate than GDP growth (i.e., more in line with recent trends), public health care spending would increase by 4 to 5 percent of GDP by 2030, whereas public health spending would be largely contained around current levels if per capita health costs grow 1 percent slower than GDP growth. See Deborah Roseveare, Willi Leibfritz, Douglas Fore, and Eckhard Wurzel, "Ageing Populations, Pension Systems and Government Budgets: Simulations for 20 OECD countries," OECD Economics Department Working Paper No. 168 (Paris: Organization for Economic Cooperation and Development, September 1996).

[45]In particular, the OECD estimates include a "debt containment" rule, whereby the increase in net public debt is limited to six times the increase in net public spending (as shares of GDP). In Japan, the policy approach is to raise social security contribution rates as needed to ensure the solvency of the system. If this approach is maintained, the impact on the fiscal position would therefore be less than that suggested by the OECD and EU estimates.

[46]Kieran McMorrow and Werner Roger, "The Economic Consequences of Ageing Populations."

[47]Laurence Kotlikoff and Willi Leibfritz, "An International Comparison of Generational Accounts," in *Generational Accounting around the World*, ed. by Alan Auerbach, Laurence Kotlikoff, and Willi Leibfritz (Chicago: University of Chicago Press, 1999). See also "Uses and Limitations of Generational Accounting," Box 5 in the May 1996 *World Economic Outlook*.

nation of these measures.[48] As noted earlier, delaying such policy reforms would only increase the scale of the required adjustments.

Saving Public Pension Systems

The demographic trends outlined above are expected to lead to significantly slower growth rates of aggregate output and average living standards over the next half century. For example, in the OECD scenario discussed earlier, growth in per capita GDP is projected to fall to around 1 percent a year in the United States, the European Union, and Japan over the next two to three decades, compared with growth in the 1990s averaging around 1½ to 2 percent. Regardless of whether pension systems are public or private, funded or unfunded, the fundamental concern arising from rising dependency ratios is how a potentially more slowly growing pool of output will be shared between a relatively smaller workforce and a relatively larger dependent population. From this perspective, policy responses to the fiscal and broader economic consequences of aging populations need to be assessed not only in terms of how they will affect *claims* on future output, but also how they will influence the *level* of future output that will be available. Policies affecting output shares may become less burdensome and divisive, the greater the total output that is available.

As considered in subsequent sections, a range of reforms to domestic pension systems has aimed to reduce claims of current and prospective retirees on future output. But, in addition, there is substantial scope for reform to counteract the projected slowing in growth of output and living standards, particularly by improving labor market performance. Increased pre-

funding of pension liabilities could also help to ease the sharing of the pension burden across generations and, by increasing national saving and lowering interest rates, could contribute to faster output growth. Setting the output constraint described above in an international context provides a further perspective on policies that could help address the challenge of aging populations. In this case, the focus needs to be on production and distribution of global rather than national output. In particular, increasing globalization offers the prospect of larger saving flows from the advanced economies supporting investment and growth in more slowly aging developing countries. These saving patterns would then reverse as output slows in fast-aging regions, with domestic consumption in these countries supported through increased imports. These points are considered in more detail below.

Domestic Reforms

National responses to pension system imbalances have in many cases focused on reducing pension entitlements of future retirees. For example, pension replacement rates compared with past earnings have been reduced by linking pensions to lifetime earnings rather than to earnings just in the years immediately preceding retirement. In some countries (e.g., Australia and New Zealand), flat rate rather than earnings-linked pensions are provided. Pensions have been increasingly indexed to prices rather than wages. This implies that, with productivity growth, the purchasing power of pensioners relative to wage earners would fall over time, although some countries have introduced measures to limit the extent of this decline.

In addition, however, more attention could be focused on reforms aimed at improving labor market performance, which could go a long way toward supporting output growth and fiscal positions as populations age. This is particularly the case in Europe, where the scope for increasing the employment of older age groups (e.g., 55–64), both through higher participation and lower unemployment, appears to be substantially

---

[48]For example, under the assumptions employed by Kotlikoff and Leibfritz in "An International Comparison of Generational Accounts," immediate cuts of around 20 to 40 percent in transfer spending would be needed in most of the large industrialized economies, or across-the-board tax increases of 10 to 15 percent in the United States, Japan, and Germany, and over 60 percent in Italy.

greater than in the United States and Japan (Figure 3.9). Female participation rates also remain low in some euro area countries (for example, Spain), due in part to restrictions on the use of part-time employment. Simulations by the European Union indicate that a comprehensive package of labor market reforms that led to a 10 percentage point increase in the overall labor force participation rate—bringing it to around the same level as in the United States and Japan—would largely eliminate the adverse impact of aging on future GDP growth. Similarly, projected pension expenditures in Germany, France, and Italy would take on a much flatter profile if participation and unemployment in these countries gradually converged on rates recently reached by the best three EU performers.[49]

A moderate extension of the retirement age (or contribution period) needed to obtain a full pension could form part of such a package. Various studies have indicated that this reform would substantially reduce the fiscal burden of pensions, both by increasing labor force participation, output, and hence government revenues, and by reducing pension payouts.[50] In the OECD projections discussed earlier, a gradual increase of five years in the retirement age in the United States, Japan, and the European Union would roughly halve the fiscal deficits projected

Figure 3.9. Employment—Population Ratios by Age, Selected Countries, 1999
(Percent)

There is substantial scope for reforms, especially in the euro area, to boost employment among older age groups.

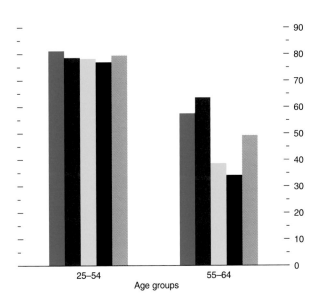

Sources: OECD Labor Force Statistics; and United States Census Bureau.

[49]Specifically, these adjustments imply an increase of close to 10 percentage points in the EU employment rate by 2010 (from 61 to around 70 percent), and a further increase of nearly 10 percentage points by 2045. Stronger productivity growth and more favorable demographic trends (than in the baseline scenario) are also assumed. With economic growth strengthening as a result, pension expenditures in Germany would rise by a peak level of just under 2½ percent of GDP over their 2000 level (compared with a rise of nearly 4½ percent of GDP without these labor market improvements); the corresponding peak increase would be 2½ percent of GDP for France and ½ percent for Italy, compared with 4 percent of GDP for France and 1½ percent for Italy without reforms.

[50]See, for example, Dave Turner and others, "The Macroeconomic Implications of Ageing in a Global Context;" and Sheetal K. Chand and Albert Jaeger, "Aging Populations and Public Pension Schemes," IMF Occasional Paper No. 147 (Washington: International Monetary Fund, 1996).

for 2050. This reform, as with other labor market measures noted above, would need to be coordinated with reductions in the strong disincentives that exist under current tax and transfer systems for labor force participation by older workers.[51]

Pre-Funding Pension Liabilities

If the government seeks to smooth welfare across generations, then part of the future increase in transfers and expenditures would be met by increased net taxes (or "mandatory savings") on current workers. Primary fiscal surpluses would rise during the working lives of the current large cohort, enabling public debt to be reduced and, in some cases, allowing a buildup of net public financial assets at home and abroad. During the retirement of this baby boom generation, part of the cost of its pension benefits will be financed by public dissaving and part through taxes paid by the working generation. Implicitly, then, this approach would be equivalent to adding a funded component to the largely unfunded pension system that currently prevails.

Pre-funding future pension liabilities would provide a further means of increasing future output, to the extent that national saving and capital accumulation rise in response. With tax rates smoothed over time, the welfare costs of tax distortions would be minimized.[52] Reducing public debt prior to the retirement of the baby boomers would also provide greater scope for covering higher pension costs out of concurrent government expenditure, given the induced decline in real interest rates and reduction in debt servicing costs.

International Dimensions

With public policy discussions on pension reform usually taking a country-by-country perspective, the open economy aspects of aging populations have been relatively neglected.[53] Illustrating the importance of these international dimensions, the projected increase in overall dependency rates (of young and old relative to the 20- to 64-year-old group) in the major industrial economies and other fast-aging countries is partially offset by the fall in dependency rates in countries that, by 2050, will account for nearly half of world GDP (Figure 3.10).[54] In view of the negative effect of rising dependency rates on private and national saving, the financing of public pension obligations in the aging countries will affect the distribution of trade balances and capital flows within the global economy.[55]

Output, Trade, and Capital Flows

In a closed national economy, the growth rate of average per capita consumption across generations would be likely to fall as the dependency ratio increased, driven by the lower pace of output growth. Hence, maintaining the living standards of retirees in an aging society would eventually come at the cost of relatively lower living standards of workers and the young.[56] In an

[51]See Jonathan Gruber and David Wise, "An International Perspective on Policies for an Aging Society," NBER Working Paper No. 8103 (Cambridge, Mass.: National Bureau of Economic Research, January 2001), and references therein.
[52]See Robert Barro, "On the Determination of Public Debt;" and V. V. Chari and Patrick Kehoe, "Optimal Fiscal and Monetary Policy," in *Handbook of Macroeconomics*, ed. by Michael Woodford and John Taylor (New York: North Holland, 1999).

[53]These multilateral issues have established a foothold in the research literature, however, and have been incorporated into econometric models of the OECD, European Union, and IMF that generate some of the simulations referred to in this chapter. See also Robin Brooks, "Population Aging and Global Capital Flows in a Parallel Universe," IMF Working Paper 00/151 (Washington: International Monetary Fund, 2000); and Credit Suisse First Boston, *Euro Area Weekly*, "Re-centering the Debate on Pensions," (London: CSFB, November 2000).
[54]The fall in the total dependency rate in developing countries is due to a relatively slow increase in the old-age dependency rate (compared with the industrial countries) and to a significant decline in the youth dependency rate.
[55]See, for example, Paul Masson, Tamim Bayoumi, and Hossein Samiei, "Saving Behavior in Industrial and Developing Countries," *Staff Studies for the World Economic Outlook*, (Washington: International Monetary Fund, 1995).
[56]If retirees seek to reduce their assets to maintain consumption, these competing claims would be equilibrated in part by rising real interest rates.

Figure 3.10. Total Dependency Ratios[1]
(Percent)

Rising dependency ratios among industrial and other fast aging countries will be partly offset by declining rates of dependency in the rest of the world.

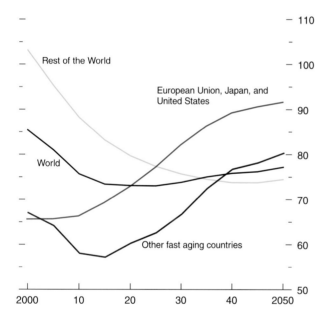

Source: United States Census Bureau.
[1]Ratio of 0–19 and 65+ age groups to 20–64 age group.

open economy, however, a much smoother path of consumption (and real interest rates) over the life cycle may be feasible for all generations following a fertility boom. This is particularly the case if there is some degree of complementarity between fast- and slow-aging economies regarding saving and investment flows. With international trade in goods, services, and financial assets, the growth rate of national absorption per capita does not need to match the growth rate of output per capita as the dependency ratio falls and then rises. Openness can allow the industrialized countries to continue to provide stable rates of per capita consumption growth even as the share of employment falls. These countries can in fact accumulate foreign assets, through an increase in the current account balance, over the working life of the baby boomers. As this generation retires and the dependency ratio rises, running down these assets, as well as additional foreign borrowing, can then sustain consumption via a decrease in the current account balance.

An approximate assessment of these flows is provided by the OECD study discussed earlier, which projects saving and current account balances. In the reference scenario, the industrial countries will substantially increase their current account positions in the first few decades of the twenty-first century, reaching peak levels of about 2 percent of GDP in both the United States and Japan, and 3 percent in the euro area, in the 2010s (Figure 3.11).

This would allow a large increase in net foreign assets, of around 40 to 50 percent of GDP in the United States, Japan, and the euro area, by the 2030s. Developing countries (both fast and slow aging) will absorb these capital inflows, whether in the form of debt or equity, to sustain their relatively rapid investment growth.

The situation will then reverse. As the population ages and output growth slows, industrial countries will progressively sustain consumption by increasing imports of goods and services. Current accounts will rapidly turn into deficits for several decades, reaching average levels of 3 to 4 percent of GDP. Such imbalances will not only exhaust the foreign assets accumulated earlier in the century but will also induce industrial countries to borrow heavily, creating net foreign liabilities of around 50 percent of GDP by the third quarter of the century. Developing countries will be able to sustain saving and share their production with industrial countries thanks to a slower aging pattern as well as higher output growth and (by then) larger economic size: their combined current account surpluses would barely reach 2 percent of GDP.

The extent of these projected capital movements between industrial and developing countries would be unprecedented in recent times. In the last 30 years, net foreign asset positions of industrial countries declined from about plus 4 percent of their combined GDP in 1970 to approximately minus 4 percent in 1998, largely driven by the increase in U.S. foreign liabilities.[57] Capital flows of the projected size were, however, seen during the gold standard, indicating that such sustained flows could again be accommodated within the international financial system.[58]

In the context of such an increase in international financial integration, a central issue concerns the quality of capital markets and policies in developing countries. The large capital flows projected above would be warranted on the basis of an efficient global allocation of resources, given the higher productivity in developing countries and the outlined demographic trends. However, the risks associated with poorer institutional frameworks and higher economic and pol-

[57]Individual countries, however, experienced larger changes in net foreign asset positions. Extreme cases include Ireland, whose net foreign asset position has increased from –80 percent of GDP in 1970 to approximate balance in 1998, and Switzerland, whose position declined from about 70 percent in 1970 to about 20 percent in 1980. For estimates of historical data of stocks of foreign assets and liabilities, see Philip Lane and Gian Maria Milesi-Ferretti, "The External Wealth of Nations," *Journal of International Economics* (forthcoming).

[58]See Charles Bean, "The External Constraint in the U.K.," in *External Constraints on Macroeconomic Policy: The European Experience,* ed. by George Alogoskoufis, Lucas Papademos, and Richard Portes (Cambridge, England: Cambridge University Press, 1991).

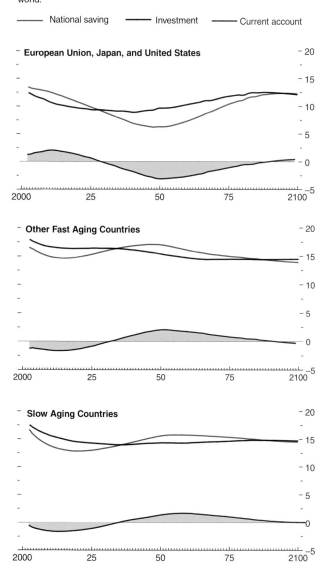

Figure 3.11. Saving, Investment, and Current Account Balances in the Reference Scenario
(Percent of GDP)

A buildup of foreign assets by the industrial countries over the next 20–30 years would help both to sustain consumption in these countries as their populations age and to finance investment in the rest of the world.

Source: Dave Turner, Claude Giorno, Alain de Serres, Ann Vourc'h and Pete Richardson, "The Macroeconomic Implications of Aging in a Global Context," OECD Economics Department Working Paper No. 193 (Paris: OECD, 1998).

Table 3.1. Net Migration Flows to Major Industrial Economies in 2000 to 2050
(Average Annual Number: thousands)

	Scenario I Constant Total Population	Scenario II Constant 15–65 Age Group	Scenario III Constant Dependency Ratio[1]	Scenario IV Average Net Migration 1990–1998
United States	128	359	11,851	1,015
Japan	343	647	10,471	−3
European Union	949	1,588	13,480	857
Germany	344	487	3,630	404
France	29	109	1,792	59
Italy	251	372	2,268	114
United Kingdom	53	125	1,194	73

Source: United Nations Population Division
[1]65+ age group relative to 15–64 group.

icy uncertainty in developing economies may discourage flows toward these countries and even induce, at times, sudden and massive reversal. Further development of capital markets and institutions in developing countries would be required in order to improve protection of property rights, strengthen supervisory and regulatory regimes, enhance transparency in financial intermediation, and ensure that financial flows are properly channeled to productive investment activities. Although sound macroeconomic policies would raise the confidence of international investors, vigilance and the assistance of the international financial institutions would also play a role in preventing possible financial crises.

International Migration

Migration of labor provides a potential mechanism for reducing the level of capital flows that would be needed to smooth consumption over demographic cycles in the industrialized economies. In particular, migration from countries with younger populations to those with aging populations would help to reduce dependency ratios and increase output and consumption in faster-aging countries. Immigration should slow the growth of labor costs in the most industrialized countries as the labor pool shrinks. Global output could also increase, to the extent that labor productivity of immigrants is higher in the recipient country than in the home country. A source of concern may be the loss of human capital (or "brain drain") from developing countries, although increased labor mobility might also facilitate the return of skilled workers to their home countries.

Hence, governments may have an incentive to relax restrictions on immigration as their populations age.[59] By increasing the tax base, immigration would help ease fiscal constraints on making public pension payments to retirees. In contrast, borrowing to finance the consumption of an aging population may be costly, as this could compete with high demand for investment in the middle- and low-income countries with rapid technological progress and development.

Increased migration would need to be part of a broader package of reform measures, however, rather than the principal means by which aging populations are supported. This point is illustrated by recent United Nations' projections indicating the level of migration that would be required over the next half century to either maintain a constant total population (Scenario I in Table 3.1), stabilize the working age population (Scenario II), or keep a constant elderly dependency ratio (Scenario III). For the United States and the European Union, the migration required to stabilize the population is not out of line with inflows during the 1990s (shown in column IV of Table 3.1); in the United States, re-

---

[59]The negative impact of immigration on wages could strengthen the lobby against relaxing immigration restrictions. The tightening of restrictions on immigration, however, are most often associated with periods of falling real wages rather with periods of rising real wages.

cent immigration flows in fact exceed the level needed to maintain a constant working age population. But the migration inflows needed to stabilize dependency ratios—in the range of 10 to 13 million people a year in the United States, Japan, and the European Union—are clearly far above recent levels, and probably higher than would be politically and economically feasible in the foreseeable future.

Globalization provides an important route through which future pension costs can be absorbed. As with the essential domestic reforms discussed earlier, the size of adjustment in any one dimension—accumulation and decumulation of net foreign assets, the associated trade flows, and migration—implies that all of these channels need to be involved to some extent in resolving the pension problem.

CHAPTER IV

THE DECLINE OF INFLATION IN EMERGING MARKETS: CAN IT BE MAINTAINED?

Recent years have witnessed a dramatic decline in inflation in emerging market economies.[1] By the end of 2000, average inflation in emerging markets had declined from triple-digit figures in the late 1980s to some 5 percent excluding a few outlier cases—Indonesia, Turkey, and Venezuela (Table 4.1). Such low levels of inflation have not been seen since before World War II, when, mostly under the discipline of the gold standard system of fixed exchange rates, prices were roughly stable and episodes of deflation were not uncommon. The recent decline of inflation in emerging markets looks all the more impressive against the background of the 1970s and 1980s. Inflation began to rise gradually in the 1950s, but it accelerated dramatically in the 1970s and early 1980s, culminating in several episodes of triple-digit annual inflation and four major hyperinflations in the late 1980s/early 1990s (Figure 4.1).[2] From that point on, disinflation was steep.

This rise and fall of inflation in emerging markets appears to reflect in part changes in the international monetary system and inflation trends in advanced countries. One notable feature of the post-World War II period was an increase in inflation persistence compared with earlier historical eras, when inflation was either generalized and gradual (e.g., following the gold discoveries of the fifteenth through the nineteenth century), or rapid and specific, reflecting exceptional fiscal strains (as during or immediately after wars).[3] This gradual increase in the persistence of inflation, combined with the breakup of the Bretton Woods international system of commodity-based money and the associated removal of external constraints on accommodative monetary policies, made it possible for the supply shocks of the 1970s to push world inflation to unprecedented peacetime levels, producing the "Great Inflation" of the 1970s and early 1980s.[4] To the extent that emerging markets imported this inflation, loosened fiscal policies, and also adopted increasingly accommodative monetary policies during the period, these external trends were reflected in those countries' prices and magnified further. Conversely, as governments in advanced countries responded to public dissatisfaction with inflation, and institutional and operational changes were put in place to foster monetary and fiscal policy discipline, this helped bring inflation in advanced countries back under control. This combination of falling external inflation and the adoption of sounder macroeconomic policies, also in response to public dissatisfaction with high inflation, explains much of the recent fall in inflation in emerging markets.

---

[1]For the purposes of this chapter, the following 24 countries are defined as emerging markets: Argentina, Brazil, Bulgaria, Chile, China, Colombia, Czech Republic, Egypt, Hungary, India, Indonesia, Israel, Korea, Malaysia, Mexico, Pakistan, Peru, Philippines, Poland, Russia, South Africa, Thailand, Turkey, and Venezuela. This group comprises countries that either have small economies with relatively high per capita income or large economies with lower per capita income. All of them have nominal GDP in excess of $50 billion (in 1999 PPP-adjusted terms) with the exception of Bulgaria, which has a nominal GDP of $12 billion but is usually classified as an emerging market.

[2]The underlying definition of hyperinflation follows that of Phillip Cagan's seminal work, which defines hyperinflation as consumer price increases in excess of 50 percent *per month*. See Phillip Cagan, "The Monetary Dynamics of Hyperinflation," in *Studies in the Quantity Theory of Money*, ed. by Milton Friedman (Chicago: University of Chicago Press, 1956). Those four episodes were: Argentina (May 1989–March 1990), Brazil (December 1989–March 1990), Peru (July–August 1990), and Russia (April 1991–January 1992).

[3]See Barry Eichengreen and Nathan Sussman, "The International System in the (Very) Long Run," *World Economic Outlook Supporting Studies* (Washington: International Monetary Fund, 2000) for a historical overview and bibliographical references.

[4]For an account of the rise and fall of inflation in advanced countries since the 1970s, see the October 1996 issue of the *World Economic Outlook*.

Table 4.1. Inflation in Industrial Countries and Emerging Markets[1]

(Annual percent)

	1900–13	1930–39	1950–60	1961–70	1971–80	1981–90	1991–95	1996–2000	2000
Advanced Economies	1.5	0.2	4.3	4.0	10.8	8.1	3.9	2.0	2.5
Selected Emerging Markets	1.2	1.6	15.2	18.3	29.8	139.7	94.4	23.4	7.8
Selected Emerging Markets, excluding Bulgaria, Indonesia, Venezuela, and Turkey	1.2	2.8	15.0	9.2	31.4	161.1	100.0	9.1	5.2

Sources: Brian Mitchell, *International Historical Statistics* (New York: Stockton Press, 1998); and IMF staff estimates.
[1]Average of annual percent change of the consumer price index over the specified period.

Within this broad picture, inflation performance has varied widely across emerging market countries and regions (Table 4.2). Asia has had the lowest inflation during much of the post-World War II period—a development associated with fiscal prudence and sound macroeconomic policies. Latin America has had the highest inflation, featuring several cases of long-lasting triple-digit inflation and hyperinflations associated with deep-seated fiscal problems and monetary accommodation. In between the Asian and Latin American extremes lie the experiences of the emerging markets of Africa, the Middle East, and Eastern Europe. Inflation has been persistently high in some (as in Israel through the early 1990s and Turkey to date), while in others, such as the Czech Republic, Poland, and Hungary, the combination of dismantling of price controls, nominal rigidities, and fiscal problems produced brief episodes of high inflation followed by gradual disinflation from the mid-1990s.

Given the harm caused by high inflation (see in Box 4.1), the recent decline of inflation in emerging markets is clearly welcome. Whether this more stable price environment is likely to be permanent and what steps need to be taken to keep inflation under control are questions of considerable policy relevance that have yet to be settled. This chapter aims to shed light on these issues by reviewing the cross-country evidence and by highlighting the main threats to the current low inflation environment. Four broad questions are addressed:

- Why has inflation been historically high in emerging markets and why has it declined sharply in recent years?

- Has there been a systematic relationship between fiscal performance and inflation?
- Which monetary regime has been better in controlling money growth and inflation?
- What additional steps need to be taken to curb inflation in some countries and to keep inflation at current low levels in others?

Why Do Countries Inflate?

The literature provides two main motives as to why inflation strikes: the need of governments to finance persistent fiscal deficits through seigniorage and the time inconsistency of economic policies.[5] Governments have financed persistent fiscal deficits by issuing money since time immemorial—witness coin clipping that occurred in Roman times. At the root of the seigniorage motive is the government's unwillingness or incapacity to avoid persistent deficits or to resort to other sources of financing to make up for the shortfall.[6] Governments generally resort to seigniorage because, compared to other revenue sources, it tends to be easier to

[5]For a survey and references see Stanley Fischer, "Modern Central Banking," in *The Future of Central Banking*, ed. by Forrest Capie, Charles Goodhart, Stanley Fischer, and Norbert Schnadt (New York: Cambridge University Press, 1994), pp. 262–308.

[6]In any period of time, seigniorage—the revenues the government obtains from issuing money—comprises both the "inflation tax"—the purchasing power losses that inflation causes to the holders of real money balances—and the change in real money balances. As the inflation tax is usually the main component of seigniorage, both terms are often used equivalently in the literature. In steady state, inflation tax and seigniorage are equal, as real balances are constant.

Figure 4.1. Inflation Over Time
(Percent change)

Emerging markets in Latin America, Europe, Africa, and the Middle East have recently accomplished a marked reduction in inflation, while Asia continues to sustain moderate to low inflation.

— Selected advanced economies
— Selected emerging markets
— Selected emerging markets—Latin America
— Selected emerging markets—Asia
— Selected emerging markets—Europe
— Selected emerging markets—Africa and the Middle East

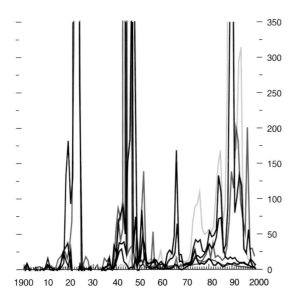

Sources: Brian Mitchell, *International Historical Statistics* (New York: Stockton Press, 1998); and IMF staff estimates.

collect and enforce and does not require the approval of the legislative body, which can be lengthy and politically difficult.

Seigniorage has varied widely across countries and over time. Reasons that might account for such wide variations in seigniorage include different spending needs (as a ratio to GDP) and the relative cost of funding those needs through a variety of taxes and borrowing instruments, with the cost of using a particular instrument rising in proportion to its use. Accordingly, incentives to use seigniorage will be lower in countries where collection of formal taxes is more efficient and borrowing is cheaper due to more developed capital markets. Seigniorage will also tend to be lower in countries where public tolerance for inflation is lower (itself a function of institutional and historical factors), and where governments' capacity to enhance the use of high-powered money (the tax base for seigniorage) is more limited—this being the case, for instance, in highly "dollarized" small open economies relative to large economies in which domestic transactions in foreign currency are rarer. In addition to these country specific factors, seigniorage has also varied over time with the advent of paper money and, even more important, with changes in the international monetary system. In particular, the breakup of the Bretton Woods fixed exchange rate system in the early 1970s, by ending the long period in which the international monetary system was commodity-based, reduced the external constraint on seigniorage. This made it easier for many countries to explore this source of revenue in the 1970s and 1980s, until public antipathy to inflation became an increasingly binding domestic constraint.

Relative to advanced countries, seigniorage has been a significant source of government revenue in many developing countries.[7] Asian coun-

---

[7]See, for instance, Berthold Herrendorf, "Time Consistent Collection of Optimal Seigniorage: A Unifying Framework," *Journal of Economic Surveys*, Vol. 11 (March, 1997), pp. 1–46; and Alex Cukierman, Sebastian Edwards, and Guido Tabellini, "Seigniorage and Political Instability," *The American Economic Review*, Vol. 82 (June 1992), pp. 537–55.

Table 4.2. Inflation in Emerging Markets
(Annual percent change in the consumer price index)

	1961–70	1971–80	1981–90	1991–95	1996–2000	2000
Africa/Middle East						
Egypt	3.2	9.5	17.0	13.9	4.4	2.7
Israel	5.6	45.0	118.3	12.9	6.4	1.1
South Africa	2.8	10.7	14.7	11.3	6.5	4.5
Asia						
China	. . .	4.1	7.2	13.1	1.8	0.3
India	6.4	8.2	8.9	10.5	7.5	3.4
Indonesia	210.6	17.5	8.6	8.9	19.1	2.5
Korea	14.8	16.5	6.4	6.2	4.0	2.3
Malaysia	0.9	6.0	3.2	4.3	3.1	1.3
Pakistan	3.5	12.4	7.0	11.2	7.3	4.4
Philippines	5.7	14.9	13.7	10.1	7.1	4.4
Thailand	2.3	10.0	4.4	4.8	4.3	1.5
Emerging Europe						
Bulgaria	. . .	. . .	7.6	132.1	242.3	10.4
Czech Republic[1]	1.0	1.1	3.4	19.2	6.8	3.9
Hungary	10.3	9.7	10.9	25.4	15.1	9.7
Poland	. . .	4.7	107.7	44.0	12.8	10.1
Russia[2]	1.2	3.3	2.0	583.7	39.3	20.8
Turkey	4.0	33.6	46.3	79.3	74.1	54.9
Latin America						
Argentina	21.5	141.7	787.0	42.9	−0.1	−0.8
Brazil	33.6	41.7	613.8	1113.8	7.6	7.5
Chile	27.2	174.8	20.4	13.9	5.2	3.8
Colombia	11.5	21.3	23.7	25.0	16.0	9.5
Mexico	2.7	16.8	69.1	18.0	19.4	9.5
Peru	9.4	31.9	1223.6	113.3	6.9	3.8
Venezuela	1.1	8.5	24.9	44.9	45.1	16.2

[1]Before 1993, the data refers to Czechoslovakia.
[2]Before 1991, the data refers to the Soviet Union.

tries have generally collected the lowest levels and Latin America the highest (Figure 4.2). In extreme cases, such as in Argentina, Chile, Egypt, and Israel at various times during the 1970s and 1980s, seigniorage as a share of GDP reached the double-digits. Interestingly, despite the higher inflation rates, seigniorage in Latin America has not been substantially higher than that of other regions except Asia. This suggests that some Latin American countries operated beyond the point where revenues from seigniorage are maximized (i.e., the peak of the inflation-tax collection curves depicted in Figure 4.2), due to the shrinking of the tax base caused by falling real money balances as inflation kept rising. This implies that high inflation cannot be entirely explained as a result of efficient taxation.

While the seigniorage theory emphasizes the behavior of the fiscal authority, the time inconsistency theory focuses on the behavior of the monetary authority. The theory highlights the inflationary bias to monetary policy from not being able to credibly commit to low inflation. The perception that output can be raised in the short-run by expansionary monetary policies may induce the central bank to run a looser monetary policy than is consistent with low inflation. This is particularly likely if the central bank is not independent from the rest of the government and when political considerations, such as electoral cycles, may influence policy. By the same token, the theory also helps explain why central banks may adopt an accommodative policy stance once inflation is triggered by other factors, such as adverse supply shocks.

Once triggered, higher inflation can also lead to the development of various indexation mechanisms that tie subsequent price and wage increases to past inflation, which can help to maintain existing inflationary momentum. In

Box 4.1. Why Emerging Market Countries Should Strive to Preserve Lower Inflation

Following the decline in inflation in emerging markets in recent years, a widespread consensus has emerged among policymakers and the public that one of the key policy challenges is now to preserve these gains. Why is there so much concern about inflation, especially for emerging markets, where fostering economic growth and reducing poverty and unemployment might be considered to be of greater intrinsic importance?

Most economists agree that inflation, especially high inflation, harms economic efficiency and growth, but the nature and magnitude of these costs are not yet entirely understood. Several costs of inflation have been identified, including:

- High inflation may distort relative prices of different goods and services, thereby lowering economic efficiency.
- People devote time and resources to economizing on money balances whose real value is eroding over time.
- Unexpected inflation leads to arbitrary redistribution: for example, from fixed interest rate lenders to borrowers.
- Higher inflation is typically associated with higher uncertainty about future inflation, forcing people to spend time and resources protecting themselves from future changes in inflation.
- High inflation may interfere with the financial system's ability to allocate resources effectively, for example because of distortions to accounting and tax rules.
- That said, moderate levels of inflation may also have benefits, such as facilitating needed relative price adjustment if the flexibility of nominal wages to downward adjustments is limited.

While few doubt that extremely high inflation is bad for economic growth and efficiency, there is a debate on whether moderate inflation is harmful and on exactly where the threshold lies between moderate, tolerable inflation and high, harmful inflation.[1] The empirical literature on

this issue is not conclusive, with estimates ranging from 2 to 7 percent a year in many studies to, as high as 40 percent a year according to one study. Nevertheless, recent trends in emerging markets reveal a clear preference for single-digit inflation levels.[2] The costs of inflation will also differ across countries depending on specific characteristics, such as the degree of indexation and the ways in which the financial system has developed to cope with the uncertainties associated with inflation. Countries with a recent history of high inflation typically still have in place indexation mechanisms that may reduce the annual costs of inflation but may also make inflation—and its associated costs—more persistent.

Inflation and Financial Sector Development

The effects of inflation on the development of the financial system are complex and especially relevant for emerging markets. High inflation may be expected to increase the resources a country devotes to financial services. High expected inflation will lead households to make smaller cash withdrawals with greater frequency; banks will therefore need to build more branches and make more investments in automation and technology in order to satisfy increased customer activity. Higher and more volatile inflation will raise the demand for financial sector services aimed at protecting economic agents from the associated uncertainty. One study confirms that countries with higher inflation devote a greater share of their GDP to

---

[1] Indeed, one of the most common arguments that is put forward in favor of maintaining inflation at a low level (say 2–4 percent a year) rather than letting it increase to a moderate level (say 10–20 percent) is simply that it is important to avoid taking a slippery slope

where moderate inflation might degenerate into excessive, harmful inflation.

[2] See Michael Bruno and William Easterly, "Inflation Crises and Long-Run Growth," *Journal of Monetary Economics*, Vol. 41 (February 1998), pp. 3–26; Atish Ghosh and Steven Phillips, "Warning: Inflation May Be Harmful to Your Growth," *IMF Staff Papers*, International Monetary Fund, Vol. 45, (December 1998), pp. 672–713; Mohsin S. Khan and Abdelhak S. Senhadji, "Threshold Effects in the Relationship Between Inflation and Growth," IMF Working Paper 00/110 (Washington: International Monetary Fund, June 2000); and Peter Christoffersen and Peter Doyle, "From Inflation to Growth: Eight Years of Transition," *The Economics of Transition*, Vol. 8, No. 2 (2000), pp. 421–451.

financial services.[3] However, it seems that these resources, while protecting agents from inflation uncertainty, do not result in genuine financial development. Indeed private credit, bank assets, financial sector liquid liabilities, and stock market capitalization (all as a share of GDP) tend to be lower in countries with high inflation, with a marked drop in financial sector development around a threshold of 15 percent inflation.[4]

Inflation and the Poor

A possible cost of inflation, which is particularly relevant in developing countries, relates to its effects on the poor. There are a number of reasons why inflation often hurts the poor more than it hurts the rich. The poor have less access to financial instruments used to hedge against inflation. Moreover, the poor are more likely to rely on sources of income—such as pensions, subsidies, and transfers—that may be only partially indexed to inflation. There are, of course, counterarguments. First, in those countries where rural poverty remains widespread, poor households are likely to be engaged in subsistence farming, which is less affected by developments in the monetized economy: while inflation is likely to hurt the urban poor, it may have a smaller impact on the poor living in rural areas. Second, those below the poverty line in developing countries may have small cash hold-

ings, no pensions, and no transfers or subsidies from the state. Finally, policies aimed at boosting aggregate demand may raise inflation but may also temporarily assist the poor by reducing unemployment.

Current evidence suggests that inflation tends to hurt the poor to a greater extent than it hurts the rich. Drawing on a polling data survey of more than 30,000 households in 38 countries, and controlling for other factors, a recent paper finds that [relatively] poor people are more likely to mention inflation as one of their top concerns.[5] Moreover, the authors report that direct measures of improvement in the well-being of the poor are negatively correlated with inflation in cross-country samples for the past few decades. Another study confirms that, in an international panel, higher inflation is associated with lower income of the poor over the longer term.[6] Using U.S. data over time, it also finds that any benefits to the poor of expansionary policies leading to higher inflation and lower unemployment are minor and short-lived. Such studies relying on data from developing countries are subject to a number of caveats, in particular whether surveys capture a sufficiently large share of the rural population, where many of the poor are to be found.

[3]William B. English, "Inflation and Financial Sector Size," *Journal of Monetary Economics*, Vol. 44, (December 1999), pp. 379–400.

[4]John H. Boyd, Ross Levine, and Bruce D. Smith, "The Impact of Inflation on Financial Sector Performance," *Journal of Monetary Economics* (forthcoming).

[5]William Easterly and Stanley Fischer, "Inflation and the Poor," Policy Research Working Paper No. 2335 (Washington: The World Bank, 2000), forthcoming in the *Journal of Money, Credit, and Banking*.

[6]Christina Romer and David Romer, "Monetary Policy and the Well-Being of the Poor," NBER Working Paper No. 6793 (Cambridge, Mass.: National Bureau for Economic Research, 1998).

addition, other factors may contribute.[8] One is the so-called province effect, where local governments have an incentive to increase expenditure,

overlooking the impact on the national government deficit because they only pay part of the cost. As the resulting fiscal deficit is higher, so tends to be the resort to seigniorage. In addition, a war of attrition between social groups can also make it difficult for the government to reach a consensus on appropriate macroeconomic policies, leading to increased use of

[8]For a more detailed discussion and references, see Guillermo Calvo and Carlos Végh, "Inflation Stabilization and BOP Crises in Developing Countries," in *Handbook of Macroeconomics*, ed. by John Taylor and Michael Woodford (New York: North-Holland, 1999), pp. 1531–1614.

Figure 4.2. Seigniorage in Emerging Market Economies, 1950–2000[1]
(Three-year moving averages; percent of GDP)

Seigniorage has displayed a Laffer-curve shape, the peak of which has varied widely across countries.

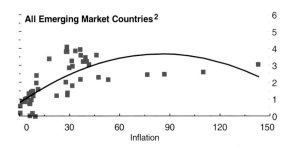

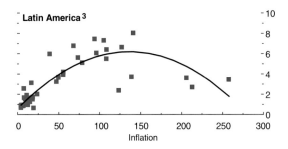

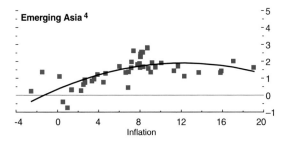

seigniorage.[9] Finally, persistent inflation can arise out of the dynamics of interest payments on government debt. Once the nominal interest rate on the debt is given by private sector expectations of future inflation, the government will have an incentive to validate those expectations or inflate further, as disinflation increases the real value of the debt service.

These considerations reveal the complexity of inflationary processes. Inflation can be triggered by a host of factors—ranging from higher fiscal deficits to oil price shocks—and since the government, including the central bank, has a variety of incentives to accommodate such impulses, a complex inflationary dynamic can result with little connection to its original cause. Thus, any analysis of the determinants of inflation must look at several variables and recognize that, even then, a satisfactory explanation of specific developments in certain countries during certain periods might prove elusive.

The complexity of persistent high inflation can make it harder for governments to create consensus to stabilize the economy, underscoring the importance of reacting quickly to early signs of inflationary pressures. Failure to do so may mean that the macroeconomic situation will have to become clearly unsustainable—as under high and hyperinflation—before such a consensus is reached. Indeed, the difficulty in forging a consensus to lower inflation helps explain why many emerging market countries have tolerated moderate to high inflation rates until recently.

Empirical Evidence on the Determinants of Inflation

The extensive literature on the determinants of inflation across countries has explored the roles of fiscal deficits, monetary policy, and the combination of external shocks and inflation inertia in producing inflation. Studies that fo-

[9]See Alberto Alesina and Allan Drazen, "Why Are Stabilizations Delayed?" *American Economic Review*, Vol. 81 (December 1991), pp.1170–88; and Alejandro M. Werner, "Building Consensus for Stabilizations," *Journal of Development Economics*, Vol. 59 (August 1999), pp.319–336.

cused on the relationship between deficits, seigniorage, and inflation have yielded mixed results, with little evidence of a strong connection across a wide range of countries and inflation rates.[10] On time inconsistency, the empirical literature has focused on two implications of the theory—namely, that central bank independence and greater openness to trade are associated with lower inflation. Such studies have found a negative relationship between inflation and central bank independence, while the results on openness have been found to be sensitive to the sample, specification, and period of estimation.[11] Other studies have examined the role of monetary expansion, price inertia, and changes in nominal exchange rates and the world price of oil and other commodities. Inflation inertia and changes in money supply have been found to be key determinants of inflation, with oil and other world prices playing a less important role.[12]

Given the widespread view that fiscal policy is closely connected with the inflationary experience of many emerging market countries, the IMF has reexamined the relationship between fiscal deficits and inflation, focusing only on emerging markets (Box 4.2). This study finds a significant and relatively consistent long-run relationship between the size of government

---

[10]See Robert King and Charles Plosser, "Money, Deficits, and Inflation," *Carnegie-Rochester Conference Series on Public Policy*, Vol. 22 (1985), pp. 147–96; and Stanley Fischer, Ratna Sahay, and Carlos Végh, "Modern Hyper—and High Inflations," *Journal of Economic Literature* (forthcoming).

[11]See the large literature referenced in Sylvester C. Eijffinger, *Independent Central Banks and Economic Performance* (United Kingdom: Edward Elgar, 1997); and Marta Campillo and Jeffrey Miron, "Why Does Inflation Differ Across Countries," in *Reducing Inflation: Motivation and Strategy*, ed. by Christina Romer and David Romer (Chicago: University of Chicago Press, 1997); and Christina Terra, "Openness an Inflation: A New Assessment," *Quarterly Journal of Economics*, Vol. 113 (May 1998), pp. 641–80.

[12]See Prakash Loungani and Phillip Swagel, "Sources of Inflation in Developing Countries," IMF Working Paper (Washington, International Monetary Fund, forthcoming); and "The Rise and Fall of Inflation," Chapter VI in the October 1996 *World Economic Outlook*.

Figure 4.2 *(concluded)*

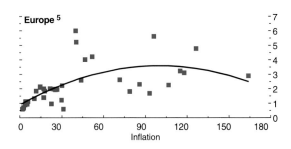

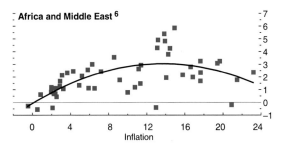

Source: IMF, *International Financial Statistics*.
[1]Seigniorage is calculated as the annual change in reserve money divided by nominal GDP.
[2]Excluding three outlying observations with inflation rates greater than 200 percent as well as inflation and seigniorage in Israel for the period 1977 to 1985.
[3]Excluding four outlying observations with inflation rates greater than 300 percent.
[4]Excluding three outlying observations with inflation rates greater than 70 percent.
[5]Availability of data for emerging Europe is as follows Czech Republic (1994–99), Hungary (1983–99), Poland (1980–99), Russia (1994–99), and Turkey (1962–99).
[6]Excluding inflation and seigniorage in Israel for the period 1977 to 1985.

Box 4.2. Is There a Relationship Between Fiscal Deficits and Inflation?

Economists generally agree that fiscal deficits are one of the main causes of inflation, particularly high and hyper inflation. By creating excessive aggregate demand pressures recurrent fiscal deficits can both spark and sustain inflationary processes.[1] Typically, governments facing persistent fiscal imbalances are incapable (or unwilling) to create the political consensus needed to increase taxes and/or reduce expenditures and find borrowing increasingly difficult. As a result, these governments pressure the central bank to finance those deficits by printing money. Indeed, there is a large literature documenting the crucial role played by fiscal deficits during the hyperinflation episodes of the 1920s, 1970s, and 1980s and high and moderate inflation episodes of the 1970s, 1980s, and 1990s.[2]

Despite these case studies, more formal empirical analysis has had only limited success in establishing the existence of a relationship between the size of fiscal deficits and inflation.[3]

Long-Run Relationship Between Inflation, Fiscal Deficits, and Changes in World Prices[1]

Government deficit/narrow money	
Coefficient	0.32
t-ratio	(18.1)
Change in world oil prices	
Coefficient	0.08
t-ratio	(9.4)
World inflation	
Coefficient	0.29
t-ratio	(7.3)

[1]The sample covered Argentina, Brazil, Chile, China, Colombia, Egypt, Hungary, India, Indonesia, Israel, Korea, Malaysia, Mexico, Morocco, Pakistan, Peru, Philippines, South Africa, Thailand, Turkey, Uruguay, Venezuela, and Zimbabwe.

In general, this relationship is complex, and an important distinction needs to be made between the short and long run. In the short run, higher deficits do not necessarily lead to higher inflation, as they can be financed by additional borrowing. In the long run, however, high deficits will generally lead to higher inflation, as governments use seigniorage to finance them, although there will also be reverse causation through the impact of inflation on nominal interest rates. Because of this, it is useful to focus on the long-run relationship between fiscal deficits and inflation.

Some initial work by IMF staff indicates there is a positive long-run relationship between the size of fiscal deficits scaled by narrow money (as defined by the IMF's *International Finance Statistics*) and inflation for a sample of 23 emerging market economies during the period of 1970–99 (see the Table).[4] The econometric specification used in this study has been derived from a small open economy that predicts that in the long run the ratio of government deficits to narrow money should be directly related to inflation. In other words, inflation will be higher the larger are the fiscal imbalances (as

---

[1]Inflation, by affecting government revenues and expenditures, also changes the size of the fiscal deficits, albeit in an uncertain direction. There is some evidence, however, that fiscal deficits tend to increase with high inflation because of high nominal interest payments. To eliminate the effects of inflation on the deficit, alternative deficit definitions have been proposed, including that of the operational fiscal deficit; however, these definitions are not problem free. See Vito Tanzi, Mario Blejer, and Mario Teijeiro, "Effects of Inflation on Measurement of Fiscal Deficits: Conventional Versus Operational Measures" in *How to Measure the Fiscal Deficit*, ed. by Mario Blejer and Adrienne Cheasty (Washington: International Monetary Fund, 1993).

[2]See, for instance, Thomas Sargent, "The Ends of Four Big Inflations," in *Inflation, Causes, and Effects*, ed. by Robert Hall (Chicago: University of Chicago Press,1982), pp. 41–97; and Rudiger Dornbusch and Stanley Fischer, "Stopping Hyperinflation Past and Present," *Weltwirtschaftliches Archiv*, Vol. 122, (1986) and "Moderate Inflation," *World Bank Economic Review*, Vol.7 (January 1993).

[3]See for instance Robert King and Charles Plosser, "Money, Deficits, and Inflation," *Carnegie-Rochester Conference Series on Public Policy*, Vol. 22 (Spring 1985), pp. 147–96; and Stanley Fischer, Ratna Sahay, and Carlos Végh, "Modern Hyper–and High Inflations" (unpublished; Washington: International Monetary Fund, 2000).

[4]See Luis Catão and Marco Terrones, "Government Deficits and Inflation: A New Look at the Emerging Markets Evidence," IMF Working Paper (Washington: International Monetary Fund, forthcoming).

measured by the ratio of government deficit over GDP) and/or the lower the size of the inflation tax base (proxied by the ratio of narrow money to GDP).[5] The existence of a long-run deficit-inflation relationship was tested using a dynamic panel regression.[6] Despite the wide variety of inflation experiences in emerging market economies, a statistically significant long-run relationship between the ratio of government deficits to narrow money and inflation was found and was superior to including only the deficit as a ratio for GDP or narrow money as a ratio to GDP. Moreover, the hypothesis of long-run coefficient homogeneity could not be rejected.

This relationship is quite stable to the inclusion of other variables, as well as to the exclusion of countries that experienced hyperinflation episodes in the late 1980s/early 1990s (Argentina, Brazil, and Peru). The stability of the long-run relationship between deficits and inflation was explored by introducing into the long-run econometric specification indicators of openness, political instability, exchange rate regime, changes in oil prices, changes in non-oil commodity prices, and world inflation—variables that have featured prominently in previous empirical

studies.[7] In addition to government deficits, changes in world oil prices and world inflation were found to be significant, suggesting that external factors matter, including overall global monetary stability. As in other studies, a negative long-run association between openness and inflation was found; however, once the fiscal deficit is introduced in the specification, openness changes sign and becomes statistically insignificant, suggesting that the effect of openness on inflation is indirect and in the long run works mainly through the fiscal channel. The analysis also found no evidence of a statistically significant relationship between pegged exchange rate regimes (as measured by a dummy variable created from the *de jure* exchange rate classification compiled by the IMF) and inflation, although other studies have found this link in the short run.

These results point to a significant long-run relationship between deficits and inflation. Based on the estimated parameters, the model predicts that a (permanent) reduction in the government deficit by 1 percentage point of GDP is associated with a drop in inflation by 2 to 6 percentage points depending on the level of private sector's holdings of narrow money. Likewise, a 10 percent reduction in oil prices changes would lead to a four-fifths of a percentage point reduction in the inflation rate, while a 10 percent change in world inflation translates into a reduction in domestic inflation of almost 3 percent.[8]

---

[5]A battery of tests confirmed that the specification derived from theory was statistically superior to other ones that included deficit over GDP and narrow money over GDP.

[6]A pooled mean group (PMG) estimator technique was used, as this is particularly good at dealing with dynamic processes and outliers, such as hyper inflation episodes. In addition, the PMG estimator is flexible enough to constrain the long-run parameters to be equal across countries while allowing other parameters (intercepts, short-run coefficients, and error variances) to vary freely from country to country. See M. Hashem Pesaran, Yongcheol Shin, and Ron Smith, "Pooled Mean Group Estimation of Dynamic Heterogeneous Panels,"*Journal of the American Statistical Association*, Vol. 94 (June 1999), pp. 621–34.

[7]See, for instance, Martha Campillo and Jeffrey Miron, "Why Does Inflation Differ Across Countries," in *Reducing Inflation: Motivation and Strategy*, ed. by Christina Romer and David Romer (Chicago: University of Chicago Press, 1997); and Chapter VI of the October 1996 *World Economic Outlook*.

[8]Short-run estimates are less informative, as they are country specific. The lag structure for each country was selected using the Schwarz Bayesian criterion, subject to a maximum lag of two (because of data considerations). In more than half of the countries at least one lag of inflation was included.

deficits—scaled by narrow money—and inflation. These results indicate that long-term inflation is positively related to fiscal deficits (measured as a ratio to GDP) and inversely related to the size of the inflation tax base (proxied by the ratio of narrow money to GDP).

As also discussed in Box 4.2, the same empirical study on emerging markets explored the stability of the long-run relationship between the fiscal deficit and inflation to the inclusion of other variables that have featured prominently in the literature. Among those, change in world oil prices and world inflation were the other variables found to have a long-run bearing on inflation, suggesting that global monetary stability also matters for emerging market inflation performance. In some specifications of the model, a negative long-run relationship between openness and inflation was also found, but became insignificant once the fiscal deficit variable was introduced. Similarly, no statistically significant relationship between (*de jure*) pegged exchange rate regimes was found, in contrast with the results of an earlier study.[13] These results suggest that the influence of openness and exchange rate regimes on inflation may, over the long term, occur largely through fiscal policy and financial developments that affect the size of the inflation tax base.[14]

What Explains the 1990s Inflation Performance in Emerging Markets?

As noted above, inflation was reduced in almost all emerging countries in the 1990s, but the extent and speed at which countries reined it in varied considerably. Looking across the different regions, a variety of experiences can be identified.

In Latin America, *Argentina, Brazil, and Peru* experienced periods of hyperinflation during 1989–90. In each case, this had been preceded by persistent high inflation from the mid-1970s through the late 1980s, partly as a result of high fiscal deficits (itself reflecting political factors) and indexation in labor and financial markets. Moreover, access to international markets was limited in most cases following the 1980s debt crisis, forcing these countries to rely more on domestic financing of fiscal deficits, including seigniorage. As inflation increased, many of these economies saw money aggregates shrink as a ratio of GDP while the maturity of government debt shortened rapidly, laying the preconditions for hyperinflation. In these cases, the macroeconomic chaos and sharp collapse of output and employment associated with hyperinflation helped create political consensus over a relatively short time span for the ensuing stabilization. By the end of the 1990s, inflation in all three countries had been reduced to single digits (despite a sharp devaluation in Brazil in early 1999).

Other countries in Latin America, as well as Israel and Turkey, also experienced sustained moderate to high inflation—typically in the range of 20 to 80 percent—during the 1970s and 1980s, but without degenerating into hyperinflation. Most of these inflations were also reduced in the 1990s, although inflation remains high in Turkey (notwithstanding considerable progress before the collapse of its recent stabilization program—see Chapter 1) and to a lesser extent Venezuela.

In *Asia,* following some pickup in the wake of the oil price shocks of the 1970s, inflation was generally held at low levels during the 1980s and the 1990s. China experienced a marked but short-lived pickup in inflation during the early 1990s, associated with a surge in domestic investment, and a few countries—including Pakistan, the Philippines, India, and Indonesia—experienced persistent inflation in the high single or low double digits. With the exception of

---

[13]See Atish Ghosh, Anne-Marie Gulde, Jonathan Ostry, and Holger Wolf, "Does the Nominal Exchange Rate Regime Matter?," IMF Working Paper 95/121 (Washington: International Monetary Fund, 1995).

[14]Indeed, a recent study has found a positive correlation between openness and government size. This correlation may reflect the use of government spending as an external risk-reducing device. See Dani Rodrik, "Why Do More Open Economies Have Bigger Governments?" *Journal of Political Economy,* Vol. 106 (October 1998), pp. 997–1032.

Table 4.3. Emerging Market Countries: Selected Variables

Periods	Inflation[1]	Deficit/GDP	Expenditures/GDP	Oil Prices[1]	Imports/GDP	Narrow Money/GDP
All Emerging Markets						
1971–80	22.8	5.1	23.5	43.9	24.0	14.8
1981–85	52.7	5.7	32.8	−5.7	26.1	15.6
1986–90	188.3	3.9	29.7	2.2	24.9	13.9
1991–95	93.4	2.6	28.1	−5.3	29.5	13.3
1996–2000	23.1	2.7	27.7	15.1	32.8	14.7
Latin America						
1971–80	58.0	2.1	14.2	43.9	15.2	11.2
1981–85	107.9	4.1	20.8	−5.7	14.2	9.1
1986–90	681.6	4.9	20.0	2.2	15.3	7.7
1991–95	195.9	1.0	18.1	−5.3	17.9	7.0
1996–2000	14.2	2.0	18.2	15.1	20.0	8.1
Asia						
1971–80	10.2	3.5	16.7	43.9	19.9	13.4
1981–85	8.3	5.0	20.1	−5.7	25.4	14.5
1986–90	6.5	3.2	19.8	2.2	26.4	15.8
1991–95	8.6	1.2	18.7	−5.3	33.5	17.3
1996–2000	6.8	2.8	18.9	15.1	38.5	19.7
Europe						
1971–80	6.1	2.5	18.6	43.9	24.4	16.2
1981–85	14.2	2.4	38.0	−5.7	24.3	18.5
1986–90	44.9	2.5	39.1	2.2	24.2	14.4
1991–95	156.6	4.4	37.9	−5.3	34.4	13.7
1996–2000	65.3	3.4	36.1	15.1	41.1	12.9
Africa and the Middle East						
1971–80	16.9	12.4	44.3	43.9	36.6	18.5
1981–85	80.2	11.2	52.2	−5.7	40.4	20.3
1986–90	20.3	5.3	39.8	2.2	33.4	17.6
1991–95	12.4	3.7	37.6	−5.3	32.0	15.3
1996–2000	6.0	2.4	37.8	15.1	31.4	17.9

Sources: IMF, *International Financial Statistics*; and IMF staff estimates.
[1]Average annual percent change of the consumer price index.

Indonesia, low inflation was generally maintained during the Asian crisis, notwithstanding substantial currency devaluations.

Among *transition countries*, almost all experienced a sharp burst of inflation in the early 1990s, reflecting price liberalization, the unwinding of the monetary overhang inherited from the period of central planning, and fiscal pressures caused by the collapse of central planning.[15] In many respects, these inflations are more reminiscent of historical bouts of inflation due to war and political collapse—as for example following the breakup of the Austro-Hungarian empire in the early twentieth century. In most cases, aided by strong macroeconomic policies, inflation had been reduced to moderate double-digit levels in the mid-1990s and to close to single digit levels by 2000.[16]

While the forces behind disinflation in all these groups varied, fiscal consolidation in each case played a crucial role. Indeed, as shown in Table 4.3, fiscal deficits in emerging markets as a whole were reduced by about one-half from the levels observed in the 1970s and 1980s. On average, calculations based on the IMF's empirical

[15]See, for instance, Carlo Cottarelli and Peter Doyle, *Disinflation in Transition 1993–97*, Occasional Paper No. 179 (Washington: International Monetary Fund, 1999).

[16]The two important relapses in the fight against inflation have been Bulgaria (1996) and Russia (1998–99). Since then, Bulgaria has managed to stabilize prices under a currency board arrangement, and Russia has made considerable progress in lowering inflation under a floating exchange rate regime.

Figure 4.3. Inflation and Its Determinants in Emerging Markets
(Simple annual averages)

In the late 1990s, improved fiscal balances and restrained monetary growth have lowered inflation in Latin America, Europe, and the Africa/Middle East regions. Other factors, such as world inflation and oil prices, have also played a role.

■ Central government deficit, percent of narrow money (left scale)

■ Narrow money, percent of GDP (left scale)

▢ APSP oil price index, percent change (left scale)

— Inflation, percent change (right scale)

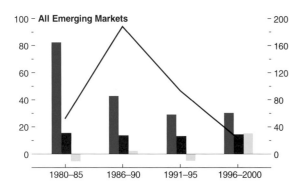

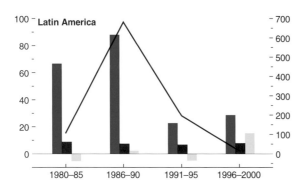

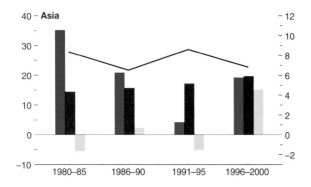

estimates reported in Box 4.2 suggest that the 2½ percentage points of GDP deficit reduction observed for the group of emerging markets (excluding transition economies) has led to a 5 to 15 percentage point reduction in inflation rates. With fiscal deficits in Asia already low, this fiscal consolidation effort in the emerging markets took place primarily in the Africa/Middle Eastern and Latin American regions (Figure 4.3 and Table 4.3).[17] While the extent of fiscal adjustment is much more difficult to measure in transition economies—given the extent of quasi-fiscal activities, especially during the centrally planned period—it is clear that fiscal consolidation also played a central role in the disinflation process.[18] Particularly in the second half of the 1990s, this was accompanied by financial deepening in all regions, which further reduced the need for seigniorage.

External developments also contributed to falling inflation in the 1990s. First, as discussed in the previous section, the decline in global inflation, both through its direct impact on import prices as well as indirectly (through, among other things, pressure on emerging markets' external competitiveness and demonstration effects of the virtues of low inflation), clearly helped. Second, the decline in oil prices in the first half of the 1990s also provided modest support to disinflation programs at that time (although, with prices rising thereafter, oil prices likely had an adverse effect for the decade as a whole).

A number of other forces—while not directly captured in the econometric model described earlier—also contributed, although their impact likely varied considerably across different countries. These included:

- *Institutional reforms.* In most emerging markets, the independence of the central bank

---

[17]Fiscal deficits in Asia were mostly low to begin with, and only rose substantially during the 1997–98 financial crisis.

[18]See Stanley Fischer and Ratna Sahay, "The Transition Economies After Ten Years," IMF Working Paper 00/30 (Washington: International Monetary Fund, 2000). The slight deterioration of the fiscal position indicator (scaled by M1) for merging Europe depicted in Figure 4.3 is entirely due to Turkey.

was enhanced, helping to address the time inconsistency problem discussed above. Many countries (most notably Argentina and Brazil) also greatly reduced or eliminated indexation of wage and financial sector contracts, helping to reduce inflation inertia. This was accompanied by some increase in political stability, primarily in emerging markets of Europe, Africa, and the Middle East.

- *Structural reforms.* Most countries undertook wide-ranging structural reforms in trade, product, and labor markets, which tend to reduce inflationary pressures. One outcome of these reforms was the substantial rise in trade openness for emerging markets as a group (Table 4.3), particularly in Asia and emerging Europe (less so in Latin America and the Middle East). In addition, financial sector regulations and supervisory frameworks were improved, fostering discipline in credit markets that, together with widespread privatization of public banks, posed an additional constraint on fiscal profligacy.

- *Access to global capital markets.* Capital flows to emerging markets substantially increased, particularly to Asia and Latin America in the first half of the 1990s, as well as to a number of emerging European countries, particularly Hungary and the Czech Republic. While this should in principle be beneficial for disinflation—for instance by reducing the need for seigniorage—it also contributed to overheating and inflationary pressures in countries with fixed exchange rate regimes or where the authorities were reluctant to let the exchange rate appreciate. The important role of capital inflows in slowing down the disinflation process has been observed in Eastern Europe.

A particular issue of importance in a number of Asian and Latin American countries in recent years has been the behavior of the exchange pass-through. While inflation picked up in all countries in the wake of dramatic currency devaluations, the effect was relatively short-lived and far from one-to-one in most countries

Figure 4.3 *(concluded)*

■ Central government deficit, percent of narrow money (left scale)
■ Narrow money, percent of GDP (left scale)
▢ APSP oil price index, percent change (left scale)
— Inflation, percent change (right scale)

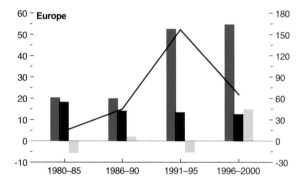

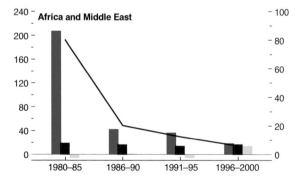

Sources: IMF, *International Financial Statistics;* and IMF staff estimates.

Figure 4.4. Exchange Rate Pass-Through in Emerging Markets in the 1990s[1]
(Inflation as a percent of change in nominal effective exchange rate)

Exchange rate pass-through has been well below unity in most emerging market countries in the aftermath of major devaluations.

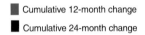

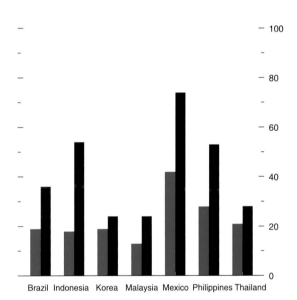

Source: IMF staff estimates.
[1]Calculated as the ratio of cumulative percentage change in the consumer price index over 12- and 24- month periods by the one-month lagged percentage change in the nominal effective exchange rate over 12- and 24- month periods, respectively.

(Figure 4.4). Recent studies, including work by IMF staff, have sought to explain this limited exchange rate pass-through in a broad sample of advanced and developing countries.[19] They find that, in general, the extent of the pass-through is positively related to the size of the output gap and negatively related to the degree of real exchange rate appreciation immediately preceding the devaluation, with some evidence that it may also be a negative function of average inflation levels in the years preceding the devaluation. Since all emerging market countries that experienced sharp devaluations in the 1990s had already achieved low inflation levels and displayed some degree of real exchange rate appreciation on the eve of the devaluation, these two factors plus the severity of the subsequent output contractions explain the limited pass-through.

To summarize, lower rates of inflation in emerging markets during the 1990s appear to have been closely linked to domestic fiscal consolidation, aided by falling world inflation, and—in some cases—limited exchange rate pass-through. Other factors—such as institutional strengthening, financial sector development, trade, and product and labor market reforms—also played a role as well, although the precise extent is difficult to quantify. This is partly because of indirect effects through the fiscal channel, the lack of better proxy variables, and the fact that these contributions varied widely from country to country, making it harder to derive accurately their average impact from a wide range of countries.

Monetary Regimes and Inflation Performance

Although inflation is a monetary phenomenon, fiscal deficits are a key long-run determi-

---

[19]Ilan Goldfajn and Sergio R. C. Werlang, "The Pass-Through From Depreciation to Inflation: A Panel Study," (unpublished; Brasilia: Central Bank of Brazil, 2000); and Eduardo Borensztein and José de Gregorio, "Devaluation and Inflation," (unpublished; Washington: International Monetary Fund, March 2000).

nant of inflation through the seigniorage channel. The conduct and institutions of monetary policy, however, clearly play a central role in price determination, particularly in the short to medium term. As has already been noted, in the short run the relationship between fiscal deficits and inflation may be relatively weak, since in most cases governments have access to noninflationary sources of financing. Moreover, the conduct and institutions of monetary policy may themselves influence fiscal policy. For example, a currency board tends to discourage persistently large fiscal deficits and the use of inflation tax, which are incompatible with sustainable pegs. This section reviews the record with the use of different monetary policy regimes, and the extent to which they have contributed to falling inflation rates during the 1990s.

What Does the Recent Record Tell Us?

The past 15 years or so witnessed a significant broadening of possible choices of monetary regimes and far-reaching institutional changes in the arrangements underpinning those regimes in emerging markets. Moving along the spectrum ranging from strict rules to full discretion, these regimes can be grouped as:

- Hard exchange rate pegs, which comprise currency unions, the use of foreign currency as the only legal tender, and currency board arrangements;

- Soft exchange rate pegs, including crawling pegs or bands, where the parity can be changed at the sole discretion of the monetary authority without violating any national law or international agreement;

- Floating exchange rate regimes where the monetary authority has a statutory mandate to target inflation directly (inflation targeting); and

- Other floating exchange rate regimes, including those where the monetary authority specifically targets the growth of monetary aggregates (monetary targeting), as well as hybrid arrangements whereby no

single nominal anchor is systematically targeted.[20]

At one extreme—under hard pegs—the monetary authority has virtually no room for discretion, as domestic monetary conditions are strictly linked to those of the foreign country (or countries) through a rigid peg. Seigniorage and monetary accommodation are constrained through a visible and strict rule. At the other extreme—a floating exchange rate with no explicit nominal targeting—room for discretion is considerable, allowing monetary policy to be tailored to domestic business cycle conditions or respond to other considerations. In between, seigniorage and monetary accommodation are somewhat constrained either by a fixed peg (which can be adjusted within limits and often at a cost) or by a set of domestic laws and institutional arrangements, such as those that underpin an inflation targeting regime (Box 4.3).

Figure 4.5 summarizes trends in the use of four main competing regimes since the mid-1980s. Two main developments stand out. One is the continuing move toward more flexible exchange rate regimes and the erosion of soft pegs—an ongoing trend since the early 1970s that has been accelerated in recent years by greater international integration (notably through higher capital mobility and more open capital accounts) and by the exchange rate and financial crises of the mid and late 1990s.[21] Second, there is a gradual emergence of a bipolar distribution among countries with more open

[20]The main features of the operation of each of these regimes are extensively described elsewhere. Useful reviews can be found in Carlo Cottarelli and Curzio Giannini, *Credibility Without Rules? Monetary Frameworks in the Post-Bretton Woods Era*, IMF Occasional Paper No. 154 (Washington: International Monetary Fund, 1997); and Frederic Mishkin, "International Experiences with Different Monetary Policy Regimes," NBER Working Paper No. 7044 (Cambridge, Mass.: National Bureau of Economic Research, September 2000).

[21]See Cottarelli and Giannini, *Credibility Without Rules*; and Michael Mussa, Paul Masson, Alexander Swoboda, Esteban Jadresic, Paolo Mauro, and Andrew Berg, *Exchange Rate Regimes in an Increasingly Integrated World Economy*, IMF Occasional Paper No. 193 (Washington: International Monetary Fund, 2000).

Box 4.3. Inflation Targeting in Emerging Market Economies: Implementation and Challenges

In recent years, several emerging market countries have joined a number of industrial countries in adopting monetary frameworks that formally target inflation. Brazil, Chile, the Czech Republic, Israel, Poland, and South Africa have adopted full-fledged inflation targeting, while others are moving toward this framework.[1]

The experience of the countries that have adopted inflation targeting suggests that the foundations for successful inflation targeting are built on the following:

- a mandate to achieve price stability;
- central bank instrument independence;
- transparent policies to build accountability and credibility;
- a good framework for forecasting inflation;
- a reasonable understanding of transmission channels between policy instruments and inflation;
- a well-developed financial system;
- absence of fiscal dominance (i.e., and the conduct of domestic monetary policy should not be dictated by fiscal needs);
- a reasonable degree of macroeconomic stability.

Although these elements need not be considered prerequisites for beginning the transition toward full-fledged inflation targeting, they can pose important challenges for many emerging market countries seeking to go down this path. In many cases, central banks have yet to be granted the operational independence (i.e., an ability to set policy instruments without government oversight) needed to set monetary policy in accordance with a price stability objective, and they are often reluctant to communicate their economic outlooks and policy intentions in a transparent manner. Ongoing structural change in their economies may impede their ability to forecast inflation, while weak links between monetary policy and inflation often associated with underdeveloped financial systems or partial dollarization complicate the assessment

of the appropriate policy response. In addition, it might take some time to establish the credibility of an inflation targeting framework, particularly in cases where there are large fiscal debt burdens or an inadequate track record of entrenched macroeconomic stability. That said, it is also true that many of these issues pose similar challenges for other monetary regimes, particular those using floating exchange rates.

An examination of the differences between emerging market countries that target inflation and those that do not sheds some light on the preferred starting point and conditions that favor the choice of inflation targeting among other alternative monetary policy regimes. Usually, inflation targeting countries are relatively well developed and have more complex domestic financial systems, suggesting these attributes should be considered by other countries thinking of adopting this monetary framework. They are also countries that have opted for significant exchange rate flexibility, in part because their terms of trade may follow different cycles than those of their major trading partners.[2]

The legal frameworks of all inflation targeting countries give the central bank instrument independence, and make price stability a primary objective.[3] A comparison suggests that emerging market countries tend to prefer a more formal institutional framework in support of inflation targeting than industrial countries. Emerging market countries usually modify the central bank legal framework before adopting inflation targeting, and all emerging market countries explicitly limit central bank financing of govern-

[1]For further reading, see Andrea Schaechter, Mark R. Stone, and Mark Zelmer, *Adopting Inflation Targeting: Practical Issues for Emerging Market Countries*, IMF Occasional Paper No. 202 (Washington: International Monetary Fund, 2000).

[2]For example, as a major exporter of precious metals, South Africa's terms of trade are significantly affected by swings in commodity prices. A floating exchange rate regime anchored by an inflation targeting framework helps it manage the effects of commodity price movements on its economy.

[3]In most inflation targeting frameworks, the inflation target is announced by the government or jointly by the government and the central bank. Thus, while the government can play an active role in setting the objectives for monetary policy, the central bank has the discretion to take the monetary actions it judges necessary to achieve the target, and is publicly held accountable for its actions.

ment deficits in the primary market. The more formal inflation targeting frameworks in emerging market countries compared to their industrial counterparts may reflect histories of greater government intervention in monetary policy, higher and more variable rates of inflation, less developed financial systems, greater vulnerability to inflationary monetization of government debt, greater susceptibility to exchange rate crises, and IMF involvement.

There are also differences in the operation and design of inflation targeting between emerging market and industrial countries. Central banks in emerging market countries tend to rely less on statistical models in the conduct of monetary policy, intervene more frequently in foreign exchange markets, use shorter horizons to achieve their objectives, and target wider bands than industrial countries. These differences presumably reflect underlying differences between the two groups of countries. Structural changes in underlying economic relationships are more prevalent in emerging market countries, and they are inclined to be more vulnerable to shocks, especially those emanating from volatile capital flows. By mixing and matching the elements of the framework (such as the choice of the price index to be targeted, a point target or a range, and escape clauses) an inflation targeting central bank can design a framework that gives it the appropriate trade-off between credibility and the discretion needed to respond to shocks, such as unexpected hikes in oil prices.[4]

Volatile capital flows are usually associated with rapid movements in the exchange rate and pronounced swings in the spreads between domestic and international interest rates, which can be particularly disruptive for countries that are relatively open to trade or are large borrowers. In an inflation targeting framework, clear explanations by the central bank of the rationale underlying its policy stance may help to ensure

that such shocks are not compounded by uncertainty regarding the conduct of monetary policy. Over time, a proven track record of attaining the inflation targets should help financial markets develop greater confidence in the motivations underpinning monetary actions.[5] Nonetheless, central banks that target inflation have occasionally found it prudent to take action to moderate exchange rate movements to ensure that excessive changes do not destabilize inflation expectations or the domestic financial system while retaining exchange rate flexibility. Taking steps to moderate a rapid depreciation of the exchange rate can thus help to avoid the more dramatic tightening that might otherwise occur in response to financial instability, rather than because a tighter monetary stance is desired. This can be particularly important for partially dollarized economies, where the financial condition of the private sector is often sensitive to exchange rate fluctuations. However, it is important to unwind such actions as soon as practical to avoid moving away from the inflation target.

The transition to full-fledged inflation targeting is also an issue in many emerging market economies. Several countries have confronted the challenge of introducing this framework before they exited from an exchange rate targeting regime. The experiences of Israel and Poland suggest that a gradual shift from a fixed exchange rate regime to a looser exchange rate regime to an inflation targeting framework is feasible, but needs sound and supportive fiscal and structural policies to manage the transition and minimize the risk of undermining the credibility and effectiveness of the new framework by saddling the central bank with conflicting objectives.

---

[4]Issues surrounding the design of inflation targeting frameworks are discussed in Ben Bernanke, Thomas Laubach, Frederic Mishkin, and Adam Posen, *Inflation Targeting: Lessons from the International Experience* (Princeton: Princeton University Press, 1999) and associated references.

[5]It is worth noting that many inflation targeting countries, such as Australia, Chile, and New Zealand, have found that the pass-through effects from exchange rate movements to domestic inflation declined as their inflation rates fell and inflation targeting frameworks gained credibility, implying that over time they can be more tolerant of exchange rate movements. However, it must be recognized that this fall in pass-through has also occurred in several countries that did not adopt inflation targeting frameworks but have been successful in lowering inflation.

Figure 4.5. Monetary Regimes in Emerging Market Countries[1]
(Percent of all emerging market countries)

In recent years, countries have been moving away from "soft" pegs and instead gravitating toward either floating exchange rates in conjunction with inflation targeting or "hard" pegged exchange rates.

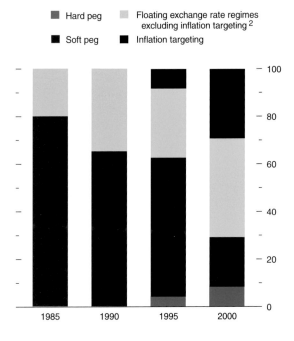

■ Hard peg   ▨ Floating exchange rate regimes
              excluding inflation targeting [2]
■ Soft peg   ■ Inflation targeting

Source: IMF staff estimates.
[1]Based on "de facto" classification following the method used in Stanley Fischer's "Exchange Rate Regimes: Is the Bipolar View Correct?" (speech to the American Economic Association, Jan. 6, 2001).
[2]Including monetary targeting regimes.

capital accounts, which have been leaning toward *either* hard exchange pegs or floating exchange rates, with inflation targeting being increasingly popular among the latter.[22]

Partly reflecting these significant changes in the use of monetary and exchange rate regimes and the failure of many countries to reduce inflation on a sustained basis in the 1970s and 1980s, important institutional changes have taken place in recent years in central bank charters as well as in the overall design and goals of monetary policy in emerging markets. One of them is greater central bank independence and transparency. Following the pioneering experience of New Zealand and its adoption by other advanced countries, a growing number of emerging markets have given their central banks complete control over the instruments used to achieve a low inflation goal.

Along with central bank instrument independence, several emerging markets—inflation targeters or not—have also greatly increased the transparency and accountability of goals and procedures of monetary policy, often in the form of statutory arrangements, giving the central bank a well-defined mandate to pursue price stability. In Latin America, for instance, the Argentine central bank law of 1991 explicitly prescribes that "the primary and fundamental mission of the Bank is to preserve the value of the currency," while Chile's central bank act of the same year restricted the objectives of the central bank to "oversee monetary stability and the proper functioning of the internal and external payments system." In a similar vein, the new central bank charters for most transition economies—including the Czech Republic, Hungary, Poland, and Russia—which were passed into law in the early 1990s, clearly stated that the main goal for monetary policy was low inflation. In the particular case of countries

[22]Reasons for this growing bipolar outlook are discussed in Stanley Fischer, "Exchange Rate Regimes: Is the Bipolar View Correct?" address to the American Economic Association Meeting (January 2001), available at http://www.imf.org/external/np/speeches/2001/010601a.htm.

WHAT DOES THE RECENT RECORD TELL US?

adopting inflation targeting, such as Israel, Chile, and, more recently, Brazil, Colombia, Korea, Mexico, and South Africa, these statutory changes have been combined with the public announcement of multiyear targets for inflation. This has helped to reduce the room for monetary policy discretion in the medium to long run, thus helping anchor long-term inflation expectations. To the extent that these institutional changes limit the scope for seigniorage, they are clearly conducive to greater fiscal discipline.

The other change in monetary arrangements introduced by several emerging markets has been to allow domestic bank accounts and transactions to be conducted in either domestic or foreign currency.[23] Such a dual currency arrangement has often been coupled with hard exchange rate pegs (as in Hong Kong SAR since 1982, Argentina since 1991, and Bulgaria from 1997) or floating exchange rate regimes (as in Peru from the early 1990s). In most cases, foreign currency denominated assets and liabilities in the domestic financial system have expanded very rapidly, so that some of these economies have become highly "dollarized" or "euroized" (Figure 4.6). Once such freedom to choose between foreign and domestic currency denominated assets is combined with the elimination of capital account restrictions, allowing residents to switch freely between onshore and offshore asset holdings—as has been the case in most of these countries—a significant constraint on monetary policy discretion is imposed. Not only is the monetary authority given control of a smaller share of the money supply but also this share can rapidly shrink (via currency switching) if the credibility of domestic policies falters. Indeed, in

[23]A few emerging market economies in the Western Hemisphere started allowing domestic banks to take foreign currency deposits and supply foreign currency denominated loans to residents already in the early 1970s, mainly to retain foreign exchange reserves within the country. However, in Argentina, Peru, and Mexico, for instance, the convertibility of foreign currency denominated deposits was temporarily suspended during macroeconomic crises in the 1980s, entailing a *de facto* partial confiscation of those deposits. Since the early 1990s, this arrangement been fully honored in those countries.

Figure 4.6. Foreign Currency Deposits
(Percent of M3)

The share of foreign currency deposits in the domestic banking systems rose significantly in recent years.

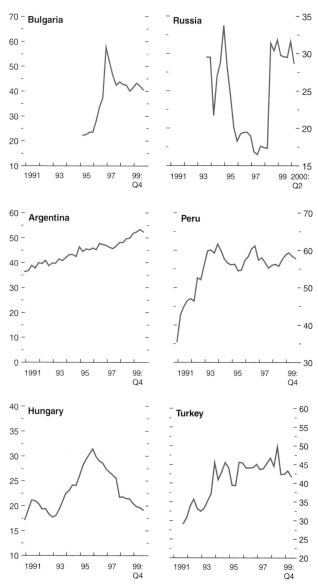

Sources: IMF, *International Financial Statistics;* and IMF staff estimates.

Table 4.4. Major Emerging Markets Exchange-Rate and Money-Based Stabilization Programs Since the 1970s

| Country | Beginning Date | Exchange Rate/Monetary Arrangement[1] | 12-Month Inflation | | | Did the Program End in a Currency Crash? |
			At start of program	Third year of program	In 2000	
Chile	April 1975	Managed/Monetary aggregates	394.3	—	—	No. Ended December 1977.
Chile (Tablita)	February 1978	Crawling peg, peg.	52.1	28.7	4.5	Yes (February 1983).
Argentina (Tablita)	December 1978	Crawling peg	169.9	131.3	—	Yes (April 1982).
Argentina (Austral)	June 1985	Peg, crawling peg	1,128.9	—	—	Yes (September 1987).
Israel	July 1985	Peg, horizontal band, crawling band.	445.4	16.0	0.3	No
Brazil (Cruzado)	February 1986	Peg.	286.0	—	—	Yes (March 1987).
Mexico	December 1987	Peg, crawling peg, widening band.	143.7	29.9	8.9	Yes (December 1994).
Argentina (Bonex)	December 1989	Float/Monetary aggregates	4,923.3	—	—	No. Ended February 1991.
Poland	January 1990	Peg, crawling peg, widening band.	639.6	39.8	8.6	No
Brazil (Collor)	March 1990	Managed/Monetary aggregates	5,747.3	—	—	No. Ended January 1991.
Peru	August 1990	Float/Monetary aggregates	12,377.8	48.5	3.7	No.
Argentina (Convertibility)	April 1991	Currency board.	287.4	4.3	0.1	No.
Brazil (Cardoso)	July 1994	Managed float, crawling peg.	4,922.6	6.1	6.0	Yes (January 1999).
Russia	July 1995	Band, crawling band.	225.0	5.5	20.2	Yes (August 1998).
Bulgaria	July 1997	Currency board.	1,502.8	8.6	11.4	No.
Turkey	January 1998	Crawling peg.	99.1	—	39.0	Yes (February 2001).

Sources: G. Calvo and C. Végh, "Inflation Stabilization and BOP Crises in Developing Countries," in *Handbook of Macroeconomics,* ed. by John Taylor and Michael Woodford (New York, North Holland, 1999), pp. 1531–1614; and IMF staff estimates.
[1]Where more than one arrangement is listed, the sequence of arrangements is indicated.

several countries the dollarization of financial intermediation appears to be quite sensitive to interest rate differentials, exchange rate volatility, and changes in devaluation risk.[24] At the same time, to the extent that partial dollarization reduces the scope for monetary policy discretion and the base for seigniorage, it also helps foster fiscal discipline.

How do these different monetary regimes (and the new institutional arrangements underpinning them) fare relative to each other in terms of: (1) the speed at which inflation is brought down after the regime is adopted; (2) the output cost of the policies designed to drive down inflation (the so-called "sacrifice" ratio);

and (3) their ability to foster fiscal discipline and *sustain* low inflation in the longer-term?

Most countries that experienced high inflation have at some point used exchange-rate-based stabilization programs to reduce price increases (see Table 4.4). Examples of soft pegs used to lower inflation from very high rates include the three attempted stabilizations in Argentina (including the Tablita and Austral plans) as well as stabilization programs in Brazil, Bulgaria, Chile, Israel, Mexico, Poland, Russia and, most recently, Turkey. In addition, some countries with moderate inflation also used soft pegs to help reduce it (e.g., Egypt, Pakistan, and Hungary), whereas others—notably in east Asia—pegged their exchange rates as much to achieve foreign trade stability as to keep inflation low. Examples of exchange-rate-based stabilizations using hard pegs include Argentina from 1991 and Bulgaria since 1997.

Exchange-rate-based stabilization programs generally succeeded in bringing inflation down rapidly in the short term, often accompanied by dramatic initial expansions in activity and appreciation of the real exchange rate (Figure 4.7), as inflation in the tradable goods sector slowed at a much faster

[24]The response of dollarization to interest rate differential in a few European emerging markets is examined in Fischer, Sahay, and Végh, "Modern Hyper—and High Inflations." Evidence on the impact of real exchange volatility on dollarization in large cross-section of countries is provided in Alain Ize and Eduardo Levy-Yeyati, "Dollarization of Financial Intermediation: Causes and Policy Implications," IMF Working Paper 98/28 (Washington: International Monetary Fund, 1998). For a theoretical analysis see Luis Catão and Marco Terrones, "Determinants of Dollarization: The Banking Side," IMF Working Paper 00/146 (Washington: International Monetary Fund, 2000).

rate than in nontradable goods.[25] This appreciation of the real exchange rate often led to unsustainable increases in domestic demand, output, and imports (as consumers and firms took advantage of the lower prices of foreign goods by accelerating such purchases), posing a clear threat to the balance of payments. Less credible pegs have been particularly susceptible to this effect, leading to a sharply negative short-run sacrifice ratio (the ratio of lost output to inflation reduction) at first, but at the cost of a significant recession later, particularly if the peg is abandoned.

Regarding the long-term impact on inflation, the difference between soft and hard pegs is important. In the case of soft pegs, growing balance of payments pressures have often led to their demise. This was so, for instance, in Argentina following the stabilization programs of 1978–81 (the *tablita*) and the 1985–86 Austral plan; Brazil during the 1986 cruzado plan and (to a lesser extent) the 1994–98 Real plan; the Chilean tablita program of 1978–82; Mexico following the 1987–94 stabilization; Russia in 1995–98; and it was a contributing factor in Turkey more recently.[26] In addition, because fixed exchange rate regimes tend to encourage unhedged foreign currency borrowing (often backed by implicit or explicit government guarantees), the collapse of the peg has tended to produce severe domestic banking crises—as, for instance, in Mexico during the 1994–95 "Tequila" crisis, in several Asian emerging markets during 1997–98, and in Turkey more recently.[27]

[25]For a stylized graphical description of the main macroeconomic regularities of exchange-rate-based stabilizations, see Guillermo Calvo and Carlos Végh, "Inflation Stabilization and BOP crises in Developing Countries;" and Mussa and others, *Exchange Rate Regimes in an Increasingly Integrated World Economy.*

[26]In recognition of such concerns, the Turkish program included an exit strategy to a floating exchange rate system (see Chapter I for more details). However, the pegged exchange rate collapsed before the exit strategy could be implemented.

[27]The frequent juxtaposition of currency and banking crises (the so-called "twin crises") has been documented in Graciela Kaminsky and Carmen Reinhart, "The Twin Crisis: The Causes of Banking and Balance-of-Payments Problems," *American Economic Review*, Vol. 89 (June 1999), pp. 473–500.

Figure 4.7. Selected Exchange Rate Stabilization Programs, 1985–98[1]
(Simple averages, three years prior and four years after program initiation, t)

Exchange rate stabilization has been generally associated with output growth in the early stages and a marked appreciation of the real exchange rate.

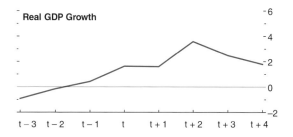

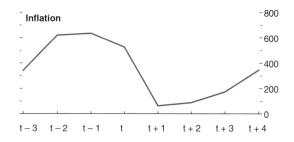

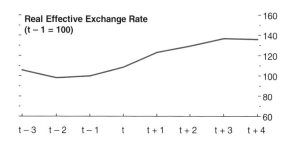

Source: IMF staff estimates.
[1]Simple averages for the following nine exchange rate stabilization programs: Israel, July 1985; Brazil (Cruzado), February 1986; Mexico, December 1987; Poland, January 1990; Argentina (Convertibility), April 1991; Brazil (Cardoso), July 1994; Russia, July 1995; Bulgaria, July 1997; and Turkey, January 1998.

Part—but certainly not all—of the sustainability problem with soft pegs seems related to the ambiguous relationship between pegged exchange rate regimes and fiscal discipline.[28] On the one hand, fixed exchange rates should be expected to foster fiscal discipline, given that policymakers know all too well that fiscal discipline is required to maintain the peg and that failure to do so is likely to result in politically and economically costly devaluations.[29] On the other hand, one can argue that fixed exchange rates can (temporarily) mask excesses in fiscal policy that would manifest themselves much faster in a floating exchange rate regime.[30] This masking effect can be particularly hazardous at the onset of stabilization programs where inflation drops sharply following the introduction of the peg, giving a false impression that the stabilization gains are permanent and leading to procrastination in undertaking the necessary but unpopular fiscal measures. Indeed, a common pattern of several stabilization programs is that of monetary discipline being enforced first and fiscal adjustment coming later—sometimes too little and too late.[31] This is largely because, as discussed earlier, consensus on fiscal adjustment and supportive reforms generally takes longer, is harder to achieve, and can be politically very costly. Consistent with these arguments about the ambiguous relationship between fiscal deficits and exchange rate regimes, a recent empirical study has found that the magnitude of fiscal deficits (measured as a ratio to GDP) has varied widely across pegged exchange rate regimes, that differences in fiscal performance between pegged and floating regimes are not statistically significant, and that the net effect depends on the choice of group of countries.[32]

That said, some soft exchange rate pegs have succeeded in bringing inflation down on a more sustained basis, particularly in the 1990s. Common general features of these experiences include fiscal restraint, broader structural and institutional reforms, and actions to break inflation inertia, such as wage freezes and labor market reform.[33] In addition, a variety of macroeconomic strategies have accompanied these stabilizations. In Egypt, inflation was reduced through an exchange-rate-based stabilization program and adherence to a soft-peg regime, which was supported by strong fiscal consolidation and gradually made more flexible. In other cases, such as Israel and Poland, inflation was reined in through a gradual loosening of the exchange rate band and, over time, the adoption of an inflation targeting regime (in Israel, capital controls also played a part). In Hungary, however the appreciation of the real exchange rate following stabilization was successfully contained through tight fiscal and monetary policies. In several Asian countries (notably Malaysia, Korea, and Thailand until the 1997–98 crisis), exchange rate

---

[28]Other sustainability problems are discussed in Stanley Fisher and Ratna Sahay, "The Transition Economies After Ten Years."

[29]Paul Krugman first formalized the relationship between fiscal deficits and speculative attacks in what became subsequently known as a "first-generation" model of currency crises. See Paul Krugman, "A Model of Balance-of-Payments Crises," *Journal of Money, Credit and Banking*, Vol. 11 (November 1979), pp.311–25.

[30]This argument has been made by Aaron Tornell and Andres Velasco, "Fixed versus Flexible Exchange Rates: Which Provides More Fiscal Discipline?," *Journal of Monetary Economics*, Vol. 45 (April 2000), pp.399–436. In other words, under flexible exchange rates the excesses of fiscal policy tend to be paid immediately, providing greater incentives to fiscal rectitude.

[31]This was the case, for instance, in Mexico in 1988–94, Brazil during 1994–98, and Turkey through much of the 1990s.

[32]See Antonio Fatás, and Andrew K. Rose, "Do Monetary Handcuffs Restrain Leviathan? Fiscal Policy in Extreme Exchange Rate Regimes," CEPR Discussion Paper No. 2692 (London: Centre for Economic Policy Research, 2001). A study for Latin America found no evidence that fixed exchange rates brought about greater fiscal discipline. See Michael Gavin and Roberto Perotti, "Fiscal Policy in Latin America," in *NBER Macroeconomics Annual*, ed. by Ben Bernanke and Julio Rotemberg (Cambridge, Mass.: The MIT Press, 1997). At the other extreme, Aaron Tornell and Andrés Velasco, "Fixed versus Flexible Exchange Rates: Which Provides More Fiscal Discipline?," find that floating exchange rate regimes have been more conducive to fiscal discipline in their sample of sub-Saharan African countries.

[33]See Stanley Fischer and David Orsmond, "Israeli Inflation from an International Perspective," IMF Working Paper 00/178 (Washington: International Monetary Fund, 2000).

pegs were also associated with low inflation. This history of monetary stability helped limit the exchange rate pass-through in the Asian crisis, enabling these countries to preserve low inflation.

In the case of hard pegs, devaluations have been much less frequent in both the recent and the distant past.[34] One reason is that a government's reputation tends to suffer following an exit from a hard peg; therefore, governments have been reluctant to abandon their hard pegs. The other reason is that countries under hard pegs have become highly "dollarized" or "euroized" following their adoption of dual currency arrangements in domestic banking and extensive foreign currency borrowing by the public and private sectors. As a result, the benefits of a devaluation on external competitiveness are smaller, while the impact on balance sheets can be highly contractionary if the nonfinancial private sector has a net short position in foreign currency. Yet, short-run output costs of sticking to the peg have at times been significant, as witnessed for instance by the experiences of Hong Kong SAR in 1997–98 and Argentina during the 1994–1995 "Tequila" crisis, as well as following the large external shocks associated with the Asian crisis of 1997–98 and the Russian crisis of 1998.

Until recently, the use of *floating exchange rate regimes* in stabilization programs has been mostly associated with the use of a monetary anchor. In this case, rather than pegging the exchange rate to that of a low inflation country, the central bank targets a monetary aggregate such as the monetary base or broad money, seeking to slow down its growth rate. Three main stylized facts have been generally associated with the use of monetary targeting in stabilization programs in emerging markets (Figure 4.8): (1) the slow convergence of inflation to the growth rate of the money supply, implying that dramatic monetary

[34]In the case of currency boards, the historical record indicates that most exits from the regime have been voluntary, and primarily reflecting political factors rather than external macroeconomic shocks. See Atish Ghosh, Anne-Marie Gulde, and Holger Wolf, "Currency Boards: More than a Quick Fix?," *Economic Policy: A European Forum* (October 2000).

Figure 4.8. Selected Monetary Stabilization Programs, 1975–90[1]
(Simple averages, three years prior and four years after program initiation, t)

Money-based stabilization programs have been generally associated with sharp output losses at their initial stages and limited appreciation of the real exchange rate.

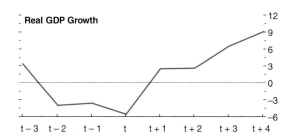

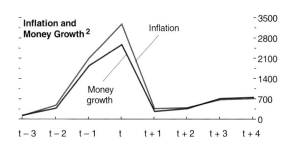

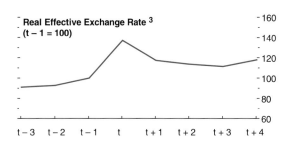

Source: IMF staff estimates.
[1]Simple averages for the following four monetary stabilization programs: Chile, April 1975; Argentina (Bonex), December 1989; Brazil (Collar), March 1990; Peru, August 1990. Data for Argentina in years t + 1, t + 2, t + 3, and t + 4 excluded because it adopted a new exchange rate stabilization program in t + 1 (1991).
[2] Money growth measured as annual percent change in M1.
[3] Excludes Peru for which real effective exchange rate data was not available prior to 1979.

tightening is typically needed to produce a significant drop in inflation; (2) a real appreciation of the currency but without leading to a clear-cut deterioration of the current account; and (3) an initial contraction (often dramatic) in economic activity. The third item implies that, in contrast with exchange-rate-based stabilizations, recessions will come earlier rather than later, in line with the kind of Phillips curve trade-offs observed in industrial countries.[35] The initial recession tends to be very sharp.[36] Partly for this reason, and in marked contrast with exchange rate pegs, the external trade and current account balances do not typically move sharply into deficits that bring into question the sustainability of the regime.

There is also consensus that the use of monetary targeting to maintain low inflation has become increasingly problematic in emerging markets. As amply demonstrated by the experience of industrial countries, a major issue is the instability of the relationship between monetary aggregates and inflation, often exacerbated by growing international capital mobility and financial innovation.[37] The issue is likely to be even more acute among emerging markets with long histories of monetary instability (which, among other things, makes it difficult to characterize the money-inflation relationship using long time series data) and where continuing currency substitution, the dollarization of bank deposits (in countries where they are allowed), and large swings in capital inflows stemming from changes in external interest rates complicate the control of domestic money growth.[38] In addition, grow-

ing dollarization in several of these countries and associated currency mismatches in private sector balance sheets can make it very difficult for central banks to focus solely on the pre-set monetary target at the expense of exchange rate stability when conflict between them arises.[39] For these reasons, monetary targeting regimes seem a clearly inferior alternative to other existing regimes outside the realm of stabilization programs in emerging markets—a contention supported by the fact that they have been largely abandoned in both advanced and emerging market economies.

The international experience with *inflation targeting*, albeit very recent, has been so far significantly more favorable. Regarding its capacity to lower inflation, a recent study including both industrial countries and emerging markets that have adopted inflation targeting over the past decade finds that it has taken about 10 quarters (2½ years) on average for a country to achieve stationary inflation levels following the adoption of inflation targeting.[40] Among emerging markets, however, the variance has been higher—with Chile and Israel having experienced the longest transition periods (nine and six years, respectively) since they began to publicly announce inflation targets in the early 1990s—partly reflecting the wider discrepancies in inflation levels at the starting point of the new regime. Countries that adopted inflation targeting have also been generally successful in meeting their announced targets, a feature that stands in sharp contrast with the international experience with mone-

---

[35]This difference in output performance between the two types of stabilization strategies has been dubbed in the literature as the "recession now vs. recession later" hypothesis.

[36]See Guillermo Calvo and Carlos Végh, "Inflation Stabilization and BOP Crisis in Developing Countries."

[37]Between the early 1970s and early 1980s, about half of the industrial countries adopted monetary targeting, but most of them discontinued the practice since. See Cottarelli and Giannini, "Credibility Without Rules."

[38]See, for instance, Guillermo Calvo and Carlos Végh, "Currency Substitution in Developing Countries: An Introduction," *Revista de Análisis Económico*, Vol. 7 (June 1992), pp. 3–28; Ratna Sahay and Carlos Végh,

"Dollarization in Transition Economies: Evidence and Policy Implications," and Miguel Savastano, "Dollarization in Latin America: Recent Evidence and Policy Issues," both in *The Macroeconomics of International Currencies: Theory, Policy, and Evidence,* ed. by Paul Mizen and Eric Pentecost (Gloucertershire, UK: Edward Elgar), pp. 193–224.

[39]As discussed later, a similar trade-off may arise under inflation targeting.

[40]See Vittorio Corbo, Oscar Landerretche Moreno, and Klaus Schmidt-Hebbel, "Does Inflation Targeting Make a Difference?," (unpublished; Santiago: Central Bank of Chile, 2000).

tary targets, which were frequently breached and revised.[41]

Sacrifice ratios have also been considerably lower under inflation targeting than under monetary targeting, though not as favorable as under exchange-rate-based stabilizations. In countries that have been under inflation targeting for several years (Chile and Israel, among emerging markets, and Australia, Canada, Chile, Finland, New Zealand, Spain, Sweden, and the United Kingdom), the sacrifice ratio has been estimated at 0.6 percent of annual GDP. For emerging market countries that adopted the framework over the past two years (Brazil, Colombia, Korea, Mexico, and South Africa) the average sacrifice ratio has to date been slightly negative (–0.4 of GDP).[42] Both figures are substantially lower than traditional benchmark estimates of sacrifice ratios in advanced countries.[43]

Inflation targeting's effect on fiscal performance is harder to establish, though the evidence is consistent with the hypothesis that it helps foster fiscal discipline. Table 4.5 shows that all countries that adopted inflation targeting experienced some improvement in their fiscal balances, typically with a one-to two-year lag (al-

though in some cases the improvement preceded the introduction of inflation targeting). As the absence of fiscal dominance appears to be a pre-condition to successful inflation targeting (Box 4.3), fiscal discipline and maintenance of a targeting regime should be linked without necessarily implying that one causes the other.[44] In any event, it is significant that in none of the countries where inflation targeting has been introduced has there been any evidence of a subsequent loosening of the fiscal stance.[45]

Some aspects of inflation targeting remain controversial. First, in virtually all countries that adopted inflation targeting, inflation had already been slowing and several of them embarked upon the new regime with single-digit inflation levels. In two emerging markets where inflation was in the double-digits prior to the adoption of inflation targeting (Chile and Israel), the transition period was rather protracted, even though inflation had been already trending down. This may suggest that the main strength of inflation targeting as a monetary policy regime lies in its capacity to keep inflation under control *once it is already low.*

Second, economic theory maintains that a key ingredient to reduce inflation is regime credibility. This raises the question of where monetary policy credibility will come from in the case of emerging markets that are considering adopting inflation targeting following a long history of monetary instability and/or large devaluations. In this regard, a comparison between inflation targeting and its main competitor—exchange rate pegs—is illustrative. Under exchange rate pegging, credibility is largely imported—that is, it comes from a tangible (and hence credible) restraint on the behavior of tradable prices. In

---

[41]Corbo, Moreno, and Schmidt-Hebbel, "Does Inflation Targeting Make a Difference?," estimate an annual absolute average deviation between actual and target inflation of 66 basis points during the period 1989–2000 for a sample of countries consisting of Australia, Canada, Chile, Finland, Israel, New Zealand, Spain, Sweden, and the United Kingdom. Regarding the experience of emerging markets that have joined the sample more recently (Brazil, Colombia, Korea, Mexico, and South Africa) those deviations have averaged 2.74 percentage points. Another related indicator is the frequency of quarterly breaches in inflation targets. These have been relatively infrequent during both the disinflation period and the long-run target period. See Andrea Schaechter, Mark R. Stone, and Mark Zelmer, "Adopting Inflation Targeting: Practical Issues for Emerging Market Countries," IMF Occasional Paper No. 202 (Washington: International Monetary Fund, 2000).

[42]See Corbo, Moreno, and Schmidt-Hebbel, "Does Inflation Targeting Make a Difference?"

[43]Estimates of sacrifice ratios in developed countries are provided in Laurence Ball, "What Determines the Sacrifice Ratio?," in *Monetary Policy*, ed. by Gregory Mankiw (Chicago: The University of Chicago Press, 1994), pp. 155–188.

[44]It may simply be that a country decides to adopt inflation targeting once the fiscal situation is reasonably under control or there is already a firm resolve to lower the deficit.

[45]Ideally, the way to measure the performance would be based on cyclical adjusted measures of the fiscal stance, rather than based on actual fiscal deficits scaled by nominal GDP. However, as previously noted, such measures are hard to obtain for emerging markets, partly due to a lack of consensual estimates of the output gap.

Table 4.5. Fiscal Balances of Countries That Adopted Inflation Targeting[1]
(Annual percent)

Country	1985–89	1990	1991	1992	1993	1994	1995	1996	1997	1998	1999	2000
Early inflation targeters												
Chile[2]	1.01	**3.48**	**2.38**	**3.02**	**1.75**	**2.26**	**3.63**	**2.58**	**2.10**	**-0.11**	**-2.37**	**-1.06**
Israel[2]	-3.49	**-4.35**	**-6.08**	**-3.65**	**-2.50**	**-2.30**	**-4.10**	**-3.70**	**-2.70**	**-2.30**	**-2.25**	**-0.61**
Australia	-0.18	0.91	-1.39	-3.44	-3.90	-3.27	-2.37	-1.48	-0.29	0.66	1.46	1.32
Canada	-5.33	**-4.91**	**-5.45**	**-5.12**	**-5.48**	**-4.57**	**-3.93**	**-2.04**	**0.50**	**0.52**	**0.62**	**1.43**
Finland	0.98	1.02	-4.54	**-8.11**	**-10.65**	**-10.77**	**-8.72**	**-7.20**	**-3.67**	**-1.48**	**-0.78**	**1.34**
New Zealand	-2.66	**-1.68**	**-4.48**	**-4.61**	**-0.69**	**2.20**	**3.61**	**2.72**	**1.64**	**0.97**	**0.43**	**0.30**
Spain	-3.84	-2.80	-2.20	-2.67	-5.91	-4.92	-5.92	-3.93	-2.67	-2.14	-1.09	-0.72
Sweden	-0.48	1.33	-3.93	**-9.76**	**-14.66**	**-11.27**	**-8.72**	**-3.77**	**-1.79**	**0.64**	**3.66**	**3.92**
United Kingdom	-1.42	-0.84	-2.78	**-7.24**	**-8.18**	**-6.91**	**-5.48**	**-4.16**	**-1.48**	**0.25**	**1.48**	**3.80**
Average	-1.71	-0.87	-3.16	-4.62	-5.58	-4.39	-3.55	-2.33	-0.93	-0.33	0.13	1.09
Newcomers												
Brazil	-1.51	2.64	0.19	-0.87	-0.10	0.10	-2.27	-2.57	-2.63	-5.40	**-6.89**	**-3.20**
Colombia[3]	-1.56	-0.68	0.01	-1.81	-1.02	-1.47	-3.37	-4.63	-3.41	-5.37	-7.43	-6.05
Czech Republic	2.52	-2.07	4.15	-0.62	0.46	1.24	-0.25	-0.10	-0.94	**-1.63**	**-1.61**	**-2.30**
Mexico[3]	-9.79	-2.60	0.20	1.46	0.77	-0.58	-1.74	-1.00	-1.86	-2.27	-2.22	-0.94
Poland	-2.03	0.71	-7.24	-7.27	-3.92	-3.39	-3.67	-3.53	-2.61	-2.97	**-4.98**	**-5.28**
South Africa	-4.46	-3.11	-4.76	-8.73	-9.42	-5.24	-5.19	-4.51	-3.84	-2.34	-2.06	**-2.65**
Thailand	-2.43	4.73	4.81	2.83	2.19	1.92	2.97	2.47	-0.86	-2.55	-2.94	**-2.24**
Average	-2.80	-0.85	-1.24	-2.97	-2.20	-1.56	-2.75	-2.72	-2.55	-3.33	-4.20	-3.40

[1]Years under inflation targeting in bold.
[2]Date for starting with inflation targeting at the point inflation targets began to be publicly announced.
[3]Inflation targeting starting in 2001. Previously, monetary targets were announced.

particular, under currency unions or unilateral adoption of the currency of a low inflation country, credibility clearly stems from national constitutional arrangements and/or international agreements that tend to be hard to revoke. In the absence of those, inflation targeting countries have to rely on the various institutional arrangements discussed above, such as greater transparency and accountability of monetary policies, granting the central bank operational (instrument) independence, and giving the central bank a clear mandate to lower inflation above anything else. As noted before, there is evidence that such arrangements have played a significant role in helping to control inflation; yet, building such credibility may take a significant time and, hence, protract stabilization.[46]

Third, inflation targeting may be a problem in countries that must maintain exchange rate sta-bility to protect the unhedged balance sheet positions of the private sector. Indeed, because of potential financial fragilities arising out of large exchange rate movements, it has been argued that most developing countries tend to display a "fear of floating."[47] In principle, inflation targeting does not rule out some attention being paid to exchange rate movements by the central bank to the extent that they have a bearing on future inflation. This generally produces a pattern of monetary tightening when the exchange rate depreciates, a similar response (but not necessarily of the same magnitude) to that if the exchange rate were being targeted directly. So, inflation targeting does take into account the "fear of floating" argument, but only indirectly. To the extent that conflicting objectives between exchange rate stability and inflation arise or the magnitude of tightening needed to stabilize the exchange rate differs substantially from that needed to achieve the inflation targets, balance sheet considerations

[46]One possible alternative is to borrow temporarily such credibility from an external institution, such as the IMF, until the "nuts and bolts" of inflation targeting are put in place. Countries that adopted inflation targeting or started moving toward it while under IMF-supported programs include Brazil, Colombia, and Thailand.

[47]See Guillermo Calvo and Carmen M. Reinhart, "Fear of Floating," NBER Working Paper No. 7993 (Cambridge, Mass.: National Bureau of Economic Research, 2000).

(as in several partially dollarized emerging market economies) may become paramount, limiting the use of inflation targeting and undermining the transparency of monetary policy.

Finally, successful inflation targeting has generally been associated with significant preconditions that some other emerging markets currently may find difficult to meet (see Box 4.3). Particular examples are the existence of well-developed financial markets, absence of fiscal dominance, reasonably well-understood transmission mechanisms, and central bank instrument independence.

Safeguarding Low Inflation in Emerging Markets

As discussed above, the decline in world inflation and greater monetary stability in advanced countries, together with the strengthening of institutional arrangements in recent years, have helped to address one of the main causes of emerging market inflation in previous decades—namely, the lack of a credible nominal anchor for private sector inflation expectations. In addition, the substantial progress made over the past decades in the theory and practice of monetary policy has undoubtedly contributed to sounder central banking practices. This includes not only more sophisticated forecasting tools and a better understanding of policy instruments, but also—and perhaps more crucially—the emphasis on transparency and accountability of central bank decisions and awareness of the perils of saddling the monetary authority with multiple objectives other than that of preserving price stability. Finally, other structural policies have helped by making economies more efficient and reducing inflation inertia, such as labor market and trade reform.

However, lower external inflation, sounder central bank arrangements, and better understanding of monetary policy do not guarantee price stability. Because monetary and fiscal policies are intrinsically linked through the budget constraint of the consolidated government, monetary policy soundness, and hence a country's inflation performance, are dependent on

the stance of its fiscal policy. While recent institutional changes in monetary policy arrangements do appear to have helped curb fiscal excesses, they cannot of themselves prevent persistent fiscal deficits. Indeed, history points to episodes of significant loosening of fiscal policies under currency boards, central bank independence, and partial and even full dollarization; moreover, significant reductions in fiscal deficits in several countries that adopted inflation targeting in recent years are yet to be seen. This suggests that monetary arrangements *per se* have only limited power to fix "real" problems arising from a fiscal regime inconsistent with the goal of price stability.

There have, of course, been other general developments that have helped restrain fiscal excesses in emerging markets, some of which may be of a more permanent nature. One of them is the rapid growth of domestic financial systems. As mentioned above, inflation appears to be inversely related to the depth of domestic financial markets, insofar as the latter lowers the cost of noninflationary financing of fiscal deficits and reduces the need of seigniorage. Financial sector concerns about inflation, combined with the sector's growing economic importance, are also a contributing factor.[48] A second key development is greater financial integration of emerging market countries within the world economy. To the extent that national governments compete among themselves for a given pool of world savings, and international capital markets monitor country-specific fiscal developments and price the respective sovereign spreads accordingly, this provides a clear incentive for fiscal prudence. Third, public tolerance for inflation appears to be lower. This may be merely due to a demonstration effect stemming from low inflation in in-

---

[48]The argument about financial sector distaste for inflation and its impact on macroeconomic discipline has been made by Adam Posen, "Why Central Bank Independence Does Not Cause Low Inflation: There Is No Institutional Fix for Politics," in *Finance and the International Economy: The AMEX Bank Review Prize Essays,* ed. by Richard O'Brien, Vol.1 (New York: Oxford University Press, 1993).

dustrial countries, but it may also reflect greater political weight in newly democratic regimes of lower income groups that are bound to lose more from inflation (see Box 4.1).

Other factors, however, may pose a threat to recent gains in price stabilization. First, some of the underlying institutional arrangements now in place in several emerging markets—notably those underpinning inflation targeting—are fairly new and have not been extensively tested. It remains to be seen whether they will be sustainable and effective in controlling inflation under a variety of crisis situations, such as those that plagued many emerging markets over the past decade. Second, despite substantial improvement in recent years, fiscal deficits remain relatively high in several emerging market countries, and in some countries public debt/GDP ratios are approaching those of advanced economies that have much more extensive welfare systems and a significant elderly population. Perhaps even more worrisome, fiscal consolidation efforts have been halted in quite a few countries over the past five years (see Table 4.3). Reasons for concern seem especially justified in some countries with hard exchange rate pegs where the accompanying requirement of stringent fiscal discipline has been somewhat lacking. To the extent that fail-ure in taking bold steps in this direction increase the temptation to tackle the fiscal problem by resorting to the inflation tax, long-term price stability could be threatened.

Finally, consensus on how to distribute the fiscal cost of price stabilization remains hard to forge. This has been particularly the case in emerging markets with wide income disparities, long histories of fiscal and monetary imbalances, and sharply divided governments—factors that no doubt increase the political cost of monetary and fiscal prudence. Although low inflation *per se* may help create a strong constituency in favor of price stability, this cannot be taken for granted, at least on the basis of historical experiences to date.[49] These political economy complications indicate that the achievement and preservation of price stability in those countries will require a firm political resolve and strong institutional arrangements to limit the discretion of *both* the monetary and the fiscal authorities.

---

[49]This point is vividly illustrated in the words of Brazilian finance minister Pedro Malan in the wake of the 1994 Brazilian stabilization program: "We made a bet that the initial success at bringing down inflation would create the political support for the reforms required to consolidate those gains. This is a bet that's still on the table," *Wall Street Journal*, October 4, 1995, quoted in Alejandro M. Werner, "Building Consensus for Stabilization."

Directors agreed that prospects for global growth have weakened significantly, led by a marked slowdown in the United States, the stalling recovery in Japan, and a slowing of growth in Europe and in a number of emerging market countries. They noted that some slowdown from the rapid rates of global growth of late 1999 and early 2000 is both desirable and expected, especially in those countries most advanced in the cycle, but that the deceleration is proving to be steeper than earlier thought. At the same time, while headline inflation in most advanced economies has begun to stabilize, with moderate wage increases and declining oil prices, underlying inflation remains generally subdued, except perhaps in a number of faster growing European and emerging market economies.

Given the rapid policy response by several central banks in both advanced and emerging economies, Directors thought the chances are reasonable that the slowdown in global activity will be relatively short lived, although the pace of recovery may be slowed by the continuing decline in global equity markets. Declining short- and long-term interest rates should provide support to activity in the second half of 2001, and, with inflationary risks receding, policymakers in most advanced countries—with the important exception of Japan—have substantial room for further easing. Moreover, given the remarkable strengthening in fiscal positions in recent years, most advanced countries also have room for fiscal easing as a second line of defense, which the United States in particular is expected to use. In addition, while a number of emerging market countries continue to face serious difficulties, external and financial vulnerabilities have generally been reduced since the 1997–98 crises as a result of wide-ranging structural reforms, and the shift away from soft exchange rate pegs to flexible exchange rate systems has improved countries' ability to manage external shocks.

Most Directors agreed, however, that the outlook remains subject to considerable uncertainty, and that a deeper and more prolonged downturn is possible. They noted that the adjustment process in the United States could be complicated by the substantial imbalances that developed during the expansion, including the large current account deficit, the apparent overvaluation of the U.S. dollar, and the negative household savings rate, as well as by the risk of possible further declines in equity markets.

Directors emphasized that the extent of the downturn will be affected by policy decisions by all countries. In the advanced economies, a more proactive approach to macroeconomic policies, particularly on the monetary side, may well be required, and should be pursued consistently with their respective cyclical positions and without compromising medium-term stabilization objectives. Where needed, these policies should be complemented with the determined pursuit of structural reforms. In view of the present fragility of external financing conditions, prospects in emerging markets depend critically on maintaining investor confidence. For these countries, Directors underscored the need to maintain prudent macroeconomic policies and to press ahead with corporate, financial and—especially in the transition economies—institutional reforms.

Directors noted with concern that the slowdown in global growth will adversely affect the low-income countries, both directly and through lower commodity prices. The need for countries to sustain strong policies is even greater in such circumstances, both in countries receiving debt relief under the Enhanced HIPC Initiative and in others. Directors stressed that to assist the efforts of low-income countries, the advanced economies have a special responsibility to increase aid flows, to support initiatives promoting peace and domestic stability, and to provide further assistance to fight the spread of the HIV/AIDS epidemic. They especially emphasized the importance, at the present juncture, of further reducing barriers to the exports of the developing countries, and of the poorest countries in particular. In this connection, the recent initiative of the European Union to eliminate tariffs on almost all exports of the least developed countries was welcomed.

Directors considered that, given the change in the global economic outlook, it is particularly important that the Fund, in its dialogue with member countries, as well as through its multilateral surveillance, continue to support actively the implementation of policies that promote economic stability and prosperity. A number of Directors emphasized the need for the Fund to continue to strengthen its surveillance activities.

Major Currency Areas

For the United States, Directors noted that the outlook is subject to more than the usual amount of uncertainty. While growth is likely to remain weak in the first half of 2001, reflecting rapid inventory adjustment, most Directors believed that activity, supported by lower short- and long-term interest rates, will pick up in the second half, although the rate of pickup may be slowed by the lagged effect of the recent decline in equity prices. However, Directors also acknowledged that there is a significant risk that the imbalances built up during the long expansion could unwind in a less orderly fashion, accompanied by further declines in confidence and increases in risk aversion in financial markets. With the balance of risks shifting increasingly toward weaker aggregate demand, Directors strongly welcomed the timely and significant easing of monetary policy in the first quarter. If economic and financial conditions remain weak, some further easing would be appropriate. While monetary policy remains the preferred instrument for responding actively to

cyclical developments, Directors believed that, given the sustained fiscal surpluses in prospect in coming years, moderate and front-loaded tax cuts would also be appropriate from a cyclical perspective. These tax cuts should preferably be enacted in phases, with each phase put in place only once it is clear that sufficient budgetary resources will be available to finance it. The surpluses of the Social Security and Medicare Health Insurance trust funds should be preserved in order to help meet future pension and health care costs.

Directors expressed considerable concern at the renewed setback to recovery in Japan, which could exacerbate the slowdown and have a particularly serious impact on a number of Asian countries. While this setback partly reflects the slowdown elsewhere, especially the weakening of global demand for electronics equipment, it is also due to continued weak consumer confidence and underlying structural weaknesses, especially in the Japanese corporate and financial sectors. Given the deteriorating outlook and continued deflation, Directors welcomed the recent introduction of a new monetary policy framework, which effectively returns to the zero-interest rate policy and includes a commitment to maintain the new framework until consumer prices have stopped declining, and (if needed) will step up outright purchases of long-term government bonds. They urged that the framework be forcefully implemented. Given the high level of public debt, Directors believed that the very gradual fiscal consolidation currently underway remains appropriate, and that further fiscal easing should be considered only as a last resort. They stressed, however, that the prospects for a return to sustained growth in the medium term depend most critically on determined action to address weaknesses in banks and life insurance companies, including through the vigorous application of the regulatory and supervisory framework, along with measures to further encourage corporate restructuring. In this respect, Directors looked forward to the staff's assessment of the new reform package announced by the Japanese government.

Directors observed that while growth in the euro area remains relatively well sustained, signs of slowing activity have intensified in recent months and confidence has weakened. While headline inflation remains above the ECB's target, underlying price pressures are muted, with little evidence thus far of pass-through effects of higher energy prices and the weaker euro on wages. Against this background, many Directors believed that a moderate cut in interest rates is now appropriate, with a further cut being in order if the exchange rate were to appreciate sharply or if indications of slowing growth were to mount. Directors considered that, while recent tax cuts in some countries would provide helpful stimulus, there is no further need to use fiscal policy actively to support output at this stage, although fiscal execution should allow the full play of automatic stabilizers. While welcoming the important progress that has been made in some areas of structural reform, Directors underscored that further deepening and acceleration of market-oriented reforms, especially of pension systems, labor markets, and product markets, is necessary both to raise potential output growth over the medium term, and to address the challenges posed by aging populations. They also underscored the need, over the medium term, to further reduce tax burdens, which remain very high in a number of euro area countries. Such reductions would need to be accompanied by spending restraint in order to allow medium-term budget targets to be met.

Emerging Economies

Directors observed that following a rapid recovery from the recent regional crisis, growth in emerging Asia has weakened as a result of higher oil prices, slowing growth in the United States and Japan, the downturn in the global electronics cycle, and—in some countries—the lagging pace of corporate and financial restructuring. They noted that growth is expected to slow most in the Newly Industrialized Economies and ASEAN countries, particularly those more advanced in the recovery and where the process

of corporate and financial restructuring has lagged. In these countries, it will be crucial to restore the momentum of structural reforms. For countries with low inflation and sustainable fiscal positions, Directors recommended moderate interest rate reductions, coupled in some cases with an easier pace of fiscal consolidation. Directors noted that growth is expected to be relatively well maintained in China and India. In China, a gradual shift to a more neutral fiscal policy stance is appropriate given considerations of medium-term sustainability. In India, the recent monetary policy easing should be supported by continued improvements in the environment for private investment and a substantial reduction, over the medium term, in the overall public sector deficit.

Directors noted that growth in Latin America rebounded in 2000 following the sharp slowdown in 1999, in part reflecting strong adjustment measures put in place in many countries. In 2001, the direct impact of weakening external demand on activity is likely to be largest in Mexico and in several countries in the Andean region and Central America, but more moderate in those countries—such as Brazil and Argentina—that are less open and where trade links with the United States are less important. However, given Latin America's large external financing requirements, the impact of the U.S. slowdown on financial markets will be critical. While a number of countries had been able to cover a substantial part of their annual public sector financing needs in early 2001, Directors expressed concern that, despite the easing of U.S. monetary policy, financing conditions have deteriorated following the latest crises in Argentina and Turkey, reflecting a rise in investor risk aversion and possible concerns about a slowdown in inward foreign direct investment. With intensifying scrutiny from global financial markets, it will be important to maintain prudent fiscal policies, along with structural reforms—particularly in financial and corporate sectors and labor markets. Directors generally welcomed the recent initiatives to strengthen the policy framework in Argentina, while stressing the need for continued fiscal restraint and strict adherence to the economic program at all levels of government.

Directors observed that growth in Africa has been constrained by war and civil conflict in some countries, weak commodity prices, and, for oil-importing countries, by higher oil prices. While countries that implement sound macroeconomic and structural policies and maintain political stability have been able to achieve relatively strong rates of growth, Directors were concerned that the outlook for the region could be adversely affected by the current global slowdown, particularly through a further weakening of commodity prices. Directors welcomed the recent strengthening of economic policies in many countries, which has been supported by debt relief through the Enhanced HIPC Initiative and the Poverty Reduction and Growth Facility. It will be important to sustain the momentum for reform in the years ahead, particularly by improving the environment for private investment, strengthening public service delivery, improving tax administration and infrastructure, and enhancing governance. Directors generally endorsed the conclusions of the staff analysis of trade integration in Sub-Saharan Africa, noting in particular the scope for further reductions in trade barriers by African countries. They agreed that a lasting improvement in Africa's trade performance will depend on a broader mix of macroeconomic policies and structural reforms that will be key to improved efficiency and external competitiveness. Directors also welcomed the staff's suggestions for rationalizing the current regional trade arrangements to allow them to reach their intended objectives.

Directors noted that, in the Middle East, higher oil prices combined with increased oil production have generally boosted activity and improved fiscal and external balances in 2000. With the windfall gains from higher oil prices having been prudently used, the projected decline in oil prices in 2001 and 2002 appears generally manageable. Nonetheless, a prudent approach to fiscal policy remains desirable, especially in those countries where government

debt needs to be reduced. More generally, Directors underscored the need for continued reforms to promote economic diversification and growth, including the removal of remaining impediments to trade and foreign direct investment. Growth in most of the non-oil producing countries in the region is expected to remain stable, although it could be affected by a steeper-than-anticipated global slowdown. Directors considered that reform of trade and foreign direct investment regimes is also a priority in many of these countries, which have yet to share fully in the benefits of globalization.

Directors observed that the situation in Turkey remains very difficult. They welcomed the steps taken to reform the financial system, particularly with regard to state banks, but noted that further decisive policy measures are needed to resolve the problems in the banking sector, strengthen the fiscal accounts, and achieve broad-based structural reforms. In central and eastern Europe, growth is expected to remain reasonably well sustained in 2001, although activity will be vulnerable to a greater-than-expected slowdown in Western Europe. Against the background of weakening external demand and large current account deficits, Directors favored a rebalancing of the policy mix toward relatively tighter fiscal policy, which would help restrain domestic demand while limiting upward pressure on interest rates and exchange rates. They also noted that further structural and institutional reforms are needed, especially with respect to privatization, enterprise restructuring, and financial regulation and supervision, to promote sustainable growth in the medium term and facilitate accession to the European Union.

Directors welcomed the recent improvement in growth performance and external positions in the countries of the Commonwealth of Independent States (CIS), which reflects mainly higher world energy prices and buoyant growth in Russia. In Russia, growth is expected to moderate from the very rapid pace in 2000, as a result in part of lower oil prices and some real appreciation of the ruble, as well as the global slowdown. The government's long-term reform plan is an important step forward, but Directors agreed that it needs to be both firmly implemented and significantly developed in a number of key areas, including banking reform and payments arrears and restructuring of infrastructural monopolies. Accelerating structural and institutional reform also remains the central challenge in most other CIS countries.

Maintaining Improved Fiscal and Monetary Policies

Directors welcomed the comprehensive discussion in the World Economic Outlook of the recent improvements in fiscal performance and the decline in inflation in many countries. They noted that the durability of recent fiscal consolidation in advanced economies is likely to be improved by the associated reductions in public expenditure (as a share of GDP) and the strengthening of fiscal frameworks over the past decade. Directors emphasized that fiscal discipline will be vital in the years ahead, given the substantial increases expected in public spending on pensions and health care as populations age. In order to meet pension liabilities and enhance output growth as dependency ratios rise, the policy response should be broad-based, encompassing both pension reform and structural reforms, including labor market improvements. Consideration should be given to directing a part of recent and projected fiscal improvements to increased pre-funding of future pension liabilities. Directors took note of the global perspective of population aging: as dependency ratios decline in many developing countries, in-

creased saving by countries with aging populations could support growth in emerging markets and future consumption in advanced economies.

Directors reviewed the analysis of the decline in inflation in emerging economies in recent years. Improved monetary stability in advanced economies and substantial progress in institutional reform in emerging economies, including more independent central banks and improved knowledge about monetary policy transmission, have played an important contributing role in achieving this outcome. Directors noted that prudent fiscal policies have also been a key factor in achieving lower inflation and allowing the conduct of a stable monetary policy in the long run. While observing that experience with the more frequent use of inflation targeting to accompany flexible exchange rates has been generally encouraging so far, Directors considered that a more definitive verdict on inflation targeting will need to await further experience, particularly with the maintenance of price stability during sustained periods that include episodes of financial stress and exchange rate instability.

Finally, Executive Directors wished to take this opportunity to express their deep appreciation to Michael Mussa for his outstanding contribution as Economic Counsellor and Director of the Research Department to the Fund's multilateral surveillance over the past ten years, especially through his oversight and direction of the World Economic Outlook, and his regular informal briefings on World Economic and Market Developments, which have been a highlight of the Board agenda.

STATISTICAL APPENDIX

The statistical appendix presents historical data, as well as projections. It comprises four sections: Assumptions, Data and Conventions, Classification of Countries, and Statistical Tables.

The assumptions underlying the estimates and projections for 2001–2002 and the medium-term scenario for 2003–2006 are summarized in the first section. The second section provides a general description of the data and of the conventions used for calculating country group composites. The classification of countries in the various groups presented in the *World Economic Outlook* is summarized in the third section. Note that the group of advanced economies now includes Cyprus.

The last, and main, section comprises the statistical tables. Data in these tables have been compiled on the basis of information available through the end of March 2001. The figures for 2001 and beyond are shown with the same degree of precision as the historical figures solely for convenience; since they are projections, the same degree of accuracy is not to be inferred.

Assumptions

Real effective *exchange rates* for the advanced economies are assumed to remain constant at their average levels during the period February 19–March 16, 2001. For 2001 and 2002, these assumptions imply average U.S. dollar/SDR conversion rates of 1.292 and 1.294, respectively.

Established *policies* of national authorities are assumed to be maintained. The more specific policy assumptions underlying the projections for selected advanced economies are described in Box A1.

It is assumed that the *price of oil* will average $25.50 a barrel in 2001 and $22.50 a barrel in 2002.

With regard to *interest rates*, it is assumed that the London interbank offered rate (LIBOR) on six-month U.S. dollar deposits will average 4.5 percent in 2001 and 4.3 percent in 2002; that the three-month certificate of deposit rate in Japan will average 0.3 percent in 2001 and 0.5 in 2002; and that the three-month interbank deposit rate for the euro will average 4.4 percent in 2001 and 4.1 percent in 2002.

With respect to *introduction of the euro*, on December 31, 1998 the Council of the European Union decided that, effective January 1, 1999, the irrevocably fixed conversion rates between the euro and currencies of the member states adopting the euro are:[1]

1 euro	=	13.7603	Austrian schillings
	=	40.3399	Belgian francs
	=	1.95583	Deutsche mark
	=	5.94573	Finnish markkaa
	=	6.55957	French francs
	=	340.750	Greek drachma
	=	0.787564	Irish pound
	=	1,936.27	Italian lire
	=	40.3399	Luxembourg francs
	=	2.20371	Netherlands guilders
	=	200.482	Portuguese escudos
	=	166.386	Spanish pesetas

See Box 5.4 in the October 1998 *World Economic Outlook* for details on how the conversion rates were established.

Data and Conventions

Data and projections for 182 countries form the statistical basis for the *World Economic Outlook* (the World Economic Outlook database). The data are maintained jointly by the IMF's Research Department and area departments, with the latter regularly updating

---

[1]The conversion rate for Greece was established prior to inclusion in the euro area on January 1, 2001.

Box A1. Economic Policy Assumptions Underlying the Projections for Selected Advanced Countries

The short-term fiscal policy assumptions used in the *World Economic Outlook* are based on officially announced budgets, adjusted for differences between the national authorities and the IMF staff regarding macroeconomic assumptions and projected fiscal outturns. The medium-term fiscal projections incorporate policy measures that are judged likely to be implemented. In cases where the IMF staff has insufficient information to assess the authorities' budget intentions and prospects for policy implementation, an unchanged structural primary balance is assumed, unless otherwise indicated. Specific assumptions used in some of the advanced economies follow (see also Tables 14–16 in the Statistical Appendix for data on fiscal and structural balances).[1]

United States. The fiscal projections are based on the budget proposals made in the Administration's FY2002 Budget (February 28, 2001), adjusted for the IMF staff's macroeconomic assumptions.

Japan. The projections take account of the FY2000 supplementary budget and the FY2001 draft budget. The ¥11 trillion stimulus package of November 2000 includes additional public investment of ¥5 trillion (headline figure), most of which is projected to take place in the first two quarters of FY2001. Local governments are projected to largely offset their share in the

stimulus package with cuts in own-account expenditures elsewhere. A "typical" supplementary budget of ¥1 trillion is included in the calculations for FY2001. The improvement in the fiscal balance in FY2001 is mainly on account of a decline in the use of public funds for the resolution of banking sector problems.

Germany. The fiscal projections incorporate the government's fiscal consolidation package for 2000 and beyond and the income tax reform package 2001–2005 that were approved by Parliament in December 1999 and July 2000, respectively. The fiscal projections for 2000 also include the proceeds from the August 2000 sale of mobile phone licenses (UMTS) of DM 99.4 billion (US$ 46.9 billion), which amounts to 2.5 percent of GDP.

France. The projections are based on the national authorities' targets. For 2001, the projections are adjusted for the Constitutional Court's rejection of the targeted reduction in the generalized social contribution, for the introduction of the *prime pour l'emploi*, and for the IMF staff's weaker macroeconomic projections. For the medium term, the projections are broadly consistent with the government's stability program, adjusted for the differences between the IMF staff's and the authorities' macroeconomic assumptions.

Italy. The fiscal projections are based on the 2001 budget approved in December 2000 by parliament, the updated medium-term fiscal plan (*DPEF*) covering the period 2001–2004, and the 2001 stability program. The fiscal measures included in the 2001 budget are assumed to be implemented fully and to have the impact as indicated in the government's fiscal plan. For the years 2002–2004, the IMF staff's projections build on the authorities' projections at unchanged legislation (*tendenziale*) and factor in differences in the macroeconomic assumptions for the medium term, the effect of changes in legislation needed on the basis of current policies (in particular, expected wage increases and new capital spending), and the announced fiscal targets (*quadro programmatico*). For the years 2005–06, the projections assume an unchanged

---

[1]The output gap is actual less potential output, as a percent of potential output. Structural balances are expressed as a percent of potential output. The structural budget balance is the budgetary position that would be observed if the level of actual output coincided with potential output. Changes in the structural budget balance consequently include effects of temporary fiscal measures, the impact of fluctuations in interest rates and debt-service costs, and other noncyclical fluctuations in the budget balance. The computations of structural budget balance are based on IMF staff estimates of potential GDP and revenue and expenditures elasticities (see the October 1993 *World Economic Outlook*, Annex I). Net debt is defined as gross debt less financial assets of the general government, which include assets held by the social security insurance system. Estimates of the output gap and of the structural budget balance are subject to significant margins of uncertainty.

primary structural balance. Details on the measures for 2002 will be unveiled in the budget law to be submitted to parliament in September. The estimates for 2000 include receipts from the sale of Universal Mobile Telecommunications Service (UMTS) licenses of about lire 23 trillion, or 1 percent of GDP.

United Kingdom. The fiscal projections are based on the November 2000 pre-budget, the July 2000 spending review, and the March 2000 budget. Additionally, the projections incorporate more recent statistical releases from the Office for National Statistics, including provisional budgetary outturns through December 2000. The main differences between the national authorities' and the IMF staff's projections are as follows: the IMF staff projections are based on potential growth of 2 percent rather than the 2¼ percent underlying the official projections, and the IMF staff projections assume that the fuel tax cut (about 0.2 percent of GDP a year starting in 2001/02) proposed for consultation in November 2000 is implemented. The IMF staff's projections also include an adjustment for the proceeds of the recent UMTS license auction (about 2.4 percent of GDP) received in fiscal year 2001/02 to conform to the Eurostat accounting guidelines (the proceeds are not included in the computation of the structural balance).

Canada. The fiscal outlook prepared by the IMF staff assumes tax and expenditure policies in line with those outlined in the budget plan 2000 and the October 2000 economic statement and budget update, adjusted for the IMF staff's macroeconomic projections. In line with the announcement in the October 2000 update, the staff expects a federal government budget surplus of Can\$10 billion for the fiscal year 2000/01, reflecting the government's new policy of announcing a debt reduction target each October for the current fiscal year. Over the medium term, the IMF staff assumes that the federal government budget will be in surplus by Can\$3 billion a year, an amount equivalent to the contingency reserve. The consolidated fiscal

position for the provinces is assumed to evolve in line with their stated medium-term targets.

Australia. The fiscal projections through FY2004 are based on the 2000/01 budget, which was released in May 2000. For the remainder of the projection period, the IMF staff's projections assume unchanged policies.

Belgium. Fiscal projections through 2005 are based on the government's medium-term tax and expenditure plans announced in the 2001 budget and on the targets and rules for the fiscal balance presented in the 2001–05 stability program. The projections incorporate the IMF staff's assumptions for economic growth and interest rates, and assume resulting budgetary windfalls are devoted to improving the fiscal balance.

Greece. The fiscal projections are based on the authorities' policies presented in the 2001 budget, adjusted for different macroeconomic assumptions. For the 2002–06 period, primary current expenditures are assumed to maintain their share of GDP, while the current revenue share is projected to decline slightly (by ¼ percent of GDP), as social insurance contributions—which are tied to wages—are expected to grow less rapidly than output. Thus, the overall surplus is projected to grow largely in line with a reduction in interest expenditures, which is the result of euro area membership.

Netherlands. The 2000 budget estimate includes revenues from the sale of mobile phone licenses of NLG 5.9 billion (0.7 percent of GDP). The fiscal projections through 2002 reflect the government's rules-based approach to fiscal policy, which comprises medium-term real expenditure ceilings, and a baseline path for revenues adjusted for the IMF staff's growth projections. As permitted under the rules, spending is projected to be increased up to the ceiling, thereby offsetting any growth-related windfalls. The revenue baseline path includes the effects of planned tax cuts in conjunction with the tax reform package implemented in 2001. For the period after 2002, real expenditures are assumed to grow by an annual average of 1.8 percent. The revenue ratio is projected to

Box A1 *(concluded)*

fall by 0.35 percent of GDP annually, reflecting the notion that part of the current revenue windfalls are not permanent.

Spain. Fiscal projections through 2004 are based on the policies outlined in the national authorities' updated stability program of January 2001. Projections for subsequent years assume no significant changes in those policies.

Sweden. The fiscal data for 2000 are based on the general government budget outturn for January–November 2000 and preliminary full-year figures for the central government. Projections for 2001 are based on the national authorities' policies as presented in the 2001 budget adopted by the parliament. IMF staff projections for 2002–2005 take into account the ministry of finance's medium-term projections and nominal ceilings on central government expenditures, both available through 2003. The authorities' medium-term fiscal objective calls for achieving a general government surplus of 2 percent of GDP over the economic cycle. The projected substantial surpluses also take into account the authorities' announced medium-term program of tax reductions.

Switzerland. The projections for 2001–04 are based on official budget plans that include measures to balance the Confederation's budget in 2001 and strengthen the finances of the social security system. Privatization receipts and windfall revenue from the withholding tax and the stamp duty are assumed to be applied to debt

reduction. Beyond 2004, the general government's structural balance is assumed to remain unchanged.

Monetary policy assumptions are based on the established framework for monetary policy in each country. In most cases, this implies a nonaccommodative stance over the business cycle, so that official interest rates will increase when economic indicators suggest that inflation will rise above its acceptable rate or range, and decrease when indicators suggest that prospective inflation will not exceed the acceptable rate or range, that prospective output growth is below its potential rate, and that the margin of slack in the economy is significant. On this basis, the London interbank offered rate (LIBOR) on six-month U.S. dollar deposits is assumed to average 4.5 percent in 2001 and 4.3 percent in 2002. The projected path for U.S. dollar short-term interest rates reflects the assumption that the U.S. Federal Reserve will lower the target Federal Funds rate by another 25 basis points in the first half of 2001, with no further decreases in the remainder of 2001 and 2002. The rate on six-month Japanese yen deposits is assumed to average 0.3 percent in 2001, with the current accommodative policy stance being maintained, and 0.5 percent in 2002. The rate on six-month euro deposits is assumed to average 4.4 percent in 2001, reflecting the assumption of moderate easing in the course of the year, and 4.1 percent in 2002. Changes in interest rate assumptions compared with the October 2000 *World Economic Outlook* are summarized in Table 1.1.

country projections based on consistent global assumptions.

Although national statistical agencies are the ultimate providers of historical data and definitions, international organizations are also involved in statistical issues, with the objective of harmonizing methodologies for the national compilation of statistics, including the analytical frameworks, concepts, defi-

nitions, classifications, and valuation procedures used in the production of economic statistics. The *World Economic Outlook* database reflects information from both national source agencies and international organizations.

The completion in 1993 of the comprehensive revision of the standardized *System of National Accounts 1993* (*SNA*) and the IMF's

Balance of Payments Manual (*BPM*) represented important improvements in the standards of economic statistics and analysis.[2] The IMF was actively involved in both projects, particularly the new *Balance of Payments Manual,* which reflects the IMF's special interest in countries' external positions. Key changes introduced with the new *Manual* were summarized in Box 13 of the May 1994 *World Economic Outlook.* The process of adapting country balance of payments data to the definitions of the new *BPM* began with the May 1995 *World Economic Outlook.* However, full concordance with the *BPM* is ultimately dependent on the provision by national statistical compilers of revised country data, and hence the *World Economic Outlook* estimates are still only partially adapted to the *BPM.*

The members of the European Union have recently adopted a harmonized system for the compilation of the national accounts, referred to as ESA 1995. All national accounts data from 1995 onward are now presented on the basis of the new system. Revision by national authorities of data prior to 1995 to conform to the new system has progressed, but has in some cases not been completed. In such cases, historical *World Economic Outlook* data have been carefully adjusted to avoid breaks in the series. Users of EU national accounts data prior to 1995 should nevertheless exercise caution until such time as the revision of historical data by national statistical agencies has been fully completed. See Box 1.2, *Revisions in National Accounts Methodologies,* in the May 2000 *World Economic Outlook.*

Composite data for country groups in the *World Economic Outlook* are either sums or weighted averages of data for individual countries. Arithmetically weighted averages are used for all data except inflation and money growth for the developing and transition country groups, for which geometric averages are used. The following conventions apply.

- Country group composites for exchange rates, interest rates, and the growth rates of monetary aggregates are weighted by GDP converted to U.S. dollars at market exchange rates (averaged over the preceding three years) as a share of world or group GDP.
- Composites for other data relating to the domestic economy, whether growth rates or ratios, are weighted by GDP valued at purchasing power parities (PPPs) as a share of total world or group GDP.[3]
- Composite unemployment rates and employment growth are weighted by labor force as a share of group labor force.
- Composites relating to the external economy are sums of individual country data after conversion to U.S. dollars at the average market exchange rates in the years indicated for balance of payments data and at end-of-year market exchange rates for debt denominated in currencies other than U.S. dollars. Composites of changes in foreign trade volumes and prices, however, are arithmetic averages of percentage changes for individual countries weighted by the U.S. dollar value of exports or imports as a share of total world or group exports or imports (in the preceding year).

For central and eastern European countries, external transactions in nonconvertible currencies (through 1990) are converted to U.S. dollars at the implicit U.S. dollar/ruble con-

---

[2]Commission of the European Communities, International Monetary Fund, Organization for Economic Cooperation and Development, United Nations, and World Bank, *System of National Accounts 1993* (Brussels/Luxembourg, New York, Paris, and Washington, 1993); and International Monetary Fund, *Balance of Payments Manual, Fifth Edition* (Washington: IMF, 1993).

[3]See Box A1 of the May 2000 *World Economic Outlook* for a summary of the revised PPP-based weights and Annex IV of the May 1993 *World Economic Outlook.* See also Anne Marie Gulde and Marianne Schulze-Ghattas, "Purchasing Power Parity Based Weights for the *World Economic Outlook,*" in *Staff Studies for the World Economic Outlook* (Washington: International Monetary Fund, December 1993), pp. 106–23.

version rates obtained from each country's national currency exchange rate for the U.S. dollar and for the ruble.

Unless otherwise indicated, multiyear averages of growth rates are expressed as compound annual rates of change.

Classification of Countries
Summary of the Country Classification

The country classification in the *World Economic Outlook* divides the world into three major groups: advanced economies, developing countries, and countries in transition.[4] Rather than being based on strict criteria, economic or otherwise, this classification has evolved over time with the objective of facilitating analysis by providing a reasonably meaningful organization of data. A few countries are presently not included in these groups, either because they are not IMF members, and their economies are not monitored by the IMF, or because databases have not yet been compiled. Cuba and the Democratic People's Republic of Korea are examples of countries that are not IMF members, whereas San Marino, among the advanced economies, is an example of an economy for which a database has not been completed. It should also be noted that, owing to a lack of data, only three of the former republics of the dissolved Socialist Federal Republic of Yugoslavia (Croatia, the former Yugoslav Republic of Macedonia, and Slovenia) are included in the group composites for countries in transition.

Each of the three main country groups is further divided into a number of subgroups. Among the advanced economies, the seven largest in terms of GDP, collectively referred to

as the major advanced countries, are distinguished as a subgroup, and so are the 15 current members of the European Union, the 12 members of the euro area,[5] and the four newly industrialized Asian economies. The developing countries are classified by region, as well as into a number of analytical and other groups. A regional breakdown is also used for the classification of the countries in transition. Table A provides an overview of these standard groups in the *World Economic Outlook*, showing the number of countries in each group and the average 2000 shares of groups in aggregate PPP-valued GDP, total exports of goods and services, and population.

General Features and Compositions of Groups in the *World Economic Outlook* Classification
Advanced Economies

The 29 advanced economies are listed in Table B. The seven largest in terms of GDP—the United States, Japan, Germany, France, Italy, the United Kingdom, and Canada—constitute the subgroup of *major advanced economies,* often referred to as the Group of Seven (G-7) countries. The current members of the *European Union* (15 countries), the *euro area* (12 countries), and the *newly industrialized Asian economies* are also distinguished as subgroups. Composite data shown in the tables for the European Union and the euro area cover the current members for all years, even though the membership has increased over time.

In 1991 and subsequent years, data for *Germany* refer to west Germany *and* the eastern Länder (i.e., the former German Democratic Republic). Before 1991, economic data are not available on a unified basis or in a consistent manner. Hence, in tables featuring data expressed as annual percent change, these apply to west Germany in years up to and

---

[4]As used here, the term "country" does not in all cases refer to a territorial entity that is a state as understood by international law and practice. It also covers some territorial entities that are not states, but for which statistical data are maintained on a separate and independent basis.

[5]Data shown are aggregates of country data and do not reflect official statistics at this time.

Table A. Classification by *World Economic Outlook* Groups and Their Shares in Aggregate GDP, Exports of Goods and Services, and Population, 2000[1]
(Percent of total for group or world)

	Number of Countries	GDP		Exports of Goods and Services		Population	
		Share of total for					
		Advanced economies	World	Advanced economies	World	Advanced economies	World
Advanced economies	**29**	**100.0**	**57.1**	**100.0**	**75.7**	**100.0**	**15.4**
Major advanced economies	7	79.5	45.4	62.9	47.7	74.3	11.5
United States		38.5	22.0	18.8	14.2	29.7	4.6
Japan		12.8	7.3	9.2	7.0	13.6	2.1
Germany		8.1	4.6	11.0	8.4	8.9	1.4
France		5.6	3.2	6.6	5.0	6.3	1.0
Italy		5.4	3.1	5.1	3.9	6.1	0.9
United Kingdom		5.5	3.1	6.7	5.1	6.3	1.0
Canada		3.5	2.0	5.5	4.2	3.3	0.5
Other advanced economies	22	20.5	11.7	37.1	28.1	25.7	4.0
Memorandum							
European Union	15	35.0	20.0	47.6	36.0	40.2	6.2
Euro area	12	28.0	16.0	37.9	28.7	32.3	5.0
Newly industrialized Asian economies	4	6.0	3.4	13.1	9.9	8.6	1.3
		Developing countries	World	Developing countries	World	Developing countries	World
Developing countries	**125**	**100.0**	**37.0**	**100.0**	**20.0**	**100.0**	**77.9**
Regional groups							
Africa	51	8.6	3.2	10.3	2.1	15.7	12.2
Sub-Sahara	48	6.6	2.4	7.6	1.5	14.2	11.1
Excluding Nigeria and South Africa	46	3.8	1.4	3.8	0.8	10.5	8.2
Developing Asia	25	58.3	21.6	46.19	9.2	66.8	52.0
China		31.2	11.6	18.4	3.7	27.0	21.1
India		12.6	4.6	3.9	0.8	21.4	16.6
Other developing Asia	23	14.5	5.4	23.7	4.7	18.4	14.3
Middle East, Malta, and Turkey	16	10.5	3.9	20.9	4.2	6.6	5.1
Western Hemisphere	33	22.6	8.4	22.7	4.5	10.9	8.5
Analytical groups							
By source of export earnings							
Fuel	18	9.0	3.3	21.5	4.3	7.0	5.4
Nonfuel	109	91.0	33.7	78.5	15.7	93.0	72.4
of which, primary products	42	6.5	2.4	5.9	1.2	10.9	8.5
By external financing source							
Net debtor countries	113	97.3	36.0	87.8	17.6	99.3	77.3
of which, official financing	43	5.6	2.1	5.1	1.0	13.8	10.8
Net debtor countries by debt-servicing experience							
Countries with arrears and/or rescheduling during 1994-98	55	24.6	9.1	24.0	4.8	29.0	22.6
Other groups							
Heavily indebted poor countries	40	5.1	1.9	4.3	0.9	13.6	10.6
Middle East and north Africa	21	10.3	3.8	20.3	4.1	7.5	5.9
		Countries in transition	World	Countries in transition	World	Countries in transition	World
Countries in transition	**28**	**100.0**	**5.9**	**100.0**	**4.3**	**100.0**	**6.7**
Central and eastern Europe	16	39.2	2.3	51.4	2.2	29.7	2.0
CIS and Mongolia	12	61.1	3.6	48.8	2.1	71.4	4.8
Russia		42.0	2.5	34.3	1.5	36.8	2.5
Excluding Russia	11	19.1	1.1	14.5	0.6	34.6	2.3

[1]The GDP shares are based on the purchasing-power-parity (PPP) valuation of country GDPs.

Table B.   Advanced Economies by Subgroup

	European Union		Euro Area	Newly Industrialized Asian Economies	Other Countries
Major advanced economies					
	France Germany Italy United Kingdom		France Germany Italy		Canada Japan United States
Other advanced economies					
	Austria Belgium Denmark Finland Greece Ireland	Luxembourg Netherlands Portugal Spain Sweden	Austria Belgium Finland Greece Ireland Luxembourg Netherlands Portugal Spain	Hong Kong SAR[1] Korea Singapore Taiwan Province of China	Australia Cyprus Iceland Israel New Zealand Norway Switzerland

[1]On July 1, 1997, Hong Kong was returned to the People's Republic of China and became a Special Administrative Region of China.

including 1991, but to unified Germany from 1992 onward. In general, data on national accounts and domestic economic and financial activity through 1990 cover west Germany only, whereas data for the central government and balance of payments apply to west Germany through June 1990 and to unified Germany thereafter.

Developing Countries

The group of developing countries (125 countries) includes all countries that are not classified as advanced economies or as countries in transition, together with a few dependent territories for which adequate statistics are available.

The *regional breakdowns* of developing countries in the *World Economic Outlook* conform to the IMF's *International Financial Statistics (IFS)* classification—*Africa, Asia, Europe, Middle East,* and *Western Hemisphere*—with one important exception. Because all of the non-advanced countries in Europe except Malta and Turkey are included in the group of countries in transition, the *World Economic Outlook* classification places these two countries in a combined *Middle East, Malta, and Turkey* region. In both classifications, Egypt and the Libyan Arab Jamahiriya are included in this region, not in

Africa. Three additional regional groupings—two of them constituting part of Africa and one a subgroup of Asia—are included in the *World Economic Outlook* because of their analytical significance. These are *sub-Sahara, sub-Sahara excluding Nigeria and South Africa,* and *Asia excluding China and India.*

The developing countries are also classified according to *analytical criteria* and into *other groups.* The analytical criteria reflect countries' composition of export earnings and other income from abroad, a distinction between net creditor and net debtor countries, and, for the net debtor countries, financial criteria based on external financing source and experience with external debt servicing. Included as "other groups" are currently the heavily indebted poor countries (HIPCs), and Middle East and north Africa (MENA). The detailed composition of developing countries in the regional, analytical, and other groups is shown in Tables C, D and E.

The first analytical criterion, by *source of export earnings,* distinguishes between categories: *fuel* (Standard International Trade Classification—SITC 3) and nonfuel and then focuses on *nonfuel primary products* (SITC 0,1,2,4, and 68).

The financial criteria focus on *net debtor countries* which are differentiated on the basis

Table C. Developing Countries by Region and Main Source of Export Earnings

	Fuel	Nonfuel, Of Which Primary Products
Africa		
Sub-Sahara	Angola	Benin
	Congo, Rep. of	Botswana
	Equatorial Guinea	Burkina Faso
	Gabon	Burundi
	Nigeria	Central African Rep.
		Chad
		Congo, Democratic Rep. of
		Côte d'Ivoire
		Gambia, The
		Ghana
		Guinea
		Guinea-Bissau
		Liberia
		Madagascar
		Malawi
		Mali
		Mauritania
		Namibia
		Niger
		Somalia
		Sudan
		Swaziland
		Tanzania
		Togo
		Zambia
		Zimbabwe
North Africa	Algeria	
Developing Asia	Brunei Darussalam	Bhutan
		Cambodia
		Myanmar
		Papua New Guinea
		Solomon Islands
		Vanuatu
		Vietnam
Middle East, Malta, and Turkey	Bahrain	
	Iran, Islamic Rep. of	
	Iraq	
	Kuwait	
	Libya	
	Oman	
	Qatar	
	Saudi Arabia	
	United Arab Emirates	
Western Hemisphere	Trinidad and Tobago	Belize
	Venezuela	Bolivia
		Chile
		Guyana
		Honduras
		Nicaragua
		Paraguay
		Peru
		Suriname

of two additional financial criteria: by *official external financing* and by *experience with debt servicing.*[6]

The *other groups* of developing countries (see Table E) constitute the HIPCs and MENA countries. The first group comprises 40 of the countries (all except Nigeria) considered by the IMF and the World Bank for their debt initiative, known as the HIPC Initiative.[7] Middle East and north Africa, also referred to as the MENA countries, is a *World Economic Outlook* group, whose composition straddles the Africa and Middle East and Europe regions. It is defined as the Arab League countries plus the Islamic Republic of Iran.

Countries in Transition

The group of countries in transition (28 countries) is divided into two regional subgroups: *central and eastern Europe, and the Commonwealth of Independent States and Mongolia.* The detailed country composition is shown in Table F.

One common characteristic of these countries is the transitional state of their economies from a centrally administered system to one based on market principles. Another is that this transition involves the transformation of sizable industrial sectors whose capital stocks have proven largely obsolete. Although several other countries are also "in transition" from partially command-based economic systems toward market-based systems (including China, Cambodia, the Lao People's Democratic Republic, Vietnam, and a number of African countries), most of these are largely rural,

[6]During the 1994–98 period, 55 countries incurred external payments arrears or entered into official or commercial bank debt-rescheduling agreements. This group of countries is referred to as *countries with arrears and/or rescheduling during 1994–98.*

[7]See David Andrews, Anthony R. Boote, Syed S. Rizavi, and Sukwinder Singh, *Debt Relief for Low-Income Countries: The Enhanced HIPC Initiative,* Pamphlet Series, No. 51 (Washington: International Monetary Fund, November 1999)

Table D. Developing Countries by Region and Main External Financing Source

Countries	Net debtor countries	Of which, official financing
Africa		
Sub-Sahara		
Angola	•	
Benin	•	•
Burkina Faso	•	•
Burundi	•	•
Cameroon	•	•
Central African Rep.	•	•
Chad	•	•
Comoros	•	•
Congo, Democratic Rep. of	•	•
Congo, Rep. of	•	•
Côte d'Ivoire	•	
Djibouti	•	
Equatorial Guinea	•	
Eritrea	•	
Ethiopia	•	•
Gabon	•	
Gambia, The	•	•
Ghana	•	
Guinea	•	•
Guinea-Bissau	•	
Kenya	•	
Lesotho	•	
Liberia	•	•
Madagascar	•	•
Malawi	•	•
Mali	•	•
Mauritania	•	•
Mauritius	•	
Mozambique, Rep. of	•	•
Namibia	•	
Niger	•	•
Nigeria	•	
Rwanda	•	•
São Tomé and Príncipe	•	•
Senegal	•	•
Seychelles	•	
Sierra Leone	•	
Somalia	•	
South Africa	•	
Sudan	•	
Tanzania	•	•
Togo	•	•
Uganda	•	•
Zambia	•	•
Zimbabwe	•	
North Africa		
Algeria	•	•
Morocco	•	
Tunisia	•	
Developing Asia		
Afghanistan, Islamic State of	•	
Bangladesh	•	•
Bhutan	•	•
Cambodia	•	•
China	•	
Fiji	•	
India	•	
Indonesia	•	
Kiribati	•	
Lao People's Democratic Rep.	•	•

Countries	Net debtor countries	Of which, official financing
Malaysia	•	
Maldives	•	
Myanmar	•	
Nepal	•	•
Pakistan	•	
Papua New Guinea	•	
Philippines	•	
Samoa	•	•
Solomon Islands	•	
Sri Lanka	•	
Thailand	•	
Tonga	•	•
Vanuatu	•	
Vietnam		
Middle East, Malta, and Turkey		
Bahrain	•	
Egypt	•	
Iran, Islamic Rep. of	•	
Iraq	•	
Jordan	•	
Kuwait		
Lebanon	•	•
Libya	•	•
Malta	•	
Oman		•
Qatar		
Saudi Arabia		
Syrian Arab Rep.	•	
Turkey	•	•
United Arab Emirates		
Yemen, Rep. of	•	
Western Hemisphere		
Antigua and Barbuda	•	•
Argentina	•	•
Bahamas, The	•	•
Barbados	•	
Belize	•	•
Bolivia	•	
Brazil	•	•
Chile	•	•
Colombia	•	•
Costa Rica	•	•
Dominica	•	
Dominican Rep.	•	•
Ecuador	•	•
El Salvador	•	
Grenada	•	
Guatemala	•	•
Guyana	•	•
Haiti	•	•
Honduras	•	•
Jamaica	•	
Mexico	•	•
Netherlands Antilles	•	•
Nicaragua	•	•
Panama	•	
Paraguay	•	
Peru	•	
St. Kitts and Nevis	•	
St. Lucia	•	
St. Vincent and the Grenadines	•	
Suriname	•	
Trinidad and Tobago	•	
Uruguay	•	
Venezuela	•	

Table E. Other Developing Country Groups

Countries	Heavily Indebted Poor Countries	Middle East and North Africa
Africa		
Sub-Sahara		
Angola	•	
Benin	•	
Burkina Faso	•	
Burundi	•	
Cameroon	•	
Central African Rep.	•	
Chad	•	
Congo, Democratic Rep. of	•	
Congo, Rep. of	•	
Côte d'Ivoire	•	
Djibouti		•
Ethiopia	•	
Ghana	•	
Guinea	•	
Guinea-Bissau	•	
Kenya	•	
Liberia	•	
Madagascar	•	
Malawi	•	
Mali	•	
Mauritania	•	•
Mozambique, Rep. of	•	
Niger	•	
Rwanda	•	
São Tomé and Príncipe	•	
Senegal	•	
Sierra Leone	•	
Somalia	•	•
Sudan	•	•
Tanzania	•	
Togo	•	
Uganda	•	
Zambia	•	

Countries	Heavily Indebted Poor Countries	Middle East and North Africa
North Africa		
Algeria		•
Morocco		•
Tunisia		•
Developing Asia		
Lao People's Democratic Rep.	•	
Myanmar	•	
Vietnam	•	
Middle East, Malta and Turkey		
Bahrain		•
Egypt		•
Iran, Islamic Rep. of		•
Iraq		•
Jordan		•
Kuwait		•
Lebanon		•
Libya		•
Oman		•
Qatar		•
Saudi Arabia		•
Syrian Arab Rep.		•
United Arab Emirates		•
Yemen, Rep. of	•	•
Western Hemisphere		
Bolivia	•	
Guyana	•	
Honduras	•	
Nicaragua	•	

Table F. Countries in Transition by Region

Central and Eastern Europe		Commonwealth of Independent States and Mongolia
Albania	Lithuania	Armenia
Belarus	Macedonia, former	Azerbaijan
Bosnia and Herzegovina	Yugoslav Republic of	Belarus
Bulgaria	Poland	Georgia
Croatia	Romania	Kazakhstan
Czech Republic	Slovak Republic	Kyrgyz Republic
Estonia	Slovenia	Moldova
Hungary	Yugoslavia, Federal Republic of	Mongolia
Latvia	(Serbia/Montenegro)	Russia
		Tajikistan
		Turkmenistan
		Ukraine
		Uzbekistan

low-income economies for whom the principal challenge is one of economic development. These countries are therefore classified in the developing country group rather than in the group of countries in transition.

List of Tables

163

Table 1. Summary of World Output[1]

(Annual percent change)

	Ten-Year Averages		1993	1994	1995	1996	1997	1998	1999	2000	2001	2002
	1983–92	1993–2002										
World	**3.4**	**3.6**	**2.3**	**3.7**	**3.6**	**4.0**	**4.2**	**2.8**	**3.5**	**4.8**	**3.2**	**3.9**
Advanced economies	**3.3**	**2.9**	**1.4**	**3.4**	**2.7**	**2.9**	**3.5**	**2.7**	**3.4**	**4.1**	**1.9**	**2.7**
United States	3.4	3.5	2.7	4.0	2.7	3.6	4.4	4.4	4.2	5.0	1.5	2.5
European Union	2.6	2.3	–0.4	2.8	2.4	1.6	2.6	2.9	2.6	3.4	2.4	2.8
Japan	3.9	1.2	0.5	1.0	1.6	3.3	1.9	–1.1	0.8	1.7	0.6	1.5
Other advanced economies	4.7	4.3	4.1	5.9	5.0	4.1	4.6	1.1	5.6	5.9	2.9	4.0
Developing countries	**4.7**	**5.5**	**6.3**	**6.7**	**6.1**	**6.5**	**5.8**	**3.5**	**3.8**	**5.8**	**5.0**	**5.6**
Regional groups												
Africa	2.0	3.1	0.2	2.4	2.9	5.7	2.9	3.3	2.3	3.0	4.2	4.4
Developing Asia	7.3	7.2	9.4	9.6	9.0	8.2	6.6	4.0	6.1	6.9	5.9	6.3
Middle East, Malta, and Turkey	3.4	3.5	3.3	0.3	4.3	4.8	5.4	3.6	0.8	5.4	2.9	4.6
Western Hemisphere	2.3	3.4	4.1	5.0	1.7	3.6	5.3	2.3	0.2	4.1	3.7	4.4
Analytical groups												
By source of export earnings												
Fuel	2.6	2.8	0.6	0.1	2.8	3.5	4.6	2.9	1.0	4.3	4.3	3.9
Nonfuel	5.0	5.8	7.0	7.4	6.5	6.8	5.9	3.6	4.1	5.9	5.0	5.7
of which, primary products	2.6	4.5	3.9	5.3	6.4	5.9	5.5	3.1	2.1	4.0	4.1	5.3
By external financing source												
Net debtor countries	4.8	5.6	6.5	6.9	6.3	6.6	5.9	3.6	4.0	5.8	5.0	5.6
of which, official financing	2.8	3.9	1.4	2.5	5.4	5.3	4.0	3.9	3.3	4.0	4.6	5.0
Net debtor countries by debt-servicing experience												
Countries with arrears and/or rescheduling during 1994–98	2.7	3.7	3.5	4.6	5.1	5.0	4.4	–0.6	2.0	4.3	4.2	4.7
Countries in transition	**–0.4**	**–0.1**	**–7.5**	**–7.6**	**–1.5**	**–0.5**	**1.6**	**–0.9**	**2.6**	**5.8**	**4.0**	**4.2**
Central and eastern Europe	. . .	3.2	0.3	3.5	5.5	4.0	2.5	2.1	1.8	3.8	3.9	4.4
Commonwealth of Independent States and Mongolia	. . .	–1.9	–10.9	–13.3	–5.5	–3.3	1.0	–2.8	3.1	7.1	4.1	4.1
Russia	. . .	–1.7	–10.4	–11.6	–4.2	–3.4	0.9	–4.9	3.2	7.5	4.0	4.0
Excluding Russia	. . .	–2.3	–11.8	–17.0	–8.6	–3.1	1.4	1.6	2.7	6.3	4.2	4.4
Memorandum												
Median growth rate												
Advanced economies	3.2	3.1	0.7	4.1	2.9	3.0	3.7	3.3	3.9	3.9	2.6	2.8
Developing countries	3.4	3.9	2.9	3.8	4.3	4.6	4.4	3.7	3.2	3.9	4.0	4.5
Countries in transition	–0.1	2.0	–7.8	–1.9	1.9	3.0	3.7	3.8	3.1	5.0	4.7	5.0
Output per capita												
Advanced economies	2.9	2.3	0.8	2.7	2.1	2.3	2.8	2.1	2.8	3.6	1.4	2.2
Developing countries	2.4	3.9	4.4	4.8	4.4	4.8	4.1	2.0	2.4	4.3	3.5	4.2
Countries in transition	–1.1	—	–7.6	–7.6	–1.4	–0.2	2.0	–0.7	2.6	6.0	4.1	4.3
World growth based on market exchange rates	**3.0**	**2.8**	**1.1**	**3.0**	**2.8**	**3.2**	**3.5**	**2.3**	**3.0**	**4.2**	**2.3**	**3.0**
Value of world output in billions of U.S. dollars												
At market exchange rates	18,063	29,607	24,418	26,228	29,086	29,801	29,680	29,473	30,536	31,400	31,929	33,520
At purchasing power parities	22,806	39,476	30,467	32,170	33,996	36,032	38,227	39,652	41,585	44,549	47,473	50,612

[1]Real GDP.

Table 2. Advanced Economies: Real GDP and Total Domestic Demand

(Annual percent change)

	Ten-Year Averages		1993	1994	1995	1996	1997	1998	1999	2000	2001	2002	Fourth Quarter[1]		
	1983–92	1993–2002											2000	2001	2002
Real GDP															
Advanced economies	**3.3**	**2.9**	**1.4**	**3.4**	**2.7**	**2.9**	**3.5**	**2.7**	**3.4**	**4.1**	**1.9**	**2.7**	...	...	...
Major advanced economies	3.2	2.6	1.3	3.1	2.3	2.7	3.3	2.8	3.0	3.8	1.6	2.4	3.1	1.5	2.9
United States	3.4	3.5	2.7	4.0	2.7	3.6	4.4	4.4	4.2	5.0	1.5	2.5	3.4	1.4	3.0
Japan	3.9	1.2	0.5	1.0	1.6	3.3	1.9	−1.1	0.8	1.7	0.6	1.5	2.8	0.3	2.6
Germany	3.1	1.6	−1.1	2.3	1.7	0.8	1.4	2.1	1.6	3.0	1.9	2.6	2.7	2.3	2.8
France	2.2	2.1	−0.9	1.8	1.9	1.0	1.9	3.3	3.2	3.2	2.6	2.6	2.8	2.2	2.9
Italy	2.3	1.8	−0.9	2.2	2.9	1.1	2.0	1.8	1.6	2.9	2.0	2.5	2.7	2.1	3.0
United Kingdom	2.5	2.9	2.3	4.4	2.8	2.6	3.5	2.6	2.3	3.0	2.6	2.8	2.6	2.7	2.8
Canada	2.7	3.3	2.3	4.7	2.8	1.5	4.4	3.3	4.5	4.7	2.3	2.4	4.0	1.7	2.7
Other advanced economies	3.9	3.8	1.9	4.6	4.3	3.8	4.2	2.2	4.8	5.2	3.0	3.8	...	...	...
Spain	3.2	2.9	−1.0	2.4	2.8	2.4	3.9	4.3	4.0	4.1	2.9	3.2	3.8	2.5	3.6
Netherlands	2.8	3.1	0.8	3.2	2.3	3.0	3.8	4.1	3.9	3.9	2.9	2.7	3.4	2.6	2.5
Belgium	2.3	2.2	−1.5	3.0	2.6	1.2	3.4	2.4	2.7	3.9	2.4	2.4	...	...	...
Sweden	1.7	2.5	−2.2	4.1	3.7	1.1	2.1	3.6	4.1	3.6	2.6	2.8	...	...	...
Austria	2.6	2.2	0.5	2.4	1.7	1.8	1.3	3.3	2.8	3.2	2.2	2.6	...	...	...
Denmark	1.9	2.6	—	5.5	2.8	2.5	3.0	2.8	2.1	2.9	2.1	2.3	2.3	2.1	2.3
Finland	1.6	4.0	−1.1	4.0	3.8	4.0	6.3	5.3	4.2	5.7	4.2	4.0	5.5	4.1	3.6
Greece[2]	2.1	2.6	−1.6	2.0	2.1	2.4	3.5	3.1	3.4	4.0	3.8	3.8	...	...	...
Portugal	3.0	2.6	−1.4	2.4	2.9	3.4	3.7	4.2	2.8	3.0	2.4	2.8	2.7	1.6	2.8
Ireland	3.7	7.9	2.7	5.8	9.7	7.7	10.7	8.6	9.8	10.7	7.0	6.2	...	...	...
Luxembourg	5.5	5.5	8.5	4.1	3.5	2.9	7.3	5.0	7.3	8.5	4.2	4.3	...	...	...
Switzerland	1.9	1.4	−0.5	0.5	0.5	0.3	1.7	2.3	1.5	3.4	2.0	2.0	2.6	1.9	2.0
Norway	2.9	3.1	2.7	5.5	3.8	4.9	4.7	2.0	0.9	2.2	1.9	2.3	...	...	...
Israel	4.4	4.2	3.7	7.1	6.5	5.0	3.3	2.4	2.3	6.0	1.8	4.3	...	...	...
Iceland	1.8	3.1	0.6	4.5	0.1	5.2	4.7	4.5	4.1	3.6	1.9	2.1	...	...	...
Cyprus	6.3	4.0	0.7	5.9	6.1	1.9	2.4	5.0	4.5	5.0	4.5	4.0	...	...	...
Korea	8.7	5.5	5.5	8.3	8.9	6.8	5.0	−6.7	10.9	8.8	3.5	5.5	4.6	5.3	3.5
Australia	3.1	4.0	3.8	5.0	4.4	3.7	3.8	5.6	4.7	3.7	1.9	3.5	2.0	2.3	4.3
Taiwan Province of China	8.5	5.9	6.5	7.6	6.4	6.1	6.7	4.6	5.4	6.0	4.1	5.6	4.1	4.5	6.0
Hong Kong SAR	6.4	4.1	6.1	5.4	3.9	4.5	5.0	−5.3	3.1	10.5	3.5	4.8	6.8	7.0	0.3
Singapore	7.0	7.4	12.7	11.4	8.0	7.5	8.4	0.3	5.9	9.9	5.0	5.8	11.0	2.5	7.0
New Zealand	1.8	3.4	5.2	5.8	4.3	3.6	2.2	−0.1	3.9	3.5	2.6	2.7	1.6	3.0	2.7
Memorandum															
European Union	2.6	2.3	−0.4	2.8	2.4	1.6	2.6	2.9	2.6	3.4	2.4	2.8	...	...	...
Euro area	2.7	2.2	−0.8	2.3	2.3	1.5	2.4	2.9	2.6	3.4	2.4	2.8	...	...	...
Newly industrialized Asian economies	8.2	5.6	6.4	7.9	7.5	6.3	5.7	−2.4	7.9	8.2	3.8	5.5	5.5	5.4	4.4
Real total domestic demand															
Advanced economies	**3.4**	**2.9**	**1.1**	**3.4**	**2.7**	**3.0**	**3.3**	**3.0**	**4.0**	**4.1**	**2.2**	**2.7**	...	...	...
Major advanced economies	3.3	2.8	1.1	3.1	2.2	2.8	3.2	3.5	3.7	4.1	2.0	2.4	3.3	1.9	2.8
United States	3.4	4.0	3.3	4.4	2.5	3.7	4.7	5.5	5.2	5.7	2.1	2.7	4.2	1.8	3.2
Japan	3.9	1.1	0.4	1.3	2.1	3.8	1.0	−1.4	0.9	1.3	0.8	1.2	2.8	0.1	2.6
Germany	3.0	1.5	−1.1	2.3	1.7	0.3	0.6	2.4	2.4	2.0	1.8	2.5	2.2	2.1	2.5
France	2.1	1.9	−1.6	1.8	1.8	0.7	0.6	4.0	3.2	3.2	3.0	2.6	2.9	2.7	2.6
Italy	2.7	1.4	−5.1	1.7	2.0	0.9	2.7	3.1	3.0	2.3	1.7	2.3	1.1	3.2	2.0
United Kingdom	2.7	3.2	2.2	3.4	1.8	3.1	3.7	4.6	3.8	3.7	3.1	3.1	2.9	3.4	2.8
Canada	3.1	3.1	1.4	3.2	1.7	1.4	6.2	2.2	4.2	5.5	2.6	2.7	3.4	3.0	2.9
Other advanced economies	4.1	3.5	1.0	4.8	4.6	3.8	3.7	1.1	4.9	4.4	2.8	3.8	...	...	...
Memorandum															
European Union	2.8	2.2	−1.6	2.4	2.1	1.4	2.3	3.8	3.3	3.0	2.5	2.7	...	...	...
Euro area	2.8	2.0	−2.2	2.1	2.2	1.1	2.0	3.7	3.2	2.9	2.4	2.7	...	...	...
Newly industrialized Asian economies	8.4	4.6	5.9	8.7	7.8	6.8	4.0	−9.2	7.5	6.7	3.0	5.6	...	...	...

[1]From fourth quarter of preceding year.
[2]Based on revised national accounts for 1988 onward.

Table 3. Advanced Economies: Components of Real GDP
(Annual percent change)

| | Ten-Year Averages | | 1993 | 1994 | 1995 | 1996 | 1997 | 1998 | 1999 | 2000 | 2001 | 2002 |
	1983–92	1993–2002										
Private consumer expenditure												
Advanced economies	**3.4**	**2.9**	**1.9**	**3.0**	**2.6**	**2.7**	**2.8**	**3.0**	**4.0**	**3.7**	**2.4**	**2.6**
Major advanced economies	3.2	2.7	1.9	2.8	2.3	2.4	2.6	3.3	3.8	3.6	2.3	2.4
United States	3.4	3.7	3.4	3.8	3.0	3.2	3.6	4.7	5.3	5.3	2.5	2.4
Japan	3.6	1.4	2.0	2.5	1.5	1.9	1.1	0.2	1.2	0.5	1.0	1.7
Germany	3.1	1.6	0.1	1.0	2.0	1.0	0.7	2.0	2.6	1.6	2.4	3.0
France	1.8	1.7	−0.1	0.6	1.6	1.3	0.1	3.6	2.7	2.4	2.3	2.4
Italy	2.9	1.6	−3.7	1.5	1.7	1.2	3.2	3.1	2.3	2.9	2.0	2.4
United Kingdom	3.0	3.3	2.9	2.9	1.7	3.6	3.9	4.0	4.4	3.7	2.9	2.9
Canada	3.0	3.0	1.8	3.1	2.1	2.5	4.4	2.9	3.5	4.0	3.2	2.6
Other advanced economies	3.9	3.5	1.8	4.1	3.8	3.9	3.6	1.7	4.9	4.3	3.0	3.5
Memorandum												
European Union	2.8	2.2	−0.4	1.6	1.8	2.0	2.1	3.4	3.2	2.8	2.5	2.8
Euro area	2.7	2.0	−0.9	1.3	1.9	1.6	1.8	3.3	3.0	2.7	2.4	2.8
Newly industrialized Asian economies	8.2	5.1	7.1	8.0	7.0	6.6	5.2	−4.6	7.4	6.6	3.8	4.9
Public consumption												
Advanced economies	**2.7**	**1.5**	**0.9**	**1.0**	**1.1**	**1.7**	**1.3**	**1.6**	**2.2**	**2.2**	**1.3**	**2.1**
Major advanced economies	2.4	1.4	0.7	0.9	0.8	1.2	1.0	1.3	2.3	2.2	1.2	2.2
United States	2.4	1.1	−0.4	0.2	—	0.5	1.8	1.5	2.1	2.0	0.7	2.8
Japan	3.1	2.8	3.2	2.8	4.3	2.8	1.3	1.9	4.0	3.6	1.9	1.8
Germany	1.7	0.7	0.1	2.4	1.5	1.8	−0.9	0.5	−0.1	1.4	−0.3	0.2
France	2.5	1.6	4.2	0.6	−0.1	2.2	2.1	0.3	2.5	1.5	1.6	1.4
Italy	2.5	0.4	−0.2	−0.8	−2.1	1.1	0.3	0.4	1.6	1.7	1.2	1.2
United Kingdom	1.2	1.8	−0.8	1.4	1.6	1.7	−1.4	1.1	4.0	2.7	4.1	4.0
Canada	2.5	0.5	0.1	−1.2	−0.5	−1.4	−1.2	1.6	1.3	2.4	2.3	1.5
Other advanced economies	3.8	2.2	2.0	1.3	2.0	3.6	2.3	2.7	1.9	2.4	1.7	1.6
Memorandum												
European Union	2.2	1.3	1.0	1.0	0.8	1.6	0.5	1.3	2.0	1.9	1.5	1.6
Euro area	2.4	1.2	1.3	1.0	0.7	1.6	1.0	1.2	1.7	1.8	1.0	1.1
Newly industrialized Asian economies	6.4	2.6	3.7	0.8	2.6	8.0	3.3	1.8	−0.7	2.5	2.1	1.7
Gross fixed capital formation												
Advanced economies	**4.1**	**4.4**	**—**	**4.7**	**4.0**	**5.8**	**5.7**	**5.5**	**5.8**	**6.2**	**2.8**	**3.6**
Major advanced economies	3.9	4.3	0.2	4.2	3.1	5.9	5.6	6.3	6.2	6.2	2.7	3.0
United States	3.9	7.1	5.7	7.3	5.4	8.4	8.8	10.7	9.1	8.8	3.3	3.8
Japan	5.1	−0.1	−3.1	−1.2	0.1	7.3	0.7	−4.2	−0.8	1.1	−0.4	−0.1
Germany	3.7	1.2	−4.5	4.0	−0.7	−0.8	0.6	3.0	3.3	2.4	1.9	3.2
France	2.5	2.7	−6.5	1.5	2.1	−0.1	—	6.6	7.3	6.7	6.3	4.3
Italy	2.3	1.9	−10.9	0.1	6.0	3.6	2.1	4.3	4.6	6.1	2.0	2.4
United Kingdom	3.6	4.4	0.8	3.6	2.9	4.9	7.5	10.1	5.4	2.6	3.2	3.2
Canada	3.5	5.6	−2.7	7.4	−1.9	5.8	15.4	3.4	10.1	11.2	4.0	4.3
Other advanced economies	4.9	4.6	−1.0	6.6	7.4	5.2	6.0	2.4	4.1	6.0	3.3	5.8
Memorandum												
European Union	3.3	2.9	−5.6	2.6	3.6	2.3	3.5	6.3	5.5	4.7	3.5	3.6
Euro area	3.3	2.6	−6.5	2.2	3.3	1.7	2.7	5.5	5.5	4.9	3.5	3.6
Newly industrialized Asian economies	9.9	5.0	7.3	10.9	10.4	7.2	4.5	−9.1	—	9.4	2.9	8.2

Table 3 *(concluded)*

	Ten-Year Averages		1993	1994	1995	1996	1997	1998	1999	2000	2001	2002
	1983–92	1993–2002										
Final domestic demand												
Advanced economies	**3.7**	**2.9**	**1.2**	**2.9**	**2.6**	**3.2**	**3.1**	**3.1**	**4.0**	**4.1**	**2.3**	**2.8**
Major advanced economies	3.6	2.8	1.2	2.6	2.1	3.0	2.9	3.5	4.0	4.0	2.2	2.5
United States	3.3	4.0	3.1	3.8	2.9	3.7	4.3	5.4	5.6	5.6	2.5	2.8
Japan	3.9	1.2	0.6	1.5	1.5	3.6	1.0	–0.8	1.1	1.2	0.8	1.2
Germany	5.9	1.3	–1.0	2.0	1.3	0.7	0.3	1.9	2.2	1.7	1.7	2.5
France	2.1	1.9	–0.4	0.8	1.3	1.2	0.6	3.4	3.5	3.0	2.9	2.6
Italy	2.7	1.5	–4.5	0.8	1.7	1.7	2.4	2.8	2.6	3.3	1.8	2.2
United Kingdom	2.7	3.2	1.8	2.7	1.9	3.4	3.5	4.5	4.5	3.3	3.2	3.1
Canada	3.0	3.0	0.6	2.8	0.8	2.2	5.2	2.8	4.4	5.2	3.2	2.8
Other advanced economies	4.1	3.5	1.3	4.2	4.3	4.1	3.9	1.7	4.1	4.5	2.9	3.9
Memorandum												
European Union	3.6	2.2	–1.2	1.7	1.9	1.9	2.1	3.5	3.5	3.0	2.5	2.7
Euro area	3.7	2.0	–1.7	1.4	1.9	1.6	1.8	3.3	3.3	3.0	2.4	2.7
Newly industrialized Asian economies	8.4	4.7	6.6	8.0	7.6	7.1	4.6	–5.7	4.0	6.9	3.3	5.6
Stock building[1]												
Advanced economies	**0.1**	**—**	**–0.1**	**0.5**	**0.1**	**–0.2**	**0.2**	**—**	**–0.1**	**0.1**	**–0.2**	**–0.1**
Major advanced economies	0.1	—	–0.1	0.5	—	–0.2	0.3	0.1	–0.3	0.1	–0.2	–0.1
United States	0.1	—	—	0.7	–0.5	—	0.4	0.2	–0.4	0.2	–0.4	–0.1
Japan	—	—	–0.2	–0.2	0.6	0.3	—	–0.6	–0.2	0.1	0.1	—
Germany	0.1	0.1	–0.1	0.3	0.3	–0.5	0.2	0.4	0.2	0.2	—	—
France	0.1	—	–1.2	1.0	0.5	–0.6	0.1	0.6	–0.3	0.2	—	—
Italy	—	—	–0.7	0.8	0.2	–0.7	0.3	0.3	0.4	–1.0	–0.2	0.2
United Kingdom	—	0.1	0.4	0.7	—	–0.4	0.3	0.1	–0.7	0.4	—	—
Canada	0.1	0.1	0.8	0.3	0.9	–0.8	1.0	–0.5	–0.2	0.3	–0.5	–0.1
Other advanced economies	0.1	—	–0.3	0.5	0.2	–0.3	–0.2	–0.6	0.7	–0.1	—	—
Memorandum												
European Union	—	—	–0.4	0.7	0.2	–0.5	0.2	0.3	–0.2	—	—	—
Euro area	0.1	—	–0.6	0.6	0.3	–0.5	0.2	0.4	—	–0.1	—	—
Newly industrialized Asian economies	0.1	–0.2	–0.6	0.7	0.3	–0.3	–0.6	–3.3	2.7	–0.3	–0.3	–0.1
Foreign balance[1]												
Advanced economies	**–0.1**	**–0.1**	**0.3**	**–0.1**	**0.1**	**—**	**0.2**	**–0.4**	**–0.6**	**–0.1**	**–0.2**	**—**
Major advanced economies	–0.1	–0.2	0.2	—	0.2	–0.1	0.1	–0.8	–0.8	–0.4	–0.3	–0.1
United States	–0.1	–0.5	–0.6	–0.4	0.1	–0.1	–0.3	–1.3	–1.2	–1.0	–0.4	–0.2
Japan	0.1	0.1	0.1	–0.2	–0.5	–0.4	1.0	0.3	–0.1	0.4	–0.2	0.3
Germany	–0.3	0.2	—	0.1	0.1	0.5	0.8	–0.3	–0.8	1.0	0.1	0.2
France	0.1	0.2	0.7	—	0.1	0.4	1.3	–0.6	0.1	—	–0.3	0.1
Italy	–0.3	0.4	4.3	0.6	1.0	0.2	–0.6	–1.2	–1.3	0.6	0.3	0.2
United Kingdom	–0.4	–0.4	0.1	0.9	1.0	–0.5	–0.3	–2.0	–1.5	–0.8	–0.8	–0.5
Canada	–0.3	0.2	0.9	1.5	1.0	0.2	–1.8	1.1	0.4	–0.7	–0.2	–0.2
Other advanced economies	–0.1	0.4	1.0	–0.1	–0.1	—	0.7	1.0	0.4	1.1	0.3	0.1
Memorandum												
European Union	–0.2	0.1	1.2	0.4	0.4	0.2	0.4	–0.9	–0.6	0.3	–0.1	—
Euro area	–0.2	0.2	1.4	0.3	0.2	0.3	0.5	–0.7	–0.5	0.5	—	0.1
Newly industrialized Asian economies	0.2	1.4	0.6	–0.8	0.1	–0.3	1.9	6.5	1.8	2.8	0.8	0.5

[1]Changes expressed as percent of GDP in the preceding period.

Table 4. Advanced Economies: Unemployment, Employment, and Real Per Capita GDP
(Percent)

	Ten-Year Averages[1]		1993	1994	1995	1996	1997	1998	1999	2000	2001	2002
	1983–92	1993–2002										
Unemployment rate												
Advanced economies	**7.0**	**6.7**	**7.5**	**7.4**	**7.1**	**7.1**	**6.9**	**6.8**	**6.4**	**5.9**	**5.9**	**5.9**
Major advanced economies	6.9	6.4	7.2	7.0	6.7	6.8	6.6	6.3	6.1	5.7	5.9	6.0
United States[2]	6.8	5.1	6.9	6.1	5.6	5.4	5.0	4.5	4.2	4.0	4.4	5.0
Japan	2.5	3.9	2.5	2.9	3.1	3.3	3.4	4.1	4.7	4.7	5.3	5.2
Germany	7.3	8.2	7.6	8.2	7.9	8.6	9.5	9.0	8.3	7.8	7.6	7.4
France	9.7	11.0	11.6	12.3	11.7	12.4	12.5	11.6	11.3	9.7	8.8	8.2
Italy[3]	10.7	10.9	10.1	11.1	11.6	11.6	11.7	11.8	11.4	10.6	9.9	9.5
United Kingdom	9.0	7.3	10.4	9.7	8.7	8.2	7.1	6.3	6.0	5.6	5.3	5.4
Canada	9.7	8.7	11.4	10.4	9.4	9.6	9.1	8.3	7.6	6.8	7.2	7.1
Other advanced economies	7.3	7.5	8.7	8.8	8.2	8.1	7.8	8.1	7.3	6.3	6.1	5.7
Spain	18.9	18.5	22.7	24.2	22.9	22.2	20.8	18.8	15.9	14.1	12.7	11.7
Netherlands	7.9	4.9	6.5	7.6	7.1	6.6	5.5	4.1	3.2	2.8	3.0	3.0
Belgium	9.0	8.7	8.8	10.0	9.9	9.7	9.4	9.5	8.8	7.0	7.0	7.0
Sweden	2.7	6.5	8.2	8.0	7.7	8.1	8.0	6.5	5.6	4.7	4.1	4.0
Austria	3.5	3.9	4.0	3.8	3.9	4.3	4.4	4.5	3.8	3.3	3.4	3.3
Denmark	9.3	7.8	12.0	11.9	10.1	8.6	7.8	6.5	5.6	5.2	5.3	5.3
Finland	5.5	12.5	16.4	16.6	15.4	14.6	12.6	11.4	10.3	9.8	9.2	8.8
Greece	7.7	10.4	9.7	9.6	10.0	10.3	9.6	10.8	11.7	11.1	10.9	10.7
Portugal	6.7	5.5	5.5	6.8	7.2	7.3	6.7	5.0	4.4	4.1	4.0	4.0
Ireland	15.5	8.7	15.5	14.1	12.1	11.5	9.8	7.4	5.6	4.3	3.7	3.7
Luxembourg	1.5	2.9	2.1	2.7	3.0	3.3	3.3	3.3	2.9	2.6	2.7	2.6
Switzerland	0.9	3.5	4.5	4.7	4.2	4.7	5.2	3.9	2.7	1.9	1.9	1.8
Norway	3.8	4.2	6.1	5.5	5.0	4.9	4.1	3.2	3.2	3.4	3.5	3.5
Israel	7.7	8.3	10.0	7.8	6.9	6.7	7.7	8.5	8.9	8.8	9.4	8.6
Iceland	1.3	3.2	4.4	4.8	5.0	4.3	3.9	2.7	1.9	1.3	1.8	2.1
Cyprus	2.9	3.2	2.7	2.7	2.6	3.1	3.4	3.4	3.6	3.5	3.6	3.8
Korea	3.1	3.7	2.8	2.4	2.0	2.0	2.6	6.8	6.3	4.1	4.2	3.5
Australia	8.4	8.2	10.9	9.8	8.5	8.6	8.5	8.0	7.2	6.6	7.0	6.7
Taiwan Province of China	2.1	2.5	1.5	1.6	1.8	2.5	2.3	2.7	2.7	3.2	3.4	3.2
Hong Kong SAR	2.3	3.7	2.0	1.9	3.2	2.8	2.2	4.7	6.3	5.0	4.7	4.1
Singapore	3.3	2.7	2.7	2.6	2.7	2.0	1.8	3.2	3.5	3.1	2.7	2.5
New Zealand	6.6	6.9	9.5	8.2	6.3	6.1	6.7	7.5	6.8	6.0	5.8	5.9
Memorandum												
European Union	9.4	9.6	10.6	11.1	10.7	10.8	10.6	9.8	9.1	8.2	7.8	7.5
Euro area	9.7	10.2	10.7	11.5	11.2	11.5	11.4	10.7	9.9	9.0	8.4	8.1
Newly industrialized Asian economies	2.8	3.3	2.4	2.2	2.1	2.2	2.4	5.4	5.2	3.9	4.0	3.4
Growth in employment												
Advanced economies	**1.3**	**1.0**	**−0.1**	**1.1**	**1.2**	**1.0**	**1.5**	**1.0**	**1.3**	**1.4**	**0.9**	**0.8**
Major advanced economies	1.2	0.9	0.1	1.0	0.8	0.8	1.5	1.0	1.1	1.2	0.7	0.6
United States	1.8	1.4	1.5	2.3	1.5	1.5	2.3	1.5	1.5	1.3	0.6	0.5
Japan	1.3	0.1	0.2	0.1	0.1	0.5	1.1	−0.7	−0.8	−0.2	0.1	0.4
Germany	0.9	0.3	−1.4	−0.2	0.1	−0.3	−0.2	0.9	1.1	1.5	1.2	0.6
France	0.2	1.0	−1.0	0.9	0.7	—	1.0	1.8	2.2	2.2	1.6	1.1
Italy	0.4	—	−4.1	−1.6	−0.6	0.5	0.4	1.1	1.3	1.9	1.0	0.6
United Kingdom	0.5	0.9	−0.9	1.0	1.4	1.1	2.0	1.1	1.3	1.0	0.5	0.5
Canada	1.5	1.9	0.8	2.0	1.9	0.8	2.3	2.6	2.8	2.6	1.8	1.8
Other advanced economies	1.4	1.5	−0.4	1.3	2.2	1.7	1.6	1.0	2.1	2.1	1.5	1.4
Memorandum												
European Union	0.6	0.8	−1.9	—	0.8	0.6	1.0	1.9	1.8	1.9	1.2	0.9
Euro area	0.6	0.8	−2.0	−0.2	0.6	0.6	0.9	2.0	1.9	2.1	1.4	1.0
Newly industrialized Asian economies	2.5	1.4	1.5	2.8	2.5	2.1	1.7	−2.7	1.5	1.3	1.7	1.6

Table 4 *(concluded)*

	Ten-Year Averages[1]		1993	1994	1995	1996	1997	1998	1999	2000	2001	2002
	1983–92	1993–2002										
Growth in real per capita GDP												
Advanced economies	**2.9**	**2.3**	**0.8**	**2.7**	**2.1**	**2.3**	**2.8**	**2.1**	**2.8**	**3.6**	**1.4**	**2.2**
Major advanced economies	2.8	2.1	0.7	2.4	1.7	2.1	2.6	2.2	2.5	3.3	1.1	1.9
United States	2.4	2.6	1.5	3.0	1.7	2.6	3.4	3.4	3.2	4.2	0.7	1.8
Japan	3.4	1.0	0.2	0.7	1.3	3.1	1.7	–1.3	0.7	1.5	0.4	1.3
Germany	5.1	1.4	–1.8	2.1	1.4	0.5	1.2	2.1	1.5	2.9	1.8	2.5
France	1.8	1.7	–1.3	1.4	1.5	0.6	1.5	2.9	2.7	2.8	2.3	2.3
Italy	2.3	1.9	0.5	1.9	2.7	1.0	1.8	1.7	2.1	3.0	2.1	2.6
United Kingdom	2.2	2.7	2.1	4.0	2.4	2.2	3.1	2.9	2.5	2.9	2.4	2.7
Canada	1.5	2.3	1.2	3.5	1.7	0.4	3.3	2.4	3.7	3.7	1.3	1.5
Other advanced economies	3.2	3.1	1.3	3.8	3.5	3.0	3.5	1.4	4.1	4.6	2.5	3.3
Memorandum												
European Union	3.0	2.1	–0.4	2.4	2.1	1.4	2.3	2.7	2.5	3.2	2.3	2.7
Euro area	3.2	2.0	–0.8	2.0	2.0	1.2	2.1	2.7	2.5	3.3	2.3	2.7
Newly industrialized Asian economies	7.0	4.4	5.4	6.5	6.0	5.0	4.3	–3.8	6.7	7.1	2.8	4.5

[1]Compound annual rate of change for employment and per capita GDP; arithmetic average for unemployment rate.
[2]The projections for unemployment have been adjusted to reflect the new survey techniques adopted by the U.S. Bureau of Labor Statistics in January 1994.
[3]New series starting in 1993, reflecting revisions in the labor force surveys and the definition of unemployment to bring data in line with those of other advanced economies.

Table 5. Developing Countries: Real GDP

(Annual percent change)

	Ten-Year Averages		1993	1994	1995	1996	1997	1998	1999	2000	2001	2002
	1983–92	1993–2002										
Developing countries	**4.7**	**5.5**	**6.3**	**6.7**	**6.1**	**6.5**	**5.8**	**3.5**	**3.8**	**5.8**	**5.0**	**5.6**
Regional groups												
Africa	2.0	3.1	0.2	2.4	2.9	5.7	2.9	3.3	2.3	3.0	4.2	4.4
Sub-Sahara	1.8	3.1	0.6	2.0	3.8	5.2	3.5	2.6	2.2	3.1	3.9	4.6
Excluding Nigeria and South Africa	1.9	3.5	−0.2	1.7	4.4	5.5	4.1	3.9	2.6	3.0	4.5	5.4
Developing Asia	7.3	7.2	9.4	9.6	9.0	8.2	6.6	4.0	6.1	6.9	5.9	6.3
China	10.2	9.2	13.5	12.6	10.5	9.6	8.8	7.8	7.1	8.0	7.0	7.1
India	5.4	6.2	5.0	6.7	7.6	7.1	4.9	6.0	6.6	6.4	5.6	6.1
Other developing Asia	5.3	4.3	6.3	6.9	7.7	6.7	3.8	−5.2	3.5	5.0	3.9	4.9
Middle East, Malta, and Turkey	3.4	3.5	3.3	0.3	4.3	4.8	5.4	3.6	0.8	5.4	2.9	4.6
Western Hemisphere	2.3	3.4	4.1	5.0	1.7	3.6	5.3	2.3	0.2	4.1	3.7	4.4
Analytical groups												
By source of export earnings												
Fuel	2.6	2.8	0.6	0.1	2.8	3.5	4.6	2.9	1.0	4.3	4.3	3.9
Nonfuel	5.0	5.8	7.0	7.4	6.5	6.8	5.9	3.6	4.1	5.9	5.0	5.7
of which, primary products	2.6	4.5	3.9	5.3	6.4	5.9	5.5	3.1	2.1	4.0	4.1	5.3
By external financing source												
Net debtor countries	4.8	5.6	6.5	6.9	6.3	6.6	5.9	3.6	4.0	5.8	5.0	5.6
of which, official financing	2.8	3.9	1.4	2.5	5.4	5.3	4.0	3.9	3.3	4.0	4.6	5.0
Net debtor countries by debt-servicing experience												
Countries with arrears and/or rescheduling during 1994–98	2.7	3.7	3.5	4.6	5.1	5.0	4.4	−0.6	2.0	4.3	4.2	4.7
Other groups												
Heavily indebted poor countries	2.2	4.3	1.6	2.9	5.8	6.0	4.9	4.0	3.6	4.0	4.8	5.6
Middle East and north Africa	2.9	3.6	1.5	2.2	2.5	4.8	4.1	4.3	2.7	4.5	4.9	4.4
Memorandum												
Real per capita GDP												
Developing countries	2.4	3.9	4.4	4.8	4.4	4.8	4.1	2.0	2.4	4.3	3.5	4.2
Regional groups												
Africa	−0.7	0.7	−2.3	−0.1	0.9	3.1	0.5	0.9	−0.4	0.4	1.8	2.0
Developing Asia	5.4	5.8	7.6	8.0	7.4	6.8	5.1	2.8	4.8	5.7	4.7	5.2
Middle East, Malta, and Turkey	0.2	1.4	1.0	−2.2	1.6	2.3	2.3	2.0	−0.2	3.3	1.0	2.7
Western Hemisphere	0.2	1.8	2.2	3.3	0.2	1.8	3.7	0.7	−1.3	2.6	2.2	2.9

Table 6. Developing Countries—by Country: Real GDP[1]

(Annual percent change)

	Average 1983–92	1993	1994	1995	1996	1997	1998	1999	2000
Africa	**2.0**	**0.2**	**2.4**	**2.9**	**5.7**	**2.9**	**3.3**	**2.3**	**3.0**
Algeria	1.9	−2.1	−0.9	3.8	3.8	1.1	5.1	3.2	3.0
Angola	2.1	−24.0	1.3	7.1	7.9	6.2	3.1	3.4	2.1
Benin	1.6	3.5	4.4	4.6	5.5	5.7	4.5	5.0	5.3
Botswana	9.8	2.0	3.4	4.7	6.8	7.6	6.2	7.3	8.5
Burkina Faso	3.6	−0.8	1.2	4.0	6.0	4.8	6.2	5.8	4.0
Burundi	4.0	−5.9	−3.7	−7.3	−8.4	0.4	4.5	−0.8	—
Cameroon	0.3	−3.2	−2.5	3.3	5.0	5.1	5.0	4.4	4.2
Cape Verde	1.3	12.7	11.5	3.8	3.8	4.7	7.6	7.9	6.7
Central African Republic	0.6	2.7	2.2	8.0	−4.6	4.5	5.2	3.6	3.3
Chad	6.3	−2.1	5.7	1.3	2.4	4.5	6.7	0.5	0.6
Comoros	1.7	3.0	−5.3	−3.9	−1.2	0.3	−1.2	−0.4	1.7
Congo, Dem. Rep. of	−1.4	−13.5	−3.9	0.7	0.9	−8.2	−3.5	−14.0	−4.9
Congo, Rep. of	5.8	−1.0	−5.5	4.0	4.3	−0.6	3.7	−3.0	4.5
Côte d'Ivoire	0.6	−0.2	2.0	7.1	6.9	6.2	5.8	1.6	−2.0
Djibouti	0.1	−6.7	−0.9	−3.5	−4.1	−0.7	0.1	2.2	0.7
Equatorial Guinea	3.7	6.7	59.3	10.0	63.7	73.9	30.0	10.1	48.2
Eritrea	...	−2.5	9.8	2.9	6.8	7.9	3.9	0.8	−9.0
Ethiopia	0.4	6.5	3.9	8.5	7.8	1.8	2.4	3.0	4.6
Gabon	1.9	3.9	3.7	5.0	3.6	5.7	3.5	−9.6	−2.9
Gambia, The	3.2	1.8	3.8	−3.4	6.2	4.9	3.5	6.4	5.3
Ghana	4.1	5.0	3.3	4.0	4.6	4.2	4.7	4.4	3.7
Guinea	3.8	5.0	4.0	4.7	5.0	4.8	4.5	3.3	4.5
Guinea-Bissau	2.6	2.1	3.2	4.4	4.6	5.5	−28.1	7.8	9.3
Kenya	3.7	0.4	2.6	4.4	4.1	2.1	2.1	2.0	−0.4
Lesotho	5.3	3.7	3.7	5.9	9.5	4.6	−3.6	2.1	2.4
Liberia	...	...	...	...	...	...	...	...	...
Madagascar	1.2	2.1	—	1.7	2.1	3.7	3.9	4.7	4.8
Malawi	2.6	9.7	−10.3	16.7	7.3	3.8	2.0	4.0	3.2
Mali	4.1	−4.7	2.6	7.0	4.3	6.7	4.9	6.6	4.3
Mauritania	4.8	5.5	4.6	4.6	5.5	3.2	3.7	4.1	5.2
Mauritius	6.2	6.7	4.5	3.8	5.2	5.8	6.0	5.9	3.6
Morocco	3.5	−1.0	10.4	−6.6	12.2	−2.2	6.8	−0.7	0.8
Mozambique, Rep. of	—	8.7	7.5	4.3	7.1	11.1	11.9	7.3	3.8
Namibia	1.7	−1.6	6.2	3.2	2.1	2.6	3.0	2.9	3.5
Niger	−0.7	1.4	4.0	2.6	3.4	2.8	10.4	−0.6	3.0
Nigeria	3.8	2.2	−0.6	2.6	6.4	3.1	1.9	1.1	2.8
Rwanda	2.5	−8.3	−49.5	32.8	15.8	12.8	9.5	5.9	5.2
São Tomé and Príncipe	−0.5	1.1	2.2	2.0	1.5	1.0	2.5	2.5	3.0
Senegal	1.6	−2.2	2.9	5.2	5.1	5.0	5.7	5.1	5.5
Seychelles	5.2	6.5	−0.8	−0.6	4.7	4.3	2.3	−3.0	1.2
Sierra Leone	−1.4	0.1	3.5	−10.0	−24.8	−17.6	−0.8	−8.1	3.8
Somalia	...	...	...	...	...	...	...	...	...
South Africa	0.7	1.2	3.2	3.1	4.2	2.5	0.7	1.9	3.2
Sudan	1.7	6.2	2.0	3.0	10.5	10.2	6.1	5.1	8.3
Swaziland	6.6	3.3	3.5	3.0	3.6	4.0	2.7	3.1	3.5
Tanzania	3.4	1.2	1.6	3.6	4.5	3.5	3.3	4.8	5.1
Togo	1.4	−16.9	17.5	6.9	9.7	4.3	−2.1	2.7	−0.5
Tunisia	4.2	2.2	3.2	2.4	7.1	5.4	4.8	6.2	5.0
Uganda	3.4	8.6	6.4	11.9	8.6	5.1	4.6	7.6	4.6
Zambia	0.7	−0.1	−13.3	−2.3	6.5	3.5	−2.2	2.4	4.0
Zimbabwe	2.5	1.1	7.1	−0.6	8.7	3.7	2.5	−0.2	−5.5

Table 6 *(continued)*

	Average 1983–92	1993	1994	1995	1996	1997	1998	1999	2000
Developing Asia	**7.3**	**9.4**	**9.6**	**9.0**	**8.2**	**6.6**	**4.0**	**6.1**	**6.9**
Afghanistan, Islamic State of	...	...	...	...	...	...	...	...	...
Bangladesh	4.6	4.3	4.5	4.8	5.0	5.3	5.0	5.2	5.0
Bhutan	6.6	6.1	6.4	7.4	6.1	7.3	5.5	5.9	6.1
Brunei Darussalam	...	0.5	1.8	3.1	1.0	3.6	–4.0	2.5	3.0
Cambodia	...	4.0	3.9	6.7	5.5	3.7	1.8	5.0	4.0
China	10.2	13.5	12.6	10.5	9.6	8.8	7.8	7.1	8.0
Fiji	2.6	3.5	4.2	2.4	3.3	3.6	4.0	4.5	4.9
India	5.4	5.0	6.7	7.6	7.1	4.9	6.0	6.6	6.4
Indonesia	6.3	7.3	7.5	8.2	8.0	4.5	–13.1	0.8	4.8
Kiribati	0.2	0.8	7.2	6.5	2.6	3.3	6.1	2.5	2.0
Lao P.D. Republic	4.7	5.9	8.1	7.1	6.9	6.5	4.0	5.0	5.7
Malaysia	6.6	9.9	9.2	9.8	10.0	7.3	–7.4	5.8	8.5
Maldives	10.0	6.2	6.6	7.2	7.9	9.1	9.1	8.5	7.6
Myanmar	1.0	5.9	6.8	7.7	6.4	5.7	5.8	10.9	5.5
Nepal	4.6	3.8	8.2	3.5	5.3	5.0	3.0	3.9	6.0
Pakistan	5.8	2.7	4.4	4.9	2.9	1.8	2.6	4.3	5.1
Papua New Guinea	3.5	18.2	5.9	–3.3	7.7	–3.9	–3.8	3.2	–1.2
Philippines	1.0	2.1	4.4	4.7	5.8	5.2	–0.6	3.3	3.9
Samoa	14.3	1.7	–0.1	6.8	6.1	1.6	1.3	2.5	3.5
Solomon Islands	2.8	2.0	5.4	10.5	3.5	–2.3	0.5	–0.5	–1.0
Sri Lanka	4.1	6.9	5.6	5.5	3.8	6.4	4.7	4.3	6.0
Thailand	8.4	8.4	9.0	9.3	5.9	–1.4	–10.8	4.2	4.3
Tonga	1.8	3.7	5.0	4.8	–1.4	–4.4	–1.5	—	1.5
Vanuatu	2.8	4.5	1.3	2.3	0.4	0.6	6.0	–2.5	4.0
Vietnam	5.9	8.1	8.8	9.5	9.3	8.2	3.5	4.2	5.5
Middle East, Malta, and Turkey	**3.4**	**3.3**	**0.3**	**4.3**	**4.8**	**5.4**	**3.6**	**0.8**	**5.4**
Bahrain	3.5	12.9	–0.2	3.9	4.1	3.1	4.8	4.0	3.9
Egypt	3.5	2.5	3.9	4.7	5.0	5.3	5.7	6.0	5.1
Iran, Islamic Republic of	2.6	2.1	0.9	2.9	5.5	3.4	2.2	2.5	3.6
Iraq	...	...	...	...	...	...	...	...	...
Jordan	9.0	5.6	5.0	6.4	2.1	3.1	2.9	3.1	4.0
Kuwait	–1.5	45.1	2.3	4.0	1.2	2.3	2.0	–2.4	3.6
Lebanon	2.2	7.0	8.0	6.5	4.0	4.0	3.5	1.0	—
Libya	0.5	–9.7	–2.7	0.9	5.2	–1.2	2.9	2.5	3.0
Malta	4.7	4.0	5.0	7.3	3.2	3.7	3.1	3.5	3.2
Oman	7.2	6.1	3.8	4.8	2.9	6.2	2.7	–1.0	4.7
Qatar	0.2	–0.6	2.3	2.9	4.8	24.0	12.3	7.6	12.9
Saudi Arabia	2.6	–0.6	0.5	0.5	1.4	2.7	1.6	–1.0	4.1
Syrian Arab Republic	2.8	5.0	7.7	5.8	4.4	1.8	7.6	–1.8	2.5
Turkey	5.0	7.7	–4.7	8.1	6.9	7.5	3.1	–4.7	7.2
United Arab Emirates	2.2	4.6	6.6	6.7	4.9	8.1	0.3	0.5	5.8
Yemen, Republic of	...	0.4	–3.6	7.9	2.9	8.1	5.3	3.8	6.5

Table 6 *(concluded)*

	Average 1983–92	1993	1994	1995	1996	1997	1998	1999	2000
Western Hemisphere	**2.3**	**4.1**	**5.0**	**1.7**	**3.6**	**5.3**	**2.3**	**0.2**	**4.1**
Antigua and Barbuda	6.8	5.1	6.2	−5.0	6.1	5.6	3.9	3.2	2.5
Argentina	1.7	6.3	5.8	−2.8	5.5	8.1	3.8	−3.4	−0.5
Bahamas, The	2.0	1.7	0.9	0.3	4.2	3.3	3.0	6.0	3.5
Barbados	0.6	0.8	4.0	3.1	1.7	6.4	4.1	1.3	3.2
Belize	6.1	3.3	1.8	3.3	2.0	3.6	4.5	4.5	6.0
Bolivia	1.2	4.3	4.7	4.7	4.4	5.0	5.5	0.6	2.5
Brazil	2.0	4.9	5.9	4.2	2.7	3.3	0.2	0.8	4.2
Chile	5.9	7.0	5.7	10.6	7.4	7.4	3.9	−1.1	5.4
Colombia	3.7	5.4	5.8	5.2	2.1	3.4	0.5	−4.3	2.8
Costa Rica	4.4	6.3	4.9	4.0	0.3	5.8	8.0	8.4	4.5
Dominica	4.0	1.7	1.4	2.3	2.1	0.6	4.8	3.5	3.5
Dominican Republic	2.7	2.9	4.3	4.7	7.2	8.3	7.3	8.0	7.8
Ecuador	2.4	2.0	4.4	2.3	2.0	3.4	0.4	−7.3	2.3
El Salvador	2.7	7.4	6.0	6.4	1.8	4.3	3.2	2.0	3.0
Grenada	5.4	−1.2	3.3	3.1	2.9	4.2	5.8	6.2	7.0
Guatemala	2.0	3.9	4.0	4.9	3.0	4.1	5.1	3.5	3.6
Guyana	−0.1	8.2	8.5	5.0	7.9	6.2	−1.7	3.0	2.5
Haiti	−0.7	−2.4	−8.3	4.4	2.7	1.1	3.0	2.0	2.0
Honduras	3.2	6.2	−1.3	4.1	3.6	5.1	2.9	−1.9	6.2
Jamaica	2.6	1.5	1.0	0.2	−1.5	−1.7	−0.5	—	1.5
Mexico	1.8	2.0	4.4	−6.2	5.2	6.8	4.9	3.8	6.9
Netherlands Antilles	0.7	0.3	2.4	0.0	−2.4	3.0	3.0	3.0	3.0
Nicaragua	−1.8	−0.2	3.3	4.2	5.0	4.9	4.2	6.7	5.9
Panama	1.7	5.5	2.9	1.8	2.4	4.4	4.0	4.1	4.5
Paraguay	2.8	4.1	3.1	4.7	1.3	2.6	−0.4	0.5	0.8
Peru	−1.2	6.4	13.1	7.3	2.5	6.8	−0.4	1.4	3.6
St. Kitts and Nevis	5.0	6.7	5.1	3.7	6.5	6.8	1.1	2.8	2.6
St. Lucia	7.1	2.0	2.1	4.1	1.4	2.1	2.9	3.1	4.1
St. Vincent and the Grenadines	6.1	2.3	−2.0	8.3	1.2	3.1	5.7	4.0	3.5
Suriname	0.2	−9.5	−5.4	7.1	6.7	5.6	1.9	5.0	2.9
Trinidad and Tobago	−3.1	−1.4	3.6	4.0	3.8	3.1	4.8	6.8	5.6
Uruguay	2.5	2.7	7.3	−1.4	5.6	4.9	4.6	−3.2	−1.0
Venezuela	2.4	0.3	−2.3	4.0	−0.2	6.4	0.2	−6.1	3.2

[1]For many countries, figures for recent years are IMF staff estimates. Data for some countries are for fiscal years.

Table 7. Countries in Transition: Real GDP[1]

(Annual percent change)

	Average 1983–92	1993	1994	1995	1996	1997	1998	1999	2000
Central and eastern Europe	...	**0.3**	**3.5**	**5.5**	**4.0**	**2.5**	**2.1**	**1.8**	**3.8**
Albania	–3.6	9.6	9.4	8.9	9.1	–7.0	8.0	7.3	7.8
Bosnia and Herzegovina	...	...	...	32.4	85.8	39.9	12.8	8.6	13.7
Bulgaria	–0.9	–1.5	1.7	2.2	–10.9	–6.9	3.5	2.4	5.0
Croatia	...	–8.0	5.9	6.8	6.0	6.6	2.5	–0.4	3.5
Czech Republic	...	0.1	2.2	5.9	4.8	–1.0	–2.2	–0.8	3.1
Estonia	...	–8.2	–2.0	4.3	3.9	10.6	4.7	–1.1	6.4
Hungary	–1.0	–0.6	2.9	1.5	1.3	4.6	4.9	4.5	5.3
Latvia	...	–14.9	0.6	–0.8	3.3	8.6	3.9	1.1	5.5
Lithuania	...	–16.2	–9.8	3.3	4.7	7.3	5.1	–4.2	2.7
Macedonia, former Yugoslav Rep. of	...	–7.5	–1.8	–1.1	1.2	1.4	2.9	2.7	6.0
Poland	0.9	4.3	5.2	6.8	6.0	6.8	4.8	4.1	4.1
Romania	–2.0	1.5	3.9	7.1	3.9	–6.1	–5.4	–3.2	2.0
Slovak Republic	...	–3.7	4.9	6.9	6.6	6.5	4.1	1.9	2.2
Slovenia	...	2.8	5.3	4.1	3.5	4.6	3.8	5.2	4.9
Commonwealth of Independent States and Mongolia	...	**–10.9**	**–13.3**	**–5.5**	**–3.3**	**1.0**	**–2.8**	**3.1**	**7.1**
Russia	...	–10.4	–11.6	–4.2	–3.4	0.9	–4.9	3.2	7.5
Excluding Russia	...	–11.8	–17.0	–8.6	–3.1	1.4	1.6	2.7	6.3
Armenia	...	–14.1	5.4	6.9	5.9	3.3	7.3	3.3	6.0
Azerbaijan	...	–23.1	–19.7	–11.8	1.3	5.8	10.0	7.4	10.3
Belarus	...	–7.0	–12.6	–10.4	2.8	11.4	8.3	3.4	6.0
Georgia	...	–29.3	–10.4	2.6	10.5	10.7	2.9	2.9	1.5
Kazakhstan	...	–9.2	–12.6	–8.2	0.5	1.7	–1.9	2.8	9.4
Kyrgyz Republic	...	–15.5	–19.8	–5.8	7.1	10.0	2.1	3.7	5.0
Moldova	...	–1.1	–31.1	–1.4	–5.9	1.6	–6.5	–3.4	1.9
Mongolia	1.6	–3.0	2.3	6.3	2.4	4.0	3.5	3.2	3.0
Tajikistan	...	–11.1	–21.4	–12.5	–4.4	1.7	5.3	3.7	8.3
Turkmenistan	...	–10.0	–17.3	–7.2	–6.7	–11.3	5.0	16.0	17.6
Ukraine	...	–14.2	–22.9	–12.2	–10.0	–3.3	–1.9	–0.4	4.2
Uzbekistan	...	–2.3	–4.2	–0.9	1.6	2.5	4.3	4.3	4.0
Memorandum EU accession candidates	...	2.8	1.1	6.3	4.8	4.1	2.4	–0.1	4.8

[1]Data for some countries refer to real net material product (NMP) or are estimates based on NMP. For many countries, figures for recent years are IMF staff estimates. The figures should be interpreted only as indicative of broad orders of magnitude because reliable, comparable data are not generally available. In particular, the growth of output of new private enterprises of the informal economy is not fully reflected in the recent figures.

Table 8. Summary of Inflation

(Percent)

| | Ten-Year Averages | | 1993 | 1994 | 1995 | 1996 | 1997 | 1998 | 1999 | 2000 | 2001 | 2002 |
	1983–92	1993–2002										
GDP deflators												
Advanced economies	**4.5**	**1.8**	**2.7**	**2.2**	**2.3**	**1.9**	**1.7**	**1.4**	**0.9**	**1.3**	**1.6**	**1.6**
United States	3.3	1.9	2.4	2.1	2.2	1.9	1.9	1.3	1.5	2.0	2.0	2.1
European Union	5.5	2.2	3.5	2.7	3.1	2.5	1.9	2.0	1.5	1.5	1.9	1.8
Japan	1.8	–0.5	0.5	0.1	–0.4	–0.6	0.3	–0.1	–1.4	–1.7	–1.2	–0.4
Other advanced economies	7.8	2.3	3.8	3.2	3.4	3.0	2.2	1.5	0.1	1.4	2.0	2.0
Consumer prices												
Advanced economies	**4.6**	**2.2**	**3.1**	**2.6**	**2.6**	**2.4**	**2.1**	**1.5**	**1.4**	**2.3**	**2.1**	**1.8**
United States	4.0	2.6	3.0	2.6	2.8	2.9	2.3	1.5	2.2	3.4	2.6	2.2
European Union	5.1	2.3	3.8	3.0	2.9	2.5	1.8	1.5	1.4	2.3	2.3	1.8
Japan	1.8	0.3	1.2	0.7	–0.1	0.1	1.7	0.6	–0.3	–0.6	–0.7	—
Other advanced economies	7.9	2.7	3.4	3.3	3.8	3.2	2.4	2.6	1.0	2.2	2.8	2.3
Developing countries	**46.9**	**17.0**	**43.2**	**55.3**	**23.2**	**15.4**	**9.9**	**10.4**	**6.7**	**6.1**	**5.7**	**4.8**
Regional groups												
Africa	22.4	21.3	39.0	54.8	35.1	30.1	14.4	9.1	11.5	13.5	9.6	5.7
Developing Asia	9.9	7.0	10.8	16.0	13.2	8.3	4.8	7.7	2.5	1.9	2.8	3.3
Middle East, Malta, and Turkey	22.9	26.4	29.4	37.3	39.1	29.6	27.7	27.6	23.2	20.7	18.4	13.5
Western Hemisphere	173.8	35.1	152.1	200.3	36.0	21.2	12.9	9.8	8.8	8.1	6.3	4.8
Analytical groups												
By source of export earnings												
Fuel	15.3	22.8	29.2	36.1	42.6	35.0	19.3	17.2	16.2	14.6	12.4	10.6
Nonfuel	52.3	16.5	45.0	57.6	21.3	13.5	8.9	9.7	5.8	5.3	5.0	4.3
of which, primary products	75.2	22.3	46.7	62.9	29.6	27.0	15.8	12.0	12.2	13.1	9.4	5.6
By external financing source												
Net debtor countries	49.0	17.5	44.9	57.4	23.9	15.9	10.2	10.7	6.9	6.3	5.8	4.9
of which, official financing	37.2	19.7	37.5	63.5	30.4	23.4	11.4	8.1	10.8	10.8	7.4	4.8
Net debtor countries by debt-servicing experience												
Countries with arrears and/or rescheduling during 1994–98	109.8	41.4	200.5	221.7	40.0	21.0	11.9	17.8	13.3	11.5	9.8	6.7
Countries in transition	**42.4**	**77.5**	**634.3**	**274.2**	**133.5**	**42.4**	**27.4**	**21.8**	**43.9**	**20.1**	**15.3**	**10.0**
Central and eastern Europe	...	25.6	79.9	45.6	24.7	23.3	41.8	17.1	10.9	12.8	9.8	6.3
Commonwealth of Independent States and Mongolia	...	111.7	1,242.3	508.0	235.2	55.6	19.1	24.9	70.4	25.0	19.0	12.4
Russia	...	94.0	874.7	307.4	197.4	47.6	14.7	27.7	85.7	20.8	17.6	12.3
Excluding Russia	...	154.6	2,440.9	1,334.5	338.8	75.5	29.6	19.3	41.8	34.6	22.2	12.8
Memorandum												
Median inflation rate												
Advanced economies	4.7	2.2	3.0	2.4	2.5	2.1	1.8	1.7	1.5	2.7	2.5	2.2
Developing countries	9.4	6.5	9.3	10.6	10.0	7.5	6.2	5.7	3.8	4.2	4.1	4.0
Countries in transition	95.8	72.4	472.3	132.1	40.1	24.1	14.8	10.0	8.0	10.0	7.3	5.3

Table 9. Advanced Economies: GDP Deflators and Consumer Prices
(Annual percent change)

	Ten-Year Averages		1993	1994	1995	1996	1997	1998	1999	2000	2001	2002	Fourth Quarter[1]		
	1983–92	1993–2002											2000	2001	2002
GDP deflators															
Advanced economies	**4.5**	**1.8**	**2.7**	**2.2**	**2.3**	**1.9**	**1.7**	**1.4**	**0.9**	**1.3**	**1.6**	**1.6**	...	...	...
Major advanced economies	3.7	1.5	2.3	1.8	1.9	1.7	1.5	1.1	0.9	1.1	1.3	1.5	1.2	1.6	1.5
United States	3.3	1.9	2.4	2.1	2.2	1.9	1.9	1.3	1.5	2.0	2.0	2.1	2.3	2.0	2.1
Japan	1.8	−0.5	0.5	0.1	−0.4	−0.6	0.3	−0.1	−1.4	−1.7	−1.2	−0.4	−2.0	−0.4	−0.6
Germany	2.8	1.5	3.7	2.5	2.0	1.0	0.8	1.1	0.9	−0.4	1.6	1.5	−0.3	2.4	1.2
France	4.4	1.1	2.4	1.8	1.7	1.4	1.2	0.7	0.2	0.5	0.4	0.6	0.6	0.6	0.6
Italy	8.3	3.0	3.9	3.5	5.0	5.3	2.4	2.7	1.6	2.2	2.1	1.7	2.5	2.1	1.6
United Kingdom	5.6	2.4	2.7	1.5	2.5	3.3	2.9	3.0	2.3	1.8	1.9	2.5	1.3	2.2	2.6
Canada	3.5	1.6	1.5	1.1	2.3	1.7	1.0	−0.6	1.6	3.6	2.1	1.9	3.2	2.2	1.8
Other advanced economies	8.0	2.7	4.5	3.8	3.9	3.0	2.5	2.3	0.9	1.7	2.4	2.2	...	...	...
Spain	8.2	3.3	4.5	3.9	4.9	3.5	2.2	2.3	2.9	3.5	3.0	2.5	...	...	...
Netherlands	1.4	2.3	1.9	2.3	1.8	1.2	2.0	2.0	1.7	3.1	4.3	2.6	...	...	...
Belgium	3.1	1.7	3.7	1.9	1.8	1.2	1.3	1.6	1.0	1.3	1.9	1.3	...	...	...
Sweden	7.1	1.7	2.6	2.4	3.5	1.4	1.7	0.9	0.5	1.3	1.3	1.6	...	...	...
Austria	3.2	1.6	2.8	2.8	2.3	1.3	1.2	0.7	0.9	1.3	1.4	1.7	...	...	...
Denmark	4.5	2.2	1.4	1.7	1.8	2.5	2.2	1.9	3.0	3.7	2.1	1.8	...	...	...
Finland	5.3	2.0	2.3	2.0	4.1	−0.2	2.1	3.0	0.5	2.9	1.6	1.9	...	...	...
Greece	17.3	6.7	14.5	11.2	11.2	7.3	6.8	5.1	2.8	3.1	3.1	3.0	...	...	...
Portugal	16.1	4.6	7.0	6.1	7.4	3.5	3.2	4.3	3.6	3.2	4.7	3.0	...	...	...
Ireland	4.3	3.9	5.2	1.7	3.0	2.3	4.4	5.8	3.8	5.5	4.0	3.8	...	...	...
Luxembourg	3.4	2.2	0.8	4.9	4.3	1.7	3.3	1.5	1.1	1.4	1.5	1.5	...	...	...
Switzerland	3.3	1.1	2.7	1.6	1.1	0.4	−0.2	0.2	0.6	1.6	1.4	1.3	...	...	...
Norway	4.1	3.2	2.1	−0.2	3.1	4.3	3.0	−0.8	6.6	15.1	0.8	−1.1	...	...	...
Israel	68.5	7.6	11.2	13.2	9.8	10.9	8.4	8.3	6.6	1.7	1.9	4.2	...	...	...
Iceland	23.8	3.4	2.3	1.9	2.8	1.9	3.5	5.3	3.8	3.6	4.1	4.3	...	...	...
Cyprus	5.1	3.2	4.9	5.1	3.6	1.9	2.6	2.3	2.1	3.9	2.7	2.7	...	...	...
Korea	6.9	3.5	7.1	7.7	7.1	3.9	3.1	5.1	−2.0	−1.6	2.8	2.3	...	...	...
Australia	5.8	1.6	1.6	0.8	1.5	2.2	1.6	0.1	1.0	3.3	2.3	2.3	...	...	...
Taiwan Province of China	2.2	1.4	4.0	1.5	2.0	3.1	1.7	2.6	−1.4	−1.6	1.4	1.2	...	...	...
Hong Kong SAR	8.0	2.2	8.5	6.9	2.6	5.9	5.8	0.4	−5.1	−6.5	1.0	3.7	...	...	...
Singapore	2.2	1.1	3.3	2.9	2.6	1.3	0.7	−1.7	−3.1	1.8	1.9	1.9	...	...	...
New Zealand	7.3	1.8	2.3	1.6	2.0	2.0	0.9	1.0	−0.3	2.0	3.5	3.2	...	...	...
Memorandum															
European Union	5.5	2.2	3.5	2.7	3.1	2.5	1.9	2.0	1.5	1.5	1.9	1.8	...	...	...
Euro area	5.5	2.2	3.8	2.9	3.2	2.4	1.7	1.8	1.3	1.4	1.9	1.6	...	...	...
Newly industrialized Asian economies	5.4	2.6	6.1	5.4	4.7	3.7	2.9	3.2	−2.3	−1.9	2.1	2.1	...	...	...
Consumer prices															
Advanced economies	**4.6**	**2.2**	**3.1**	**2.6**	**2.6**	**2.4**	**2.1**	**1.5**	**1.4**	**2.3**	**2.1**	**1.8**	...	...	...
Major advanced economies	3.9	2.0	2.8	2.2	2.3	2.2	2.0	1.3	1.4	2.3	1.9	1.7	2.4	1.6	1.8
United States	4.0	2.6	3.0	2.6	2.8	2.9	2.3	1.5	2.2	3.4	2.6	2.2	3.4	2.2	2.3
Japan	1.8	0.3	1.2	0.7	−0.1	0.1	1.7	0.6	−0.3	−0.6	−0.7	—	−0.6	−0.7	0.4
Germany[2]	2.3	1.8	4.5	2.7	1.7	1.2	1.5	0.6	0.7	2.1	2.0	1.3	2.4	1.4	1.3
France	4.4	1.5	2.1	1.7	1.8	2.1	1.3	0.7	0.6	1.8	1.5	1.4	2.0	1.5	1.2
Italy	7.4	3.0	4.6	4.1	5.2	4.0	1.9	2.0	1.7	2.6	2.2	1.6	2.8	1.7	1.8
United Kingdom[3]	5.3	2.6	3.0	2.4	2.8	3.0	2.8	2.7	2.3	2.1	2.2	2.4	2.1	2.3	2.5
Canada	4.4	1.8	1.8	0.2	1.9	1.6	1.6	1.0	1.7	2.7	3.0	2.2	3.1	2.6	2.0
Other advanced economies	7.7	2.9	4.2	4.1	3.8	3.2	2.3	2.4	1.3	2.4	2.8	2.3	...	...	...
Memorandum															
European Union	5.1	2.3	3.8	3.0	2.9	2.5	1.8	1.5	1.4	2.3	2.3	1.8	...	...	...
Euro area	5.0	2.3	4.0	3.2	3.0	2.5	1.7	1.3	1.2	2.4	2.3	1.7	...	...	...
Newly industrialized Asian economies	4.3	3.3	4.6	5.7	4.6	4.3	3.4	4.4	—	1.1	2.8	2.3	...	...	...

[1]From fourth quarter of preceding year.
[2]Based on the revised consumer price index for united Germany introduced in September 1995.
[3]Retail price index excluding mortgage interest.

Table 10. Advanced Economies: Hourly Earnings, Productivity, and Unit Labor Costs in Manufacturing

(Annual percent change)

| | Ten-Year Averages | | 1993 | 1994 | 1995 | 1996 | 1997 | 1998 | 1999 | 2000 | 2001 | 2002 |
	1983–92	1993–2002										
Hourly earnings												
Advanced economies	**6.0**	**3.3**	**4.0**	**3.4**	**3.2**	**2.9**	**2.9**	**3.3**	**3.1**	**3.5**	**3.4**	**3.2**
Major advanced economies	5.1	3.0	3.6	2.9	2.7	2.3	2.5	3.3	2.8	3.6	3.4	3.0
United States	4.1	3.4	2.8	2.8	2.1	1.3	1.9	5.3	4.0	5.2	5.1	3.7
Japan	3.9	1.1	2.7	2.3	2.4	1.7	3.1	0.9	−0.6	−0.1	−1.5	0.3
Germany	5.2	3.2	7.0	2.2	4.0	4.7	1.1	2.0	2.4	2.4	2.8	3.0
France	5.8	3.1	3.9	3.7	1.6	2.6	3.2	2.7	2.5	3.6	3.8	3.5
Italy	9.9	3.2	5.4	3.1	4.7	5.8	4.6	−2.0	2.4	2.5	3.0	2.7
United Kingdom	8.4	4.4	4.7	5.0	4.4	4.3	4.2	4.5	4.1	4.6	4.5	4.1
Canada	5.0	1.9	1.9	1.7	2.2	−0.9	3.0	2.8	1.7	0.9	2.1	3.6
Other advanced economies	10.2	4.5	5.9	5.9	5.2	5.7	4.3	3.0	4.4	3.2	3.6	3.8
Memorandum												
European Union	7.3	3.6	5.5	3.7	3.9	4.4	3.3	2.3	2.9	3.4	3.5	3.4
Euro area	7.1	3.4	5.7	3.4	3.8	4.3	3.1	1.8	2.6	3.1	3.4	3.2
Newly industrialized Asian economies	13.4	6.3	9.2	11.4	7.9	10.2	5.6	0.9	7.8	2.1	3.8	4.6
Productivity												
Advanced economies	**3.3**	**3.6**	**2.1**	**4.9**	**3.7**	**3.2**	**4.2**	**2.5**	**4.5**	**5.7**	**2.8**	**2.6**
Major advanced economies	3.3	3.6	1.6	4.5	3.6	3.2	4.2	2.8	4.3	6.0	2.9	2.5
United States	3.0	4.2	1.9	3.0	3.9	3.4	3.8	6.2	5.8	7.2	4.1	3.0
Japan	2.9	2.1	−1.0	3.3	4.7	3.8	4.8	−4.2	3.5	6.6	−0.1	0.5
Germany	3.9	5.0	3.1	8.8	4.5	6.0	7.0	4.7	2.9	6.2	3.5	3.2
France	3.8	3.9	0.4	9.0	3.9	2.9	6.4	4.0	2.9	3.6	2.8	3.4
Italy	3.3	2.3	0.6	6.0	3.6	3.7	2.7	−1.9	1.1	4.0	1.5	2.0
United Kingdom	4.8	2.1	4.9	4.5	−0.5	−1.0	0.6	−0.4	3.7	4.1	3.1	2.1
Canada	2.6	2.0	4.4	5.2	1.0	−1.3	3.0	−0.3	2.4	0.3	2.0	3.0
Other advanced economies	3.3	3.8	4.0	6.7	4.0	2.8	4.4	1.4	5.3	4.7	2.2	2.7
Memorandum												
European Union	3.6	3.5	3.0	7.7	3.2	2.8	4.4	2.1	2.5	4.3	2.5	2.5
Euro area	3.5	3.7	2.3	8.0	3.9	3.8	5.0	2.5	2.3	4.3	2.5	2.6
Newly industrialized Asian economies	7.9	6.5	4.7	7.1	7.9	6.3	7.1	−1.6	14.8	10.6	3.7	5.0
Unit labor costs												
Advanced economies	**2.7**	**−0.3**	**1.9**	**−1.4**	**−0.5**	**−0.2**	**−1.3**	**0.8**	**−1.3**	**−2.1**	**0.6**	**0.6**
Major advanced economies	1.8	−0.5	2.0	−1.6	−0.9	−0.9	−1.5	0.6	−1.5	−2.3	0.4	0.5
United States	1.0	−0.8	0.8	−0.1	−1.7	−2.1	−1.8	−0.8	−1.7	−1.8	1.0	0.7
Japan	1.0	−1.0	3.8	−0.9	−2.2	−2.0	−1.6	5.3	−4.0	−6.2	−1.4	−0.2
Germany	1.2	−1.7	3.8	−6.1	−0.4	−1.2	−5.5	−2.6	−0.4	−3.6	−0.7	−0.2
France	1.9	−0.8	3.6	−4.9	−2.3	−0.3	−3.0	−1.2	−0.4	—	1.0	0.1
Italy	6.4	0.9	4.8	−2.7	1.1	2.0	1.8	−0.2	1.3	−1.5	1.5	0.7
United Kingdom	3.4	2.3	−0.2	0.5	4.9	5.4	3.6	4.9	0.3	0.4	1.4	1.9
Canada	2.3	−0.1	−2.4	−3.4	1.3	0.4	—	3.1	−0.7	0.6	0.2	0.5
Other advanced economies	6.8	0.7	1.8	−0.8	0.9	2.6	−0.2	1.7	−0.6	−1.3	1.4	1.1
Memorandum												
European Union	3.6	0.2	2.5	−3.6	0.8	1.6	−0.9	0.2	0.4	−0.8	1.0	0.8
Euro area	3.5	−0.2	3.4	−4.2	−0.1	0.6	−1.7	−0.7	0.4	−1.1	0.9	0.5
Newly industrialized Asian economies	4.3	−0.4	3.5	2.6	−1.0	2.6	−1.5	2.7	−5.1	−7.0	0.2	−0.2

Table 11. Developing Countries: Consumer Prices
(Annual percent change)

	Ten-Year Averages		1993	1994	1995	1996	1997	1998	1999	2000	2001	2002
	1983–92	1993–2002										
Developing countries	**46.9**	**17.0**	**43.2**	**55.3**	**23.2**	**15.4**	**9.9**	**10.4**	**6.7**	**6.1**	**5.7**	**4.8**
Regional groups												
Africa	22.4	21.3	39.0	54.8	35.1	30.1	14.4	9.1	11.5	13.5	9.6	5.7
Sub-Sahara	26.3	25.8	47.9	68.7	40.7	36.4	17.6	10.7	14.5	17.4	11.5	6.4
Excluding Nigeria and South Africa	34.7	38.4	73.7	121.7	57.1	58.4	25.2	13.0	21.7	26.8	14.9	7.2
Developing Asia	9.9	7.0	10.8	16.0	13.2	8.3	4.8	7.7	2.5	1.9	2.8	3.3
China	7.6	6.4	14.7	24.1	17.1	8.3	2.8	−0.8	−1.4	0.4	1.0	1.5
India	9.3	7.4	6.4	10.2	10.2	9.0	7.2	13.2	4.7	4.0	3.8	5.9
Other developing Asia	13.0	8.5	8.3	7.9	9.2	8.0	6.8	22.1	9.1	3.5	5.9	5.2
Middle East, Malta, and Turkey	22.9	26.4	29.4	37.3	39.1	29.6	27.7	27.6	23.2	20.7	18.4	13.5
Western Hemisphere	173.8	35.1	152.1	200.3	36.0	21.2	12.9	9.8	8.8	8.1	6.3	4.8
Analytical groups												
By source of export earnings												
Fuel	15.3	22.8	29.2	36.1	42.6	35.0	19.3	17.2	16.2	14.6	12.4	10.6
Nonfuel	52.3	16.5	45.0	57.6	21.3	13.5	8.9	9.7	5.8	5.3	5.0	4.3
of which, primary products	75.2	22.3	46.7	62.9	29.6	27.0	15.8	12.0	12.2	13.1	9.4	5.6
By external financing source												
Net debtor countries	49.0	17.5	44.9	57.4	23.9	15.9	10.2	10.7	6.9	6.3	5.8	4.9
of which, official financing	37.2	19.7	37.5	63.5	30.4	23.4	11.4	8.1	10.8	10.8	7.4	4.8
Net debtor countries by debt-servicing experience												
Countries with arrears and/or rescheduling during 1994–98	109.8	41.4	200.5	221.7	40.0	21.0	11.9	17.8	13.3	11.5	9.8	6.7
Other groups												
Heavily indebted poor countries	51.5	31.7	60.4	92.4	49.4	46.4	21.5	14.7	17.0	18.9	11.9	7.1
Middle East and north Africa	15.5	13.8	19.5	21.8	24.2	16.7	11.2	10.4	10.1	9.2	8.4	7.7
Memorandum												
Median												
Developing countries	9.4	6.5	9.3	10.6	10.0	7.5	6.2	5.7	3.8	4.2	4.0	4.0
Regional groups												
Africa	9.5	8.5	9.7	24.7	11.8	7.7	7.4	5.8	3.9	5.1	4.6	4.2
Developing Asia	8.1	6.5	6.7	8.4	9.1	8.5	6.4	8.2	4.4	3.9	5.0	4.5
Middle East, Malta, and Turkey	7.0	3.9	5.9	4.6	6.4	6.8	3.1	3.0	2.1	1.7	2.7	2.8
Western Hemisphere	14.6	6.4	10.7	8.3	10.2	7.4	7.0	5.1	3.5	4.6	3.8	3.7

Table 12. Developing Countries—by Country: Consumer Prices[1]

(Annual percent change)

	Average 1983–92	1993	1994	1995	1996	1997	1998	1999	2000
Africa	**22.4**	**39.0**	**54.8**	**35.1**	**30.1**	**14.4**	**9.1**	**11.5**	**13.5**
Algeria	12.3	20.5	29.0	29.8	18.7	5.7	5.0	2.6	0.3
Angola	23.9	1,379.5	949.8	2,672.2	4,146.0	221.5	107.4	248.2	325.0
Benin	1.6	0.4	38.5	14.5	4.9	3.8	5.8	0.3	4.2
Botswana	12.4	14.3	10.5	10.5	10.1	8.8	6.5	7.2	5.6
Burkina Faso	0.4	0.6	24.7	7.8	6.1	2.3	5.0	–1.1	–0.2
Burundi	7.1	9.7	14.7	19.4	26.4	31.1	12.5	3.6	31.9
Cameroon	4.8	–3.7	12.7	25.8	6.6	5.2	—	2.9	0.8
Cape Verde	10.0	5.8	3.3	8.4	6.0	8.6	4.4	4.4	–2.5
Central African Republic	1.4	–2.9	24.5	19.2	3.7	1.6	–1.9	–1.5	3.0
Chad	2.4	31.4	41.3	9.1	11.8	5.9	4.4	–8.0	3.1
Comoros	1.1	2.0	25.3	7.1	2.0	3.0	3.5	3.5	3.5
Congo, Dem. Rep. of	200.5	1,893.1	23,760.5	541.8	616.8	198.5	29.1	284.9	555.7
Congo, Rep. of	–1.2	5.0	42.9	8.6	10.2	13.2	1.8	3.1	3.0
Côte d'Ivoire	3.8	2.1	26.0	14.3	2.7	4.2	4.5	0.7	2.5
Djibouti	5.3	4.4	6.5	4.9	3.5	2.5	2.2	2.0	2.4
Equatorial Guinea	13.0	1.6	38.9	11.4	6.0	3.0	3.0	3.0	3.0
Eritrea	...	4.6	11.6	10.7	9.3	1.3	9.5	9.0	20.3
Ethiopia	7.3	10.0	1.2	13.4	–2.3	–1.6	3.8	1.9	4.2
Gabon	2.2	0.6	36.1	10.0	4.5	4.1	2.3	–0.7	1.0
Gambia, The	17.7	5.9	4.0	4.0	4.8	3.1	1.1	2.5	2.5
Ghana	33.2	24.9	24.9	59.5	46.6	27.9	19.3	12.4	25.0
Guinea	28.2	7.2	4.2	5.6	3.0	1.9	5.1	4.6	6.8
Guinea-Bissau	61.9	48.2	15.2	45.4	50.7	49.1	8.0	–2.1	9.1
Kenya	13.6	45.9	28.8	1.5	9.0	11.2	6.6	3.5	6.2
Lesotho	14.3	13.8	7.2	9.9	9.1	8.5	7.8	8.7	6.0
Liberia	...	...	...	...	...	...	...	...	...
Madagascar	14.0	9.3	39.0	49.0	19.8	4.5	6.2	9.9	11.9
Malawi	17.1	22.8	34.7	83.1	37.7	9.1	29.8	44.8	29.6
Mali	0.8	–0.6	24.8	12.4	6.5	–0.7	4.1	–1.2	1.2
Mauritania	8.2	9.3	4.1	6.5	4.7	4.5	8.0	4.1	3.3
Mauritius	6.9	8.9	9.4	6.0	5.9	7.9	5.4	7.9	5.3
Morocco	6.4	5.2	5.1	6.1	3.0	1.0	2.7	0.7	2.0
Mozambique, Rep. of	48.1	42.3	63.1	54.4	44.6	6.4	0.6	3.1	12.3
Namibia	12.8	8.5	10.8	10.0	8.0	8.8	6.2	8.6	4.5
Niger	–0.8	–0.6	24.8	11.2	5.3	2.9	4.5	2.9	2.9
Nigeria	22.3	57.2	57.0	72.8	29.3	8.5	10.0	6.6	6.9
Rwanda	5.3	12.5	64.0	22.0	8.9	11.7	6.8	–2.4	4.0
Sâo Tomé and Príncipe	24.6	25.5	51.2	36.8	42.0	69.0	42.1	16.3	10.7
Senegal	3.4	–0.6	32.0	8.1	2.8	1.7	2.4	0.8	0.7
Seychelles	2.6	1.3	1.8	–0.3	–1.1	0.6	2.7	6.3	6.7
Sierra Leone	81.2	22.2	24.2	26.0	23.1	14.9	35.5	34.1	5.0
Somalia	...	...	...	...	...	...	...	...	...
South Africa	14.5	9.7	9.0	8.6	7.4	8.6	6.9	5.2	5.4
Sudan	60.2	101.3	115.5	68.4	132.8	46.7	17.1	16.0	8.0
Swaziland	13.0	12.0	13.8	12.3	6.4	7.1	8.1	6.1	6.5
Tanzania	29.9	23.6	37.1	26.5	21.0	16.1	12.6	6.3	6.2
Togo	1.7	2.4	48.5	6.4	2.5	5.5	–1.4	4.5	–2.5
Tunisia	7.4	4.0	4.5	6.3	3.8	3.7	3.1	2.7	3.0
Uganda	92.3	30.0	6.5	6.1	7.5	7.8	5.8	–0.2	6.3
Zambia	67.5	183.3	54.6	34.9	43.1	24.4	24.5	26.8	22.3
Zimbabwe	17.8	27.6	22.2	22.6	21.4	18.8	32.3	57.8	55.9

Table 12 *(continued)*

	Average 1983–92	1993	1994	1995	1996	1997	1998	1999	2000
Developing Asia	**9.9**	**10.8**	**16.0**	**13.2**	**8.3**	**4.8**	**7.7**	**2.5**	**1.9**
Afghanistan, Islamic State of	...	...	...	...	...	...	...	...	...
Bangladesh	8.8	3.5	3.1	10.0	8.8	4.8	8.0	6.3	4.7
Bhutan	9.9	11.2	7.0	9.5	8.8	6.5	10.6	6.8	4.8
Brunei Darussalam	...	4.3	2.4	6.0	2.0	1.7	−0.4	−0.1	1.5
Cambodia	...	114.3	9.4	1.3	7.2	8.0	14.8	4.0	1.0
China	7.6	14.7	24.1	17.1	8.3	2.8	−0.8	−1.4	0.4
Fiji	6.7	6.5	4.9	5.2	0.6	—	2.2	2.2	2.4
India	9.3	6.4	10.2	10.2	9.0	7.2	13.2	4.7	4.0
Indonesia	8.1	9.7	8.5	9.4	7.9	6.2	58.0	20.7	3.8
Kiribati	2.7	6.1	5.3	4.1	−1.5	2.2	4.7	2.0	3.0
Lao P.D. Republic	34.7	6.3	6.8	19.4	13.0	19.3	87.4	134.0	27.1
Malaysia	2.6	3.5	3.7	3.4	3.5	2.7	5.3	2.8	1.5
Maldives	6.7	20.1	3.4	5.5	6.2	7.6	−1.4	3.0	2.0
Myanmar	16.8	33.6	22.4	21.7	20.0	33.9	49.1	11.4	10.3
Nepal	8.6	5.9	9.1	8.7	9.2	8.1	8.4	11.4	3.4
Pakistan	7.3	10.0	12.4	12.3	10.4	11.4	6.2	4.1	4.4
Papua New Guinea	5.6	5.0	2.9	17.3	11.6	3.9	13.6	14.9	16.2
Philippines	13.5	6.9	8.4	8.0	9.0	5.9	9.7	6.6	4.3
Samoa	3.4	1.7	12.1	−2.9	5.4	6.9	2.2	3.0	3.0
Solomon Islands	11.2	9.2	13.3	9.6	11.8	8.1	12.4	8.3	6.0
Sri Lanka	11.7	11.7	8.4	7.7	15.9	9.6	9.4	4.7	6.2
Thailand	3.7	3.4	5.1	5.8	5.9	5.6	8.1	0.3	1.5
Tonga	10.0	3.1	2.4	0.5	2.6	2.0	3.1	3.9	5.3
Vanuatu	6.3	3.6	2.3	2.2	0.9	2.9	3.2	2.0	2.0
Vietnam	124.6	8.4	9.5	16.9	5.6	3.1	7.9	4.1	−1.7
Middle East, Malta, and Turkey	**22.9**	**29.4**	**37.3**	**39.1**	**29.6**	**27.7**	**27.6**	**23.2**	**20.7**
Bahrain	−0.2	2.6	0.4	3.1	−0.1	1.5	−0.3	−1.6	−0.4
Egypt	18.6	11.0	9.0	9.4	7.1	6.2	4.2	3.8	2.8
Iran, Islamic Republic of	18.6	22.9	35.2	49.4	23.2	17.3	20.0	20.4	18.5
Iraq	...	...	...	...	...	...	...	...	...
Jordan	5.0	3.3	3.6	2.3	6.5	3.0	3.1	0.6	0.7
Kuwait	8.1	0.4	2.5	2.7	3.6	0.7	0.1	1.8	1.5
Lebanon	89.9	24.7	8.0	10.6	8.9	7.7	4.5	−2.7	−0.4
Libya	7.7	7.5	10.7	8.3	4.0	3.6	3.7	2.6	−3.0
Malta	1.0	4.0	4.1	4.0	2.4	3.1	2.4	2.5	2.5
Oman	1.4	1.1	−0.7	−1.1	0.3	−0.2	−0.5	0.5	−1.0
Qatar	3.0	−0.9	1.4	3.0	7.1	2.7	2.9	2.2	2.4
Saudi Arabia	−0.4	0.8	0.6	5.0	0.9	−0.4	−0.2	−1.2	−0.6
Syrian Arab Republic	20.6	23.6	3.9	7.7	8.9	1.9	−0.4	−2.1	1.5
Turkey	52.4	66.1	106.3	93.7	82.3	85.7	84.6	64.9	54.9
United Arab Emirates	3.9	4.4	5.0	4.4	2.6	2.1	2.0	2.0	2.0
Yemen, Republic of	...	62.4	71.3	62.5	40.0	4.6	11.5	9.2	8.0

Table 12 *(concluded)*

	Average 1983–92	1993	1994	1995	1996	1997	1998	1999	2000
Western Hemisphere	**173.8**	**152.1**	**200.3**	**36.0**	**21.2**	**12.9**	**9.8**	**8.8**	**8.1**
Antigua and Barbuda	3.6	3.1	6.5	2.7	3.0	0.3	3.3	1.6	2.0
Argentina	413.1	10.6	4.2	3.4	0.2	0.5	0.9	−1.2	−0.7
Bahamas, The	5.1	2.7	1.3	2.1	1.4	0.5	1.3	1.5	1.4
Barbados	4.5	1.2	−0.1	1.9	2.4	7.7	−1.3	1.6	2.6
Belize	2.9	1.4	2.5	2.9	6.3	1.1	−0.9	−1.0	2.0
Bolivia	198.9	8.5	7.9	10.2	12.4	4.7	7.7	2.2	4.6
Brazil	475.8	1,927.4	2,075.8	66.0	15.8	6.9	3.2	4.9	7.0
Chile	21.1	12.7	11.4	8.2	7.4	6.1	5.1	3.3	3.8
Colombia	24.2	22.5	22.8	20.9	20.8	18.5	18.7	10.9	9.2
Costa Rica	19.3	9.8	13.5	23.2	17.6	13.3	11.7	10.1	11.5
Dominica	4.0	1.6	—	1.3	1.7	2.4	0.9	1.6	1.9
Dominican Republic	27.1	5.3	8.3	12.5	5.4	8.3	4.8	6.5	7.7
Ecuador	43.7	45.0	27.3	22.9	24.4	30.6	36.1	52.2	96.2
El Salvador	19.0	18.5	10.6	10.1	9.8	4.5	2.5	0.6	2.5
Grenada	3.2	2.8	2.6	2.2	2.8	1.3	1.4	0.5	0.8
Guatemala	15.5	13.4	12.5	8.4	11.0	9.2	6.6	5.3	7.0
Guyana	38.4	12.0	12.4	12.2	7.1	3.6	4.6	7.5	6.6
Haiti	10.1	18.8	37.4	30.2	21.9	16.2	10.0	10.0	10.0
Honduras	10.2	10.7	18.2	29.5	23.8	20.2	13.7	11.6	10.5
Jamaica	27.6	24.3	33.2	21.7	21.5	9.1	8.1	6.3	7.7
Mexico	59.3	9.8	7.0	35.0	34.4	20.6	15.9	16.6	9.5
Netherlands Antilles	2.5	1.9	1.9	2.7	3.5	3.5	3.5	3.5	3.5
Nicaragua	910.3	20.4	7.7	11.2	11.6	9.2	13.0	11.2	9.7
Panama	1.0	0.5	1.3	0.9	1.3	1.3	0.6	1.3	1.4
Paraguay	23.7	18.3	20.6	13.4	9.8	7.0	11.6	6.8	9.2
Peru	383.7	48.6	23.7	11.1	11.5	8.5	7.3	3.5	3.8
St. Kitts and Nevis	2.5	1.8	1.4	3.0	2.0	8.7	3.7	3.5	—
St. Lucia	3.1	0.8	2.7	5.9	0.9	—	2.8	1.0	1.5
St. Vincent and the Grenadines	3.4	4.3	1.0	1.7	4.4	0.4	2.1	1.0	0.8
Suriname	17.9	143.4	368.5	235.5	−0.8	7.2	20.8	28.7	16.8
Trinidad and Tobago	9.6	13.2	3.7	5.3	−2.7	3.6	5.7	3.4	3.4
Uruguay	73.2	54.2	44.7	42.2	28.3	19.8	10.8	5.7	4.8
Venezuela	27.4	38.1	60.8	59.9	99.9	50.0	35.8	23.6	16.2

[1]For many countries, figures for recent years are IMF staff estimates. Data for some countries are for fiscal years.

Table 13. Countries in Transition: Consumer Prices[1]

(Annual percent change)

	Average 1983–92	1993	1994	1995	1996	1997	1998	1999	2000
Central and eastern Europe	...	**79.9**	**45.6**	**24.7**	**23.3**	**41.8**	**17.1**	**10.9**	**12.8**
Albania	16.0	85.0	22.6	7.8	12.7	32.1	20.9	0.4	−0.2
Bosnia and Herzegovina	...	...	...	0.2	−13.7	9.5	0.6	3.4	4.6
Bulgaria	28.4	72.8	96.0	62.1	123.0	1,061.2	18.8	2.6	10.4
Croatia	...	1,516.6	97.5	2.0	3.5	3.6	5.7	4.2	6.2
Czech Republic	...	20.8	10.0	9.1	8.8	8.5	10.7	2.1	3.9
Estonia	...	89.8	47.7	29.0	23.1	11.2	8.1	3.3	4.0
Hungary	15.1	22.4	18.8	28.3	23.5	18.3	14.3	10.0	9.8
Latvia	...	109.2	35.9	25.0	17.6	8.4	4.7	2.4	2.7
Lithuania	...	410.4	72.1	39.5	24.7	8.8	5.1	0.8	1.0
Macedonia, former Yugoslav Rep. of	...	338.7	127.5	15.7	2.3	2.6	−0.1	−0.7	6.1
Poland	71.8	35.3	32.2	27.9	19.9	14.9	11.8	7.3	10.1
Romania	35.1	256.1	136.7	32.3	38.8	154.8	59.1	45.8	45.7
Slovak Republic	...	23.0	13.4	9.9	5.8	6.1	6.7	10.7	12.0
Slovenia	...	31.9	21.5	13.5	9.9	8.4	7.9	6.2	8.9
Commonwealth of Independent States and Mongolia	...	**1242.3**	**508.0**	**235.2**	**55.6**	**19.1**	**24.9**	**70.4**	**25.0**
Russia	...	874.7	307.4	197.4	47.6	14.7	27.7	85.7	20.8
Excluding Russia	...	2,440.9	1,334.5	338.8	75.5	29.6	19.3	41.8	34.6
Armenia	...	3,731.8	5,273.4	176.7	18.7	14.0	8.7	0.7	−0.8
Azerbaijan	...	1,129.7	1,664.0	411.8	19.8	3.7	−0.8	−8.5	1.8
Belarus	...	1,190.2	2,434.1	709.3	52.7	63.8	73.0	293.7	169.0
Georgia	...	3,125.4	15,606.5	162.7	39.3	7.0	3.6	19.1	4.0
Kazakhstan	...	1,662.3	1,879.9	176.3	39.1	17.4	7.3	8.4	13.4
Kyrgyz Republic	...	772.4	190.1	40.7	31.3	22.6	12.0	36.8	18.7
Moldova	...	788.5	329.6	30.2	23.5	11.8	7.7	39.3	31.3
Mongolia	13.7	268.4	87.6	56.8	46.8	36.6	9.4	7.6	11.6
Tajikistan	...	2,194.9	350.4	610.0	418.2	88.0	43.2	27.6	34.0
Turkmenistan	...	3,102.4	1,748.3	1,005.2	992.4	83.7	16.8	23.5	8.0
Ukraine	...	4,734.9	891.2	376.4	80.2	15.9	10.6	22.7	28.2
Uzbekistan	...	534.2	1,568.3	304.6	54.0	70.9	29.0	29.1	25.4
Memorandum									
EU accession candidates	...	64.9	59.1	42.8	39.4	55.4	35.6	25.3	24.4

[1]For many countries, inflation for the earlier years is measured on the basis of a retail price index. Consumer price indices with a broader and more up-to-date coverage are typically used for more recent years.

Table 14. Summary Financial Indicators
(Percent)

	1993	1994	1995	1996	1997	1998	1999	2000	2001	2002
Advanced economies										
Central government fiscal balance[1]										
Advanced economies	−4.3	−3.7	−3.3	−2.7	−1.6	−1.6	−1.4	−0.3	−0.8	−0.9
United States	−4.2	−3.0	−2.6	−1.8	−0.6	0.6	1.3	2.3	2.2	1.5
European Union	−5.9	−5.3	−4.6	−4.1	−2.4	−1.7	−1.0	0.5	−0.8	−0.8
Euro area	−5.3	−4.8	−4.3	−4.1	−2.7	−2.3	−1.7	−0.4	−1.3	−1.2
Japan	−2.6	−3.4	−3.9	−4.2	−3.9	−8.9	−11.8	−12.1	−11.5	−10.5
Other advanced economies	−2.0	−1.5	−1.0	−0.2	0.6	−0.2	−0.1	1.5	0.8	0.9
General government fiscal balance[1]										
Advanced economies	−4.7	−4.0	−3.8	−3.1	−1.7	−1.2	−0.8	0.3	−0.1	−0.3
United States	−5.1	−3.8	−3.3	−2.4	−1.3	—	0.7	1.7	1.6	0.8
European Union	−6.3	−5.6	−5.3	−4.3	−2.4	−1.6	−0.6	1.3	−0.3	−0.3
Euro area	−5.9	−5.3	−5.3	−4.4	−2.6	−2.2	−1.2	0.3	−0.8	−0.6
Japan	−1.6	−2.2	−3.5	−4.2	−3.2	−4.5	−7.0	−8.2	−6.8	−5.9
Other advanced economies	−2.5	−1.9	−1.1	−0.2	0.6	−0.5	0.2	2.2	1.5	1.5
General government structural balance[2]										
Advanced economies	−3.8	−3.3	−3.2	−2.4	−1.2	−0.7	−0.5	−0.3	−0.1	−0.2
Growth of broad money										
Advanced economies	3.8	2.6	4.4	4.9	5.0	6.8	. . .	. . .	. . .	. . .
United States	1.3	0.6	3.9	4.5	5.6	8.5	6.3	6.2	. . .	. . .
Euro area	6.3	2.3	5.7	4.0	4.6	4.6	7.3	6.0	. . .	. . .
Japan	1.4	2.9	3.2	2.9	3.8	4.4	2.6	2.2	. . .	. . .
Other advanced economies	8.0	9.5	8.8	8.7	6.4	10.3	. . .	. . .	. . .	. . .
Short-term interest rates[3]										
United States	3.5	3.1	4.4	5.7	5.1	4.9	4.8	6.0	4.1	3.8
Japan	2.4	1.9	0.8	0.3	0.3	0.2	—	0.2	0.1	0.3
Euro area	8.7	6.5	6.3	4.7	4.2	4.0	3.1	4.5	4.4	4.1
LIBOR	3.4	5.1	6.1	5.6	5.9	5.6	5.5	6.7	4.5	4.3
Developing countries										
Central government fiscal balance[1]										
Weighted average	−3.3	−2.8	−2.6	−2.2	−2.4	−3.9	−4.2	−3.2	−3.2	−3.0
Median	−4.2	−3.8	−3.4	−2.5	−2.4	−3.0	−3.0	−3.0	−2.5	−2.3
General government fiscal balance[1]										
Weighted average	−3.6	−3.8	−3.2	−2.7	−3.1	−4.6	−5.0	−3.7	−3.8	−3.5
Median	−4.0	−3.7	−3.2	−2.7	−2.3	−3.2	−2.9	−2.7	−2.1	−1.7
Growth of broad money										
Weighted average	115.6	95.1	23.2	22.3	22.3	17.6	15.0	13.0	12.2	11.0
Median	16.1	20.0	16.3	14.4	16.4	10.2	12.0	9.9	10.0	9.3
Countries in transition										
Central government fiscal balance[1]	−6.2	−7.4	−4.7	−4.6	−4.7	−3.7	−2.5	−0.5	−1.5	−1.3
General government fiscal balance[1]	−6.8	−7.5	−4.7	−5.9	−5.3	−5.0	−2.2	0.2	−1.5	−2.2
Growth of broad money	428.6	195.2	75.5	32.3	33.1	20.4	38.9	35.1	20.0	18.8

[1]Percent of GDP.
[2]Percent of potential GDP.
[3]For the United States, three-month treasury bills; for Japan, three-month certificates of deposit; for LIBOR, London interbank offered rate on six-month U.S. dollar deposits.

Table 15. Advanced Economies: General and Central Government Fiscal Balances and Balances Excluding Social Security Transactions[1]

(Percent of GDP)

	1993	1994	1995	1996	1997	1998	1999	2000	2001	2002
General government fiscal balance										
Advanced economies	**−4.7**	**−4.0**	**−3.8**	**−3.1**	**−1.7**	**−1.2**	**−0.8**	**0.3**	**−0.1**	**−0.3**
Major advanced economies	−5.0	−4.2	−4.1	−3.4	−1.9	−1.3	−1.0	0.1	−0.4	−0.7
United States	−5.1	−3.8	−3.3	−2.4	−1.3	—	0.7	1.7	1.6	0.8
Japan	−1.6	−2.2	−3.5	−4.2	−3.2	−4.5	−7.0	−8.2	−6.8	−5.9
Germany[2]	−3.1	−2.4	−3.3	−3.4	−2.7	−2.1	−1.4	1.5	−2.0	−1.5
France[2,3]	−6.0	−5.5	−5.5	−4.1	−3.0	−2.7	−1.6	−1.3	−0.6	−0.8
Italy[2]	−9.4	−9.1	−7.6	−7.1	−2.7	−2.8	−1.8	−0.3	−1.3	−1.2
United Kingdom[2,4]	−7.8	−6.9	−5.4	−4.1	−1.5	0.3	1.5	5.9	1.3	0.3
Canada	−8.7	−6.7	−5.4	−2.8	0.2	0.2	2.2	3.4	2.7	2.5
Other advanced economies	−3.5	−3.0	−2.7	−1.5	−0.7	−0.9	−0.2	1.4	1.0	1.1
Spain	−6.7	−6.1	−7.0	−4.9	−3.2	−2.6	−1.1	−0.3	—	0.2
Netherlands	−3.1	−3.6	−4.2	−1.8	−1.1	−0.7	1.0	2.2	0.7	1.0
Belgium	−7.3	−5.0	−4.3	−3.8	−1.9	−0.9	−0.7	—	0.3	0.3
Sweden	−11.9	−10.8	−7.9	−3.4	−2.0	1.8	1.9	3.4	3.2	3.0
Austria	−4.2	−4.8	−5.1	−3.8	−1.7	−2.3	−2.1	−1.1	−0.7	—
Denmark	−2.8	−2.4	−2.3	−1.0	0.5	1.1	3.1	2.9	2.8	2.5
Finland	−7.3	−5.7	−3.7	−3.2	−1.5	1.3	1.8	6.7	5.5	5.5
Greece	−13.8	−10.0	−10.2	−7.4	−4.0	−2.5	−1.8	−0.9	0.5	1.2
Portugal	−6.1	−6.0	−4.6	−4.0	−2.6	−1.9	−2.1	−1.4	−1.5	−1.4
Ireland	−2.3	−1.7	−2.2	−0.2	0.7	2.1	3.9	4.5	3.7	3.6
Luxembourg	5.2	4.2	2.2	2.7	3.6	3.3	2.3	4.1	4.2	4.6
Switzerland	−3.8	−2.8	−1.9	−2.0	−2.4	−0.4	−0.4	1.8	0.3	0.2
Norway	−1.4	0.4	3.5	6.6	7.9	3.6	4.8	14.1	12.2	10.2
Israel	−2.7	−3.3	−4.4	−5.6	−4.0	−3.6	−4.7	−2.8	−4.0	−2.4
Iceland	−4.5	−4.7	−3.0	−1.6	—	0.4	2.2	2.8	2.7	2.9
Cyprus	−2.4	−1.4	−1.0	−3.4	−5.3	−5.5	−4.0	−2.7	−2.6	−2.3
Korea[5]	1.3	1.0	1.3	1.0	−0.9	−3.8	−2.7	2.5	1.1	0.9
Australia[6]	−4.4	−3.5	−2.1	−0.9	—	0.2	0.9	1.1	0.5	0.7
Taiwan Province of China	0.6	0.2	0.4	0.2	0.1	1.4	0.1	−0.5	−0.4	−0.4
Hong Kong SAR	5.1	1.3	−0.3	2.2	6.1	−2.6	−0.9	−0.9	−0.2	−0.3
Singapore	14.4	13.9	12.2	9.3	9.2	3.6	4.5	7.0	6.4	7.7
New Zealand[7]	−0.7	2.2	3.6	2.7	1.6	0.9	0.4	0.3	0.8	1.4
Memorandum										
European Union	−6.3	−5.6	−5.3	−4.3	−2.4	−1.6	−0.6	1.3	−0.3	−0.3
Euro area	−5.9	−5.3	−5.3	−4.4	−2.6	−2.2	−1.2	0.3	−0.8	−0.6
Newly industrialized Asian economies	2.5	1.7	1.6	1.5	1.0	−1.5	−1.1	1.5	0.9	0.9
Fiscal balance excluding social security transactions										
United States	−5.3	−4.2	−3.7	−2.7	−1.7	−0.7	−0.3	0.1	0.1	−0.4
Japan	−4.7	−5.0	−6.3	−6.7	−5.8	−6.5	−8.8	−9.5	−7.7	−6.6
Germany	−3.3	−2.5	−2.9	−3.1	−2.8	−2.2	−1.7	1.3	−2.1	−1.5
France	−5.1	−5.0	−4.8	−3.6	−2.6	−2.6	−1.8	−1.5	−1.0	−1.4
Italy	−5.4	−4.5	−5.6	−5.3	−0.7	1.3	2.6	3.6	3.1	3.2
Canada	−5.9	−3.9	−2.7	—	3.0	2.8	4.5	5.3	4.2	3.7

Table 15 *(concluded)*

	1993	1994	1995	1996	1997	1998	1999	2000	2001	2002
Central government fiscal balance										
Advanced economies	**−4.3**	**−3.7**	**−3.3**	**−2.7**	**−1.6**	**−1.6**	**−1.4**	**−0.3**	**−0.8**	**−0.9**
Major advanced economies	−4.5	−3.8	−3.4	−3.0	−1.7	−1.8	−1.7	−0.6	−1.1	−1.3
United States[8]	−4.2	−3.0	−2.6	−1.8	−0.6	0.6	1.3	2.3	2.2	1.5
Japan[9]	−2.6	−3.4	−3.9	−4.2	−3.9	−8.9	−11.8	−12.1	−11.5	−10.5
Germany[10]	−2.1	−1.5	−1.4	−2.2	−1.7	−1.5	−1.3	1.3	−1.3	−1.0
France[10]	−4.6	−4.6	−4.2	−4.6	−3.6	−3.0	−3.2	−2.3	−1.4	−1.7
Italy	−9.9	−9.1	−7.1	−6.8	−2.9	−2.8	−1.4	−1.0	−2.4	−2.3
United Kingdom	−8.2	−6.9	−5.5	−4.2	−1.5	0.3	1.4	4.1	0.7	0.3
Canada	−5.5	−4.6	−3.9	−2.0	0.5	0.5	0.6	1.4	0.9	0.6
Other advanced economies	−3.8	−3.2	−2.8	−1.7	−1.0	−1.1	−0.6	0.8	0.4	0.6
Memorandum										
European Union	−5.9	−5.3	−4.6	−4.1	−2.4	−1.7	−1.0	0.5	−0.8	−0.8
Euro area	−5.3	−4.8	−4.3	−4.1	−2.7	−2.3	−1.7	−0.4	−1.3	−1.2
Newly industrialized Asian economies	1.2	1.0	1.0	1.0	0.8	−1.4	−1.4	0.7	0.2	0.2

[1]On a national income accounts basis except as indicated in footnotes. See Box A1 for a summary of the policy assumptions underlying the projections.

[2]Includes one-off receipts from the sale of mobile telephone licenses equivalent to 2.5 percent of GDP in 2000 for Germany, 0.6 percent of GDP in 2001 for France, 1.2 percent of GDP in 2000 for Italy, and 2.4 percent of GDP in 2000 for the United Kingdom.

[3]Adjusted for valuation changes of the foreign exchange stabilization fund.

[4]Excludes asset sales.

[5]Data include social security transactions (that is, the operations of the public pension plan).

[6]Data exclude net advances (primarily privatization receipts and net policy-related lending).

[7]Data from 1992 onward are on an accrual basis and are not strictly comparable with previous cash-based data.

[8]Data are on a budget basis.

[9]Data are on a national income basis and exclude social security transactions.

[10]Data are on an administrative basis and exclude social security transactions.

Table 16. Advanced Economies: General Government Structural Balances[1]

(Percent of potential GDP)

	1993	1994	1995	1996	1997	1998	1999	2000	2001	2002
Structural balance[2]										
Advanced economies	**-3.8**	**-3.3**	**-3.2**	**-2.4**	**-1.2**	**-0.7**	**-0.5**	**-0.3**	**-0.1**	**-0.2**
Major advanced economies	-3.8	-3.3	-3.2	-2.6	-1.2	-0.7	-0.6	-0.4	-0.2	-0.3
United States	-3.8	-2.8	-2.2	-1.5	-0.7	0.2	0.6	1.0	1.5	1.0
Japan	-1.5	-1.9	-3.1	-4.2	-3.3	-3.4	-5.7	-7.2	-5.6	-4.8
Germany[3,4]	-3.0	-2.4	-3.3	-2.7	-1.6	-1.1	-0.4	-0.5	-1.3	-1.0
France[4]	-3.9	-3.9	-4.0	-2.3	-1.4	-1.7	-0.8	-0.9	-0.9	-0.6
Italy[4]	-8.2	-7.9	-7.0	-6.2	-1.7	-1.8	-0.6	-0.7	-0.5	-0.6
United Kingdom[4]	-6.6	-5.5	-4.4	-3.4	-1.0	0.5	1.5	3.4	1.3	0.4
Canada	-4.4	-3.9	-2.9	0.1	2.2	1.9	3.0	3.3	2.9	2.9
Other advanced economies	-3.9	-3.6	-3.2	-1.7	-0.7	-0.4	0.1	0.4	0.3	0.6
Spain	-5.0	-5.2	-5.1	-3.1	-1.8	-1.9	-1.0	-0.8	-0.1	0.2
Netherlands	-1.9	-2.7	-3.0	-0.9	-0.8	-1.0	—	0.1	-0.8	-0.4
Belgium	-5.2	-3.1	-2.7	-1.6	-0.5	0.4	0.4	-0.1	—	0.1
Sweden	-5.9	-6.7	-5.2	0.2	1.7	5.1	4.1	3.8	3.0	3.0
Austria	-3.7	-4.6	-4.9	-3.6	-1.2	-1.7	-1.6	-1.5	-0.5	0.2
Denmark	-1.1	-1.2	-1.7	-0.7	0.5	0.6	2.3	1.7	1.7	1.5
Finland	-0.9	-0.7	0.3	0.4	0.2	2.1	2.4	6.7	5.6	5.6
Greece	-5.9	-3.9	-3.5	-2.4	-1.2	-0.7	-0.5	-0.3	—	0.2
Portugal	-5.4	-5.0	-3.5	-3.1	-2.1	-1.9	-2.0	-1.4	-1.2	-0.9
Ireland	-0.1	0.4	-1.5	0.3	0.3	1.5	3.0	3.0	2.5	2.8
Norway[5]	-7.9	-6.7	-4.5	-3.4	-2.6	-3.6	-3.5	-3.3	-2.9	-3.0
Australia[6]	-2.7	-2.2	-1.5	-0.7	0.2	0.3	0.8	0.9	0.4	0.8
New Zealand[7]	-0.3	-0.1	1.2	0.8	0.7	0.7	0.3	0.7	1.2	1.9
Memorandum										
European Union[8]	-4.8	-4.4	-4.3	-3.1	-1.3	-0.8	-0.1	0.3	-0.2	-0.1
Euro area[8]	-4.5	-4.2	-4.3	-3.2	-1.4	-1.3	-0.5	-0.5	-0.6	-0.4

[1]On a national income accounts basis.

[2]The structural budget position is defined as the actual budget deficit (or surplus) less the effects of cyclical deviations of output from potential output. Because of the margin of uncertainty that attaches to estimates of cyclical gaps and to tax and expenditure elasticities with respect to national income, indicators of structural budget positions should be interpreted as broad orders of magnitude. Moreover, it is important to note that changes in structural budget balances are not necessarily attributable to policy changes but may reflect the built-in momentum of existing expenditure programs. In the period beyond that for which specific consolidation programs exist, it is assumed that the structural deficit remains unchanged.

[3]The estimate of the fiscal impulse for 1995 is affected by the assumption by the federal government of the debt of the Treuhandanstalt and various other agencies, which were formerly held outside the general government sector. At the public sector level, there would be an estimated withdrawal of fiscal impulse amounting to just over 1 percent of GDP.

[4]Excludes mobile telephone license receipts.

[5]Excludes oil.

[6]Excludes commonwealth government privatization receipts.

[7]Excludes privatization proceeds.

[8]Excludes Luxembourg.

Table 17. Advanced Economies: Monetary Aggregates

(Annual percent change)[1]

	1993	1994	1995	1996	1997	1998	1999	2000
Narrow money[2]								
Advanced economies	**8.1**	**4.4**	**5.3**	**4.4**	**4.1**	**5.3**	...	...
Major advanced economies	7.6	4.0	4.7	3.6	3.7	5.0	...	...
United States	10.6	2.5	−1.6	−4.5	−1.3	2.1	1.8	−1.6
Japan	3.4	4.9	12.8	10.0	8.9	6.1	11.8	4.1
Euro area	6.0	4.4	6.4	7.5	7.1	9.5	10.3	5.7
Germany	8.5	5.2	6.8	12.4	2.3	11.1	...	...
France	1.4	2.8	7.7	0.8	6.5	3.1	...	...
Italy	7.6	3.4	1.4	3.9	7.7	9.0	...	...
United Kingdom	6.0	6.8	5.6	6.7	6.4	5.4	11.6	4.6
Canada	14.4	8.7	7.6	17.8	10.6	8.7	8.5	14.2
Other advanced economies	10.8	6.6	8.3	8.3	6.2	6.4	...	...
Memorandum								
Newly industrialized Asian economies	18.0	9.3	10.5	5.8	−3.8	0.9	19.7	3.2
Broad money[3]								
Advanced economies	**3.8**	**2.6**	**4.4**	**4.9**	**5.0**	**6.8**	...	...
Major advanced economies	2.6	1.7	3.7	4.2	4.6	6.5	...	...
United States	1.3	0.6	3.9	4.5	5.6	8.5	6.3	6.2
Japan	1.4	2.9	3.2	2.9	3.8	4.4	2.6	2.2
Euro area	6.3	2.3	5.7	4.0	4.6	4.6	7.3	6.0
Germany	10.9	1.6	3.6	8.7	3.6	7.3	...	...
France	−2.9	1.8	4.6	−3.3	2.0	2.7	...	...
Italy	3.8	1.0	−1.9	3.8	9.0	5.6	...	...
United Kingdom	4.9	4.2	9.9	9.6	5.7	8.4	4.0	8.0
Canada	2.7	2.8	4.1	2.1	−1.3	1.4	5.1	5.5
Other advanced economies	9.3	6.6	7.6	8.8	7.0	8.4	...	...
Memorandum								
Newly industrialized Asian economies	15.6	16.6	13.0	11.4	11.3	19.8	16.9	13.5

[1]Based on end-of-period data except for Japan which is based on monthly averages.

[2]M1 except for the United Kingdom, where M0 is used here as a measure of narrow money; it comprises notes in circulation plus bankers' operational deposits. M1 is generally currency in circulation plus private demand deposits. In addition, the United States includes traveler's checks of nonbank issues and other checkable deposits and excludes private sector float and demand deposits of banks. Japan includes government demand deposits and excludes float. Germany includes demand deposits at fixed interest rates. Canada excludes private sector float.

[3]M2, defined as M1 plus quasi-money, except for Japan, Germany, and the United Kingdom, for which the data are based on M2 plus certificates of deposit (CDs), M3, and M4, respectively. Quasi-money is essentially private term deposits and other notice deposits. The United States also includes money market mutual fund balances, money market deposit accounts, overnight repurchase agreements, and overnight Eurodollars issued to U.S. residents by foreign branches of U.S. banks. For Japan, M2 plus CDs is currency in circulation plus total private and public sector deposits and installments of Sogo Banks plus CDs. For Germany M3 is M1 plus private time deposits with maturities of less than four years plus savings deposits at statutory notice. For Italy, M2 comprises M1 plus term deposits, passbooks from the Postal Office, and CDs with maturities of less than 18 months. For the United Kingdom, M4 is composed of non-interest-bearing M1, private sector interest-bearing sterling sight bank deposits, private sector sterling time banks deposits, private sector holdings of sterling bank CDs, private sector holdings of building society shares and deposits, and sterling CDs less building society holdings of banks deposits and bank CDs and notes and coins.

Table 18. Advanced Economies: Interest Rates

(Percent a year)

	1993	1994	1995	1996	1997	1998	1999	2000	March 2001
Policy-related interest rate[1]									
Major advanced economies	**4.7**	**4.5**	**5.4**	**4.4**	**4.2**	**4.3**	...	...	...
United States	3.0	4.2	5.9	5.3	5.5	5.4	5.0	6.3	5.7
Japan	3.0	2.1	1.2	0.4	0.4	0.4	0.1	0.1	0.2
Euro area	...	...	...	...	...	3.3	2.7	4.0	4.8
Germany	7.4	5.3	4.4	3.2	3.1	3.3	...	...	...
France	8.6	5.6	6.3	3.7	3.3	3.4	...	...	...
Italy	10.5	8.8	10.7	8.6	6.6	4.8	...	...	...
United Kingdom	5.9	5.5	6.7	6.0	6.6	7.2	5.3	6.0	6.0
Canada	4.6	5.1	6.9	4.3	3.3	4.9	4.7	5.5	5.5
Short-term interest rate[2]									
Advanced economies	**5.5**	**4.5**	**4.7**	**4.3**	**4.0**	**4.0**	**3.5**	**4.5**	...
Major advanced economies	4.8	3.9	4.1	3.9	3.7	3.7	3.3	4.4	...
United States	3.5	3.1	4.4	5.7	5.1	4.9	4.8	6.0	4.9
Japan	2.4	1.9	0.8	0.3	0.3	0.2	0.0	0.2	0.1
Euro area	8.7	6.5	6.3	4.7	4.2	4.0	3.1	4.5	4.7
Germany	7.2	5.3	4.5	3.3	3.3	3.5	...	...	...
France	7.2	5.3	4.5	3.3	3.3	3.7	...	...	...
Italy	10.5	8.8	10.7	8.6	6.6	4.8	...	...	...
United Kingdom	5.9	5.5	6.7	6.0	6.8	7.3	5.4	6.1	5.6
Canada	4.9	5.4	7.0	4.3	3.2	4.7	4.7	5.5	4.7
Other advanced economies	8.7	7.4	7.3	6.1	5.7	5.7	4.2	5.1	...
Memorandum									
Newly industrialized Asian economies	8.5	9.0	9.2	8.7	9.4	9.8	5.5	5.7	5.1
Long-term interest rate[3]									
Advanced economies	**6.7**	**7.3**	**6.9**	**6.2**	**5.5**	**4.6**	**4.7**	**5.1**	...
Major advanced economies	6.3	6.9	6.5	5.9	5.3	4.3	4.6	5.0	...
United States	5.9	7.1	6.6	6.4	6.4	5.3	5.6	6.0	4.9
Japan	4.0	4.2	3.3	3.0	2.1	1.3	1.7	1.7	1.2
Euro area	8.3	8.4	8.7	7.2	5.9	4.8	4.6	5.4	...
Germany	6.4	7.1	6.9	6.2	5.6	4.6	...	...	...
France	6.9	7.4	7.6	6.4	5.6	4.8	...	...	...
Italy	11.3	10.6	12.2	9.4	6.9	4.9	...	...	...
United Kingdom	8.7	10.0	9.6	9.3	8.3	6.6	6.7	6.5	4.8
Canada	7.2	8.4	8.1	7.2	6.1	5.3	5.6	5.9	5.3
Other advanced economies	8.5	9.1	8.9	7.7	6.8	5.9	5.5	5.8	...
Memorandum									
Newly industrialized Asian economies	9.2	9.4	9.4	8.5	9.3	9.4	7.3	7.7	8.0

[1]For the United States, federal funds rate; for Japan, overnight call rate; for Germany, repurchase rate; for France, day-to-day money rate; for Italy, three-month treasury bill gross rate; for the United Kingdom, base lending rate; for Canada, overnight money market financing rate; for the euro area, repurchase rate.

[2]For the United States, three-month certificates of deposit (CDs) in secondary markets; for Japan three-month CDs; for Germany, France and the United Kingdom, three-month interbank deposits; for Italy, three-month treasury bills gross rate; and for Canada, three-month prime corporate paper.

[3]For the United States, yield on ten-year treasury bonds; for Japan, over-the-counter sales yield on ten-year government bonds with longest residual maturity; for Germany, yield on government bonds with maturities of nine to ten years; for France, long-term (seven- to ten-year) government bond yield (Emprunts d'Etat à long terme TME); for Italy, secondary market yield on fixed-coupon (BTP) government bonds with two to four years' residual maturity; for the United Kingdom, yield on medium-dated (ten-year) government stock; and for Canada, average yield on government bonds with residual maturities of over ten years.

Table 19. Advanced Economies: Exchange Rates

	1993	1994	1995	1996	1997	1998	1999	2000	Exchange Rate Assumption[1] 2001
				National currency units per U.S. dollar					
U.S. dollar nominal exchange rates									
Japanese yen	111.2	102.2	94.1	108.8	121.0	130.9	113.9	107.8	119.4
Euro[2]	...	...	...	...	...	...	1.07	0.92	0.92
Deutsche mark	1.65	1.62	1.43	1.50	1.73	1.76	1.84	2.12	2.12
French franc	5.66	5.55	4.99	5.12	5.84	5.90	6.16	7.12	7.10
Italian lira	1,574	1,612	1,629	1,543	1,703	1,736	1,817	2,102	2,095
Pound sterling[2]	1.50	1.53	1.58	1.56	1.64	1.66	1.62	1.51	1.46
Canadian dollar	1.29	1.37	1.37	1.36	1.38	1.48	1.49	1.49	1.55
Spanish peseta	127.3	134.0	124.7	126.7	146.4	149.4	156.2	180.6	180.0
Netherlands guilder	1.86	1.82	1.61	1.69	1.95	1.98	2.07	2.39	2.38
Belgian franc	34.6	33.5	29.5	31.0	35.8	36.3	37.9	43.8	43.6
Swedish krona	7.78	7.72	7.13	6.71	7.63	7.95	8.26	9.16	9.83
Austrian schilling	11.6	11.4	10.1	10.6	12.2	12.4	12.9	14.9	14.9
Danish krone	6.48	6.36	5.60	5.80	6.60	6.70	6.98	8.08	8.08
Finnish markka	5.71	5.22	4.37	4.59	5.19	5.34	5.58	6.45	6.43
Greek drachma	229.2	242.6	231.7	240.7	273.1	295.5	305.6	360.9	368.7
Portuguese escudo	160.8	166.0	151.1	154.2	175.3	180.1	188.2	217.6	216.9
Irish pound	0.68	0.67	0.62	0.63	0.66	0.70	0.74	0.85	0.85
Swiss franc	1.48	1.37	1.18	1.24	1.45	1.45	1.50	1.69	1.67
Norwegian krone	7.09	7.06	6.34	6.45	7.07	7.55	7.80	8.80	8.90
Israeli new sheqel	2.83	3.01	3.01	3.19	3.45	3.80	4.14	4.08	4.14
Icelandic krona	67.60	69.94	64.69	66.50	70.90	70.96	72.34	78.62	86.48
Cyprus pound	0.50	0.49	0.45	0.47	0.51	0.52	0.54	0.62	0.63
Korean won	802.7	803.4	770.8	804.5	951.2	1,401.8	1,188.8	1,131.0	1,273.5
Australian dollar	1.47	1.37	1.35	1.28	1.35	1.59	1.55	1.72	1.96
New Taiwan dollar	26.39	26.46	26.49	27.46	28.70	33.46	32.27	31.24	32.39
Hong Kong dollar	7.74	7.73	7.74	7.73	7.74	7.75	7.76	7.79	7.80
Singapore dollar	1.62	1.53	1.42	1.41	1.48	1.67	1.69	1.72	1.76
					Index, 1980–89 = 100				*Percent change from previous assumption[3]*
Real effective exchange rates[4]									
United States	74.7	73.9	69.2	73.3	79.8	85.2	85.9	91.8	1.2
Japan	145.4	154.7	161.2	136.6	126.9	115.7	129.3	137.6	−0.2
Euro[5]	109.4	107.1	112.1	112.1	99.7	95.7	89.8	79.8	−0.2
Germany	124.2	128.2	137.5	135.8	126.7	123.2	119.0	112.3	−0.1
France	92.5	91.5	92.4	89.5	85.2	84.0	81.5	78.0	−0.1
United Kingdom	90.6	91.2	86.7	88.8	108.0	119.0	123.5	133.4	−0.2
Italy	90.5	84.9	78.6	87.9	90.4	90.9	89.9	86.5	−0.1
Canada	102.2	94.3	93.8	93.6	94.7	90.1	87.4	88.4	−1.0
Spain	113.0	106.1	105.7	109.0	106.8	109.5	110.0	110.0	−0.1
Netherlands	93.3	93.1	94.0	90.6	85.4	83.0	81.6	78.9	−0.1
Belgium	99.6	99.3	102.9	100.1	95.8	94.8	93.8	90.9	−0.1
Sweden	81.4	79.1	77.7	86.1	81.5	79.1	75.6	74.5	−0.9
Austria	90.4	88.5	85.5	81.5	77.2	75.7	73.9	71.9	—
Denmark	112.8	111.4	114.3	111.6	109.2	109.6	111.9	109.0	0.1
Finland	65.9	69.4	77.4	72.6	69.1	69.0	67.1	63.8	0.1
Greece	101.9	104.2	111.1	115.1	119.1	115.0	116.2	113.1	—
Portugal	135.9	132.1	136.1	134.9	131.9	132.3	132.6	130.9	—
Ireland	70.5	67.2	64.6	64.1	62.1	57.7	55.9	53.1	−0.1
Switzerland	114.1	124.1	131.6	131.2	125.6	131.2	129.4	127.6	−0.3
Norway	99.1	100.2	107.3	111.4	116.1	115.1	119.0	120.6	0.2
Australia	89.0	93.7	93.2	109.2	113.0	101.7	102.9	97.2	−2.4
New Zealand	99.4	105.5	111.9	124.6	128.2	111.2	108.0	96.2	−0.7

[1]Average exchange rates for the period February 19–March 16, 2001. See "Assumptions" in the Introduction to the Statistical Appendix.

[2]Expressed in U.S. dollars per currency unit.

[3]In nominal effective terms. Average February 19–March 16, 2001 rates compared with December 26, 2000–January 19, 2001 rates.

[4]Defined as the ratio, in common currency, of the normalized unit labor costs in the manufacturing sector to the weighted average of those of its industrial country trading partners, using 1989–91 trade weights.

[5]An effective euro is used prior to January 1, 1999. See Box 5.5 in the *World Economic Outlook*, October 1998.

Table 20. Developing Countries: Central Government Fiscal Balances

(Percent of GDP)

	1993	1994	1995	1996	1997	1998	1999	2000	2001	2002
Developing countries	**−3.3**	**−2.8**	**−2.6**	**−2.2**	**−2.4**	**−3.9**	**−4.2**	**−3.2**	**−3.2**	**−3.0**
Regional groups										
Africa	−7.5	−5.4	−3.9	−2.9	−2.9	−4.1	−3.5	−2.0	−2.0	−1.6
Sub-Sahara	−8.0	−5.9	−4.1	−3.6	−3.6	−4.1	−4.2	−3.5	−2.6	−2.0
Excluding Nigeria and South Africa	−7.7	−6.4	−5.0	−4.4	−3.9	−4.1	−4.5	−5.0	−3.5	−3.0
Developing Asia	−3.1	−2.6	−2.5	−2.0	−2.5	−3.5	−4.2	−4.2	−4.1	−4.1
China	−1.9	−1.6	−2.1	−1.6	−1.8	−3.1	−4.1	−3.9	−3.5	−4.0
India	−6.1	−5.6	−4.6	−4.2	−4.7	−5.3	−5.5	−5.3	−5.6	−5.4
Other developing Asia	−2.6	−2.1	−1.4	−1.0	−1.9	−3.0	−3.2	−3.9	−4.1	−3.0
Middle East, Malta, and Turkey	−7.5	−5.8	−3.8	−3.5	−3.6	−6.3	−3.9	0.7	−1.8	−0.4
Western Hemisphere	−0.3	−0.9	−2.0	−1.8	−1.7	−3.4	−4.3	−2.8	−2.2	−1.8
Analytical groups										
By source of export earnings										
Fuel	−7.5	−6.8	−3.4	−0.3	−0.9	−6.5	−1.5	6.2	4.6	4.4
Nonfuel	−2.8	−2.3	−2.5	−2.4	−2.6	−3.6	−4.4	−4.1	−4.0	−3.7
of which, primary products	−5.1	−3.4	−1.9	−1.3	−1.6	−2.0	−3.2	−3.6	−3.0	−2.4
By external financing source										
Net debtor countries	−3.1	−2.6	−2.6	−2.3	−2.5	−3.8	−4.2	−3.4	−3.5	−3.2
of which, official financing	−7.0	−5.3	−3.5	−2.4	−2.7	−3.9	−3.5	−2.3	−2.5	−2.8
Net debtor countries by debt-servicing experience										
Countries with arrears and/or rescheduling during 1994–98	−3.2	−2.2	−1.8	−1.2	−1.8	−4.1	−3.6	−1.0	−1.2	−0.8
Other groups										
Heavily indebted poor countries	−7.8	−6.1	−3.7	−3.2	−3.4	−3.0	−3.3	−3.8	−3.1	−2.8
Middle East and north Africa	−7.4	−5.8	−3.6	−1.4	−1.8	−5.3	−1.3	4.0	2.3	2.2
Memorandum										
Median										
Developing countries	−4.2	−3.8	−3.4	−2.5	−2.4	−3.0	−3.0	−3.0	−2.5	−2.3
Regional groups										
Africa	−6.0	−5.2	−3.9	−4.5	−2.8	−3.4	−3.3	−3.7	−3.7	−3.0
Developing Asia	−4.2	−3.4	−3.4	−2.4	−2.2	−2.5	−2.6	−3.9	−4.4	−3.4
Middle East, Malta, and Turkey	−7.5	−6.5	−4.3	−3.3	−2.7	−6.4	−2.3	4.8	1.7	−0.2
Western Hemisphere	−1.3	−1.0	−1.8	−1.7	−1.9	−2.3	−2.8	−2.6	−2.1	−1.6

Table 21. Developing Countries: Broad Money Aggregates

(Annual percent change)

	1993	1994	1995	1996	1997	1998	1999	2000	2001	2002
Developing countries	**115.6**	**95.1**	**23.2**	**22.3**	**22.3**	**17.6**	**15.0**	**13.0**	**12.2**	**11.0**
Regional groups										
Africa	30.9	40.9	22.5	22.1	18.4	16.2	20.9	16.2	12.2	10.3
Sub-Sahara	35.7	49.8	27.0	25.8	19.7	17.5	23.2	18.5	11.6	10.5
Developing Asia	27.2	25.1	23.3	20.9	18.3	18.2	13.9	12.0	13.4	12.9
China	43.0	34.9	29.5	25.3	19.6	14.8	14.7	12.3	14.0	13.5
India	16.5	20.1	14.6	16.2	17.1	19.6	16.6	15.4	15.1	14.7
Other developing Asia	21.0	19.1	22.2	19.2	17.7	21.1	11.3	9.4	11.1	10.8
Middle East, Malta, and Turkey	26.6	41.3	33.1	34.2	25.1	30.4	29.8	20.0	15.6	11.2
Western Hemisphere	400.0	245.9	20.1	19.8	26.1	12.8	9.9	10.8	9.7	9.0
Analytical groups										
By source of export earnings										
Fuel	22.1	26.1	18.2	21.3	16.2	15.3	20.1	17.3	15.2	10.6
Nonfuel	137.3	108.0	23.9	22.4	23.1	17.8	14.3	12.4	11.8	11.1
of which, primary products	48.9	51.0	31.4	30.6	23.1	13.1	19.7	16.4	14.1	12.4
By external financing source										
Net debtor countries	126.2	102.6	24.4	23.4	23.3	18.4	15.5	13.5	12.4	11.5
of which, official financing	31.1	41.7	20.4	18.9	16.5	16.9	22.6	20.3	15.9	12.2
Net debtor countries by debt-servicing experience										
Countries with arrears and/or rescheduling during 1994–98	493.8	324.9	23.5	17.1	23.3	19.4	15.4	15.9	14.1	11.8
Other groups										
Heavily indebted poor countries	55.0	70.8	37.4	39.5	25.2	20.7	34.3	28.0	17.5	14.1
Middle East and north Africa	17.7	14.8	13.7	12.7	10.2	12.8	14.1	12.4	13.3	9.4
Memorandum										
Median										
Developing countries	16.1	20.0	16.3	14.4	16.4	10.2	12.0	9.9	10.0	9.3
Regional groups										
Africa	13.6	31.7	16.2	14.4	16.8	8.6	13.5	11.0	9.9	9.3
Developing Asia	20.4	19.4	16.7	15.0	17.0	12.4	14.9	11.1	11.8	10.6
Middle East, Malta, and Turkey	9.3	11.4	9.2	8.3	9.7	8.5	9.9	8.8	8.6	7.4
Western Hemisphere	19.6	18.3	19.5	17.0	16.4	10.3	11.3	8.2	9.6	8.9

Table 22. Summary of World Trade Volumes and Prices

(Annual percent change)

	Ten-Year Averages		1993	1994	1995	1996	1997	1998	1999	2000	2001	2002
	1983–92	1993–2002										
Trade in goods and services												
World trade[1]												
Volume	5.4	7.3	3.7	9.0	9.1	6.5	10.1	4.2	5.3	12.4	6.7	6.5
Price deflator												
In U.S. dollars	2.3	−0.7	−4.0	2.7	9.2	−1.0	−5.1	−5.4	−1.4	−0.8	−0.6	0.5
In SDRs	−0.2	0.2	−3.2	0.1	3.1	3.5	0.2	−4.0	−2.2	2.9	1.4	0.4
Volume of trade												
Exports												
Advanced economies	5.8	7.0	3.1	8.8	8.9	6.0	10.6	3.8	5.0	11.4	6.2	6.2
Developing countries	5.7	8.9	9.4	11.8	7.4	9.2	12.0	5.3	4.1	15.7	7.1	7.0
Imports												
Advanced economies	6.6	7.4	1.4	9.6	9.2	6.2	9.3	5.7	7.9	11.4	6.7	6.5
Developing countries	3.2	8.1	11.2	7.4	10.2	8.1	10.6	−0.6	1.6	16.9	8.8	7.9
Terms of trade												
Advanced economies	1.1	—	0.7	—	0.2	−0.3	−0.6	1.4	0.1	−2.2	0.2	0.8
Developing countries	−2.7	0.4	−1.3	0.7	3.6	1.4	−0.3	−7.0	3.8	6.2	−1.4	−1.6
Trade in goods												
World trade[1]												
Volume	5.6	7.7	3.8	10.0	10.0	6.2	10.4	4.6	5.6	13.4	6.7	6.5
Price deflator												
In U.S. dollars	2.1	−0.7	−4.5	2.8	9.4	−0.9	−5.5	−6.1	−1.5	−0.3	−0.3	0.5
In SDRs	−0.3	0.1	−3.6	0.2	3.2	3.5	−0.3	−4.7	−2.3	3.4	1.8	0.4
World trade prices in U.S. dollars[2]												
Manufactures	4.5	−1.1	−4.8	3.4	10.0	−2.7	−7.3	−1.7	−2.0	−6.2	0.2	1.1
Oil	−5.2	1.7	−11.8	−5.0	7.9	18.4	−5.4	−32.1	37.5	56.9	−9.6	−11.8
Nonfuel primary commodities	0.8	0.1	1.8	13.4	8.4	−1.2	−3.2	−14.7	−7.1	1.8	0.5	4.5
World trade prices in SDRs[2]												
Manufactures	2.0	−0.3	−3.9	0.9	3.8	1.7	−2.2	−0.3	−2.8	−2.8	2.2	0.9
Oil	−7.5	2.6	−11.1	−7.3	1.8	23.7	−0.2	−31.2	36.5	62.6	−7.7	−11.9
Nonfuel primary commodities	−1.6	1.0	2.7	10.6	2.3	3.3	2.2	−13.5	−7.8	5.5	2.6	4.4
World trade prices in euros[2]												
Manufactures	1.5	2.4	5.8	2.4	−0.1	−0.1	5.7	−0.1	2.3	6.6	1.3	—
Oil	−7.9	5.3	−2.0	−6.0	−2.0	21.6	7.9	−31.0	43.6	78.4	−8.6	−12.7
Nonfuel primary commodities	−2.1	3.7	13.1	12.2	−1.6	1.5	10.5	−13.3	−2.9	15.7	1.6	3.4

Table 22 *(concluded)*

	Ten-Year Averages		1993	1994	1995	1996	1997	1998	1999	2000	2001	2002
	1983–92	1993–2002										
Trade in goods												
Volume of trade												
Exports												
Advanced economies	6.1	7.3	2.7	9.5	9.8	5.7	10.9	4.3	4.9	12.7	6.4	6.1
Developing countries	6.0	9.1	8.8	12.3	8.6	9.2	12.0	4.7	5.3	17.0	6.5	6.9
Fuel exporters	4.7	3.7	4.7	2.1	0.7	7.8	2.7	1.8	0.2	9.4	5.0	2.7
Nonfuel exporters	6.9	10.6	10.4	15.8	10.9	9.5	14.8	5.6	6.4	19.0	6.9	8.0
Imports												
Advanced economies	6.8	7.8	2.0	11.0	10.1	5.6	9.8	5.9	8.5	12.2	6.6	6.5
Developing countries	3.4	8.5	11.8	8.7	10.4	8.2	9.7	–0.1	1.9	17.6	9.4	8.4
Fuel exporters	–2.0	3.6	–2.6	–13.2	6.3	0.7	11.8	4.8	2.3	15.9	9.3	3.5
Nonfuel exporters	5.7	9.6	15.8	13.7	11.2	9.4	9.4	–0.8	1.9	17.9	9.5	9.1
Price deflators in SDRs												
Exports												
Advanced economies	0.4	–0.4	–3.5	0.3	3.1	1.8	–2.2	–3.4	–3.1	0.1	1.9	0.9
Developing countries	–3.4	1.6	–3.3	0.4	5.2	7.7	1.9	–10.4	4.5	12.4	0.2	–1.1
Fuel exporters	–8.2	3.4	–9.3	–2.4	7.8	18.5	2.8	–25.6	27.7	48.7	–6.9	–8.5
Nonfuel exporters	–0.5	1.1	–1.0	1.4	4.4	4.7	1.6	–6.2	–0.3	3.1	2.4	0.8
Imports												
Advanced economies	–0.7	–0.5	–5.4	–0.1	2.7	2.8	–1.6	–5.0	–3.3	3.6	1.8	0.2
Developing countries	–0.1	1.3	–0.6	–0.7	1.7	5.9	2.6	–3.5	–0.4	5.6	1.8	0.6
Fuel exporters	–0.8	1.4	–1.7	1.3	0.9	5.9	3.2	1.2	–2.7	2.1	3.5	0.9
Nonfuel exporters	0.1	1.2	–0.3	–1.1	1.8	6.0	2.5	–4.3	—	6.2	1.5	0.6
Terms of trade												
Advanced economies	1.1	0.1	2.0	0.5	0.4	–1.0	–0.6	1.7	0.1	–3.4	0.1	0.8
Developing countries	–3.3	0.3	–2.7	1.1	3.4	1.6	–0.7	–7.1	5.0	6.4	–1.5	–1.7
Fuel exporters	–7.5	2.0	–7.7	–3.6	6.8	11.9	–0.4	–26.5	31.2	45.6	–10.0	–9.3
Nonfuel exporters	–0.6	–0.2	–0.7	2.5	2.5	–1.2	–0.9	–2.0	–0.3	–2.9	0.9	0.3
Memorandum												
World exports in billions of U.S. dollars												
Goods and services	3,311	6,783	4,707	5,266	6,263	6,581	6,839	6,720	6,940	7,707	8,125	8,683
Goods	2,645	5,445	3,707	4,188	5,036	5,274	5,475	5,356	5,544	6,239	6,594	7,039

[1]Average of annual percent change for world exports and imports. The estimates of world trade comprise, in addition to trade of advanced economies and developing countries (which is summarized in the table), trade of countries in transition.

[2]As represented, respectively, by the export unit value index for the manufactures of the advanced economies; the average of U.K. Brent, Dubai, and West Texas Intermediate crude oil spot prices; and the average of world market prices for nonfuel primary commodities weighted by their 1987–89 shares in world commodity exports.

Table 23. Nonfuel Commodity Prices[1]

(Annual percent change; U.S. dollar terms)

| | Ten-Year Averages | | 1993 | 1994 | 1995 | 1996 | 1997 | 1998 | 1999 | 2000 | 2001 | 2002 |
	1983–92	1993–2002										
Nonfuel primary commodities	**0.8**	**0.1**	**1.8**	**13.4**	**8.4**	**−1.2**	**−3.2**	**−14.7**	**−7.1**	**1.8**	**0.5**	**4.5**
Food	−0.1	−0.6	−1.3	5.2	8.1	12.2	−10.6	−12.6	−15.6	−0.5	9.2	4.6
Beverages	−6.0	1.3	6.3	74.9	0.9	−17.4	32.6	−15.2	−21.3	−16.6	−11.5	12.8
Agricultural raw materials	3.3	0.4	16.2	9.5	4.3	−2.7	−6.8	−16.4	2.2	1.8	−5.4	4.7
Metals	1.8	0.5	−14.2	16.6	19.5	−11.9	3.7	−16.2	−1.5	12.1	2.0	2.3
Fertilizers	−0.7	1.0	−15.4	8.0	10.6	13.7	1.1	2.8	−4.0	−5.0	−0.9	2.4
Advanced economies	**0.8**	**—**	**−2.5**	**13.3**	**11.1**	**−2.3**	**−3.9**	**−15.7**	**−6.8**	**4.1**	**2.2**	**3.9**
Developing countries	**0.4**	**—**	**−0.4**	**15.8**	**9.5**	**−2.6**	**−1.4**	**−16.2**	**−9.2**	**1.8**	**1.7**	**4.7**
Regional groups												
Africa	0.3	0.1	3.5	16.6	8.0	−5.2	−1.1	−14.6	−8.4	0.6	−0.1	5.0
Sub-Sahara	0.3	0.1	3.8	16.9	8.0	−5.8	−0.8	−14.7	−8.2	0.6	−0.3	5.0
Developing Asia	0.6	—	2.0	13.5	8.2	−1.3	−3.5	−14.3	−8.0	0.2	1.0	4.8
Other developing Asia	0.4	−0.2	3.1	13.9	7.4	−1.4	−4.0	−13.7	−9.3	−1.4	1.2	5.1
Middle East, Malta, and Turkey	0.6	0.1	−4.0	15.2	12.4	−3.4	−2.6	−15.4	−7.8	4.2	2.5	4.1
Western Hemisphere	0.1	—	−3.4	17.8	10.9	−2.8	0.4	−18.3	−10.6	3.2	2.7	4.6
Analytical groups												
By source of export earnings												
Fuel	1.5	0.2	−1.1	10.6	11.6	−7.2	—	−16.9	−3.5	7.3	1.3	3.5
Nonfuel	0.3	—	−0.5	16.0	9.5	−2.4	−1.5	−16.1	−9.3	1.6	1.7	4.7
of which, primary products	0.8	−0.5	−5.3	18.8	14.0	−8.7	−1.0	−16.2	−11.4	3.1	2.7	4.5
By external financing source												
Net debtor countries	0.3	—	−0.4	15.8	9.5	−2.5	−1.5	−16.1	−9.2	1.7	1.7	4.7
of which, official financing	−0.2	—	4.9	21.1	9.2	−8.1	−0.3	−13.9	−12.0	−2.5	0.2	5.9
Net debtor countries by debt-servicing experience												
Countries with arrears and/or rescheduling during 1994–98	−0.2	—	−0.7	18.6	9.2	−4.2	0.5	−15.9	−10.7	1.2	1.4	4.8
Other groups												
Heavily indebted poor countries	−1.2	−0.1	1.9	24.9	7.8	−6.9	2.0	−12.0	−14.6	−4.5	−0.1	6.3
Middle East and north Africa	0.4	0.1	−2.4	15.3	11.4	−2.7	−2.8	−15.0	−8.6	3.2	2.2	4.3
Memorandum												
Average oil spot price[2]	−14.3	21.3	−11.8	−5.0	7.9	18.4	−5.4	−32.1	37.5	56.9	−9.6	−11.8
In U.S. dollars a barrel	21.2	19.7	16.79	15.95	17.20	20.37	19.27	13.07	17.98	28.21	25.50	22.50
Export unit value of manufactures[3]	4.5	−1.1	−4.8	3.4	10.0	−2.7	−7.3	−1.7	−2.0	−6.2	0.2	1.1

[1]Averages of world market prices for individual commodities weighted by 1987–89 exports as a share of world commodity exports and total commodity exports for the indicated country group, respectively.

[2]Average of U.K. Brent, Dubai, and West Texas Intermediate crude oil spot prices.

[3]For the manufactures exported by the advanced economies.

Table 24. Advanced Economies: Export Volumes, Import Volumes, and Terms of Trade in Goods and Services

(Annual percent change)

| | Ten-Year Averages | | | | | | | | | | | |
	1983–92	1993–2002	1993	1994	1995	1996	1997	1998	1999	2000	2001	2002
Export volume												
Advanced economies	**5.8**	**7.0**	**3.1**	**8.8**	**8.9**	**6.0**	**10.6**	**3.8**	**5.0**	**11.4**	**6.2**	**6.2**
Major advanced economies	5.6	6.5	1.9	8.2	8.4	5.8	10.7	3.7	3.7	10.9	6.3	5.9
United States	7.5	6.9	3.3	8.9	10.3	8.2	12.3	2.3	2.9	9.2	5.8	6.7
Japan	5.0	4.7	1.3	4.6	5.4	6.3	11.6	−2.5	1.9	12.2	3.2	3.8
Germany	5.2	6.2	−5.5	7.6	5.7	5.1	11.3	7.0	5.1	13.2	8.3	5.6
France	5.1	6.8	—	7.7	7.7	3.5	11.8	7.7	4.0	13.6	6.9	6.0
Italy	4.7	6.4	9.0	9.8	12.6	0.6	6.4	3.6	—	10.2	6.2	6.2
United Kingdom	3.9	6.7	3.9	9.2	9.5	7.5	8.6	2.6	4.0	8.4	6.7	6.5
Canada	6.4	9.1	11.0	13.2	9.0	6.0	8.8	8.8	10.0	9.6	7.8	6.5
Other advanced economies	6.2	7.7	5.3	9.8	9.9	6.3	10.4	4.0	7.2	12.3	6.0	6.5
Memorandum												
European Union	4.9	6.9	1.3	8.9	8.9	4.8	10.2	6.0	4.9	11.3	7.0	6.0
Euro area	5.2	6.9	0.7	8.7	8.8	4.5	10.6	6.6	4.9	11.9	7.1	6.0
Newly industrialized Asian economies	9.4	9.0	10.0	11.3	12.8	7.6	10.7	0.7	8.4	16.4	5.8	7.6
Import volume												
Advanced economies	**6.6**	**7.4**	**1.4**	**9.6**	**9.2**	**6.2**	**9.3**	**5.7**	**7.9**	**11.4**	**6.7**	**6.5**
Major advanced economies	6.3	7.4	0.6	9.0	8.2	6.4	9.4	7.6	8.1	11.5	7.2	6.3
United States	7.4	10.2	9.1	12.0	8.2	8.6	13.7	11.9	10.7	13.7	7.2	7.1
Japan	5.8	4.8	−0.3	8.9	14.2	11.9	0.5	−7.6	5.3	7.7	4.0	4.8
Germany	5.5	5.9	−5.4	7.3	5.6	3.1	8.4	8.6	8.1	10.2	8.4	5.4
France	4.5	6.5	−3.7	8.2	8.0	1.6	6.9	11.3	4.0	14.7	8.8	6.0
Italy	6.7	4.8	−10.9	8.1	9.7	−0.3	10.1	9.0	5.1	8.3	5.4	5.9
United Kingdom	5.5	7.3	3.2	5.4	5.5	9.1	9.2	8.8	8.1	9.6	7.8	6.8
Canada	8.3	8.6	7.4	8.3	6.2	5.8	15.1	6.1	9.4	12.0	8.6	7.0
Other advanced economies	7.1	7.3	2.9	10.7	11.0	6.0	9.1	2.4	7.4	11.2	5.9	6.9
Memorandum												
European Union	5.6	6.5	−3.3	7.9	7.9	4.0	9.2	9.4	6.9	10.5	7.3	6.0
Euro area	5.8	6.4	−4.4	8.1	8.4	3.2	9.1	9.5	6.9	10.7	7.3	5.9
Newly industrialized Asian economies	12.8	8.1	10.7	13.1	14.5	7.7	8.1	−9.0	8.4	15.2	5.9	8.5
Terms of trade												
Advanced economies	**1.1**	**—**	**0.7**	**—**	**0.2**	**−0.3**	**−0.6**	**1.4**	**0.1**	**−2.2**	**0.2**	**0.8**
Major advanced economies	0.9	0.1	0.5	—	−0.1	−0.5	−0.6	2.0	0.3	−2.6	0.9	1.3
United States	0.1	0.9	0.9	—	−0.4	0.5	1.9	3.3	−0.7	−1.1	2.0	2.9
Japan	2.8	−0.9	1.8	1.3	—	−6.4	−4.5	2.6	1.0	−5.9	−0.1	1.3
Germany	−0.6	−0.1	2.5	0.1	0.8	−0.7	−1.8	1.8	0.9	−5.1	0.4	0.4
France	0.6	−0.3	−1.7	0.2	0.1	−1.2	—	1.1	−0.6	−2.1	1.2	0.3
Italy	2.5	−0.9	−4.4	−0.9	−2.3	4.3	−1.5	2.0	−0.5	−6.1	0.4	0.2
United Kingdom	0.3	0.5	0.3	−2.0	−2.5	1.0	2.7	2.6	1.5	0.9	1.1	−0.5
Canada	—	0.3	−1.9	−0.8	2.8	2.1	−1.0	−3.4	3.1	6.0	−2.6	−1.1
Other advanced economies	1.4	−0.2	1.0	0.1	0.5	−0.1	−0.7	0.4	−0.2	−1.6	−1.0	−0.1
Memorandum												
European Union	0.7	−0.2	—	−0.5	−0.3	0.2	−0.4	1.6	0.1	−2.7	0.3	0.1
Euro area	0.7	−0.3	0.2	−0.2	−0.1	0.1	−0.9	1.6	−0.2	−3.4	0.1	0.2
Newly industrialized Asian economies	3.7	−0.6	2.3	—	0.1	−0.6	−1.1	—	−0.9	−4.5	−1.7	0.2
Memorandum												
Trade in goods												
Advanced economies												
Export volume	6.1	7.3	2.7	9.5	9.8	5.7	10.9	4.3	4.9	12.7	6.4	6.1
Import volume	6.8	7.8	2.0	11.0	10.1	5.6	9.8	5.9	8.5	12.2	6.6	6.5
Terms of trade	1.1	0.1	2.0	0.5	0.4	−1.0	−0.6	1.7	0.1	−3.4	0.1	0.8

Table 25. Developing Countries—by Region: Total Trade in Goods
(Annual percent change)

	Ten-Year Averages		1993	1994	1995	1996	1997	1998	1999	2000	2001	2002
	1983–92	1993–2002										
Developing countries												
Value in U.S. dollars												
Exports	3.6	9.4	4.5	15.2	20.3	12.0	7.9	−7.7	9.7	25.9	4.2	5.5
Imports	4.6	8.6	9.9	9.9	19.0	9.2	6.6	−4.8	1.1	19.5	8.9	9.1
Volume												
Exports	6.0	9.1	8.8	12.3	8.6	9.2	12.0	4.7	5.3	17.0	6.5	6.9
Imports	3.4	8.5	11.8	8.7	10.4	8.2	9.7	−0.1	1.9	17.6	9.4	8.4
Unit value in U.S. dollars												
Exports	−1.0	0.7	−4.1	2.9	11.4	3.0	−3.4	−11.7	5.4	8.4	−1.8	−1.0
Imports	2.4	0.4	−1.4	1.8	7.8	1.4	−2.7	−4.9	0.4	1.8	−0.3	0.8
Terms of trade	−3.3	0.3	−2.7	1.1	3.4	1.6	−0.7	−7.1	5.0	6.4	−1.5	−1.7
Memorandum												
Real GDP growth in developing country trading partners	4.1	3.5	3.2	4.3	3.6	3.8	4.1	1.7	3.3	4.9	2.5	3.4
Market prices of nonfuel commodities exported by developing countries	0.4	—	−0.4	15.8	9.5	−2.6	−1.4	−16.2	−9.2	1.8	1.7	4.7
Regional groups												
Africa												
Value in U.S. dollars												
Exports	1.9	4.7	−5.4	3.7	18.5	11.5	1.8	−13.6	7.0	25.7	1.4	1.4
Imports	1.4	4.4	−4.0	5.4	20.4	1.2	4.3	−0.8	0.2	7.1	7.9	4.4
Volume												
Exports	2.7	4.0	2.2	0.1	9.0	7.6	5.1	−0.3	3.0	6.4	3.1	4.3
Imports	1.6	5.4	0.9	4.1	12.2	4.2	8.0	4.6	1.2	7.0	7.7	4.2
Unit value in U.S. dollars												
Exports	0.2	1.1	−7.2	6.2	8.9	3.7	−3.1	−13.4	4.2	19.0	−1.4	−2.6
Imports	1.1	−0.3	−4.5	3.5	7.3	−2.1	−3.2	−4.9	−0.6	0.7	0.5	0.5
Terms of trade	−0.9	1.4	−2.8	2.6	1.5	6.0	0.2	−9.0	4.9	18.2	−1.9	−3.1
Sub-Sahara												
Value in U.S. dollars												
Exports	2.2	4.5	−4.8	4.9	18.5	11.0	1.5	−13.8	5.6	22.0	1.3	3.1
Imports	0.9	4.5	−3.4	3.2	21.8	3.7	6.9	−2.9	−0.9	7.3	7.5	3.7
Volume												
Exports	2.9	4.0	2.2	−0.5	10.1	9.1	4.6	−1.3	1.7	6.8	3.4	4.4
Imports	2.1	5.5	1.9	2.0	14.2	8.8	9.3	2.1	0.2	6.1	7.5	3.6
Unit value in U.S. dollars												
Exports	0.3	1.0	−6.6	8.9	7.8	1.8	−3.0	−12.8	4.3	15.6	−1.8	−1.1
Imports	0.1	−0.4	−4.9	3.8	6.7	−4.1	−1.8	−4.6	−0.7	1.9	0.4	0.5
Terms of trade	0.2	1.4	−1.8	5.0	1.0	6.1	−1.2	−8.5	5.0	13.4	−2.3	−1.5

Table 25 *(concluded)*

	Ten-Year Averages		1993	1994	1995	1996	1997	1998	1999	2000	2001	2002
	1983–92	1993–2002										
Developing Asia												
Value in U.S. dollars												
Exports	10.6	12.3	11.6	23.9	23.2	10.0	12.2	−2.2	8.5	21.3	7.6	9.1
Imports	9.5	11.1	19.1	17.8	23.7	10.4	1.2	−13.5	8.9	27.6	10.9	11.2
Volume												
Exports	8.9	12.3	12.2	20.7	11.6	8.9	18.0	6.0	6.7	24.5	7.7	8.1
Imports	7.2	10.9	19.9	16.2	13.0	9.5	5.8	−6.8	6.8	24.9	11.9	10.5
Unit value in U.S. dollars												
Exports	1.9	0.3	−0.5	2.7	10.5	1.5	−4.7	−7.6	3.7	−2.4	−0.1	0.9
Imports	2.5	0.6	−0.4	1.5	9.5	1.3	−4.3	−7.6	5.0	2.7	−0.8	0.6
Terms of trade	−0.6	−0.4	−0.1	1.2	0.9	0.2	−0.4	−0.1	−1.3	−5.0	0.8	0.3
Other developing Asia												
Value in U.S. dollars												
Exports	10.2	10.3	12.5	18.8	22.4	5.7	7.4	−3.9	10.1	18.7	6.2	7.6
Imports	9.1	8.3	13.7	20.3	26.9	5.7	−0.7	−22.9	6.0	23.1	10.0	10.4
Volume												
Exports	10.2	9.6	10.4	16.6	10.3	1.8	11.0	8.6	5.6	20.0	6.3	6.5
Imports	8.2	7.2	11.5	19.8	16.4	3.5	1.8	−14.4	0.4	18.8	10.9	8.5
Unit value in U.S. dollars												
Exports	0.3	1.1	1.9	2.0	11.0	4.1	−3.2	−11.4	8.1	−1.1	−0.1	1.0
Imports	1.3	1.6	1.9	0.5	9.1	2.5	−2.4	−10.3	11.1	4.1	−0.7	1.7
Terms of trade	−0.9	−0.5	—	1.5	1.7	1.5	−0.8	−1.2	−2.7	−5.0	0.6	−0.6
Middle East, Malta, and Turkey												
Value in U.S. dollars												
Exports	−1.5	6.3	−3.2	6.7	13.5	18.1	0.7	−20.8	22.4	44.1	−0.5	−4.6
Imports	0.7	4.7	3.0	−10.3	17.8	9.3	6.9	0.7	−3.5	14.2	5.7	5.8
Volume												
Exports	5.0	4.6	5.9	5.4	0.2	8.7	3.1	2.5	0.8	10.7	6.6	2.6
Imports	−0.5	5.3	6.3	−11.2	10.6	7.4	10.4	3.8	2.1	13.6	7.0	5.4
Unit value in U.S. dollars												
Exports	−5.6	2.0	−9.2	0.7	15.5	9.4	−2.7	−21.8	20.8	30.2	−5.9	−6.6
Imports	2.3	−0.2	−2.3	2.3	6.7	2.3	−3.1	−2.0	−5.3	0.5	−0.7	0.5
Terms of trade	−7.7	2.1	−7.1	−1.6	8.2	7.0	0.4	−20.2	27.6	29.5	−5.2	−7.1
Western Hemisphere												
Value in U.S. dollars												
Exports	4.0	9.6	7.9	15.4	22.1	10.7	9.8	−4.0	4.4	20.1	3.2	9.1
Imports	5.3	9.5	9.8	17.3	10.9	10.5	18.2	4.6	−6.4	14.7	7.9	9.2
Volume												
Exports	6.5	9.5	10.6	11.4	10.5	10.9	12.4	6.5	6.6	11.7	5.3	9.0
Imports	4.2	8.5	10.3	16.1	4.9	8.1	17.6	6.9	−4.7	12.5	7.3	7.8
Unit value in U.S. dollars												
Exports	0.2	0.3	−2.8	3.8	10.8	0.1	−1.9	−10.1	−1.5	8.2	−1.9	0.3
Imports	2.9	0.9	−0.5	1.2	5.6	2.7	1.0	−2.3	−2.0	1.8	0.6	1.3
Terms of trade	−2.6	−0.6	−2.3	2.6	4.9	−2.5	−2.8	−7.9	0.5	6.3	−2.6	−1.0

Table 26. Developing Countries—by Source of Export Earnings: Total Trade in Goods
(Annual percent change)

	Ten-Year Averages		1993	1994	1995	1996	1997	1998	1999	2000	2001	2002
	1983–92	1993–2002										
Fuel												
Value in U.S. dollars												
Exports	−2.1	5.9	−5.2	1.5	13.0	21.7	0.5	−26.0	28.9	55.7	−4.5	−5.9
Imports	−1.2	3.7	−5.7	−10.4	13.4	1.5	9.2	3.3	−0.4	14.2	10.2	4.0
Volume												
Exports	4.7	3.7	4.7	2.1	0.7	7.8	2.7	1.8	0.2	9.4	5.0	2.7
Imports	−2.0	3.6	−2.6	−13.2	6.3	0.7	11.8	4.8	2.3	15.9	9.3	3.5
Unit value in U.S. dollars												
Exports	−5.9	2.5	−10.1	0.1	14.2	13.4	−2.6	−26.7	28.7	43.4	−8.8	−8.4
Imports	1.7	0.6	−2.6	3.8	6.9	1.3	−2.2	−0.2	−1.9	−1.5	1.4	1.0
Terms of trade	−7.5	2.0	−7.7	−3.6	6.8	11.9	−0.4	−26.5	31.2	45.6	−10.0	−9.3
Nonfuel												
Value in U.S. dollars												
Exports	7.3	10.6	8.4	20.1	22.5	9.4	10.2	−2.5	5.7	18.2	7.2	8.9
Imports	7.1	9.7	14.3	14.6	20.0	10.5	6.2	−6.1	1.3	20.4	8.7	9.9
Volume												
Exports	6.9	10.6	10.4	15.8	10.9	9.5	14.8	5.6	6.4	19.0	6.9	8.0
Imports	5.7	9.6	15.8	13.7	11.2	9.4	9.4	−0.8	1.9	17.9	9.5	9.1
Unit value in U.S. dollars												
Exports	1.9	0.2	−1.8	3.9	10.6	0.2	−3.7	−7.5	0.5	−0.5	0.3	1.0
Imports	2.5	0.4	−1.1	1.4	7.9	1.4	−2.8	−5.6	0.8	2.4	−0.6	0.7
Terms of trade	−0.6	−0.2	−0.7	2.5	2.5	−1.2	−0.9	−2.0	−0.3	−2.9	0.9	0.3
Primary products												
Value in U.S. dollars												
Exports	4.9	8.2	2.1	18.0	25.3	4.4	6.1	−5.6	4.7	13.9	6.7	9.4
Imports	3.9	7.7	5.7	11.6	25.9	9.3	7.5	−1.9	−7.5	11.4	7.8	10.2
Volume												
Exports	2.9	7.8	9.1	7.8	8.9	11.0	9.5	5.3	7.8	7.6	5.1	6.2
Imports	2.6	7.2	7.9	9.5	18.8	7.7	10.8	4.5	−6.0	5.5	7.1	7.9
Unit value in U.S. dollars												
Exports	3.4	0.7	−7.4	12.3	15.4	−5.0	−2.3	−10.6	−2.2	5.3	1.5	3.0
Imports	2.8	0.6	−3.4	3.1	6.2	2.1	−2.6	−6.5	−0.8	6.0	0.9	1.7
Terms of trade	0.6	0.1	−4.1	8.9	8.7	−7.0	0.3	−4.4	−1.4	−0.7	0.6	1.2

Table 27. Summary of Payments Balances on Current Account
(Billions of U.S. dollars)

	1993	1994	1995	1996	1997	1998	1999	2000	2001	2002
Advanced economies	**69.2**	**34.2**	**59.0**	**42.3**	**95.1**	**34.8**	**−133.1**	**−246.1**	**−268.7**	**−264.6**
United States	−82.7	−118.6	−109.5	−123.3	−140.5	−217.1	−331.5	−435.4	−446.0	−445.8
European Union	11.1	20.1	57.3	91.4	122.1	73.7	22.4	−24.3	−23.3	−20.5
Euro area[1]	24.9	17.3	54.1	82.1	102.1	66.6	27.0	−9.8	−6.6	3.0
Japan	132.0	130.6	111.4	65.8	94.1	121.0	106.8	117.3	115.4	124.0
Other advanced economies	8.8	2.1	−0.2	8.4	19.4	57.1	69.2	96.3	85.1	77.6
Memorandum										
Newly industrialized Asian economies	20.8	16.1	5.9	−0.9	16.8	67.2	65.2	51.7	43.2	43.0
Developing countries	**−118.5**	**−87.0**	**−96.9**	**−74.5**	**−60.5**	**−92.2**	**−18.5**	**46.0**	**—**	**−40.0**
Regional groups										
Africa	−12.3	−12.3	−16.9	−6.3	−8.0	−20.5	−15.5	1.3	−3.7	−5.5
Developing Asia	−33.0	−18.9	−42.4	−38.9	8.8	47.0	46.7	35.9	22.5	11.6
Other developing Asia	−19.4	−24.9	−38.5	−40.1	−25.2	22.5	33.8	28.4	21.1	15.6
Middle East, Malta, and Turkey	−27.3	−3.7	−0.7	9.6	5.5	−28.6	6.0	56.7	47.6	22.6
Western Hemisphere	−45.9	−52.0	−36.9	−38.9	−66.8	−90.2	−55.7	−47.9	−66.4	−68.7
Analytical groups										
By source of export earnings										
Fuel	−22.0	−4.0	2.1	30.0	19.2	−35.2	10.1	93.8	63.6	39.4
Nonfuel	−96.4	−82.9	−99.0	−104.6	−79.7	−57.0	−28.6	−47.8	−63.6	−79.3
of which, primary products	−13.7	−12.3	−14.7	−17.2	−19.2	−19.3	−9.2	−10.0	−11.3	−13.1
By external financing source										
Net debtor countries	−104.9	−78.7	−98.4	−86.6	−70.6	−71.1	−25.3	−7.3	−44.6	−65.4
of which, official financing	−9.1	−10.5	−12.1	−8.5	−4.8	−10.4	−6.1	2.6	−0.8	−5.4
Net debtor countries by debt-servicing experience										
Countries with arrears and/or rescheduling during 1994–98	−29.1	−19.1	−45.8	−41.9	−50.3	−59.4	−24.9	5.1	−14.8	−24.5
Countries in transition	**−8.1**	**2.2**	**−1.5**	**−16.8**	**−23.7**	**−28.4**	**−1.7**	**26.7**	**13.5**	**3.6**
Central and eastern Europe	−8.4	−3.4	−2.8	−15.0	−16.9	−20.3	−23.2	−20.4	−21.8	−22.7
Commonwealth of Independent States and Mongolia	0.2	5.5	1.3	−1.8	−6.8	−8.1	21.5	47.1	35.3	26.2
Russia	2.6	8.2	4.9	3.8	−0.4	−1.6	22.9	45.3	35.6	26.5
Excluding Russia	−2.4	−2.7	−3.6	−5.6	−6.4	−6.5	−1.4	1.8	−0.3	−0.3
Total[1]	**−57.4**	**−50.6**	**−39.4**	**−49.1**	**10.9**	**−85.9**	**−153.2**	**−173.5**	**−255.3**	**−301.1**
In percent of total world current account transactions	−0.6	−0.5	−0.3	−0.4	0.1	−0.6	−1.1	−1.1	−1.5	−1.7
In percent of world GDP	−0.2	−0.2	−0.1	−0.2	—	−0.3	−0.5	−0.6	−0.8	−0.9
Memorandum										
Emerging market countries, excluding Asian countries in surplus[2]	−102.5	−76.1	−76.2	−75.8	−107.7	−177.5	−68.6	32.8	−16.3	−60.4

[1]Reflects errors, omissions, and asymmetries in balance of payments statistics on current account, as well as the exclusion of data for international organizations and a limited number of countries. See "Classification of Countries" in the introduction to this Statistical Appendix.

[2]All developing and transition countries excluding China, Hong Kong SAR, Korea, Malaysia, the Philippines, Singapore, Taiwan Province of China, and Thailand.

Table 28. Advanced Economies: Balance of Payments on Current Account

	1993	1994	1995	1996	1997	1998	1999	2000	2001	2002
	Billions of U.S. dollars									
Advanced economies	**69.2**	**34.2**	**59.0**	**42.3**	**95.1**	**34.8**	**−133.1**	**−246.1**	**−268.7**	**−264.6**
Major advanced economies	18.8	−6.6	6.9	−2.5	23.4	−54.2	−219.1	−330.0	−344.6	−335.9
United States	−82.7	−118.6	−109.5	−123.3	−140.5	−217.1	−331.5	−435.4	−446.0	−445.8
Japan	132.0	130.6	111.4	65.8	94.1	121.0	106.8	117.3	115.4	124.0
Germany	−9.8	−23.9	−20.7	−7.9	−2.8	−4.6	−19.5	−21.2	−23.2	−19.4
France	9.2	7.4	10.9	20.5	39.4	37.6	37.2	27.1	28.3	32.1
Italy	7.8	13.2	25.1	40.0	32.4	20.0	6.3	−6.0	−1.8	0.7
United Kingdom	−15.9	−2.2	−5.9	−0.9	10.8	−0.1	−16.0	−24.5	−26.2	−33.3
Canada	−21.8	−13.0	−4.4	3.4	−10.1	−11.0	−2.3	12.8	8.9	5.8
Other advanced economies	50.4	40.8	52.1	44.8	71.7	88.9	86.0	83.9	75.8	71.2
Spain	−5.8	−6.6	0.2	0.4	2.5	−2.9	−12.8	−17.8	−18.0	−19.2
Netherlands	13.3	17.3	25.8	22.5	25.1	13.0	17.2	13.6	14.9	14.1
Belgium-Luxembourg	11.2	12.6	14.2	13.8	13.9	12.1	11.3	10.0	11.1	12.2
Sweden	−2.6	2.4	7.1	7.2	8.0	7.1	8.5	5.9	5.3	5.4
Austria	−1.2	−2.9	−5.4	−5.4	−6.5	−5.2	−5.8	−5.6	−5.4	−4.7
Denmark	4.7	2.7	1.9	3.1	1.1	0.3	2.9	4.2	4.2	4.4
Finland	−1.1	1.1	5.3	5.1	6.8	7.3	7.7	9.3	9.5	10.5
Greece	−0.7	−0.1	−2.9	−4.6	−4.8	−3.6	−5.1	−7.8	−8.7	−9.1
Portugal	0.2	−2.2	−0.1	−4.3	−6.0	−7.9	−10.0	−10.9	−11.0	−11.2
Ireland	1.8	1.5	1.7	2.0	1.9	0.8	0.6	−0.5	−2.2	−3.1
Switzerland	19.5	17.5	21.5	22.0	25.5	25.9	30.0	31.0	29.2	29.3
Norway	3.5	3.7	4.9	10.2	8.7	−1.9	6.0	22.2	21.6	17.4
Israel	−2.6	−3.4	−5.2	−5.4	−3.7	−1.0	−1.9	−1.9	−2.5	−2.8
Iceland	—	0.1	0.1	−0.1	−0.1	−0.6	−0.6	−0.9	−0.9	−0.7
Cyprus	0.2	0.2	−0.4	−1.0	−0.6	−1.2	−0.4	−0.7	−0.5	−0.5
Korea	1.0	−3.9	−8.5	−23.0	−8.2	40.6	24.5	11.0	10.1	5.7
Australia	−9.8	−17.2	−19.5	−15.8	−12.7	−18.4	−23.0	−15.2	−11.5	−11.6
Taiwan Province of China	7.0	6.5	5.5	10.9	7.1	3.4	8.4	9.3	7.6	8.8
Hong Kong SAR	8.6	2.1	−5.5	−1.6	−6.2	3.9	10.5	9.5	5.2	7.6
Singapore	4.2	11.4	14.4	12.8	17.9	20.3	21.8	21.8	20.3	20.9
New Zealand	−1.0	−1.9	−3.1	−3.9	−4.3	−2.2	−3.6	−2.7	−2.4	−2.2
Memorandum										
European Union	11.1	20.1	57.3	91.4	122.1	73.7	22.4	−24.3	−23.3	−20.5
Euro area[1]	24.9	17.3	54.1	82.1	102.1	66.6	27.0	−9.8	−6.6	3.0
Newly industrialized Asian economies	20.8	16.1	5.9	−0.9	16.8	67.2	65.2	51.7	43.2	43.0
	Percent of GDP									
United States	−1.2	−1.7	−1.5	−1.6	−1.7	−2.5	−3.6	−4.4	−4.3	−4.1
Japan	3.0	2.7	2.1	1.4	2.2	3.1	2.4	2.5	2.7	2.8
Germany	−0.5	−1.1	−0.8	−0.3	−0.1	−0.2	−0.9	−1.1	−1.2	−1.0
France	0.7	0.5	0.7	1.3	2.8	2.6	2.6	2.1	2.1	2.3
Italy	0.8	1.3	2.3	3.2	2.8	1.7	0.5	−0.6	−0.2	0.1
United Kingdom	−1.7	−0.2	−0.5	−0.1	0.8	—	−1.1	−1.7	−1.8	−2.2
Canada	−3.9	−2.3	−0.8	0.6	−1.6	−1.8	−0.4	1.8	1.3	0.8
Spain	−1.2	−1.3	—	0.1	0.5	−0.5	−2.1	−3.2	−3.0	−3.0
Netherlands	4.1	4.9	6.2	5.5	6.7	3.3	4.3	3.7	3.7	3.4
Belgium-Luxembourg	4.9	5.1	4.8	4.8	5.3	4.5	4.2	4.1	4.3	4.5
Sweden	−1.3	1.2	3.0	2.7	3.4	2.9	3.5	2.6	2.4	2.3
Austria	−0.6	−1.4	−2.3	−2.3	−3.2	−2.5	−2.8	−3.0	−2.8	−2.3
Denmark	3.4	1.8	1.1	1.7	0.7	0.1	1.6	2.6	2.5	2.5
Finland	−1.3	1.1	4.1	4.0	5.6	5.6	5.9	7.7	7.3	7.6
Greece	−0.8	−0.1	−2.4	−3.7	−4.0	−3.0	−4.1	−6.9	−7.3	−7.1
Portugal	0.3	−2.5	−0.1	−3.9	−5.7	−7.1	−8.7	−10.4	−9.7	−9.3
Ireland	3.6	2.7	2.5	2.8	2.4	0.9	0.6	−0.5	−2.1	−2.4
Switzerland	8.2	6.7	7.0	7.4	10.0	9.8	11.6	12.8	11.5	11.3
Norway	3.0	3.0	3.3	6.5	5.6	−1.3	3.9	13.9	13.4	10.9
Israel	−3.9	−4.5	−5.9	−5.6	−3.7	−1.0	−1.9	−1.7	−2.3	−2.5
Iceland	0.8	1.9	0.8	−1.6	−1.7	−6.9	−7.0	−10.3	−10.6	−8.2
Cyprus	3.1	2.4	−4.3	−11.4	−7.6	−13.0	−4.7	−8.0	−5.3	−4.6
Korea	0.3	−1.0	−1.7	−4.4	−1.7	12.7	6.0	2.4	2.3	1.2
Australia	−3.3	−5.1	−5.4	−3.9	−3.1	−5.0	−5.8	−4.0	−3.3	−3.2
Taiwan Province of China	3.1	2.7	2.1	3.9	2.4	1.3	2.9	3.0	2.4	2.5
Hong Kong SAR	7.4	1.6	−3.9	−1.0	−3.6	2.4	6.6	5.8	3.0	4.1
Singapore	7.3	16.3	17.3	14.0	18.9	24.6	25.9	23.6	21.0	20.2
New Zealand	−2.4	−3.8	−5.2	−6.1	−6.7	−4.2	−6.6	−5.4	−4.8	−4.2

[1]Calculated as the sum of the balances of individual euro area countries.

Table 29. Advanced Economies: Current Account Transactions

(Billions of U.S. dollars)

	1993	1994	1995	1996	1997	1998	1999	2000	2001	2002
Exports	2,935.2	3,304.9	3,962.2	4,080.0	4,192.8	4,162.2	4,262.1	4,635.0	4,919.9	5,275.5
Imports	2,847.6	3,234.6	3,874.4	4,024.0	4,123.4	4,102.1	4,338.7	4,860.4	5,166.9	5,517.4
Trade balance	87.6	70.2	87.7	55.9	69.4	60.1	−76.7	−225.4	−246.9	−241.8
Services, credits	838.0	895.1	1,013.3	1,066.7	1,098.4	1,109.8	1,150.2	1,200.7	1,238.7	1,328.1
Services, debits	775.1	825.8	941.7	986.9	1,003.5	1,036.6	1,077.1	1,113.9	1,158.4	1,236.7
Balance on services	62.8	69.2	71.5	79.8	94.9	73.2	73.1	86.8	80.3	91.3
Balance on goods and services	150.4	139.5	159.3	135.7	164.3	133.3	−3.6	−138.6	−166.6	−150.5
Income, net	−4.9	−15.4	−17.5	1.2	18.9	−3.1	−24.3	−1.0	−5.2	−14.6
Current transfers, net	−76.3	−89.9	−82.8	−94.6	−88.1	−95.4	−105.2	−106.5	−97.0	−99.5
Current account balance	**69.2**	**34.2**	**59.0**	**42.3**	**95.1**	**34.8**	**−133.1**	**−246.1**	**−268.7**	**−264.6**
Balance on goods and services										
Advanced economies	**150.4**	**139.5**	**159.3**	**135.7**	**164.3**	**133.3**	**−3.6**	**−138.6**	**−166.6**	**−150.5**
Major advanced economies	81.2	70.7	85.0	55.6	75.0	17.1	−114.8	−244.6	−256.8	−236.2
United States	−69.0	−97.0	−96.0	−102.1	−105.9	−166.9	−265.0	−368.5	−376.2	−363.5
Japan	96.5	96.4	74.7	21.2	47.3	73.2	69.1	69.5	66.8	71.8
Germany	7.4	10.0	18.0	25.2	29.0	32.3	20.6	4.8	7.4	12.6
France	24.5	25.0	28.9	31.2	45.7	42.0	39.3	28.7	29.5	33.0
Italy	32.2	37.0	45.3	62.2	47.6	39.8	23.2	10.9	15.0	17.6
United Kingdom	−10.1	−7.0	−4.4	−6.5	0.8	−11.5	−20.7	−22.1	−22.9	−27.7
Canada	−0.4	6.3	18.4	24.4	10.4	8.2	18.7	32.3	23.7	20.0
Other advanced economies	69.2	68.8	74.3	80.1	89.2	116.2	111.3	106.0	90.2	85.7
Memorandum										
European Union	91.9	110.7	147.9	175.8	187.0	155.6	108.5	55.2	57.0	63.9
Euro area	84.5	99.5	127.9	155.6	161.8	149.3	106.8	57.4	61.0	72.1
Newly industrialized Asian economies	16.9	11.9	4.3	−0.9	6.5	62.3	60.3	45.1	31.8	30.2
Income, net										
Advanced economies	**−4.9**	**−15.4**	**−17.5**	**1.2**	**18.9**	**−3.1**	**−24.3**	**−1.0**	**−5.2**	**−14.6**
Major advanced economies	21.2	15.1	5.3	32.7	32.5	21.3	−5.6	12.0	1.7	−8.3
United States	23.9	16.7	20.5	18.9	6.2	−6.2	−18.5	−13.7	−27.8	−40.3
Japan	40.6	40.3	44.4	53.6	55.6	56.6	49.7	57.6	60.4	65.3
Germany	16.6	3.0	0.1	0.9	−1.4	−6.6	−12.7	−1.1	−7.0	−8.3
France	−9.1	−6.8	−9.0	−2.7	2.6	8.6	11.0	10.3	11.0	11.8
Italy	−17.2	−16.7	−15.6	−15.0	−11.2	−12.3	−11.5	−12.6	−12.2	−12.2
United Kingdom	−12.8	−2.4	−12.4	−1.5	1.7	0.9	−2.0	−8.2	−7.2	−9.7
Canada	−20.8	−19.0	−22.7	−21.6	−21.0	−19.7	−21.7	−20.3	−15.5	−15.0
Other advanced economies	−26.0	−30.5	−22.8	−31.5	−13.6	−24.4	−18.7	−13.0	−6.9	−6.3
Memorandum										
European Union	−46.4	−45.8	−53.7	−40.7	−28.8	−38.8	−42.4	−37.8	−40.0	−43.0
Euro area	−20.2	−32.6	−30.0	−27.1	−19.9	−34.1	−34.4	−24.6	−28.4	−29.1
Newly industrialized Asian economies	4.1	5.1	5.2	3.6	14.6	5.8	7.9	11.4	17.1	18.2

Table 30. Developing Countries: Payments Balances on Current Account

	1993	1994	1995	1996	1997	1998	1999	2000	2001	2002
					Billions of U.S. dollars					
Developing countries	**−118.5**	**−87.0**	**−96.9**	**−74.5**	**−60.5**	**−92.2**	**−18.5**	**46.0**	**—**	**−40.0**
Regional groups										
Africa	−12.3	−12.3	−16.9	−6.3	−8.0	−20.5	−15.5	1.3	−3.7	−5.5
Sub-Sahara	−11.3	−9.1	−12.7	−7.1	−10.8	−18.7	−14.9	−6.7	−10.4	−9.7
Excluding Nigeria and										
South Africa	−10.6	−7.6	−9.1	−8.0	−10.8	−13.7	−11.2	−8.7	−9.8	−9.0
Developing Asia	−33.0	−18.9	−42.4	−38.9	8.8	47.0	46.7	35.9	22.5	11.6
China	−11.9	7.7	1.6	7.2	37.0	31.5	15.7	12.5	7.2	3.1
India	−1.6	−1.7	−5.6	−6.0	−3.0	−6.9	−2.8	−5.0	−5.8	−7.1
Other developing Asia	−19.4	−24.9	−38.5	−40.1	−25.2	22.5	33.8	28.4	21.1	15.6
Middle East, Malta, and Turkey	−27.3	−3.7	−0.7	9.6	5.5	−28.6	6.0	56.7	47.6	22.6
Western Hemisphere	−45.9	−52.0	−36.9	−38.9	−66.8	−90.2	−55.7	−47.9	−66.4	−68.7
Analytical groups										
By source of export earnings										
Fuel	−22.0	−4.0	2.1	30.0	19.2	−35.2	10.1	93.8	63.6	39.4
Nonfuel	−96.4	−82.9	−99.0	−104.6	−79.7	−57.0	−28.6	−47.8	−63.6	−79.3
of which, primary products	−13.7	−12.3	−14.7	−17.2	−19.2	−19.3	−9.2	−10.0	−11.3	−13.1
By external financing source										
Net debtor countries	−104.9	−78.7	−98.4	−86.6	−70.6	−71.1	−25.3	−7.3	−44.6	−65.4
of which, official financing	−9.1	−10.5	−12.1	−8.5	−4.8	−10.4	−6.1	2.6	−0.8	−5.4
Net debtor countries by debt-servicing experience										
Countries with arrears and/or										
rescheduling during 1994–98	−29.1	−19.1	−45.8	−41.9	−50.3	−59.4	−24.9	5.1	−14.8	−24.5
Other groups										
Heavily indebted poor countries	−14.7	−10.6	−12.7	−13.1	−15.0	−16.4	−13.0	−10.7	−13.3	−14.3
Middle East and north Africa	−23.5	−12.3	−5.4	11.5	9.4	−34.2	5.3	73.0	51.8	25.0

Table 30 *(concluded)*

	Ten-Year Averages		1993	1994	1995	1996	1997	1998	1999	2000	2001	2002
	1983–92	1993–2002										
	Percent of exports of goods and services											
Developing countries	**−11.6**	**−2.3**	**−15.8**	**−10.1**	**−9.4**	**−6.5**	**−4.8**	**−7.9**	**−1.5**	**3.0**	**—**	**−2.3**
Regional groups												
Africa	−11.0	−3.4	−12.5	−12.0	−14.0	−4.7	−5.9	−17.0	−12.1	0.8	−2.3	−3.4
Sub-Sahara	−14.0	−8.1	−15.1	−11.7	−13.7	−7.0	−10.4	−20.5	−15.6	−5.9	−9.0	−8.1
Excluding Nigeria and South Africa	−30.4	−14.4	−29.1	−19.9	−20.3	−16.3	−21.4	−29.9	−22.6	−15.3	−16.8	−14.4
Developing Asia	−5.0	1.4	−11.1	−5.1	−9.3	−7.7	1.6	8.7	8.0	5.2	3.0	1.4
China	8.1	0.9	−38.1	−15.9	−28.8	−22.7	4.2	22.7	21.4	13.1	7.5	3.5
India	−14.4	−9.4	−123.9	−59.9	−111.3	−94.4	19.6	102.8	89.8	59.0	33.1	15.5
Other developing Asia	−10.0	3.8	−10.6	−11.3	−14.3	−13.7	−8.0	7.8	10.9	7.8	5.5	3.8
Middle East, Malta, and Turkey	−13.8	6.8	−15.7	−2.0	−0.3	3.9	2.2	−13.4	2.5	16.7	13.9	6.8
Western Hemisphere	−19.8	−17.1	−25.2	−25.1	−15.0	−14.3	−22.5	−31.2	−18.7	−13.6	−18.0	−17.1
Analytical groups												
By source of export earnings												
Fuel	−15.6	12.2	−12.8	−2.3	1.1	12.6	7.9	−19.3	4.4	26.6	18.7	12.2
Nonfuel	−10.3	−5.7	−10.1	−5.9	−6.3	−5.9	−2.3	—	0.3	−1.6	−2.2	−2.7
of which, primary products	−24.9	−12.0	−26.8	−20.6	−19.7	−21.9	−23.1	−24.1	−11.1	−10.8	−11.4	−12.0
By external financing source												
Net debtor countries	−11.1	−4.3	−16.1	−10.3	−10.8	−8.5	−6.4	−6.7	−2.3	−0.5	−3.1	−4.3
of which, official financing	−16.1	−6.0	−21.4	−23.7	−22.5	−13.9	−7.3	−17.2	−9.2	3.0	−0.9	−6.0
Net debtor countries by debt-servicing experience												
Countries with arrears and/or rescheduling during 1994–98	−11.3	−5.9	−14.7	−8.7	−18.2	−14.8	−16.3	−21.3	−8.3	1.4	−3.8	−5.9
Other groups												
Heavily indebted poor countries	−37.6	−18.4	−43.7	−28.0	−27.3	−24.7	−27.2	−30.8	−22.4	−15.4	−18.4	−18.4
Middle East and north Africa	−14.6	7.9	−13.6	−6.9	−2.7	5.0	4.0	−18.1	2.3	21.9	15.8	7.9
Memorandum												
Median												
Developing countries	−17.4	−10.5	−19.2	−13.9	−12.9	−14.0	−11.7	−17.6	−11.1	−11.3	−10.9	−10.5

Table 31. Developing Countries—by Region: Current Account Transactions

(Billions of U.S. dollars)

	1993	1994	1995	1996	1997	1998	1999	2000	2001	2002
Developing countries										
Exports	620.5	714.9	860.1	963.5	1,039.9	960.3	1,053.8	1,326.4	1,382.2	1,457.7
Imports	662.8	728.6	866.8	946.6	1,009.2	960.7	971.1	1,160.1	1,263.8	1,378.7
Trade balance	−42.3	−13.7	−6.8	16.9	30.8	−0.4	82.7	166.4	118.4	79.0
Services, net	−49.2	−41.3	−50.5	−52.6	−58.2	−48.1	−56.4	−67.6	−63.3	−64.9
Balance on goods and services	−91.5	−55.0	−57.2	−35.7	−27.4	−48.5	26.3	98.7	55.1	14.1
Income, net	−53.9	−59.2	−72.6	−76.4	−78.8	−84.6	−88.7	−97.5	−102.7	−104.9
Current transfers, net	27.0	27.2	32.9	37.6	45.8	40.8	43.9	44.7	47.7	50.9
Current account balance	**−118.5**	**−87.0**	**−96.9**	**−74.5**	**−60.5**	**−92.2**	**−18.5**	**46.0**	**—**	**−40.0**
Memorandum										
Exports of goods and services	751.9	863.1	1,029.3	1,153.9	1,251.3	1,162.6	1,253.2	1,545.0	1,621.6	1,717.1
Interest payments	82.3	87.7	102.8	107.3	109.5	116.6	119.8	121.8	120.7	118.3
Oil trade balance	113.5	111.3	125.8	159.4	150.6	97.7	140.3	234.6	212.7	192.9
Regional groups										
Africa										
Exports	82.0	85.1	100.8	112.4	114.5	98.9	105.9	133.0	134.9	136.9
Imports	78.2	82.5	99.3	100.5	104.8	103.9	104.1	111.6	120.4	125.6
Trade balance	3.8	2.6	1.5	11.9	9.7	−5.0	1.7	21.5	14.6	11.2
Services, net	−9.2	−9.5	−11.5	−10.5	−10.5	−10.5	−10.3	−11.5	−12.8	−12.9
Balance on goods and services	−5.5	−6.9	−10.0	1.4	−0.8	−15.4	−8.6	10.0	1.8	−1.7
Income, net	−15.8	−14.8	−17.0	−18.4	−18.6	−16.8	−18.8	−21.5	−18.3	−16.7
Current transfers, net	9.0	9.4	10.2	10.7	11.4	11.8	11.9	12.7	12.8	13.0
Current account balance	**−12.3**	**−12.3**	**−16.9**	**−6.3**	**−8.0**	**−20.5**	**−15.5**	**1.3**	**−3.7**	**−5.5**
Memorandum										
Exports of goods and services	98.3	102.1	120.1	133.4	136.2	120.6	128.1	155.4	158.8	162.4
Interest payments	13.8	14.1	16.6	16.6	16.3	16.2	15.7	16.0	15.8	15.5
Oil trade balance	20.5	18.8	21.8	31.0	29.8	19.1	24.6	44.6	43.0	39.6
Developing Asia										
Exports	247.9	307.1	378.4	416.3	467.0	456.6	495.4	601.0	646.9	705.8
Imports	277.8	327.3	404.8	447.1	452.3	391.1	425.8	543.1	602.4	669.8
Trade balance	−30.0	−20.2	−26.4	−30.7	14.8	65.4	69.7	57.9	44.5	36.0
Services, net	−4.7	−4.5	−11.2	−7.0	−12.0	−12.6	−19.4	−17.6	−17.1	−18.6
Balance on goods and services	−34.6	−24.7	−37.6	−37.8	2.8	52.9	50.2	40.3	27.4	17.4
Income, net	−14.0	−13.5	−24.8	−25.2	−23.6	−28.7	−29.4	−32.5	−34.1	−36.4
Current transfers, net	15.7	19.2	20.0	24.1	29.7	22.9	25.8	28.1	29.2	30.6
Current account balance	**−33.0**	**−18.9**	**−42.4**	**−38.9**	**8.8**	**47.0**	**46.7**	**35.9**	**22.5**	**11.6**
Memorandum										
Exports of goods and services	296.8	370.5	455.0	505.5	565.3	539.6	580.4	696.2	751.1	819.2
Interest payments	21.8	24.5	26.8	29.5	26.9	30.4	34.5	30.6	25.6	24.7
Oil trade balance	−11.2	−11.5	−13.7	−19.6	−22.2	−14.5	−21.6	−38.7	−40.3	−38.6

Table 31 *(concluded)*

	1993	1994	1995	1996	1997	1998	1999	2000	2001	2002
Middle East, Malta, and Turkey										
Exports	145.6	155.4	176.4	208.4	209.8	166.2	203.4	293.0	291.6	278.2
Imports	148.6	133.3	157.0	171.7	183.5	184.8	178.2	203.6	215.3	227.7
Trade balance	–3.0	22.1	19.4	36.7	26.3	–18.6	25.2	89.4	76.3	50.5
Services, net	–27.1	–18.7	–19.7	–26.9	–23.7	–13.1	–18.9	–28.6	–24.3	–24.4
Balance on goods and services	–30.1	3.4	–0.3	9.8	2.6	–31.7	6.3	60.8	52.0	26.1
Income, net	12.3	8.1	12.8	12.6	14.2	14.8	12.8	11.3	9.9	10.0
Current transfers, net	–9.5	–15.2	–13.2	–12.9	–11.3	–11.7	–13.1	–15.4	–14.2	–13.5
Current account balance	**–27.3**	**–3.7**	**–0.7**	**9.6**	**5.5**	**–28.6**	**6.0**	**56.7**	**47.6**	**22.6**
Memorandum										
Exports of goods and services	174.3	183.0	208.1	243.2	253.1	213.7	246.3	340.3	343.2	333.4
Interest payments	11.8	12.5	15.1	15.2	16.3	16.8	13.8	15.7	19.3	20.4
Oil trade balance	90.4	89.0	99.7	122.9	119.2	78.5	114.1	189.1	178.6	161.6
Western Hemisphere										
Exports	145.0	167.4	204.4	226.4	248.7	238.7	249.2	299.4	308.8	336.8
Imports	158.2	185.5	205.8	227.3	268.6	280.9	263.0	301.8	325.8	355.6
Trade balance	–13.2	–18.1	–1.3	–1.0	–20.0	–42.2	–13.8	–2.4	–17.0	–18.8
Services, net	–8.2	–8.6	–8.0	–8.2	–12.0	–12.0	–7.7	–10.0	–9.1	–8.9
Balance on goods and services	–21.3	–26.8	–9.3	–9.2	–32.0	–54.2	–21.6	–12.4	–26.0	–27.7
Income, net	–36.4	–39.0	–43.5	–45.5	–50.7	–53.8	–53.3	–54.7	–60.2	–61.8
Current transfers, net	11.8	13.7	15.9	15.7	16.0	17.8	19.3	19.3	19.9	20.8
Current account balance	**–45.9**	**–52.0**	**–36.9**	**–38.9**	**–66.8**	**–90.2**	**–55.7**	**–47.9**	**–66.4**	**–68.7**
Memorandum										
Exports of goods and services	182.5	207.5	246.1	271.9	296.7	288.8	298.4	353.1	368.6	402.1
Interest payments	34.9	36.7	44.3	46.0	49.9	53.1	55.8	59.5	60.0	57.7
Oil trade balance	13.9	15.1	17.9	25.0	23.8	14.6	23.2	39.7	31.5	30.3

Table 32. Developing Countries—by Analytical Criteria: Current Account Transactions

(Billions of U.S. dollars)

	1993	1994	1995	1996	1997	1998	1999	2000	2001	2002
By source of export earnings										
Fuel										
Exports	161.8	164.2	185.6	225.8	226.9	167.9	216.4	337.0	321.8	302.6
Imports	124.0	111.1	126.0	127.8	139.6	144.3	143.7	164.1	180.9	188.2
Trade balance	37.8	53.1	59.6	98.0	87.3	23.6	72.7	172.9	140.9	114.5
Services, net	−45.4	−37.1	−40.1	−50.3	−51.1	−41.7	−43.0	−55.2	−55.1	−56.0
Balance on goods and services	−7.6	16.0	19.5	47.7	36.1	−18.1	29.7	117.7	85.8	58.5
Income, net	6.8	3.2	5.5	4.0	3.8	5.3	4.3	2.7	3.8	6.0
Current transfers, net	−21.3	−23.2	−22.8	−21.7	−20.8	−22.4	−23.9	−26.6	−25.9	−25.1
Current account balance	**−22.0**	**−4.0**	**2.1**	**30.0**	**19.2**	**−35.2**	**10.1**	**93.8**	**63.6**	**39.4**
Memorandum										
Exports of goods and services	172.1	174.8	197.0	237.7	241.3	182.6	231.3	352.9	339.6	322.1
Interest payments	14.6	15.2	17.9	17.3	19.1	19.5	14.9	15.1	15.9	15.4
Oil trade balance	126.1	122.9	140.3	179.4	175.8	118.4	163.8	272.2	255.1	234.0
Nonfuel exports										
Exports	458.6	550.7	674.5	737.7	813.0	792.4	837.4	989.4	1,060.4	1,155.0
Imports	538.8	617.5	740.9	818.8	869.6	816.4	827.4	996.0	1,082.9	1,190.5
Trade balance	−80.2	−66.8	−66.4	−81.1	−56.5	−24.0	10.0	−6.6	−22.5	−35.5
Services, net	−3.8	−4.1	−10.4	−2.3	−7.1	−6.4	−13.3	−12.5	−8.2	−8.9
Balance on goods and services	−83.9	−71.0	−76.7	−83.4	−63.6	−30.4	−3.4	−19.0	−30.7	−44.4
Income, net	−60.7	−62.3	−78.1	−80.5	−82.6	−89.9	−93.0	−100.2	−106.5	−110.9
Current transfers, net	48.2	50.4	55.8	59.3	66.5	63.3	67.7	71.4	73.6	76.0
Current account balance	**−96.4**	**−82.9**	**−99.0**	**−104.6**	**−79.7**	**−57.0**	**−28.6**	**−47.8**	**−63.6**	**−79.3**
Memorandum										
Exports of goods and services	579.8	688.3	832.2	916.2	1,010.0	980.0	1,021.9	1,192.1	1,282.0	1,394.9
Interest payments	67.8	72.5	84.9	90.0	90.3	97.1	104.9	106.8	104.8	102.9
Oil trade balance	−12.6	−11.6	−14.5	−20.0	−25.2	−20.7	−23.5	−37.5	−42.4	−41.1
Nonfuel primary products										
Exports	41.2	48.6	60.9	63.6	67.4	63.7	66.7	75.9	81.0	88.6
Imports	47.1	52.6	66.2	72.4	77.9	76.4	70.7	78.7	84.9	93.5
Trade balance	−6.0	−4.0	−5.4	−8.8	−10.4	−12.7	−4.0	−2.8	−3.9	−4.9
Services, net	−5.3	−5.2	−6.1	−6.3	−6.6	−5.6	−5.3	−5.9	−5.7	−5.9
Balance on goods and services	−11.3	−9.3	−11.4	−15.1	−17.1	−18.3	−9.2	−8.7	−9.6	−10.8
Income, net	−8.3	−9.1	−10.3	−10.4	−10.4	−9.9	−9.8	−11.3	−11.7	−12.4
Current transfers, net	5.9	6.1	7.1	8.3	8.3	8.9	9.9	10.1	9.9	10.1
Current account balance	**−13.7**	**−12.3**	**−14.7**	**−17.2**	**−19.2**	**−19.3**	**−9.2**	**−10.0**	**−11.3**	**−13.1**
Memorandum										
Exports of goods and services	51.2	59.6	74.6	78.7	83.4	80.2	82.9	92.5	99.4	108.7
Interest payments	7.8	8.0	9.6	9.4	9.3	9.7	9.3	10.1	10.5	10.9
Oil trade balance	−2.5	−2.5	−3.1	−3.9	−4.4	−3.8	−3.4	−3.6	−4.0	−3.8

Table 32 *(continued)*

	1993	1994	1995	1996	1997	1998	1999	2000	2001	2002
By external financing source										
Net debtor countries										
Exports	524.9	618.3	748.8	831.8	905.4	862.3	931.7	1,138.2	1,198.7	1,288.1
Imports	594.2	662.9	794.5	873.4	930.3	878.9	893.7	1,075.4	1,175.7	1,286.4
Trade balance	−69.2	−44.6	−45.8	−41.7	−24.8	−16.5	38.0	62.8	23.0	1.7
Services, net	−17.7	−16.7	−23.0	−16.0	−20.9	−19.6	−26.1	−26.4	−22.1	−22.2
Balance on goods and services	−86.9	−61.3	−68.8	−57.6	−45.8	−36.1	11.9	36.4	0.9	−20.6
Income, net	−68.9	−70.7	−87.0	−90.3	−93.8	−99.4	−104.1	−113.1	−118.1	−120.9
Current transfers, net	51.0	53.3	57.4	61.3	68.9	64.4	66.8	69.4	72.6	76.0
Current account balance	**−104.9**	**−78.7**	**−98.4**	**−86.6**	**−70.6**	**−71.1**	**−25.3**	**−7.3**	**−44.6**	**−65.4**
Memorandum										
Exports of goods and services	650.9	761.0	912.3	1,017.0	1,109.8	1,057.2	1,122.7	1,348.3	1,429.4	1,538.3
Interest payments	80.5	85.5	100.2	104.4	105.9	112.8	115.7	117.7	115.4	113.0
Oil trade balance	39.0	38.6	43.0	58.1	50.9	33.6	54.8	91.1	75.0	70.3
Official financing										
Exports	32.0	32.8	40.3	46.8	50.9	45.8	51.0	67.1	69.2	70.5
Imports	38.6	42.9	51.1	54.2	54.4	55.7	57.4	65.6	71.6	78.6
Trade balance	−6.6	−10.0	−10.8	−7.4	−3.5	−9.9	−6.3	1.5	−2.4	−8.0
Services, net	−3.0	−3.1	−3.2	−2.8	−2.8	−3.8	−3.6	−2.9	−2.9	−3.1
Balance on goods and services	−9.6	−13.1	−14.0	−10.2	−6.3	−13.8	−10.0	−1.3	−5.4	−11.1
Income, net	−6.4	−5.4	−6.7	−7.3	−7.4	−6.2	−6.7	−7.9	−7.4	−6.3
Current transfers, net	7.0	8.0	8.7	9.0	8.8	9.6	10.5	11.8	11.9	12.1
Current account balance	**−9.1**	**−10.5**	**−12.1**	**−8.5**	**−4.8**	**−10.4**	**−6.1**	**2.6**	**−0.8**	**−5.4**
Memorandum										
Exports of goods and services	42.4	44.1	53.6	61.1	65.9	60.7	66.6	83.9	86.8	89.6
Interest payments	7.1	6.7	7.4	7.4	7.6	7.4	6.8	7.1	6.8	6.7
Oil trade balance	9.4	7.6	8.6	12.2	12.8	7.7	11.2	21.4	19.8	16.5
Net debtor countries by debt-servicing experience										
Countries with arrears and/or rescheduling during 1994–98										
Exports	166.0	183.2	208.1	233.5	252.7	232.8	258.7	328.5	339.9	358.2
Imports	162.4	176.4	221.5	241.1	259.9	241.8	233.3	267.8	298.8	326.6
Trade balance	3.6	6.9	−13.4	−7.6	−7.2	−9.1	25.4	60.6	41.1	31.6
Services, net	−17.0	−14.8	−18.8	−22.3	−28.0	−32.1	−30.6	−32.0	−32.7	−33.8
Balance on goods and services	−13.4	−7.9	−32.2	−29.8	−35.3	−41.1	−5.2	28.6	8.4	−2.2
Income, net	−29.8	−26.9	−30.8	−29.3	−33.2	−35.8	−36.5	−40.6	−41.3	−41.8
Current transfers, net	14.1	15.7	17.2	17.3	18.1	17.5	16.8	17.1	18.1	19.6
Current account balance	**−29.1**	**−19.1**	**−45.8**	**−41.9**	**−50.3**	**−59.4**	**−24.9**	**5.1**	**−14.8**	**−24.5**
Memorandum										
Exports of goods and services	198.5	220.1	251.5	282.8	308.4	279.3	301.5	374.7	389.7	412.2
Interest payments	31.0	29.9	36.3	38.5	40.7	44.3	45.8	47.1	46.5	45.0
Oil trade balance	35.3	35.2	39.0	50.4	48.5	36.9	55.2	91.2	85.5	81.6

Table 32 *(concluded)*

	1993	1994	1995	1996	1997	1998	1999	2000	2001	2002
Other groups										
Heavily indebted poor countries										
Exports	26.1	29.8	36.8	42.5	44.6	42.3	46.8	57.5	59.6	63.8
Imports	33.0	35.0	42.3	47.4	50.6	51.4	53.3	59.5	64.0	69.5
Trade balance	−7.0	−5.2	−5.4	−4.9	−6.0	−9.1	−6.5	−2.0	−4.4	−5.8
Services, net	−5.8	−5.2	−6.6	−7.2	−8.2	−8.0	−7.3	−8.3	−8.4	−8.7
Balance on goods and services	−12.8	−10.4	−12.0	−12.1	−14.1	−17.1	−13.8	−10.3	−12.9	−14.5
Income, net	−8.3	−7.0	−8.6	−9.7	−9.6	−9.0	−9.6	−11.5	−11.2	−10.6
Current transfers, net	6.4	6.9	7.9	8.7	8.7	9.6	10.4	11.1	10.8	10.8
Current account balance	**−14.7**	**−10.6**	**−12.7**	**−13.1**	**−15.0**	**−16.4**	**−13.0**	**−10.7**	**−13.3**	**−14.3**
Memorandum										
Exports of goods and services	33.7	37.9	46.6	53.0	55.2	53.4	58.2	69.3	72.1	77.5
Interest payments	6.8	6.8	7.5	7.6	7.4	7.7	6.9	7.1	7.2	7.0
Oil trade balance	2.9	3.5	4.3	6.1	6.2	3.4	7.0	13.0	11.6	11.0
Middle East and north Africa										
Exports	148.7	152.2	171.7	201.1	203.1	157.3	198.9	298.3	290.5	274.7
Imports	139.6	133.6	148.2	154.1	160.3	165.9	165.1	183.1	198.0	209.8
Trade balance	9.1	18.6	23.5	47.0	42.9	−8.5	33.8	115.2	92.6	64.9
Services, net	−32.5	−22.4	−24.5	−31.0	−31.5	−23.7	−24.6	−35.3	−33.9	−34.2
Balance on goods and services	−23.4	−3.8	−1.0	16.0	11.4	−32.2	9.1	79.8	58.7	30.7
Income, net	8.8	5.1	8.6	7.7	9.1	10.1	9.5	8.9	8.3	8.8
Current transfers, net	−8.9	−13.6	−13.0	−12.2	−11.1	−12.1	−13.4	−15.8	−15.1	−14.5
Current account balance	**−23.5**	**−12.3**	**−5.4**	**11.5**	**9.4**	**−34.2**	**5.3**	**73.0**	**51.8**	**25.0**
Memorandum										
Exports of goods and services	172.0	176.7	198.3	230.0	234.7	189.3	232.2	333.5	327.7	314.7
Interest payments	−12.8	−13.1	−16.1	−16.2	−16.7	−16.7	−12.9	−13.0	−14.9	−15.5
Oil trade balance	102.9	100.1	112.2	138.8	135.7	91.8	128.8	214.4	204.1	185.6

Table 33. Summary of Balance of Payments, Capital Flows, and External Financing

(Billions of U.S. dollars)

	1993	1994	1995	1996	1997	1998	1999	2000	2001	2002
Developing countries										
Balance of payments[1]										
Balance on current account	−118.5	−87.0	−96.9	−74.5	−60.5	−92.2	−18.5	46.0	—	−40.0
Balance on goods and services	−91.5	−55.0	−57.2	−35.7	−27.4	−48.5	26.3	98.7	55.1	14.1
Income, net	−53.9	−59.2	−72.6	−76.4	−78.8	−84.6	−88.7	−97.5	−102.7	−104.9
Current transfers, net	27.0	27.2	32.9	37.6	45.8	40.8	43.9	44.7	47.7	50.9
Balance on capital and financial account	139.2	112.5	116.0	112.9	113.9	116.6	43.7	−26.5	25.5	62.4
Balance on capital account[2]	19.1	9.5	16.9	22.7	13.4	8.4	2.7	−0.1	−0.7	8.5
Balance on financial account	120.1	103.0	99.1	90.2	100.5	108.2	40.9	−26.4	26.2	53.8
Direct investment, net	50.8	74.8	85.3	108.3	129.6	127.2	125.4	113.8	119.2	123.4
Portfolio investment, net	97.7	96.9	20.7	68.9	34.7	14.0	13.5	7.5	11.1	27.7
Other investment, net	11.7	−19.1	61.4	7.9	−7.6	−49.3	−68.6	−79.2	−50.6	−30.8
Reserve assets	−40.1	−49.5	−68.3	−94.8	−56.2	16.4	−29.4	−68.5	−53.5	−66.5
Errors and omissions, net	−20.7	−25.5	−19.1	−38.4	−53.4	−24.4	−25.2	−19.5	−25.5	−22.4
Capital flows										
Total capital flows, net[3]	160.2	152.6	167.5	185.0	156.7	91.9	70.4	42.1	79.7	120.3
Net official flows	50.0	24.9	30.9	4.7	19.8	39.1	29.2	15.9	19.3	16.3
Net private flows[4]	110.2	127.7	136.5	180.3	137.0	52.8	41.2	26.2	60.4	104.0
Direct investment, net	50.8	74.8	85.3	108.3	129.6	127.2	125.4	113.8	119.2	123.4
Private portfolio investment, net	67.5	88.9	15.8	55.9	27.8	−0.1	0.5	6.3	14.6	22.1
Other private flows, net	−8.0	−36.0	35.3	16.1	−20.4	−74.3	−84.7	−93.9	−73.4	−41.4
External financing[5]										
Net external financing[6]	194.9	166.0	215.3	240.7	244.6	178.6	146.5	166.1	193.8	234.9
Nondebt-creating flows	99.3	103.6	115.3	153.5	163.2	142.3	140.7	145.0	144.8	159.7
Capital transfers[7]	19.1	9.5	16.9	22.7	13.4	8.4	2.7	−0.1	−0.7	8.5
Foreign direct investment and equity security liabilities[8]	80.2	94.1	98.4	130.8	149.7	133.9	137.9	145.1	145.5	151.2
Net external borrowing[9]	95.5	62.3	100.1	87.2	81.5	36.3	5.8	21.1	49.1	75.2
Borrowing from official creditors[10]	49.6	23.6	31.1	8.4	10.9	29.8	27.3	19.8	20.6	16.7
Of which,										
Credit and loans from IMF[11]	−0.1	−0.8	12.6	−2.9	0.8	8.5	1.3	−6.7	. . .	. . .
Borrowing from banks[12]	16.5	−30.8	20.5	25.5	28.3	24.7	−0.8	10.1	13.2	16.4
Borrowing from other private creditors	29.4	69.5	48.4	53.2	42.2	−18.3	−20.7	−8.8	15.2	42.1
Memorandum										
Balance on goods and services in percent of GDP[13]	−2.4	−1.4	−1.3	−0.7	−0.5	−1.0	0.5	1.8	1.0	0.2
Scheduled amortization of external debt	121.9	125.4	153.2	199.9	223.5	223.0	260.6	253.9	207.2	208.3
Gross external financing[14]	316.8	291.3	368.6	440.5	468.2	401.5	407.0	420.0	401.1	443.3
Gross external borrowing[15]	217.4	187.7	253.3	287.0	305.0	259.2	266.4	275.0	256.3	283.6
Exceptional external financing, net	32.0	18.1	19.1	20.4	12.9	18.1	22.7	20.1	15.7	8.8
Of which,										
Arrears on debt service	10.0	−7.5	−2.4	−3.5	−3.1	2.6	12.1	−29.9	. . .	. . .
Debt forgiveness	1.0	1.2	1.6	8.7	10.2	. . .	2.1	6.9	. . .	. . .
Rescheduling of debt service	22.3	25.0	20.4	15.8	7.2	4.9	9.4	38.8	. . .	. . .

Table 33 *(continued)*

(Billions of U.S. dollars)

	1993	1994	1995	1996	1997	1998	1999	2000	2001	2002
Countries in transition										
Balance of payments[1]										
Balance on current account	−8.1	2.2	−1.5	−16.8	−23.7	−28.4	−1.7	26.7	13.5	3.6
Balance on goods and services	−8.0	3.5	−5.0	−18.7	−20.7	−22.0	2.9	29.7	16.8	7.1
Income, net	−6.3	−5.6	−1.3	−4.0	−9.0	−13.7	−12.4	−10.7	−12.1	−12.3
Current transfers, net	6.2	4.3	4.8	5.8	5.9	7.2	7.8	7.6	8.7	8.8
Balance on capital and financial account	11.2	−0.7	5.8	23.7	26.2	35.3	5.7	−16.6	−12.2	−2.5
Balance on capital account[2]	2.5	9.9	−1.5	1.2	0.4	0.9	0.6	0.8	0.9	0.4
Balance on financial account	8.6	−10.5	7.3	22.5	25.8	34.4	5.0	−17.4	−13.1	−3.0
Direct investment, net	6.0	5.3	13.1	12.4	15.5	20.5	21.6	24.2	28.1	28.4
Portfolio investment, net	8.7	17.3	14.6	14.6	24.5	12.2	1.3	7.5	8.5	7.0
Other investment, net	4.8	−27.9	17.3	−2.5	−4.3	3.8	−11.0	−28.1	−30.2	−24.2
Reserve assets	−10.8	−5.3	−37.8	−2.0	−9.8	−2.1	−6.7	−21.0	−19.5	−14.2
Errors and omissions, net	−3.0	−1.5	−4.3	−6.9	−2.5	−6.9	−4.0	−10.0	−1.2	−1.1
Capital flows										
Total capital flows, net[3]	19.5	−5.2	45.0	24.5	35.7	36.5	11.8	3.6	6.4	11.2
Net official flows	2.1	−10.1	−4.5	4.0	33.1	17.3	−0.8	0.8	1.0	3.0
Net private flows[4]	17.4	4.8	49.6	20.5	2.5	19.2	12.5	2.8	5.4	8.2
Direct investment, net	6.0	5.3	13.1	12.4	15.5	20.5	21.6	24.2	28.1	28.4
Private portfolio investment, net	8.7	17.3	14.6	14.6	8.0	4.0	2.2	5.3	5.5	3.9
Other private flows, net	2.7	−17.8	21.9	−6.5	−20.9	−5.2	−11.2	−26.7	−28.3	−24.1
External financing[5]										
Net external financing[6]	19.8	14.1	32.5	35.2	75.5	55.3	41.1	29.1	36.8	40.3
Nondebt-creating flows	9.8	15.9	12.9	14.7	21.0	24.8	23.6	27.5	31.3	31.7
Capital transfers[7]	2.5	9.9	−1.5	1.2	0.4	0.9	0.6	0.8	0.9	0.4
Foreign direct investment and equity security liabilities[8]	7.2	6.1	14.4	13.5	20.7	23.9	22.9	26.8	30.4	31.3
Net external borrowing[9]	10.0	−1.8	19.6	20.5	54.5	30.5	17.5	1.6	5.5	8.5
Borrowing from official creditors[10]	2.1	−7.0	−3.3	4.4	33.1	17.3	−0.8	0.8	1.0	3.0
Of which,										
Credit and loans from IMF[11]	3.7	2.4	4.7	3.7	2.5	5.5	−3.6	−4.2	. . .	. . .
Borrowing from banks[12]	7.3	4.1	−2.1	1.7	3.7	2.8	—	1.4	1.5	2.6
Borrowing from other private creditors	0.6	1.2	25.0	14.4	17.7	10.4	18.3	−0.6	3.0	2.9

Table 33 *(concluded)*

	1993	1994	1995	1996	1997	1998	1999	2000	2001	2002
Memorandum										
Balance on goods and services										
in percent of GDP[13]	−1.7	0.6	−0.6	−2.1	−2.2	−2.8	0.4	4.0	2.0	0.8
Scheduled amortization of external debt	26.1	26.0	28.2	26.9	21.0	25.5	28.3	31.1	32.2	34.2
Gross external financing[14]	45.9	40.1	60.7	62.0	96.6	80.7	69.4	60.2	69.0	74.5
Gross external borrowing[15]	36.2	24.2	47.8	47.3	75.5	55.9	45.9	32.7	37.8	42.8
Exceptional external financing, net	21.6	19.4	17.4	13.1	−21.2	7.4	6.8	6.4	0.2	—
Of which,										
Arrears on debt service	0.5	3.8	−0.5	1.1	−24.8	5.1	1.7	0.8	...	...
Debt forgiveness	2.1	—	0.9	0.9	—	—	—	—	...	...
Rescheduling of debt service	1.4	13.3	13.9	9.9	3.3	2.4	4.7	4.8	...	...

[1]Standard presentation in accordance with the 5th edition of the International Monetary Fund's *Balance of Payments Manual* (1993).

[2]Comprises capital transfers—including debt forgiveness—and acquisition/disposal of nonproduced, nonfinancial assets.

[3]Comprise net direct investment, net portfolio investment, and other long- and short-term net investment flows, including official and private borrowing. In the standard balance of payments presentation above, total net capital flows are equal to the balance on financial account minus the change in reserve assets.

[4]Because of limitations on the data coverage for net official flows, the residually derived data for net private flows may include some official flows.

[5]As defined in the *World Economic Outlook* (see footnote 6). It should be noted that there is no generally accepted standard definition of external financing.

[6]Defined as the sum of—with opposite sign—the goods and services balance, net income and current transfers, direct investment abroad, the change in reserve assets, the net acquisition of other assets (such as recorded private portfolio assets, export credit, and the collateral for debt-reduction operations), and the net errors and omissions. Thus, net external financing, according to the definition adopted in the *World Economic Outlook*, measures the total amount required to finance the current account, direct investment outflows, net reserve transactions (often at the discretion of the monetary authorities), the net acquisition of nonreserve external assets, and the net transactions underlying the errors and omissions (not infrequently reflecting capital flight).

[7]Including other transactions on capital account.

[8]Debt-creating foreign direct investment liabilities are not included.

[9]Net disbursement of long- and short-term credits, including exceptional financing, by both official and private creditors.

[10]Net disbursement by official creditors, based on directly reported flows and flows derived from information on external debt.

[11]Comprise use of International Monetary Fund resources under the General Resources Account, Trust Fund, and Poverty Reduction and Growth Facility (PRGF). For further detail, see Table 37.

[12]Net disbursement by commercial banks, based on directly reported flows and cross-border claims and liabilities reported in the International Banking section of the International Monetary Fund's *International Financial Statistics*.

[13]This is often referred to as the "resource balance" and, with opposite sign, the "net resource transfer."

[14]Net external financing plus amortization due on external debt.

[15]Net external borrowing plus amortization due on external debt.

Table 34. Developing Countries—by Region: Balance of Payments and External Financing[1]

(Billions of U.S. dollars)

	1993	1994	1995	1996	1997	1998	1999	2000	2001	2002
Africa										
Balance of payments										
Balance on current account	−12.3	−12.3	−16.9	−6.3	−8.0	−20.5	−15.5	1.3	−3.7	−5.5
Balance on capital account	3.3	2.6	3.2	7.2	4.2	3.2	4.4	8.0	3.6	4.8
Balance on financial account	10.9	11.1	14.2	1.1	4.4	15.4	10.6	−10.2	−0.4	0.4
Change in reserves (− = increase)	3.2	−5.4	−2.0	−9.1	−10.6	1.9	−3.5	−14.4	−13.7	−11.0
Other official flows, net	4.5	5.0	3.9	−2.1	−1.8	2.7	1.4	−4.4	−1.5	−2.6
Private flows, net	3.2	11.4	12.3	12.3	16.8	10.9	12.7	8.6	14.7	14.0
External financing										
Net external financing	12.3	20.2	24.1	21.2	27.9	24.9	26.9	21.5	26.1	24.9
Nondebt-creating inflows	7.1	7.0	11.3	15.4	20.5	20.3	23.5	23.1	22.2	21.7
Net external borrowing	5.2	13.2	12.8	5.8	7.4	4.6	3.3	−1.5	3.9	3.2
From official creditors	4.6	5.0	4.3	−1.8	−1.7	2.9	1.6	−4.0	−1.5	−2.7
Of which,										
Credit and loans from IMF	0.2	0.9	0.8	0.6	−0.5	−0.4	−0.2	−0.1	. . .	. . .
From banks	−0.2	1.9	1.1	0.4	0.1	−0.3	1.0	0.6	1.2	1.3
From other private creditors	0.9	6.3	7.5	7.1	9.0	1.9	0.7	1.9	4.2	4.6
Memorandum										
Exceptional financing	8.0	12.5	11.2	13.5	11.7	2.0	8.2	6.3	4.9	2.0
Sub-Sahara										
Balance of payments										
Balance on current account	−11.3	−9.1	−12.7	−7.1	−10.8	−18.7	−14.9	−6.7	−10.4	−9.7
Balance on capital account	3.3	2.6	3.2	7.2	4.2	3.2	4.3	7.9	3.6	4.8
Balance on financial account	9.6	7.9	10.2	2.1	7.1	13.8	9.2	−2.2	6.3	4.7
Change in reserves (− = increase)	3.4	−3.4	−3.3	−6.3	−5.5	0.8	−3.8	−7.3	−5.9	−7.1
Other official flows, net	4.2	5.3	4.2	−1.8	−0.8	3.0	1.9	−3.9	−0.5	−1.8
Private flows, net	2.0	5.9	9.3	10.2	13.4	10.0	11.2	9.0	12.7	13.6
External financing										
Net external financing	10.9	15.9	22.0	19.8	26.3	24.2	26.3	22.3	25.0	25.0
Nondebt-creating inflows	6.0	5.7	10.7	14.3	18.8	18.8	21.8	21.7	18.4	19.1
Net external borrowing	5.0	10.1	11.4	5.4	7.5	5.4	4.5	0.6	6.5	5.8
From official creditors	4.3	5.3	4.6	−1.4	−0.8	3.3	2.1	−3.5	−0.5	−1.9
Of which,										
Credit and loans from IMF	0.7	0.5	0.6	0.1	−0.5	−0.3	−0.1	—	. . .	. . .
From banks	−0.4	1.8	1.1	0.5	—	−0.3	0.2	0.5	1.2	1.4
From other private creditors	1.0	3.0	5.7	6.4	8.2	2.4	2.3	3.7	5.8	6.4
Memorandum										
Exceptional financing	8.0	6.8	5.1	9.0	8.1	0.9	7.7	6.2	4.9	2.0
Developing Asia										
Balance of payments										
Balance on current account	−33.0	−18.9	−42.4	−38.9	8.8	47.0	46.7	35.9	22.5	11.6
Balance on capital account	12.7	4.2	11.7	13.0	5.7	—	−5.0	−8.6	−5.3	1.1
Balance on financial account	30.4	26.2	48.8	54.5	25.1	−31.0	−27.4	−13.2	−4.6	−0.8
Change in reserves (− = increase)	−25.2	−43.5	−32.7	−37.8	−20.5	−16.7	−30.1	−18.3	−14.7	−31.1
Other official flows, net	11.4	11.9	7.3	−1.2	4.6	13.6	15.5	8.7	15.0	10.2
Private flows, net	44.2	57.9	74.2	93.5	41.0	−27.9	−12.7	−3.6	−4.8	20.1
External financing										
Net external financing	75.3	75.4	93.5	106.7	96.8	39.8	37.7	61.4	66.0	86.6
Nondebt-creating inflows	49.1	49.1	64.9	74.3	66.6	57.9	40.2	54.8	56.9	66.1
Net external borrowing	26.1	26.3	28.7	32.4	30.2	−18.1	−2.5	6.7	9.1	20.5
From official creditors	10.9	11.3	6.2	−2.1	4.0	13.2	14.9	8.0	14.4	9.9
Of which,										
Credit and loans from IMF	0.6	−0.8	−1.5	−1.7	5.0	6.6	1.7	0.9	. . .	. . .
From banks	10.6	10.3	14.2	19.6	22.7	2.0	−10.8	0.5	7.8	9.7
From other private creditors	4.6	4.7	8.3	14.9	3.5	−33.4	−6.6	−1.8	−13.1	0.9
Memorandum										
Exceptional financing	1.7	1.2	0.4	0.7	0.5	14.5	14.7	14.6	10.8	6.6

Table 34 *(concluded)*

	1993	1994	1995	1996	1997	1998	1999	2000	2001	2002
Other developing Asia										
Balance of payments										
Balance on current account	−19.4	−24.9	−38.5	−40.1	−25.2	22.5	33.8	28.4	21.1	15.6
Balance on capital account	12.7	4.2	11.7	13.0	5.8	0.1	−4.9	−8.6	−5.3	1.1
Balance on financial account	6.0	24.0	27.9	38.1	35.5	−23.9	−30.8	−14.8	−12.2	−13.8
Change in reserves (− = increase)	−19.0	−3.6	−12.3	−3.4	19.9	−7.6	−15.6	−1.9	−4.6	−15.8
Other official flows, net	5.5	3.1	3.4	−3.5	3.0	8.0	8.4	4.3	8.0	2.7
Private flows, net	19.5	24.6	36.7	45.0	12.5	−24.2	−23.6	−17.2	−15.6	−0.7
External financing										
Net external financing	35.5	27.0	48.0	49.6	22.5	−5.5	−19.3	−8.6	−8.8	7.3
Nondebt-creating inflows	19.7	9.9	25.1	27.6	13.8	13.1	−2.4	2.6	4.8	14.4
Net external borrowing	15.8	17.1	22.9	22.0	8.7	−18.6	−16.9	−11.2	−13.6	−7.1
From official creditors	5.0	2.5	2.3	−4.4	2.4	7.7	7.9	3.6	7.4	2.4
Of which,										
Credit and loans from IMF	0.1	0.4	−0.3	−0.4	5.7	7.0	2.1	0.9	. . .	. . .
From banks	3.4	6.6	8.5	15.7	15.4	−0.9	−9.1	−4.8	0.1	0.9
From other private creditors	7.3	8.0	12.1	10.7	−9.1	−25.3	−15.7	−10.1	−21.1	−10.4
Memorandum										
Exceptional financing	1.7	1.2	0.4	0.7	0.5	14.5	14.7	14.6	10.8	6.6
Middle East, Malta, and Turkey										
Balance of payments										
Balance on current account	−27.3	−3.7	−0.7	9.6	5.5	−28.6	6.0	56.7	47.6	22.6
Balance on capital account	2.5	2.7	1.6	1.5	2.4	4.1	1.8	−0.7	−0.3	1.6
Balance on financial account	31.7	11.1	0.5	−5.0	0.6	27.6	0.7	−46.5	−33.5	−13.3
Change in reserves (− = increase)	2.6	−4.6	−10.3	−18.6	−11.4	12.2	−5.1	−22.9	−20.0	−12.9
Other official flows, net	3.5	0.2	2.3	2.0	0.8	7.4	4.9	−5.5	−3.4	0.3
Private flows, net	25.5	15.6	8.5	11.6	11.2	8.0	0.8	−18.1	−10.0	−0.7
External financing										
Net external financing	26.0	2.1	13.3	20.7	17.9	16.4	7.3	4.8	7.9	16.2
Nondebt-creating inflows	7.1	8.0	7.2	11.9	8.6	9.3	6.6	7.7	8.7	11.7
Net external borrowing	18.8	−5.9	6.0	8.8	9.3	7.1	0.7	−2.9	−0.8	4.5
From official creditors	1.9	−1.6	−0.3	0.4	−0.6	−1.2	−1.5	2.3	−1.1	0.6
Of which,										
Credit and loans from IMF	—	0.4	0.4	0.1	0.2	−0.1	0.6	3.3	. . .	. . .
From banks	1.1	−10.2	−0.6	−2.1	−0.2	7.1	5.2	0.9	−2.6	−2.3
From other private creditors	15.8	5.8	7.0	10.5	10.1	1.2	−3.0	−6.2	2.9	6.1
Memorandum										
Exceptional financing	13.4	4.3	3.4	1.0	0.4	0.5	0.3	0.4	0.1	0.1
Western Hemisphere										
Balance of payments										
Balance on current account	−45.9	−52.0	−36.9	−38.9	−66.8	−90.2	−55.7	−47.9	−66.4	−68.7
Balance on capital account	0.6	—	0.4	1.0	1.1	1.0	1.5	1.3	1.2	1.0
Balance on financial account	47.1	54.6	35.7	39.5	70.4	96.2	57.0	43.4	64.7	67.6
Change in reserves (− = increase)	−20.7	4.0	−23.4	−29.4	−13.8	19.0	9.3	−12.9	−5.0	−11.5
Other official flows, net	30.5	7.8	17.5	6.1	16.2	15.4	7.4	17.1	9.1	8.4
Private flows, net	37.3	42.8	41.6	62.8	68.1	61.8	40.4	39.2	60.6	70.7
External financing										
Net external financing	81.3	68.3	84.4	92.1	102.0	97.5	74.6	78.4	93.9	107.3
Nondebt-creating inflows	36.0	39.6	31.9	51.8	67.5	54.7	70.3	59.5	57.0	60.3
Net external borrowing	45.3	28.7	52.5	40.2	34.5	42.7	4.3	18.9	36.9	47.0
From official creditors	32.1	8.9	21.0	11.9	9.2	14.9	12.2	13.4	8.8	8.9
Of which,										
Credit and loans from IMF	−0.9	−1.3	12.9	−2.0	−4.0	2.5	−0.9	−10.7	. . .	. . .
From banks	5.1	−32.8	5.9	7.6	5.8	15.9	3.9	8.1	6.8	7.7
From other private creditors	8.1	52.6	25.6	20.7	19.6	12.0	−11.9	−2.7	21.3	30.4
Memorandum										
Exceptional financing	8.9	0.1	4.1	5.2	0.2	1.2	−0.4	−1.3	−0.1	0.2

[1]For definitions, see footnotes to Table 33.

Table 35. Developing Countries—by Analytical Criteria: Balance of Payments and External Financing[1]

(Billions of U.S. dollars)

	1993	1994	1995	1996	1997	1998	1999	2000	2001	2002
By source of export earnings										
Fuel										
Balance of payments										
Balance on current account	−22.0	−4.0	2.1	30.0	19.2	−35.2	10.1	93.8	63.6	39.4
Balance on capital account	0.3	0.5	1.0	4.0	−0.2	0.1	0.6	—	−0.1	1.0
Balance on financial account	31.8	21.1	5.5	−25.8	−10.0	35.1	1.4	−83.9	−50.5	−29.6
Change in reserves (− = increase)	10.4	1.0	0.7	−22.0	−13.4	18.9	5.7	−34.2	−18.9	−14.1
Other official flows, net	4.2	6.4	6.2	0.5	5.1	11.9	5.3	−6.2	−3.3	−3.5
Private flows, net	17.2	13.7	−1.3	−4.3	−1.7	4.2	−9.5	−43.5	−28.4	−12.1
External financing										
Net external financing	14.2	11.0	7.0	7.8	8.7	17.7	−0.1	−16.3	−5.4	6.0
Nondebt-creating inflows	2.3	4.1	4.3	14.6	8.1	9.3	9.3	10.5	12.8	12.9
Net external borrowing	12.0	7.0	2.7	−6.8	0.6	8.3	−9.4	−26.8	−18.2	−6.9
From official creditors	3.5	4.9	2.8	0.4	2.5	2.2	1.4	0.3	−2.0	−3.5
Of which,										
Credit and loans from IMF	−0.8	0.4	−0.2	0.7	−0.3	−0.6	−0.5	−0.6	. . .	. . .
From banks	1.7	−2.6	−2.9	−6.0	−2.7	4.4	2.5	−1.3	−0.1	−0.1
From other private creditors	6.8	4.6	2.7	−1.2	0.8	1.7	−13.4	−25.8	−16.1	−3.3
Memorandum										
Exceptional financing	16.6	12.9	11.9	9.9	7.5	5.2	4.1	2.5	1.4	−1.1
Nonfuel										
Balance of payments										
Balance on current account	−96.4	−82.9	−99.0	−104.6	−79.7	−57.0	−28.6	−47.8	−63.6	−79.3
Balance on capital account	18.8	9.0	15.9	18.7	13.6	8.3	2.1	−0.1	−0.6	7.5
Balance on financial account	88.2	81.9	93.6	116.1	110.5	73.1	39.5	57.5	76.7	83.5
Change in reserves (− = increase)	−50.6	−50.5	−69.1	−72.8	−42.9	−2.6	−35.1	−34.3	−34.6	−52.4
Other official flows, net	45.8	18.5	24.8	4.2	14.6	27.1	23.9	22.1	22.6	19.8
Private flows, net	93.0	114.0	137.9	184.6	138.7	48.6	50.7	69.7	88.8	116.1
External financing										
Net external financing	180.7	154.9	208.3	232.9	235.9	160.9	146.6	182.4	199.3	228.9
Nondebt-creating inflows	97.1	99.5	111.0	138.9	155.1	133.0	131.4	134.5	131.9	146.8
Net external borrowing	83.6	55.4	97.3	93.9	80.9	27.9	15.2	47.9	67.3	82.1
From official creditors	46.1	18.7	28.2	8.0	8.4	27.6	25.9	19.5	22.7	20.1
Of which,										
Credit and loans from IMF	0.6	−1.2	12.8	−3.6	1.2	9.1	1.8	−6.1	. . .	. . .
From banks	14.8	−28.1	23.4	31.5	31.1	20.3	−3.3	11.4	13.3	16.6
From other private creditors	22.6	64.9	45.7	54.4	41.4	−20.0	−7.3	17.0	31.3	45.4
Memorandum										
Exceptional financing	15.4	5.2	7.3	10.6	5.4	12.9	18.6	17.7	14.3	10.0
By external financing source										
Net debtor countries										
Balance of payments										
Balance on current account	−104.9	−78.7	−98.4	−86.6	−70.6	−71.1	−25.3	−7.3	−44.6	−65.4
Balance on capital account	19.3	9.7	17.0	22.9	13.6	8.3	2.2	−0.2	−0.8	8.4
Balance on financial account	97.5	84.4	90.9	91.9	105.9	85.3	37.8	19.7	59.9	69.8
Change in reserves (− = increase)	−48.3	−51.5	−68.7	−86.4	−47.8	4.8	−33.3	−58.4	−44.6	−63.1
Other official flows, net	48.1	22.9	28.2	2.6	18.6	30.6	23.7	24.6	21.9	16.9
Private flows, net	97.6	112.9	131.4	175.8	135.1	50.0	47.4	53.5	82.5	116.0
External financing										
Net external financing	188.2	160.6	211.2	232.0	241.8	171.9	149.7	177.7	200.9	235.4
Nondebt-creating inflows	99.3	103.1	114.9	149.8	161.6	141.1	139.1	143.3	141.3	156.5
Net external borrowing	88.9	57.5	96.3	82.2	80.2	30.8	10.6	34.4	59.6	78.9
From official creditors	49.4	23.5	30.9	7.9	11.0	29.9	28.1	20.6	20.9	16.9
Of which,										
Credit and loans from IMF	−0.1	−0.8	12.6	−2.9	0.8	8.5	1.3	−6.7	. . .	. . .
From banks	13.4	−29.6	19.8	25.5	27.8	21.5	−3.2	10.6	13.9	17.6
From other private creditors	26.1	63.6	45.7	48.8	41.4	−20.6	−14.3	3.2	24.8	44.3
Memorandum										
Exceptional financing	32.0	18.1	19.1	20.4	12.9	18.1	22.7	20.1	15.7	8.8

Table 35 *(continued)*

	1993	1994	1995	1996	1997	1998	1999	2000	2001	2002
Official financing										
Balance of payments										
Balance on current account	−9.1	−10.5	−12.1	−8.5	−4.8	−10.4	−6.1	2.6	−0.8	−5.4
Balance on capital account	5.0	5.4	6.4	7.1	8.2	5.7	6.6	9.9	6.6	7.4
Balance on financial account	2.8	4.3	6.0	1.6	−2.9	5.7	0.8	−12.1	−5.2	−1.7
Change in reserves (− = increase)	0.2	−3.1	−0.2	−3.3	−5.8	1.7	−1.1	−10.5	−10.0	−7.5
Other official flows, net	3.4	5.9	5.0	2.5	2.5	3.1	2.7	−3.3	3.2	3.8
Private flows, net	−0.8	1.5	1.2	2.4	0.4	0.9	−0.8	1.6	1.6	2.0
External financing										
Net external financing	7.6	12.2	13.3	11.8	11.0	9.7	9.1	8.2	11.7	13.1
Nondebt-creating inflows	5.2	7.5	8.9	10.2	11.6	9.2	10.3	14.0	11.4	13.4
Net external borrowing	2.4	4.7	4.4	1.6	−0.5	0.4	−1.2	−5.8	0.3	−0.3
From official creditors	3.4	5.7	4.8	2.3	2.4	3.0	2.6	−3.3	3.1	3.6
Of which,										
Credit and loans from IMF	−0.5	1.1	1.1	0.9	0.2	—	—	−0.1	. . .	. . .
From banks	−0.9	−0.6	0.5	1.1	0.9	0.1	—	0.3	0.4	0.5
From other private creditors	−0.1	−0.5	−0.8	−1.9	−3.8	−2.7	−3.9	−2.8	−3.1	−4.4
Memorandum										
Exceptional financing	4.6	10.3	9.9	11.3	6.9	3.9	3.8	2.4	2.7	1.7
Net debtor countries by debt-servicing experience										
Countries with arrears and/or rescheduling during 1994–98										
Balance of payments										
Balance on current account	−29.1	−19.1	−45.8	−41.9	−50.3	−59.4	−24.9	5.1	−14.8	−24.5
Balance on capital account	4.4	4.6	7.2	10.5	7.2	4.8	5.2	8.2	4.5	6.6
Balance on financial account	26.6	25.1	35.2	37.7	56.1	57.1	23.3	−7.7	15.4	22.0
Change in reserves (− = increase)	−10.1	−15.6	−23.8	−22.7	−3.1	18.7	2.9	−41.1	−25.2	−22.3
Other official flows, net	3.1	3.7	1.6	−8.8	0.7	11.4	10.8	4.1	3.0	−0.9
Private flows, net	33.5	37.1	57.4	69.2	58.4	27.1	9.6	29.4	37.6	45.2
External financing										
Net external financing	42.2	46.0	69.7	71.2	69.6	49.4	27.4	57.4	55.2	60.4
Nondebt-creating inflows	20.5	27.4	30.6	46.1	39.5	40.0	39.6	50.3	43.5	47.4
Net external borrowing	21.7	18.5	39.0	25.1	30.1	9.4	−12.3	7.1	11.7	13.0
From official creditors	3.1	3.5	1.4	−9.0	0.6	11.3	10.7	4.2	2.8	−1.1
Of which,										
Credit and loans from IMF	−0.8	1.0	0.5	0.7	3.9	10.9	5.6	−5.5	. . .	. . .
From banks	−3.4	−37.6	4.6	8.3	14.0	8.1	−6.5	−1.5	4.3	4.1
From other private creditors	22.0	52.6	33.1	25.8	15.5	−10.0	−16.5	4.4	4.6	10.0
Memorandum										
Exceptional financing	29.7	16.9	18.6	20.1	12.2	15.8	19.4	16.6	14.3	7.6
Other groups										
Heavily indebted poor countries										
Balance of payments										
Balance on current account	−14.7	−10.6	−12.7	−13.1	−15.0	−16.4	−13.0	−10.7	−13.3	−14.3
Balance on capital account	3.6	4.2	5.9	10.5	7.2	4.6	5.2	8.5	5.1	6.8
Balance on financial account	9.6	6.0	5.5	1.6	6.4	11.4	7.3	2.3	8.1	7.5
Change in reserves (− = increase)	1.8	−2.3	−1.0	−3.3	—	1.7	−2.7	−2.6	−3.3	−2.5
Other official flows, net	2.8	4.1	3.6	−1.8	0.4	3.8	3.4	−2.5	1.8	1.0
Private flows, net	5.0	4.3	2.9	6.6	6.0	5.9	6.6	7.3	9.6	9.1
External financing										
Net external financing	12.4	13.0	14.2	16.0	14.7	15.1	16.9	14.3	17.8	17.8
Nondebt-creating inflows	5.8	7.3	9.7	15.0	12.5	10.1	11.7	14.1	11.3	13.6
Net external borrowing	6.6	5.8	4.4	1.0	2.2	4.9	5.2	0.1	6.5	4.2
From official creditors	3.0	4.4	4.3	−1.2	0.8	4.2	3.8	−2.1	2.1	1.2
Of which,										
Credit and loans from IMF	−0.2	0.5	0.6	0.3	—	0.2	0.2	—	. . .	. . .
From banks	−0.2	0.7	1.0	1.6	0.4	—	0.3	0.3	0.3	0.4
From other private creditors	3.7	0.7	−0.9	0.6	1.0	0.8	1.2	1.9	4.1	2.5
Memorandum										
Exceptional financing	7.5	6.5	5.4	10.7	5.5	−1.3	5.9	4.5	4.7	2.2

Table 35 *(concluded)*

	1993	1994	1995	1996	1997	1998	1999	2000	2001	2002
Middle East and north Africa										
Balance of payments										
Balance on current account	−23.5	−12.3	−5.4	11.5	9.4	−34.2	5.3	73.0	51.8	25.0
Balance on capital account	2.5	2.7	1.6	1.5	2.4	4.1	1.8	−0.6	−0.2	1.6
Balance on financial account	25.4	20.8	6.2	−8.9	−5.8	31.4	4.0	−62.9	−37.9	−15.9
Change in reserves (− = increase)	2.8	−5.7	−4.3	−17.0	−13.0	13.6	1.2	−27.7	−21.1	−10.6
Other official flows, net	1.3	1.2	2.3	2.4	0.3	8.1	5.7	−8.8	−3.0	−0.6
Private flows, net	21.3	25.3	8.3	5.7	6.8	9.7	−2.8	−26.4	−13.8	−4.7
External financing										
Net external financing	15.3	14.8	11.0	13.7	9.3	15.4	0.2	−9.3	2.5	9.5
Nondebt-creating inflows	6.7	7.5	6.6	11.5	9.1	10.1	7.3	6.9	10.6	11.9
Net external borrowing	8.6	7.3	4.4	2.2	0.2	5.3	−7.2	−16.1	−8.1	−2.3
From official creditors	−0.3	−0.6	−0.3	0.7	−1.1	−0.5	−0.8	−1.0	−0.8	−0.2
Of which,										
Credit and loans from IMF	−0.5	0.5	0.2	0.6	0.3	−0.1	—	−0.3	. . .	. . .
From banks	−1.2	−3.1	−2.6	−5.2	−2.4	3.9	3.4	−1.2	−1.3	−1.4
From other private creditors	10.1	11.0	7.3	6.7	3.7	1.9	−9.8	−14.0	−6.1	−0.7
Memorandum										
Exceptional financing	13.6	10.1	9.6	6.8	5.4	3.0	2.2	2.0	1.6	1.5

[1]For definitions, see footnotes to Table 33.

Table 36. Developing Countries: Reserves[1]

	1993	1994	1995	1996	1997	1998	1999	2000	2001	2002
					Billions of U.S. dollars					
Developing countries	**324.7**	**380.8**	**448.9**	**541.8**	**591.6**	**604.0**	**639.4**	**705.2**	**758.7**	**824.9**
Regional groups										
Africa	19.8	24.8	26.6	31.3	42.1	39.8	39.6	53.0	66.8	77.6
Sub-Sahara	13.5	15.9	19.1	21.1	27.8	26.3	26.8	33.7	39.6	46.6
Developing Asia	125.5	174.3	200.8	246.5	264.9	289.8	322.9	339.6	354.3	385.3
Other developing Asia	91.8	100.4	106.2	118.0	96.3	112.1	131.3	132.3	136.9	152.6
Middle East, Malta, and Turkey	70.2	76.6	91.4	107.5	114.7	113.5	123.3	146.0	166.0	178.9
Western Hemisphere	109.2	105.2	130.1	156.5	169.9	160.9	153.7	166.6	171.6	183.1
Analytical groups										
By source of export earnings										
Fuel	51.7	54.2	56.6	75.2	86.9	80.0	82.5	116.3	135.2	149.1
Nonfuel	273.0	326.7	392.3	466.6	504.7	524.0	556.9	588.9	623.5	675.8
of which, primary products	39.9	49.0	53.9	58.4	62.2	59.2	59.6	61.5	68.2	73.4
By external financing source										
Net debtor countries	300.1	355.3	419.2	504.4	552.0	566.7	596.5	652.1	696.7	759.6
of which, official financing	27.6	30.7	30.8	33.2	37.3	35.1	34.6	45.0	55.0	62.4
Net debtor countries by debt-servicing experience										
Countries with arrears and/or rescheduling during 1994–98	93.2	110.6	128.7	155.2	152.7	148.3	146.0	185.7	211.0	233.1
Other groups										
Heavily indebted poor countries	22.1	24.1	26.6	28.2	28.9	27.8	29.7	31.6	34.9	37.3
Middle East and north Africa	68.8	76.4	85.0	99.9	109.1	106.0	111.1	138.1	159.2	169.8
					Ratio of reserves to imports of goods and services[2]					
Developing countries	38.5	41.5	41.3	45.5	46.3	49.9	52.1	48.8	48.4	48.4
Regional groups										
Africa	19.1	22.7	20.5	23.7	30.7	29.2	29.0	36.5	42.6	47.3
Sub-Sahara	17.1	19.6	19.4	20.7	25.8	25.1	25.7	30.2	33.0	37.4
Developing Asia	37.9	44.1	40.8	45.4	47.1	59.5	60.9	51.8	49.0	48.1
Other developing Asia	45.2	40.9	34.4	35.4	28.3	42.5	47.3	39.9	38.0	38.6
Middle East, Malta, and Turkey	34.4	42.7	43.8	46.1	45.8	46.3	51.4	52.2	57.0	58.2
Western Hemisphere	53.6	44.9	50.9	55.7	51.7	46.9	48.0	45.6	43.5	42.6
Analytical groups										
By source of export earnings										
Fuel	28.8	34.1	31.9	39.6	42.4	39.8	40.9	49.5	53.3	56.6
Nonfuel	41.1	43.0	43.2	46.7	47.0	51.9	54.3	48.6	47.5	47.0
of which, primary products	63.9	71.1	62.7	62.3	61.9	60.1	64.7	60.7	62.6	61.4
By external financing source										
Net debtor countries	40.7	43.2	42.7	46.9	47.8	51.8	53.7	49.7	48.8	48.7
of which, official financing	53.1	53.6	45.6	46.5	51.7	47.2	45.2	52.8	59.6	62.0
Net debtor countries by debt-servicing experience										
Countries with arrears and/or rescheduling during 1994–98	44.0	48.5	45.4	49.6	44.4	46.3	47.6	53.7	55.3	56.3
Other groups										
Heavily indebted poor countries	47.5	50.0	45.4	43.3	41.6	39.5	41.2	39.7	41.1	40.5
Middle East and north Africa	35.2	42.4	42.6	46.7	48.9	47.8	49.8	54.4	59.2	59.8

[1]In this table, official holdings of gold are valued at SDR 35 an ounce. This convention results in a marked underestimate of reserves for countries that have substantial gold holdings.

[2]Reserves at year-end in percent of imports of goods and services for the year indicated.

Table 37. Net Credit and Loans from IMF[1]

(Billions of U.S. dollars)

	1992	1993	1994	1995	1996	1997	1998	1999	2000
Advanced economies	**0.3**	—	—	**−0.1**	**−0.1**	**11.3**	**5.2**	**−10.3**	—
Newly industrialized Asian economies	—	—	—	—	—	11.3	5.2	−10.3	—
Developing countries	**−0.4**	**−0.1**	**−0.8**	**12.6**	**−2.9**	**0.8**	**8.5**	**1.3**	**−6.7**
Regional groups									
Africa	−0.2	0.2	0.9	0.8	0.6	−0.5	−0.4	−0.2	−0.1
Sub-Sahara	—	0.7	0.5	0.6	0.1	−0.5	−0.3	−0.1	—
Developing Asia	1.3	0.6	−0.8	−1.5	−1.7	5.0	6.6	1.7	0.9
Other developing Asia	0.1	0.1	0.4	−0.3	−0.4	5.7	7.0	2.1	0.9
Middle East, Malta, and Turkey	0.1	—	0.4	0.4	0.1	0.2	−0.1	0.6	3.3
Western Hemisphere	−1.6	−0.9	−1.3	12.9	−2.0	−4.0	2.5	−0.9	−10.7
Analytical groups									
By source of export earnings									
Fuel	−0.5	−0.8	0.4	−0.2	0.7	−0.3	−0.6	−0.5	−0.6
Nonfuel	—	0.6	−1.2	12.8	−3.6	1.2	9.1	1.8	−6.1
of which, primary products	—	−0.1	0.2	0.4	0.1	—	—	—	−0.2
By external financing source									
Net debtor countries	−0.4	−0.1	−0.8	12.6	−2.9	0.8	8.5	1.3	−6.7
of which, official financing	−0.1	−0.5	1.1	1.1	0.9	0.2	—	—	—
Net debtor countries by debt-servicing experience									
Countries with arrears and/or rescheduling during 1994–98	−1.0	−0.8	1.0	0.5	0.7	3.9	10.9	5.6	−5.5
Other groups									
Heavily indebted poor countries	−0.1	−0.2	0.5	0.6	0.3	—	0.2	0.2	—
Middle East and north Africa	−0.1	−0.5	0.5	0.2	0.6	0.3	−0.1	—	−0.3
Countries in transition	**1.6**	**3.7**	**2.4**	**4.7**	**3.7**	**2.5**	**5.5**	**−3.6**	**−4.2**
Central and eastern Europe	0.5	2.0	0.2	−2.7	−0.8	0.4	−0.4	—	−0.1
Commonwealth of Independent States and Mongolia	1.0	1.9	2.3	7.5	4.5	2.1	5.8	−3.6	−4.1
Russia	1.0	1.5	1.5	5.5	3.2	1.5	5.3	−3.6	−2.9
Excluding Russia	—	0.3	0.7	2.0	1.3	0.5	0.5	—	−1.2
Memorandum									
Total									
Net credit provided under:									
General Resources Account	0.644	3.374	0.594	15.633	0.291	14.355	18.811	−12.856	−10.741
Trust Fund	—	−0.060	−0.014	−0.015	—	−0.007	−0.001	−0.001	—
PRGF	0.733	0.253	0.998	1.619	0.325	0.179	0.374	0.194	−0.119
Disbursements at year-end under:[2]									
General Resources Account	31.217	34.503	37.276	53.275	51.824	62.703	84.961	69.913	55.756
Trust Fund	0.217	0.157	0.153	0.141	0.137	0.121	0.126	0.122	0.116
PRGF	5.041	5.285	6.634	8.342	8.392	8.049	8.788	8.761	8.199

[1]Includes net disbursements from programs under the General Resources Account, Trust Fund and Poverty Reduction and Growth Facility (formerly ESAF-Enhanced Structural Adjustment Facility). The data are on a transactions basis, with conversion to U.S. dollar values at annual average exchange rates.
[2]Converted to U.S. dollar values at end-of-period exchange rates.

Table 38. Summary of External Debt and Debt Service

	1993	1994	1995	1996	1997	1998	1999	2000	2001	2002
					Billions of U.S. dollars					
External debt										
Developing countries	**1,535.8**	**1,656.0**	**1,805.2**	**1,878.5**	**1,966.1**	**2,104.4**	**2,155.1**	**2,120.9**	**2,172.6**	**2,247.5**
Regional groups										
Africa	267.0	286.7	302.9	301.2	295.9	294.7	295.0	284.7	284.2	285.4
Developing Asia	466.7	519.9	580.0	614.5	660.1	681.9	705.4	681.6	693.8	717.6
Middle East, Malta, and Turkey	275.9	283.4	301.9	315.9	338.3	372.0	388.0	399.7	414.6	432.9
Western Hemisphere	526.2	566.0	620.4	647.0	671.8	755.8	766.6	754.9	780.0	811.6
Analytical groups										
By external financing source										
Net debtor countries	1,497.5	1,617.9	1,763.4	1,831.5	1,907.3	2,031.1	2,077.8	2,043.3	2,096.9	2,170.6
of which, official financing	162.3	176.1	183.2	182.0	178.0	179.7	178.0	164.5	163.9	165.1
Net debtor countries by debt-servicing experience										
Countries with arrears and/or rescheduling during 1994–98	683.7	727.1	766.9	797.7	831.7	890.3	910.4	883.4	898.3	915.5
Countries in transition	**235.7**	**258.7**	**276.4**	**301.7**	**314.0**	**353.7**	**355.7**	**367.3**	**370.3**	**378.5**
Central and eastern Europe	112.5	113.7	126.6	140.4	147.8	166.2	171.2	177.5	188.6	201.6
Commonwealth of Independent States and Mongolia	123.2	144.9	149.7	161.3	166.2	187.5	184.5	189.8	181.7	176.9
Russia	112.7	127.5	128.0	136.1	134.6	152.4	147.6	151.7	141.7	135.4
Excluding Russia	10.5	17.4	21.7	25.2	31.6	35.1	36.9	38.2	40.0	41.5
Debt-service payments[1]										
Developing countries	**175.4**	**195.7**	**240.3**	**283.3**	**311.2**	**310.9**	**361.6**	**347.6**	**316.2**	**318.8**
Regional groups										
Africa	29.4	29.9	33.6	30.8	28.8	28.5	27.6	28.2	29.4	27.4
Developing Asia	53.0	63.8	75.3	80.7	85.9	96.9	110.7	92.4	94.2	95.5
Middle East, Malta, and Turkey	21.7	26.3	34.4	44.6	39.3	39.1	40.5	43.6	43.0	41.6
Western Hemisphere	71.4	75.6	97.0	127.2	157.2	146.4	182.8	183.4	149.7	154.3
Analytical groups										
By external financing source										
Net debtor countries	171.9	187.9	232.2	270.4	302.6	302.7	353.3	339.2	305.4	308.0
of which, official financing	15.2	16.5	17.9	15.7	13.6	12.5	11.4	11.8	12.0	11.8
Net debtor countries by debt-servicing experience										
Countries with arrears and/or rescheduling during 1994–98	65.8	66.8	84.6	95.4	119.0	128.8	162.1	136.5	118.4	119.4
Countries in transition	**18.1**	**20.6**	**28.7**	**29.8**	**30.4**	**50.1**	**45.2**	**47.0**	**51.4**	**54.8**
Central and eastern Europe	11.3	13.8	18.8	20.0	21.0	27.9	28.5	31.0	32.6	35.5
Commonwealth of Independent States and Mongolia	6.7	6.8	9.8	9.8	9.4	22.2	16.7	16.0	18.8	19.3
Russia	6.2	4.3	6.4	6.9	5.9	16.3	12.9	11.3	14.2	14.5
Excluding Russia	0.5	2.5	3.5	2.9	3.5	5.9	3.8	4.7	4.6	4.8

Table 38 *(concluded)*

	1993	1994	1995	1996	1997	1998	1999	2000	2001	2002
					Percent of exports of goods and services					
External debt²										
Developing countries	**204.3**	**191.9**	**175.4**	**162.8**	**157.1**	**181.0**	**172.0**	**137.3**	**134.0**	**130.9**
Regional groups										
Africa	271.6	280.8	252.3	225.8	217.3	244.4	230.3	183.2	179.0	175.7
Developing Asia	157.2	140.3	127.5	121.6	116.8	126.4	121.5	97.9	92.4	87.6
Middle East, Malta, and Turkey	158.3	154.9	145.1	129.9	133.6	174.1	157.5	117.4	120.8	129.8
Western Hemisphere	288.3	272.7	252.0	238.0	226.4	261.7	256.9	213.8	211.6	201.9
Analytical groups										
By external financing source										
Net debtor countries	230.1	212.6	193.3	180.1	171.9	192.1	185.1	151.6	146.7	141.1
of which, official financing	382.9	399.1	342.0	297.9	270.1	296.0	267.2	196.1	188.7	184.3
Net debtor countries by debt-servicing experience										
Countries with arrears and/or rescheduling during 1994–98	344.4	330.3	305.0	282.0	269.7	318.7	302.0	235.8	230.5	222.1
Countries in transition	**129.9**	**127.7**	**107.0**	**107.7**	**106.1**	**124.1**	**129.6**	**112.5**	**107.6**	**104.4**
Central and eastern Europe	134.7	119.1	101.6	105.7	101.3	106.7	114.1	109.7	106.5	104.1
Commonwealth of Independent States and Mongolia	125.7	135.4	112.0	109.5	110.8	145.0	148.3	115.2	108.7	104.7
Russia	171.1	166.1	134.2	132.4	130.6	174.6	173.9	132.6	123.5	119.3
Excluding Russia	32.7	57.5	56.7	56.5	67.4	83.5	93.4	75.9	76.3	74.8
Debt-service payments										
Developing countries	**23.3**	**22.7**	**23.3**	**24.6**	**24.9**	**26.7**	**28.9**	**22.5**	**19.5**	**18.6**
Regional groups										
Africa	29.9	29.3	28.0	23.1	21.2	23.7	21.5	18.1	18.5	16.9
Developing Asia	17.8	17.2	16.5	16.0	15.2	18.0	19.1	13.3	12.5	11.7
Middle East, Malta, and Turkey	12.4	14.4	16.5	18.3	15.5	18.3	16.5	12.8	12.5	12.5
Western Hemisphere	39.1	36.4	39.4	46.8	53.0	50.7	61.3	51.9	40.6	38.4
Analytical groups										
By external financing source										
Net debtor countries	26.4	24.7	25.5	26.6	27.3	28.6	31.5	25.2	21.4	20.0
of which, official financing	35.8	37.4	33.5	25.6	20.6	20.6	17.2	14.1	13.9	13.2
Net debtor countries by debt-servicing experience										
Countries with arrears and/or rescheduling during 1994–98	33.2	30.4	33.7	33.7	38.6	46.1	53.8	36.4	30.4	29.0
Countries in transition	**10.0**	**10.2**	**11.1**	**10.6**	**10.3**	**17.6**	**16.5**	**14.4**	**14.9**	**15.1**
Central and eastern Europe	13.6	14.5	15.1	15.0	14.4	17.9	19.0	19.2	18.4	18.3
Commonwealth of Independent States and Mongolia	6.9	6.4	7.4	6.7	6.3	17.2	13.4	9.7	11.2	11.4
Russia	9.4	5.6	6.7	6.7	5.7	18.7	15.2	9.8	12.3	12.7
Excluding Russia	1.7	8.3	9.0	6.5	7.5	14.1	9.5	9.4	8.8	8.6

¹Debt-service payments refer to actual payments of interest on total debt plus actual amortization payments on long-term debt. The projections incorporate the impact of exceptional financing items.
²Total debt at year-end in percent of exports of goods and services in year indicated.

Table 39. Developing Countries—by Region: External Debt, by Maturity and Type of Creditor
(Billions of U.S. dollars)

	1993	1994	1995	1996	1997	1998	1999	2000	2001	2002
Developing countries										
Total debt	**1,535.8**	**1,656.0**	**1,805.2**	**1,878.5**	**1,966.1**	**2,104.4**	**2,155.1**	**2,120.9**	**2,172.6**	**2,247.5**
By maturity										
Short-term	243.7	237.0	282.3	307.3	368.2	369.7	295.5	271.8	274.2	281.4
Long-term	1,292.1	1,418.9	1,522.9	1,571.2	1,597.9	1,734.7	1,859.6	1,849.0	1,898.4	1,966.1
By type of creditor										
Official	725.5	787.7	827.9	886.1	852.1	902.3	929.4	918.2	946.3	966.1
Banks	379.2	373.0	410.2	459.7	525.2	552.8	542.4	544.6	556.2	579.8
Other private	431.0	495.4	567.1	532.7	588.8	649.2	683.2	658.0	670.1	701.6
Regional groups										
Africa										
Total debt	**267.0**	**286.7**	**302.9**	**301.2**	**295.9**	**294.7**	**295.0**	**284.7**	**284.2**	**285.4**
By maturity										
Short-term	28.2	31.2	34.4	37.0	45.0	43.0	46.4	24.2	26.3	28.2
Long-term	238.8	255.5	268.5	264.2	251.0	251.7	248.6	260.5	257.9	257.1
By type of creditor										
Official	184.6	201.1	213.5	213.5	206.8	212.0	210.7	199.9	198.1	195.1
Banks	43.8	44.4	44.1	43.3	40.7	36.3	36.3	34.3	31.7	31.5
Other private	38.7	41.2	45.3	44.4	48.3	46.4	48.0	50.4	54.4	58.7
Sub-Sahara										
Total debt	**211.1**	**224.8**	**236.0**	**234.5**	**234.4**	**232.8**	**235.6**	**230.9**	**232.6**	**236.5**
By maturity										
Short-term	26.0	29.1	32.5	34.6	43.0	40.9	43.8	21.5	23.4	25.1
Long-term	185.0	195.6	203.6	199.9	191.4	191.8	191.8	209.4	209.2	211.5
By type of creditor										
Official	152.4	162.8	169.1	167.8	163.8	168.4	169.6	162.4	161.5	160.0
Banks	20.0	20.8	21.7	22.4	22.3	18.0	18.0	18.1	16.7	17.8
Other private	38.7	41.2	45.3	44.4	48.3	46.4	48.0	50.4	54.4	58.7
Developing Asia										
Total debt	**466.7**	**519.9**	**580.0**	**614.5**	**660.1**	**681.9**	**705.4**	**681.6**	**693.8**	**717.6**
By maturity										
Short-term	68.3	76.3	110.2	114.6	152.9	151.2	74.0	62.4	61.2	62.9
Long-term	398.4	443.6	469.8	499.9	507.1	530.6	631.4	619.2	632.5	654.8
By type of creditor										
Official	225.4	253.8	254.3	266.0	268.8	290.5	308.9	314.6	324.0	331.6
Banks	108.3	122.1	159.3	190.2	214.5	209.3	190.4	187.3	192.1	202.6
Other private	133.0	144.1	166.3	158.4	176.8	182.1	206.1	179.8	177.6	183.4
Middle East, Malta, and Turkey										
Total debt	**275.9**	**283.4**	**301.9**	**315.9**	**338.3**	**372.0**	**388.0**	**399.7**	**414.6**	**432.9**
By maturity										
Short-term	71.9	49.6	51.3	59.8	67.3	79.3	80.9	83.8	86.1	87.4
Long-term	204.0	233.8	250.7	256.1	270.9	292.7	307.1	315.9	328.5	345.5
By type of creditor										
Official	151.8	161.7	172.6	173.1	170.8	178.1	182.8	187.7	194.8	202.7
Banks	85.5	90.0	90.9	111.4	150.0	172.4	183.3	192.0	199.0	207.8
Other private	38.6	31.7	38.5	31.4	17.4	21.4	21.9	20.0	20.8	22.4
Western Hemisphere										
Total debt	**526.2**	**566.0**	**620.4**	**647.0**	**671.8**	**755.8**	**766.6**	**754.9**	**780.0**	**811.6**
By maturity										
Short-term	75.3	80.0	86.5	96.0	102.9	96.1	94.2	101.4	100.6	102.9
Long-term	450.9	486.0	533.9	551.0	568.9	659.7	672.4	653.4	679.5	708.7
By type of creditor										
Official	163.8	171.1	187.5	233.6	205.6	221.7	227.1	216.1	229.5	236.6
Banks	141.7	116.5	115.8	114.8	120.0	134.8	132.3	131.0	133.3	137.9
Other private	220.7	278.4	317.1	298.5	346.2	399.4	407.3	407.8	417.2	437.1

Table 40. Developing Countries—by Analytical Criteria: External Debt, by Maturity and Type of Creditor

(Billions of U.S. dollars)

	1993	1994	1995	1996	1997	1998	1999	2000	2001	2002
By source of export earnings										
Fuel										
Total debt	**274.7**	**288.7**	**299.6**	**299.5**	**309.5**	**332.7**	**340.3**	**338.0**	**336.5**	**338.4**
By maturity										
Short-term	56.3	45.1	43.7	49.9	58.6	68.6	70.6	48.6	50.1	50.6
Long-term	218.4	243.5	256.0	249.6	250.9	264.1	269.7	289.5	286.5	287.7
By type of creditor										
Official	136.9	149.2	164.2	161.6	161.3	164.8	165.3	163.3	163.5	163.1
Banks	87.2	87.2	82.7	99.5	108.5	121.4	125.7	127.5	125.9	127.2
Other private	50.6	52.2	52.7	38.4	39.6	46.6	49.2	47.2	47.2	48.0
Nonfuel										
Total debt	**1,261.1**	**1,367.3**	**1,505.6**	**1,579.1**	**1,656.7**	**1,771.7**	**1,814.7**	**1,782.9**	**1,836.1**	**1,909.1**
By maturity										
Short-term	187.4	191.9	238.7	257.5	309.6	301.1	224.9	223.3	224.1	230.8
Long-term	1,073.7	1,175.4	1,266.9	1,321.6	1,347.1	1,470.6	1,589.9	1,559.6	1,611.9	1,678.4
By type of creditor										
Official	588.7	638.5	663.7	724.5	690.8	737.5	764.1	754.9	782.9	803.0
Banks	292.0	285.7	327.5	360.2	416.7	431.5	416.6	417.1	430.3	452.6
Other private	380.4	443.2	514.5	494.3	549.2	602.7	634.0	610.8	622.8	653.6
Nonfuel primary products										
Total debt	**183.0**	**196.0**	**203.5**	**203.6**	**202.3**	**211.3**	**212.3**	**213.4**	**217.6**	**225.2**
By maturity										
Short-term	17.6	18.2	19.8	19.4	19.1	16.9	14.8	17.6	16.5	16.6
Long-term	165.3	177.8	183.7	184.2	183.2	194.4	197.5	195.8	201.1	208.6
By type of creditor										
Official	122.5	132.0	136.4	132.1	131.8	133.7	137.9	138.0	141.5	145.2
Banks	28.7	31.1	33.1	34.4	31.9	31.4	31.9	30.0	26.5	26.0
Other private	31.8	32.9	33.9	37.2	38.5	46.3	42.5	45.5	49.5	54.0
By external financing source										
Net debtor countries										
Total debt	**1,497.5**	**1,617.9**	**1,763.4**	**1,831.5**	**1,907.3**	**2,031.1**	**2,077.8**	**2,043.3**	**2,096.9**	**2,170.6**
By maturity										
Short-term	220.8	211.2	259.5	279.7	335.5	329.8	255.5	231.4	232.4	239.0
Long-term	1277	1407	1504	1552	1572	1701	1822	1812	1865	1932
By type of creditor										
Official	721.0	782.9	823.0	880.5	846.5	896.2	924.1	913.4	942.1	962.0
Banks	364.0	356.5	394.9	426.7	482.6	499.0	484.5	485.2	498.9	522.2
Other private	412.5	478.4	545.5	524.3	578.3	635.9	669.2	644.7	655.9	686.4
Official financing										
Total debt	**162.3**	**176.1**	**183.2**	**182.0**	**178.0**	**179.7**	**178.0**	**164.5**	**163.9**	**165.1**
By maturity										
Short-term	9.0	8.0	8.0	5.8	5.1	5.2	5.3	5.3	5.4	5.6
Long-term	153	168	175	176	173	175	173	159	158	159
By type of creditor										
Official	128.7	142.4	149.7	150.0	148.1	151.6	151.9	141.3	142.8	145.0
Banks	27.2	27.0	23.8	22.5	19.1	18.2	16.8	14.8	12.8	11.8
Other private	6.4	6.7	9.7	9.5	10.9	9.9	9.2	8.3	8.2	8.3

Table 40 *(concluded)*

	1993	1994	1995	1996	1997	1998	1999	2000	2001	2002
Net debtor countries by debt-servicing experience										
Countries with arrears and/or rescheduling during 1994–98										
Total debt	**683.7**	**727.1**	**766.9**	**797.7**	**831.7**	**890.3**	**910.4**	**883.4**	**898.3**	**915.5**
By maturity										
Short-term	92.0	77.2	89.0	101.2	148.6	150.1	86.5	60.6	59.2	59.6
Long-term	591.6	649.9	677.9	696.4	683.1	740.2	824.0	822.8	839.1	855.9
By type of creditor										
Official	379.1	405.6	423.0	488.9	468.7	491.9	506.0	491.9	501.2	510.8
Banks	191.4	155.4	154.6	178.1	188.5	190.8	181.1	179.8	182.3	186.5
Other private	113.2	166.1	189.2	130.7	174.5	207.6	223.4	211.8	214.7	218.2
Other groups										
Heavily indebted poor countries										
Total debt	**191.2**	**202.3**	**205.0**	**202.0**	**199.3**	**200.5**	**202.5**	**193.5**	**195.0**	**198.5**
By maturity										
Short-term	9.8	8.7	9.1	8.9	8.6	5.8	5.7	4.8	5.3	5.5
Long-term	181.4	193.6	195.9	193.1	190.7	194.6	196.8	188.6	189.7	193.1
By type of creditor										
Official	156.7	167.8	171.6	166.3	158.9	162.7	165.2	157.1	159.6	162.0
Banks	17.1	18.5	18.4	19.6	18.8	15.2	15.4	15.8	14.7	15.6
Other private	17.4	16.0	15.0	16.0	21.6	22.6	21.8	20.6	20.7	21.0
Middle East and north Africa										
Total debt	**285.0**	**301.2**	**319.9**	**327.9**	**336.5**	**358.7**	**364.6**	**363.1**	**369.9**	**380.0**
By maturity										
Short-term	55.4	40.1	37.2	41.4	46.3	53.7	53.3	53.5	54.8	55.2
Long-term	229.6	261.1	282.6	286.5	290.2	305.0	311.3	309.5	315.0	324.8
By type of creditor										
Official	174.0	187.9	205.9	207.6	199.1	202.7	202.3	200.8	205.2	209.9
Banks	90.1	92.2	90.2	108.3	118.4	132.9	138.8	140.5	142.2	146.0
Other private	20.9	21.1	23.7	12.1	19.0	23.1	23.6	21.7	22.6	24.2

Table 41. Developing Countries: Ratio of External Debt to GDP[1]

	1993	1994	1995	1996	1997	1998	1999	2000	2001	2002
Developing countries	**40.6**	**41.7**	**40.3**	**38.2**	**37.8**	**41.8**	**43.4**	**39.2**	**38.2**	**36.7**
Regional groups										
Africa	70.4	77.8	73.7	69.1	66.5	69.0	69.3	66.0	64.3	61.5
Sub-Sahara	73.2	80.2	74.0	70.5	67.9	71.8	73.2	71.2	71.4	68.7
Developing Asia	32.8	35.4	32.9	31.0	32.2	35.8	34.3	30.8	29.4	28.0
Other developing Asia	53.4	53.4	53.0	51.7	58.3	81.1	72.6	65.2	61.9	56.8
Middle East, Malta, and Turkey	46.6	52.3	48.4	46.6	47.6	53.7	53.9	49.0	47.8	46.7
Western Hemisphere	37.8	35.5	36.9	35.4	33.6	37.7	43.4	38.8	38.5	37.5
Analytical groups										
By source of export earnings										
Fuel	59.4	65.3	59.1	53.4	52.4	59.9	56.6	48.2	48.1	48.3
Nonfuel	37.9	38.7	37.9	36.2	35.9	39.6	41.6	37.9	36.8	35.2
of which, primary products	87.7	87.3	76.5	71.6	67.0	71.5	75.8	74.6	73.3	70.4
By external financing source										
Net debtor countries	42.1	43.2	41.7	39.4	38.8	42.5	44.4	40.5	39.3	37.6
of which, official financing	82.4	96.4	90.5	81.7	77.5	77.3	74.5	65.7	62.2	59.4
Net debtor countries by debt-servicing experience										
Countries with arrears and/or rescheduling during 1994–98	65.4	61.9	54.2	50.9	51.8	61.7	73.7	66.8	66.0	62.3
Other groups										
Heavily indebted poor countries	120.4	132.0	124.9	116.0	108.6	107.4	106.2	99.5	94.8	89.9
Middle East and north Africa	56.3	59.6	58.1	53.6	53.4	59.3	56.3	49.7	50.3	51.6

[1]Debt at year-end in percent of GDP in year indicated.

Table 42. Developing Countries: Debt-Service Ratios[1]

(Percent of exports of goods and services)

	1993	1994	1995	1996	1997	1998	1999	2000	2001	2002
Interest payments[2]										
Developing countries	**9.0**	**8.6**	**9.0**	**8.5**	**7.8**	**9.0**	**9.1**	**7.3**	**7.1**	**7.1**
Regional groups										
Africa	9.3	9.3	9.1	9.3	7.5	8.2	7.6	6.1	6.9	7.7
Sub-Sahara	7.7	8.0	7.8	8.3	6.4	7.0	6.7	5.5	6.9	8.1
Developing Asia	6.9	6.4	6.1	6.0	4.9	5.7	6.2	4.3	3.5	3.7
Other developing Asia	6.2	6.0	6.2	6.2	6.5	7.4	7.0	5.6	5.0	5.7
Middle East, Malta, and Turkey	3.4	4.2	5.8	4.7	4.7	6.3	5.9	4.7	5.9	6.2
Western Hemisphere	17.7	16.3	16.8	16.3	15.9	17.6	18.2	16.5	15.8	14.5
Analytical groups										
By source of export earnings										
Fuel	5.2	4.8	5.0	4.8	3.9	4.9	4.2	2.8	3.6	4.2
Nonfuel	10.2	9.6	9.9	9.5	8.7	9.8	10.2	8.7	8.1	7.7
of which, primary products	9.8	8.4	8.3	7.1	6.7	7.9	7.0	6.9	7.5	7.9
By external financing source										
Net debtor countries	10.1	9.5	9.8	9.5	8.5	9.6	9.9	8.1	7.7	7.6
of which, official financing	10.4	10.8	8.8	8.9	7.5	8.2	6.6	5.4	5.1	4.9
Net debtor countries by debt-servicing experience										
Countries with arrears and/or rescheduling during 1994–98	12.0	10.4	11.5	11.9	11.1	13.2	13.3	10.3	10.3	11.4
Other groups										
Heavily indebted poor countries	10.4	11.4	8.9	10.4	6.4	6.9	5.1	4.5	4.5	6.3
Middle East and north Africa	3.4	4.0	4.8	4.1	3.9	4.6	4.4	3.0	3.6	3.9
Amortization[2]										
Developing countries	14.3	14.0	14.4	16.0	17.1	17.7	19.7	15.2	12.4	11.5
Regional groups										
Africa	20.6	20.0	18.9	13.8	13.7	15.4	14.0	12.1	11.6	9.2
Sub-Sahara	14.1	13.7	13.6	10.1	11.0	13.7	12.4	11.3	11.3	8.1
Developing Asia	10.9	10.9	10.5	10.0	10.2	12.2	12.9	9.0	9.0	8.0
Other developing Asia	12.1	12.4	11.4	11.0	13.2	17.0	18.1	12.2	12.9	11.1
Middle East, Malta, and Turkey	9.0	10.2	10.7	13.6	10.8	12.0	10.6	8.1	6.6	6.3
Western Hemisphere	21.4	20.2	22.6	30.5	37.1	33.1	43.1	35.5	24.8	23.9
Analytical groups										
By source of export earnings										
Fuel	10.9	12.6	14.3	14.8	13.4	14.0	10.8	7.0	6.9	5.9
Nonfuel	15.3	14.4	14.4	16.3	18.0	18.4	21.7	17.6	13.8	12.8
of which, primary products	14.6	13.9	15.7	15.3	11.9	13.1	13.4	12.5	13.9	11.8
By external financing source										
Net debtor countries	16.3	15.2	15.7	17.1	18.7	19.0	21.6	17.0	13.6	12.5
of which, official financing	25.4	26.7	24.7	16.7	13.2	12.4	10.5	8.7	8.8	8.3
Net debtor countries by debt-servicing experience										
Countries with arrears and/or rescheduling during 1994–98	21.2	19.9	22.2	21.8	27.5	32.9	40.5	26.1	20.1	17.6
Other groups										
Heavily indebted poor countries	23.4	24.1	21.2	11.5	12.9	16.3	14.7	13.7	12.4	6.9
Middle East and north Africa	12.2	12.7	13.6	15.6	12.2	12.5	9.4	5.8	5.8	5.8

[1]Excludes service payments to the International Monetary Fund.

[2]Interest payments on total debt and amortization on long-term debt. Estimates through 2000 reflect debt-service payments actually made. The estimates for 2001 and 2002 take into account projected exceptional financing items, including accumulation of arrears and rescheduling agreements. In some cases, amortization on account of debt-reduction operations is included.

Table 43. IMF Charges and Repurchases to the IMF[1]
(Percent of exports of goods and services)

	1993	1994	1995	1996	1997	1998	1999	2000
Developing countries	**0.9**	**0.7**	**0.9**	**0.6**	**0.7**	**0.5**	**1.0**	**1.1**
Regional groups								
Africa	1.1	0.8	2.4	0.4	0.9	1.0	0.5	0.2
Sub-Sahara	0.7	0.5	2.8	0.2	0.6	0.7	0.2	0.1
Developing Asia	0.3	0.5	0.4	0.4	0.2	0.2	0.2	0.2
Other developing Asia	0.3	0.2	0.2	0.2	0.2	0.2	0.3	0.4
Middle East, Malta, and Turkey	—	—	0.1	0.1	—	0.1	0.2	0.1
Western Hemisphere	2.6	1.5	1.6	1.6	1.9	1.1	3.2	4.2
Analytical groups								
By source of export earnings								
Fuel	0.6	0.4	0.5	0.3	0.4	0.6	0.4	0.2
Nonfuel	1.0	0.8	1.0	0.7	0.7	0.5	1.1	1.4
By external financing source								
Net debtor countries	1.1	0.8	1.0	0.7	0.7	0.6	1.1	1.3
of which, official financing	2.0	1.0	4.9	0.6	0.9	1.3	0.9	0.4
Net debtor countries by debt-servicing experience								
Countries with arrears and/or rescheduling during 1994–98	1.4	0.6	1.4	0.4	0.4	0.5	1.3	2.2
Other groups								
Heavily indebted poor countries	1.7	1.0	5.5	0.5	0.5	0.5	0.3	0.3
Middle East and north Africa	0.4	0.3	0.3	0.2	0.3	0.4	0.3	0.1
Countries in transition	**0.4**	**1.2**	**1.4**	**0.8**	**0.6**	**1.0**	**2.4**	**1.8**
Central and eastern Europe	0.8	2.3	2.7	0.9	0.4	0.5	0.4	0.4
Commonwealth of Independent States and Mongolia	0.1	0.2	0.3	0.8	0.9	1.6	4.9	3.2
Russia	0.1	0.2	0.3	1.0	1.0	1.9	5.8	3.1
Excluding Russia	—	0.1	0.3	0.4	0.5	1.2	2.8	3.4
Memorandum								
Total, billions of U.S. dollars								
General Resources Account	7.627	8.334	12.732	9.488	9.953	8.768	18.497	22.823
Charges	2.309	1.788	2.772	2.256	2.168	2.468	2.795	2.805
Repurchases	5.319	6.546	9.960	7.231	7.786	6.300	15.702	20.017
Trust Fund	0.063	0.015	0.015	—	0.007	0.001	0.001	—
Interest	0.003	—	—	—	—	—	—	—
Repayments	0.060	0.014	0.015	—	0.007	0.001	0.001	—
PRGF[2]	0.149	0.328	0.583	0.746	0.863	0.879	0.854	0.806
Interest	0.023	0.022	0.030	0.043	0.036	0.037	0.040	0.037
Repayments	0.126	0.306	0.552	0.703	0.827	0.842	0.813	0.771

[1]Excludes advanced economies. Charges on, and repurchases (or repayments of principal) for, use of International Monetary Fund credit.
[2]Poverty Reduction and Growth Facility (formerly ESAF - Enhanced Structural Adjustment Facility).

Table 44. Summary of Sources and Uses of World Saving

(Percent of GDP)

	Averages		1995	1996	1997	1998	1999	2000	2001	2002	Average 2003–2006
	1979–86	1987–94									
World											
Saving	23.0	23.0	23.4	23.2	23.7	23.0	23.0	23.6	23.4	23.1	23.4
Investment	24.2	24.1	24.3	23.9	24.1	23.3	23.0	23.4	23.6	23.7	24.2
Advanced economies											
Saving	21.9	21.6	21.3	21.4	21.9	22.0	21.6	21.6	21.4	21.0	21.3
Private	21.5	20.6	20.8	20.3	19.8	19.9	18.5	17.9	17.7	17.4	17.3
Public	0.4	1.0	0.5	1.0	2.1	2.1	3.1	3.7	3.7	3.6	4.0
Investment	23.0	22.2	21.5	21.6	21.9	21.8	21.9	22.5	22.0	21.9	22.1
Private	18.0	18.1	17.6	17.7	18.2	18.1	18.2	18.8	18.4	18.3	18.7
Public	4.7	4.1	3.9	3.9	3.7	3.6	3.8	3.7	3.6	3.5	3.4
Net lending	−1.1	−0.6	−0.2	−0.2	0.1	0.2	−0.3	−0.9	−0.6	−0.9	−0.8
Private	3.4	2.5	3.2	2.7	1.6	1.7	0.4	−0.9	−0.7	−0.9	−1.4
Public	−4.5	−3.1	−3.4	−2.9	−1.5	−1.5	−0.6	—	0.1	—	0.6
Current transfers	−0.2	−0.3	−0.3	−0.3	−0.3	−0.3	−0.4	−0.4	−0.4	−0.3	−0.3
Factor income	−0.6	−0.4	−0.4	−0.3	−0.2	−0.1	0.1	0.1	0.4	—	−0.1
Resource balance	−0.3	0.1	0.4	0.4	0.6	0.6	—	−0.6	−0.6	−0.5	−0.4
United States											
Saving	19.1	16.9	17.0	17.3	18.1	18.8	18.5	18.2	18.0	16.8	17.0
Private	19.7	17.8	17.1	16.5	16.2	15.7	14.4	13.0	13.0	12.6	12.7
Public	−0.6	−0.9	−0.1	0.8	1.9	3.2	4.0	5.2	5.0	4.2	4.3
Investment	21.0	18.6	18.7	19.1	19.9	20.8	21.1	21.8	21.0	20.5	20.8
Private	17.4	15.0	15.5	15.9	16.7	17.6	17.7	18.4	17.6	17.1	17.5
Public	3.6	3.6	3.2	3.2	3.2	3.2	3.3	3.4	3.4	3.4	3.3
Net lending	−1.9	−1.8	−1.7	−1.8	−1.8	−2.0	−2.6	−3.6	−3.0	−3.8	−3.8
Private	2.3	2.7	1.7	0.6	−0.6	−2.0	−3.3	−5.4	−4.6	−4.6	−4.8
Public	−4.2	−4.5	−3.3	−2.4	−1.3	—	0.7	1.8	1.6	0.8	1.0
Current transfers	−0.4	−0.4	−0.5	−0.5	−0.5	−0.5	−0.5	−0.5	−0.4	−0.4	−0.3
Factor income	0.2	0.2	0.1	—	−0.1	0.4	0.8	0.6	1.0	—	−0.4
Resource balance	−1.7	−1.5	−1.3	−1.3	−1.3	−1.9	−2.8	−3.7	−3.6	−3.4	−3.1
European Union											
Saving	20.4	20.5	20.7	20.4	21.0	20.9	20.8	20.9	21.0	21.3	22.0
Private	20.9	21.4	22.8	22.0	21.0	20.0	19.1	18.6	18.7	18.7	18.9
Public	−0.5	−0.9	−2.1	−1.6	−0.1	0.9	1.7	2.3	2.4	2.6	3.1
Investment	21.8	21.4	20.2	19.6	19.8	20.4	20.7	21.4	21.5	21.7	22.0
Private	17.1	18.2	17.6	17.1	17.4	18.1	18.3	19.0	19.0	19.1	19.4
Public	4.4	3.2	2.6	2.5	2.3	2.3	2.4	2.4	2.5	2.5	2.6
Net lending	−1.3	−0.9	0.5	0.8	1.2	0.5	0.1	−0.5	−0.4	−0.4	—
Private	3.6	3.3	5.3	4.9	3.6	1.9	0.8	−0.4	−0.3	−0.5	−0.5
Public	−5.1	−4.1	−4.7	−4.1	−2.4	−1.4	−0.7	−0.1	−0.2	0.1	0.5
Current transfers	−0.3	−0.4	−0.2	−0.4	−0.3	−0.4	−0.4	−0.5	−0.4	−0.4	−0.4
Factor income	−1.3	−1.1	−0.9	−0.7	−0.6	−0.8	−0.6	−0.5	−0.5	−0.5	−0.5
Resource balance	0.2	0.6	1.6	1.9	2.2	1.7	1.1	0.5	0.5	0.6	0.9
Japan											
Saving	31.3	33.0	30.2	30.6	30.9	29.9	28.6	28.6	28.4	28.1	27.7
Private	27.3	24.4	24.3	24.9	25.2	30.4	26.4	28.1	26.8	26.0	23.9
Public	4.0	8.6	5.9	5.7	5.8	−0.5	2.2	0.5	1.6	2.1	3.9
Investment	29.9	30.5	28.2	29.2	28.7	26.9	26.1	26.1	25.5	24.9	24.7
Private	21.6	23.5	19.9	20.6	21.1	19.5	18.3	18.8	18.7	18.6	19.2
Public	8.3	7.1	8.3	8.7	7.6	7.4	7.8	7.2	6.8	6.3	5.4
Net lending	1.4	2.5	2.0	1.4	2.2	3.0	2.5	2.5	2.8	3.2	3.1
Private	5.7	0.9	4.4	4.4	4.1	10.9	8.1	9.3	8.0	7.3	4.6
Public	−4.3	1.6	−2.3	−3.0	−1.9	−8.0	−5.6	−6.8	−5.2	−4.2	−1.6
Current transfers	−0.1	−0.1	−0.1	−0.2	−0.2	−0.2	−0.3	−0.2	−0.3	−0.3	−0.4
Factor income	0.2	0.8	0.8	1.1	1.3	1.3	1.3	1.2	1.6	1.8	1.8
Resource balance	1.3	1.9	1.4	0.5	1.1	1.9	1.5	1.5	1.6	1.6	1.6

Table 44 *(continued)*

	Averages		1995	1996	1997	1998	1999	2000	2001	2002	Average 2003–2006
	1979–86	1987–94									
Newly industrialized Asian economies											
Saving	...	35.1	33.4	32.3	32.3	32.6	32.2	31.0	30.3	30.4	30.1
Private	...	27.1	26.3	25.4	25.3	25.4	25.6	24.3	23.5	23.7	23.5
Public	...	8.0	7.1	6.9	7.1	7.3	6.6	6.7	6.7	6.7	6.6
	...										
Investment	...	30.8	33.2	32.7	31.6	24.2	25.9	26.9	26.1	26.6	27.0
Private	...	24.6	26.5	26.2	25.1	17.5	18.8	20.8	20.8	21.2	21.8
Public	...	6.3	6.6	6.6	6.5	6.7	7.0	6.1	5.4	5.4	5.2
Net lending	...	4.3	0.2	–0.4	0.7	8.5	6.4	4.1	4.1	3.8	3.2
Private	...	2.6	–0.3	–0.8	0.1	7.9	6.8	3.5	2.7	2.4	1.8
Public	...	1.7	0.5	0.4	0.6	0.6	–0.5	0.6	1.4	1.3	1.4
Current transfers	...	—	–0.4	–0.3	–0.4	0.1	–0.2	–0.4	–0.5	–0.4	–0.3
Factor income	...	0.3	0.3	0.2	0.6	0.1	0.3	0.5	1.5	1.6	1.6
Resource balance	...	3.9	0.3	–0.2	0.5	8.2	6.3	4.0	3.1	2.6	1.9
Developing countries											
Saving	21.8	24.2	26.8	26.4	27.0	25.5	25.3	26.3	26.1	25.9	25.9
Investment	24.0	25.9	28.8	27.6	27.5	26.1	25.1	25.3	26.1	26.4	26.8
Net lending	–2.1	–1.7	–1.9	–1.2	–0.5	–0.6	0.2	1.0	—	–0.5	–0.8
Current transfers	0.8	1.0	1.1	1.1	1.1	0.9	0.9	1.1	1.2	1.2	1.1
Factor income	–1.7	–1.7	–1.0	–1.4	–1.5	–1.7	–1.9	–1.9	–1.9	–1.7	–1.6
Resource balance	–1.2	–1.1	–2.0	–0.9	–0.1	0.3	1.2	1.8	0.7	0.1	–0.3
Memorandum											
Acquisition of foreign assets	0.8	1.4	1.2	3.1	4.2	2.5	3.0	4.0	3.3	3.1	2.4
Change in reserves	0.1	1.0	1.7	2.1	1.4	—	0.8	1.3	1.0	1.2	1.1
Regional groups											
Africa											
Saving	19.5	16.6	15.5	16.5	15.8	15.8	15.7	18.3	18.3	18.7	20.8
Investment	22.4	19.4	19.8	19.0	18.6	20.5	20.1	19.5	20.6	21.3	22.7
Net lending	–2.9	–2.9	–4.3	–2.6	–2.9	–4.7	–4.4	–1.2	–2.3	–2.6	–1.8
Current transfers	1.4	2.8	3.0	2.9	3.1	3.2	3.2	3.5	3.4	3.2	3.0
Factor income	–1.1	–3.7	–3.9	–4.9	–4.8	–3.5	–4.6	–5.2	–4.6	–4.2	–3.2
Resource balance	–3.2	–1.9	–3.4	–0.6	–1.1	–4.4	–3.1	0.5	–1.2	–1.7	–1.7
Memorandum											
Acquisition of foreign assets	0.2	0.9	1.2	3.1	3.4	0.4	1.7	3.9	4.0	3.2	2.3
Change in reserves	—	0.4	0.4	2.3	2.3	–0.4	0.6	2.9	2.9	2.2	1.5
Developing Asia											
Saving	24.9	29.7	32.9	32.1	33.2	31.7	30.9	31.3	31.2	30.5	29.8
Investment	27.1	30.7	34.6	33.1	32.1	29.2	28.7	29.6	30.0	29.8	29.6
Net lending	–2.1	–1.0	–1.7	–1.0	1.1	2.6	2.1	1.7	1.2	0.7	0.2
Current transfers	1.2	0.9	1.2	1.3	1.6	1.3	1.3	1.4	1.3	1.3	1.2
Factor income	–0.6	–0.4	–1.3	–0.7	–0.8	–1.1	–1.2	–1.1	–1.0	–1.0	–1.2
Resource balance	–2.7	–1.5	–1.6	–1.6	0.4	2.4	2.0	1.5	0.9	0.4	0.2
Memorandum											
Acquisition of foreign assets	1.8	2.1	2.9	3.3	5.7	4.3	4.1	4.2	3.6	3.6	3.0
Change in reserves	0.2	1.2	2.0	2.1	1.6	0.8	1.3	0.9	0.7	1.1	1.3
Middle East, Malta, and Turkey											
Saving	23.1	19.7	23.9	21.5	21.5	18.8	20.4	23.4	22.7	22.8	22.2
Investment	23.7	23.4	24.2	21.2	22.1	23.2	20.2	17.4	19.9	22.1	23.5
Net lending	–0.6	–3.7	–0.3	0.3	–0.6	–4.4	0.2	6.0	2.8	0.7	–1.3
Current transfers	0.1	—	–0.7	–1.3	–2.5	–3.5	–4.2	–2.6	–1.0	–0.8	–0.6
Factor income	–0.6	–1.5	7.0	0.9	0.1	–1.0	–1.0	–1.2	–1.6	–1.0	0.1
Resource balance	–0.1	–2.1	–6.5	0.8	1.8	0.1	5.4	9.8	5.4	2.5	–0.7
Memorandum											
Acquisition of foreign assets	1.8	–0.2	–10.3	2.1	2.3	–0.1	2.6	8.5	5.7	3.9	1.5
Change in reserves	0.2	0.9	2.0	2.6	0.9	–1.6	0.9	4.1	2.9	2.0	0.7

Table 44 *(continued)*

	Averages		1995	1996	1997	1998	1999	2000	2001	2002	Average 2003–2006
	1979–86	1987–94									
Western Hemisphere											
Saving	18.3	19.3	19.1	19.3	19.2	17.5	17.3	17.7	17.5	17.9	18.7
Investment	20.8	21.2	21.3	21.1	22.5	22.1	20.3	20.2	21.0	21.2	21.8
Net lending	−2.4	−1.8	−2.2	−1.9	−3.3	−4.6	−3.0	−2.5	−3.4	−3.4	−3.1
Current transfers	0.4	1.1	1.1	1.0	1.0	1.1	1.2	1.2	1.1	1.0	1.0
Factor income	−3.9	−3.3	−2.9	−2.7	−2.6	−2.7	−3.1	−3.1	−3.3	−3.1	−3.1
Resource balance	1.0	0.4	−0.5	−0.2	−1.6	−3.0	−1.1	−0.6	−1.3	−1.3	−0.9
Memorandum											
Acquisition of foreign assets	0.8	1.2	2.5	3.0	1.8	0.2	0.7	1.3	1.2	1.5	1.4
Change in reserves	−0.1	0.8	1.4	1.8	1.0	−1.0	−0.6	0.6	0.3	0.5	0.5
Analytical groups											
By source of export earnings											
Fuel											
Saving	26.0	20.0	23.7	24.2	23.5	18.6	20.7	28.0	26.9	27.3	26.6
Investment	24.2	22.7	23.3	19.8	21.3	24.1	20.0	15.6	20.1	23.4	25.9
Net lending	1.7	−2.7	0.4	4.5	2.1	−5.5	0.8	12.4	6.8	3.9	0.7
Current transfers	−2.5	−2.9	−2.4	−3.0	−4.4	−5.7	−6.5	−4.5	−2.5	−2.1	−1.6
Factor income	−0.1	−2.1	6.6	−0.6	−1.4	−1.8	−2.4	−3.0	−1.9	−1.2	−0.3
Resource balance	4.3	2.2	−3.8	8.1	7.9	2.0	9.7	19.9	11.2	7.2	2.6
Memorandum											
Acquisition of foreign assets	2.7	−0.1	−12.6	4.4	3.7	−1.4	2.1	12.4	7.4	5.6	2.2
Change in reserves	—	—	0.2	4.2	1.8	−3.0	−0.8	7.0	3.9	3.1	0.9
Nonfuel											
Saving	21.0	24.7	27.2	26.6	27.4	26.2	25.8	26.1	26.1	25.8	25.9
Investment	23.9	26.3	29.4	28.5	28.1	26.3	25.6	26.3	26.7	26.7	26.8
Net lending	−2.9	−1.6	−2.2	−1.8	−0.7	—	0.1	−0.2	−0.6	−0.9	−1.0
Current transfers	1.4	1.6	1.5	1.5	1.7	1.5	1.6	1.6	1.6	1.5	1.3
Factor income	−2.0	−1.7	−1.9	−1.5	−1.5	−1.7	−1.8	−1.8	−1.9	−1.8	−1.8
Resource balance	−2.2	−1.5	−1.8	−1.9	−0.9	0.1	0.3	—	−0.3	−0.6	−0.5
Memorandum											
Acquisition of foreign assets	0.4	1.7	2.7	3.0	4.3	2.9	3.0	3.1	2.9	2.9	2.5
Change in reserves	—	1.1	1.8	1.9	1.4	0.4	0.9	0.8	0.7	1.0	1.1
By external financing source											
Net debtor countries											
Saving	21.4	24.5	27.0	26.5	27.1	25.8	25.4	26.1	26.0	25.8	25.9
Investment	24.0	26.1	29.0	27.9	27.7	26.1	25.3	25.5	26.3	26.5	26.8
Net lending	−2.6	−1.6	−2.0	−1.4	−0.6	−0.3	0.1	0.6	−0.3	−0.7	−0.9
Current transfers	1.2	1.5	1.4	1.4	1.4	1.2	1.1	1.3	1.4	1.4	1.3
Factor income	−1.8	−2.0	−1.2	−1.6	−1.7	−1.9	−2.1	−2.1	−2.0	−1.9	−1.8
Resource balance	−1.9	−1.1	−2.3	−1.1	−0.3	0.4	1.1	1.4	0.3	−0.2	−0.4
Memorandum											
Acquisition of foreign assets	0.5	1.6	1.2	3.0	4.2	2.7	3.0	3.8	3.2	3.0	2.4
Change in reserves	—	1.0	1.7	2.1	1.4	0.2	0.8	1.3	1.0	1.2	1.1
Official financing											
Saving	14.0	13.8	14.9	15.9	17.1	15.7	18.0	20.1	19.7	19.2	21.6
Investment	20.2	19.0	22.9	21.4	20.4	21.6	21.2	21.0	22.0	23.2	24.5
Net lending	−6.2	−5.2	−8.1	−5.5	−3.3	−5.9	−3.1	−1.0	−2.4	−4.0	−2.9
Current transfers	4.2	3.8	4.5	4.3	4.1	4.4	4.6	5.0	4.9	4.6	4.3
Factor income	−5.1	−3.3	−4.8	−4.0	−3.3	−4.0	−2.9	−3.4	−3.4	−3.3	−2.4
Resource balance	−5.2	−5.7	−7.7	−5.9	−4.1	−6.3	−4.8	−2.5	−3.9	−5.4	−4.8
Memorandum											
Acquisition of foreign assets	0.6	0.7	0.8	1.4	2.5	−0.2	1.3	3.3	3.5	2.3	1.6
Change in reserves	0.2	0.6	0.3	1.4	2.1	−0.6	0.6	3.2	3.3	2.3	1.6

Table 44 *(concluded)*

	Averages		1995	1996	1997	1998	1999	2000	2001	2002	Average 2003–2006
	1979–86	1987–94									
New debtor countries by debt-servicing experience											
Countries with arrears and/or rescheduling during 1994–98											
Saving	17.6	20.0	20.8	20.0	19.6	17.1	17.4	19.5	19.7	19.9	20.6
Investment	21.0	22.6	24.6	23.0	23.3	20.9	18.5	18.1	20.3	21.3	22.7
Net lending	−3.4	−2.6	−3.8	−3.0	−3.7	−3.8	−1.1	1.4	−0.6	−1.4	−2.1
Current transfers	0.6	1.3	1.5	1.1	0.6	0.3	—	0.6	1.3	1.4	1.4
Factor income	−2.7	−2.7	0.1	−1.8	−2.5	−3.0	−2.8	−3.5	−3.1	−2.8	−2.7
Resource balance	−1.3	−0.3	−5.4	−2.3	−1.9	−1.2	1.7	4.2	1.2	—	−0.8
Memorandum											
Acquisition of foreign assets	0.3	0.7	−3.5	1.5	1.5	0.1	1.3	5.1	3.1	2.5	1.5
Change in reserves	−0.2	0.6	1.6	1.4	0.4	−0.5	0.2	3.3	2.1	1.8	1.1
Countries in transition											
Saving	...	...	23.7	22.0	21.0	17.4	22.7	27.0	25.5	24.8	24.9
Investment	...	...	24.6	24.4	24.0	21.1	20.2	21.3	22.7	23.7	25.4
Net lending	...	...	−0.9	−2.4	−3.0	−3.8	2.5	5.7	2.7	1.1	−0.5
Current transfers	...	...	0.7	0.7	0.8	0.9	1.1	1.0	1.0	0.9	1.1
Factor income	...	...	−0.7	−0.7	−0.9	−2.5	−2.7	−2.3	−2.1	−2.1	−2.0
Resource balance	...	...	−0.8	−2.5	−2.8	−2.2	4.1	7.0	3.8	2.3	0.3
Memorandum											
Acquisition of foreign assets	...	...	3.9	1.9	5.1	3.3	7.0	8.5	6.3	5.0	3.2
Change in reserves	...	...	3.7	0.2	1.2	−0.2	1.0	3.4	2.5	1.8	1.1

Note: The estimates in this table are based on individual countries' national accounts and balance of payments statistics. For many countries, the estimates of national saving are built up from national accounts data on gross domestic investment and from balance-of-payments-based data on net foreign investment. The latter, which is equivalent to the current account balance, comprises three components: current transfers, net factor income, and the resource balance. The mixing of data sources, which is dictated by availability, implies that the estimates for national saving that are derived incorporate the statistical discrepancies. Furthermore, errors, omissions, and asymmetries in balance of payments statistics affect the estimates for net lending; at the global level, net lending, which in theory would be zero, equals the world current account discrepancy. Notwithstanding these statistical shortcomings, flow of funds estimates, such as those presented in this table, provide a useful framework for analyzing development in saving and investment, both over time and across regions and countries. Country group composites are weighted by GDP valued at purchasing power parities (PPPs) as a share of total world GDP.

Table 45. Summary of World Medium-Term Baseline Scenario

	Eight-Year Averages		Four-Year Averages					Four-Year Averages
	1983–90	1991–98	1999–2002	1999	2000	2001	2002	2003–2006

Annual percent change unless otherwise noted

World real GDP	**3.8**	**3.0**	**3.8**	**3.5**	**4.8**	**3.2**	**3.9**	**4.5**
Advanced economies	3.7	2.5	3.0	3.4	4.1	1.9	2.7	3.2
Developing countries	4.5	5.7	5.0	3.8	5.8	5.0	5.6	6.2
Countries in transition	2.4	–4.9	4.2	2.6	5.8	4.0	4.2	4.9
Memorandum								
Potential output								
Major advanced economies	2.8	2.7	2.6	2.6	2.6	2.6	2.7	2.8
World trade, volume[1]	**5.6**	**6.4**	**7.7**	**5.3**	**12.4**	**6.7**	**6.5**	**6.8**
Imports								
Advanced economies	7.2	6.2	8.1	7.9	11.4	6.7	6.5	6.5
Developing countries	1.5	8.4	8.7	1.6	16.9	8.8	7.9	8.4
Countries in transition	2.1	–0.5	5.1	–7.3	13.3	8.6	6.9	6.7
Exports								
Advanced economies	5.9	6.5	7.2	5.0	11.4	6.2	6.2	6.4
Developing countries	5.2	8.8	8.4	4.1	15.7	7.1	7.0	8.3
Countries in transition	0.3	0.5	6.2	0.6	14.9	4.6	5.1	5.9
Terms of trade								
Advanced economies	1.3	0.2	–0.3	0.1	–2.2	0.2	0.8	0.3
Developing countries	–2.9	–0.9	1.7	3.8	6.2	–1.4	–1.6	–0.5
Countries in transition	–0.1	–2.3	1.2	–0.1	6.8	–0.7	–1.0	–0.4
World prices in U.S. dollars								
Manufactures	5.2	–0.1	–1.8	–2.0	–6.2	0.2	1.1	1.0
Oil	–4.2	–6.8	14.5	37.5	56.9	–9.6	–11.8	–3.5
Nonfuel primary commodities	1.7	–0.5	–0.2	–7.1	1.8	0.5	4.5	4.0
Consumer prices								
Advanced economies	4.7	2.8	1.9	1.4	2.3	2.1	1.8	2.0
Developing countries	47.9	29.4	5.8	6.7	6.1	5.7	4.8	3.9
Countries in transition	9.0	165.2	21.7	43.9	20.1	15.3	10.0	6.7
Interest rates (in percent)								
Real six-month LIBOR[2]	5.3	3.0	3.3	4.0	4.6	2.5	2.2	2.0
World real long-term interest rate[3]	5.1	4.1	2.7	3.3	2.9	2.2	2.3	2.4

Percent of GDP

Balances on current account								
Advanced economies	–0.3	0.2	–0.9	–0.5	–1.0	–1.1	–1.0	–0.9
Developing countries	–1.7	–2.2	–0.0	–0.4	0.9	0.0	–0.7	–1.2
Countries in transition	0.2	–1.4	1.3	–0.3	3.6	1.6	0.4	–1.0
Total external debt								
Developing countries	37.9	40.1	39.4	43.4	39.2	38.2	36.7	32.9
Countries in transition	8.4	38.9	47.4	53.1	49.8	44.6	42.0	35.3
Debt service								
Developing countries	4.4	5.3	6.1	7.3	6.4	5.6	5.2	4.4
Countries in transition	2.1	4.1	6.3	6.7	6.4	6.2	6.1	5.6

[1]Data refer to trade in goods and services.
[2]London interbank offered rate on U.S. dollar deposits less percent change in U.S. GDP deflator.
[3]GDP-weighted average of ten-year (or nearest maturity) government bond rates for the United States, Japan, Germany, France, Italy, the United Kingdom, and Canada.

Table 46. Developing Countries—Medium-Term Baseline Scenario: Selected Economic Indicators

	Eight-Year Averages		Four-Year Averages					Four-Year Averages
	1983–90	1991–98	1999–2002	1999	2000	2001	2002	2003–2006
			Annual percent change					
Developing countries								
Real GDP	4.5	5.7	5.0	3.8	5.8	5.0	5.6	6.2
Export volume[1]	5.2	8.8	8.4	4.1	15.7	7.1	7.0	8.3
Terms of trade[1]	−2.9	−0.9	1.7	3.8	6.2	−1.4	−1.6	−0.5
Import volume[1]	1.5	8.4	8.7	1.6	16.9	8.8	7.9	8.4
Regional groups								
Africa								
Real GDP	2.5	2.2	3.5	2.3	3.0	4.2	4.4	5.1
Export volume[1]	5.2	3.6	5.0	2.2	7.0	6.1	4.7	6.7
Terms of trade[1]	−1.2	−0.5	3.2	6.4	13.7	−3.4	−3.0	−1.1
Import volume[1]	2.4	4.7	5.0	2.1	6.4	7.6	3.9	5.6
Developing Asia								
Real GDP	7.2	7.8	6.3	6.1	6.9	5.9	6.3	7.1
Export volume[1]	8.1	12.3	11.1	6.5	22.8	7.8	8.0	9.9
Terms of trade[1]	−1.1	0.4	−1.7	−3.7	−3.9	0.8	0.3	0.4
Import volume[1]	5.7	10.3	11.9	4.9	22.0	11.2	10.1	10.6
Middle East, Malta, and Turkey								
Real GDP	3.3	3.7	3.4	0.8	5.4	2.9	4.6	5.0
Export volume[1]	3.7	6.7	4.6	−0.8	9.2	6.8	3.5	3.5
Terms of trade[1]	−6.0	−3.7	8.8	21.3	29.6	−4.6	−6.6	−2.9
Import volume[1]	−2.4	3.7	7.6	2.6	18.6	5.2	4.8	3.9
Western Hemisphere								
Real GDP	1.9	3.7	3.1	0.2	4.1	3.7	4.4	4.6
Export volume[1]	4.9	8.2	7.3	3.9	10.8	6.2	8.7	8.9
Terms of trade[1]	−1.8	−0.7	1.4	3.2	5.0	−1.9	−0.6	−0.3
Import volume[1]	1.2	11.8	5.5	−4.2	11.6	7.6	7.7	7.8
Analytical groups								
Net debtor countries by debt-servicing experience								
Countries with arrears and/or rescheduling during 1994–98								
Real GDP	2.8	3.4	3.8	2.0	4.3	4.2	4.7	5.1
Export volume[1]	5.2	6.0	6.6	0.4	10.8	8.0	7.5	8.0
Terms of trade[1]	−3.5	−1.6	1.6	2.5	8.7	−2.4	−2.0	−0.5
Import volume[1]	−1.1	6.0	4.6	−8.5	8.7	11.3	8.1	7.8

Table 46 *(concluded)*

	1990	1994	1998	1999	2000	2001	2002	2006
				Percent of exports of goods and services				
Developing countries								
Current account balance	−3.4	−10.1	−7.9	−1.5	3.0	—	−2.3	−4.4
Total external debt	191.5	191.9	181.0	172.0	137.3	134.0	130.9	106.5
Debt-service payments[2]	21.6	22.7	26.7	28.9	22.5	19.5	18.6	13.7
Interest payments	10.5	8.6	9.0	9.1	7.3	7.1	7.1	5.2
Amortization	11.1	14.0	17.7	19.7	15.2	12.4	11.5	8.6
Regional groups								
Africa								
Current account balance	−6.0	−12.0	−17.0	−12.1	0.8	−2.3	−3.4	−1.8
Total external debt	227.9	280.8	244.4	230.3	183.2	179.0	175.7	138.5
Debt-service payments[2]	16.0	29.3	23.7	21.5	18.1	18.5	16.9	14.0
Interest payments	7.2	9.3	8.2	7.6	6.1	6.9	7.7	5.2
Amortization	8.8	20.0	15.4	14.0	12.1	11.6	9.2	8.8
Developing Asia								
Current account balance	−7.5	−5.1	8.7	8.0	5.2	3.0	1.4	−0.6
Total external debt	164.0	140.3	126.4	121.5	97.9	92.4	87.6	67.9
Debt-service payments[2]	17.7	17.2	18.0	19.1	13.3	12.5	11.7	7.5
Interest payments	8.2	6.4	5.7	6.2	4.3	3.5	3.7	1.9
Amortization	9.6	10.9	12.2	12.9	9.0	9.0	8.0	5.6
Middle East, Malta, and Turkey								
Current account balance	0.3	−2.0	−13.4	2.5	16.7	13.9	6.8	−5.2
Total external debt	130.3	154.9	174.1	157.5	117.4	120.8	129.8	136.3
Debt-service payments[2]	13.7	14.4	18.3	16.5	12.8	12.5	12.5	15.0
Interest payments	6.7	4.2	6.3	5.9	4.7	5.9	6.2	7.2
Amortization	7.0	10.2	12.0	10.6	8.1	6.6	6.3	7.8
Western Hemisphere								
Current account balance	−0.7	−25.1	−31.2	−18.7	−13.6	−18.0	−17.1	−12.7
Total external debt	267.0	272.7	261.7	256.9	213.8	211.6	201.9	157.5
Debt-service payments[2]	38.3	36.4	50.7	61.3	51.9	40.6	38.4	25.8
Interest payments	19.5	16.3	17.6	18.2	16.5	15.8	14.5	10.7
Amortization	18.7	20.2	33.1	43.1	35.5	24.8	23.9	15.1
Analytical groups								
Net debtor countries by debt-servicing experience								
Countries with arrears and/or rescheduling during 1994–98								
Current account balance	−13.2	−8.7	−21.3	−8.3	1.4	−3.8	−5.9	−6.3
Total external debt	303.3	330.3	318.7	302.0	235.8	230.5	222.1	170.9
Debt-service payments[2]	27.3	30.4	46.1	53.8	36.4	30.4	29.0	21.7
Interest payments	12.0	10.4	13.2	13.3	10.3	10.3	11.4	7.2
Amortization	15.2	19.9	32.9	40.5	26.1	20.1	17.6	14.5

[1]Data refer to trade in goods and services.

[2]Interest payments on total debt plus amortization payments on long-term debt only. Projections incorporate the impact of exceptional financing items. Excludes service payments to the International Monetary Fund.

WORLD ECONOMIC OUTLOOK AND STAFF STUDIES FOR THE WORLD ECONOMIC OUTLOOK, SELECTED TOPICS, 1992–2001

I. Methodology—Aggregation, Modeling, and Forecasting

II. Historical Surveys

V. Fiscal Policy

VI. Monetary Policy; Financial Markets; Flow of Funds

VII. Labor Market Issues

VIII. Exchange Rate Issues

IX. External Payments, Trade, Capital Movements, and Foreign Debt

X. Regional Issues

XI. Country-Specific Analyses

World Economic and Financial Surveys

This series (ISSN 0258-7440) contains biannual, annual, and periodic studies covering monetary and financial issues of importance to the global economy. The core elements of the series are the *World Economic Outlook* report, usually published in May and October, and the annual report on *International Capital Markets*. Other studies assess international trade policy, private market and official financing for developing countries, exchange and payments systems, export credit policies, and issues discussed in the *World Economic Outlook*. Please consult the IMF *Publications Catalog* for a complete listing of currently available World Economic and Financial Surveys.

World Economic Outlook: A Survey by the Staff of the International Monetary Fund

The *World Economic Outlook,* published twice a year in English, French, Spanish, and Arabic, presents IMF staff economists' analyses of global economic developments during the near and medium term. Chapters give an overview of the world economy; consider issues affecting industrial countries, developing countries, and economies in transition to the market; and address topics of pressing current interest.

ISSN 0256-6877.
$42.00 (academic rate: $35.00); paper.
2001. (May). ISBN 1-58906-032-6. **Stock #WEO EA 0012001.**
2000. (Oct.). ISBN 1-55775-975-8. **Stock #WEO EA 0022000.**
2000. (May). ISBN 1-55775-936-7. **Stock #WEO EA 012000.**
1999. (Oct.). ISBN 1-55775-839-5. **Stock #WEO EA 299.**
1999. (May). ISBN 1-55775-809-3. **Stock #WEO-199.**

Official Financing for Developing Countries
by a staff team in the IMF's Policy Development and Review Department led by Anthony R. Boote and Doris C. Ross

This study provides information on official financing for developing countries, with the focus on low-income countries. It updates the 1995 edition and reviews developments in direct financing by official and multilateral sources.

$25.00 (academic rate: $20.00); paper.
1998. ISBN 1-55775-702-X. **Stock #WEO-1397.**
1995. ISBN 1-55775-527-2. **Stock #WEO-1395.**

Exchange Rate Arrangements and Currency Convertibility: Developments and Issues
by a staff team led by R. Barry Johnston

A principle force driving the growth in international trade and investment has been the liberalization of financial transactions, including the liberalization of trade and exchange controls. This study reviews the developments and issues in the exchange arrangements and currency convertibility of IMF members.

$20.00 (academic rate: $12.00); paper.
1999. ISBN 1-55775-795-X. **Stock #WEO EA 0191999.**

World Economic Outlook Supporting Studies
by the IMF's Research Department

These studies, supporting analyses and scenarios of the *World Economic Outlook,* provide a detailed examination of theory and evidence on major issues currently affecting the global economy.

$25.00 (academic rate: $20.00); paper.
2000. ISBN 1-55775-893-X. **Stock #WEO EA 0032000.**

International Capital Markets: Developments, Prospects, and Key Policy Issues
by a staff team led by Donald J. Mathieson and Garry J. Schinasi

This year's *International Capital Markets* report assesses recent developments in mature and emerging financial markets and analyzes key systemic issues affecting global financial markets. The report discusses the main risks in the period ahead; identifies sources of, and possible measures to avoid, instability in OTC derivatives markets; reviews initiatives to "involve"the private sector in preventing and resolving crises, and discusses the role of foreign-owned banks in emerging markets.

$42.00 (academic rate: $35.00); paper
2000. (Sep.). ISBN 1-55775-949-9. **Stock #WEO EA 0062000**
1999. (Sep.). ISBN 1-55775-852-2. **Stock #WEO EA 699.**
1998. (Sep.). ISBN 1-55775-770-4. **Stock #WEO-698**

Toward a Framework for Financial Stability
by a staff team led by David Folkerts-Landau and Carl-Johan Lindgren

This study outlines the broad principles and characteristics of stable and sound financial systems, to facilitate IMF surveillance over banking sector issues of macroeconomic significance and to contribute to the general international effort to reduce the likelihood and diminish the intensity of future financial sector crises.

$25.00 (academic rate: $20.00); paper.
1998. ISBN 1-55775-706-2. **Stock #WEO-016.**

Trade Liberalization in IMF-Supported Programs
by a staff team led by Robert Sharer

This study assesses trade liberalization in programs supported by the IMF by reviewing multiyear arrangements in the 1990s and six detailed case studies. It also discusses the main economic factors affecting trade policy targets.

$25.00 (academic rate: $20.00); paper.
1998. ISBN 1-55775-707-0. **Stock #WEO-1897.**

Private Market Financing for Developing Countries
by a staff team from the IMF's Policy Development and Review Department led by Steven Dunaway

This study surveys recent trends in flows to developing countries through banking and securities markets. It also analyzes the institutional and regulatory framework for developing country finance; institutional investor behavior and pricing of developing country stocks; and progress in commercial bank debt restructuring in low-income countries.

$20.00 (academic rate: $12.00); paper.
1995. ISBN 1-55775-526-4. **Stock #WEO-1595.**

Available by series subscription or single title (including back issues); academic rate available only to full-time university faculty and students. For earlier editions please inquire about prices.

The IMF *Catalog of Publications* is available on-line at the Internet address listed below.

Please send orders and inquiries to:
International Monetary Fund, Publication Services, 700 19th Street, N.W.
Washington, D.C. 20431, U.S.A.
Tel.: (202) 623-7430   Telefax: (202) 623-7201
E-mail: publications@imf.org
Internet: http://www.imf.org

For Reference

Not to be taken from this room